D1075244

THE WEIGHTIER MATTERS OF THE LAW
Essays on Law and Religion

American Academy of Religion
Studies in Religion

Lawrence Cunningham, Editor

Number 51
THE WEIGHTIER MATTERS OF THE LAW
Essays on Law and Religion

Edited by
John Witte, Jr. and Frank S. Alexander

THE WEIGHTIER MATTERS OF THE LAW
Essays on Law and Religion

A Tribute to Harold J. Berman

Edited by

John Witte, Jr. and
Frank S. Alexander

Scholars Press
Atlanta, Georgia

THE WEIGHTIER MATTERS OF THE LAW
Essays on Law and Religion

A Tribute to Harold J. Berman

Edited by

John Witte, Jr. and

Frank S. Alexander

©1988

The American Academy of Religion

Library of Congress Cataloging-in-Publication Data
Alexander, Frank, 1952-
    The weightier matters of the law.

    (Studies in religion / American Academy of
Religion ; no. 51)

    1. Religion and law.   2. Christianity and law.
3. Berman, Harold Joseph, 1918-   . I. Witte, John,
1959-   II. Berman, Harold Joseph, 1918-
III. Title.   IV. Series: Studies in religion (American
Academy of Religion) ; no. 51.
BL65.L33A45   1987   291.1'75   87-28845
ISBN 1-55540-179-1

Printed in the United States of America
on acid-free paper

HAROLD J. BERMAN

Contents

FOREWORD

My interest in the work of Harold J. Berman was whetted in 1974 when I encountered his little volume *The Interaction of Law and Religion* published that year. It seemed to me that here was a scholar at work in a field that certainly was significant but that, just as certainly, had been somewhat neglected. After all, we in the legal profession do tend to think that nothing is more important and self-sufficient than the barebones and basics of constitutional law, criminal law, international law, torts, contracts, negotiable instruments, trusts, agency, taxation, equity and all the other categories we propose and develop for our legal studies.

But Professor Berman has taken us to a higher plane. He demonstrates that, in a distinct sense, religion is law and law is religion and not merely the proverbial jealous mistress. As he has said: "At the highest level, the just and the holy are one." Theology must have its law, and faith must have its precepts. As religion and morality have an affinity, so, too, must law and morality. Although the latter are not congruent—after all, one sees little in the law as we know it that equates with the Tenth Commandment—it would be a sad legal system, indeed, that did not have its roots in moral principle.

So these essays in honor of Professor Berman's work and his 70th birthday are timely and significant. "Historical Interaction of Law and Religion" and "Religious Perspectives on Law" are ambitious but unavoidable headings. We slight legal history—or any history of man for that matter—if we ignore religion and religious thought and their influence on our conduct and habits, our progress and, on occasion, our retrogressions and failures. Such history, education, cultural development, music and the other arts are all affected and greatly shaped by religion. It is, therefore, part of us, of our being and of such happiness as we are able to attain. Law and religion enter into that important calculus of how a man should live.

I suppose I need not add—but I shall add nonetheless—that religion and law never cease to raise challenges. For those of us who labor with the First Amendment, its two religion clauses—stalwarts of liberty forged in the caldron of the late eighteenth century—with their inherent tensions, never cease to make us wonder. So much is encompassed in so few words. They carry an abiding message that law and religion need never be strangers, and cannot be, that they interact, and that they command us to our best endeavors.

Those responsible for this *Festschrift* in honor of Harold J. Berman are engaged in a good work. All of us join in a salute to this deserving scholar of great distinction.

Harry A. Blackmun
Washington, D.C.
1987

FOREWORD

Although American colleges and universities have displayed astonishing ingenuity in inventing new academic degrees, there is one European degree that is not, as far as I know, conferred by any institution in the United States: *Doctor Utriusque Juris,* "Doctor of Both Laws," namely, of civil law and of canon law. The absence of the degree is, however, symptomatic of the absence of the scholarship represented by the degree, even on university campuses where there are faculties both of law and of theology.

Harold J. Berman has made an abiding contribution to American scholarship by becoming a *Doctor Utriusque Juris,* from whose work students working in either field can learn about their own fields in ways that the existing scholarly literature does not make possible. For me, as a historian with special interest in how Christian doctrine has developed, Professor Berman's study has significantly illumined concepts, technical terms and entire periods of church history.

As a graduate student, I encountered Peter Abelard's *Sic et Non* with great excitement (although it was, of course, not then available in the fine edition painstakingly prepared by Blanche Boyer and Richard P. McKeon and published by the University of Chicago Press ten years ago). For here I found not only one of the principal avenues through which the dialectical method had become standard equipment for medieval scholasticism, but a major step forward in the history of the Christian treatment of tradition—the question that was to become in many ways the major preoccupation of my scholarly life. By setting side by side statements of the Church Fathers that appeared to contradict each other on the same subject and then considering alternative ways of resolving the contradiction, Abelard raised the questions to which, since the eighteenth century, historical methodology has been seen as providing the answers.

What I did not know at the time was that the *"sic et non"* technique had by no means been invented by Abelard but was in use before he came along. One of the principal reasons for my ignorance was that I had given no attention to the history of law during the same period and had not been compelled by my teachers to give it any attention. We studied the relation of theology to philosophy at great length, but the relation of theology to law not at all. *Concordantia discordantium,* "Harmony from dissonance," is the title of a twelfth century compend in which the contradictory decrees of canon law are subjected to the scrutiny and to the resolution which I was so excited to discover in Abelard's *Sic et Non*. When, years later and under the influence of Etienne Gilson, I studied the works of Ivo of Chartres (c. 1040–1116), the scholar whose work anticipated that compend, I found a lawyer and a theologian who belongs to the history of both fields—and, more importantly, to the history of the interrelations between the two fields. That helped me to understand scholasticism in ways that the usual polarity of Augustinianism versus Aristotelianism did not.

It would not have been necessary for me to wait until I was a mature scholar to discover Ivo of Chartes as both a lawyer and a theologian if Professor Berman's way of studying the two fields had been standard for scholars in both. More importantly, there should now be no excuse for scholars in either field to go on using a monocular instead of a binocular. The essays in this volume are examples of what happens to the study of a theologian like William of Ockham or Gerrard Winstanley, and to the study of a jurist like John Austin (whose wife translated Ranke into English) or V. F. Malinovskii, when viewed through such a binocular. Yet the finest tribute to Harold Berman, as I am sure my colleagues who have contributed to this volume would agree, will be the rise of a new generation of scholars, some in law and some in religion, who have found that they cannot make sense of their chosen field of research without a solid grasp of the other. That generation, like ours which has preceded it, will have substantial reason to be grateful to the pioneering scholarship of Harold J. Berman. In their name and in my own, I am delighted to be able to express that gratitude here to a real *Doctor Utriusque Juris*.

Jaroslav Pelikan
New Haven, CT

EDITORS' INTRODUCTION

I.

In the field of law and religion, Harold J. Berman has been an inspired and inspiring leader. He has demonstrated that religion has a legal dimension, that law has a religious dimension and that legal and religious ideas and institutions are intimately tied. He has likewise shown that jurisprudence cannot be divorced from theology, that *Rechtsgeschichte* is inseparable from *Dogmengeschichte*. Through his efforts of the past four decades, the work of generations of earlier scholars in law and religion has been brought into a common focus, and many new areas of inquiry have been opened.

Berman was eminently prepared for this task. As a student at Dartmouth College in the mid-1930s, he came under the tutelage of Eugen Rosenstock-Huessy who imbued in him a deep appreciation of the Western tradition and of its religious foundations and dimensions. Rosenstock also directed him to study Roman law and canon law and to read the great legal historians—Savigny and Gierke, Story and Maitland. As a graduate student at the London School of Economics, Berman studied medieval and early modern legal history under Theodore Plucknett and prepared an incisive analysis of the emergence and decline of courts of equity in England. He also enrolled in courses with R. H. Tawney who impressed on him the cultural influence of religious ideas and led him to the writings of von Jhering, Weber and Durkheim. Berman continued his study of Western legal history at Yale University and, under Hajo Holborn's supervision, wrote a critical appraisal of the literature describing the reception of Roman law in sixteenth century Germany.

In his first two decades of teaching at Harvard Law School (1948–1968), Berman focused primarily on the Soviet legal system and international trade law. He developed a number of new courses in Soviet law, made frequent trips to the Soviet Union, served as an expert witness in some 40 cases involving Soviet law, undertook the translation of several Soviet legal codes and produced more than 70 articles and ten books on the subject, including his path-breaking work *Justice in the U.S.S.R.: An Interpretation of Soviet Law* (1950; 2d ed., 1963) and a more popular tract *The Russians in Focus* (1953; repr. ed., 1969). After 1960, Berman also lectured widely and wrote prolifically on the *lex mercatoria* and the legal problems of trade between eastern block and western countries.

Berman's commitment to the integration of law and religion, however, manifested itself strongly throughout this early period. He insisted on viewing the Soviet legal system in light of the "secular religion of Marxist-Leninism" on which it was founded and on tracing many of its legal institutions to earlier Christian eras. He gave prominent attention to the place of the Russian Orthodox Church in Soviet culture and law and to the problems of religious freedom for Soviet Jews and Christian dissenters. He taught a number of courses in legal history and sociology of law in which he explored, *inter alia*, the influence of religious ideas and institutions on the development of the Western legal tradition.

In the past two decades, Berman has maintained an active interest in Soviet law and international trade law but has shifted the focus of his work to the interaction of law and religion. He has treated this latter subject in a variety of courses offered at Harvard and (for the past three years) at Emory University. He has lectured widely in North America and Europe on various aspects of law and religion. He has helped to establish a number of interdisciplinary institutions and colloquia devoted to the study of law and religion, notably, the Council on Religion and Law, the Law and Religion Section of the Society of Christian Ethics, the Law and Religion Section of the Association of American Law Schools, the Jurisprudence Task Force of the Christian Legal Society and the Law and Religion Program at Emory University. He has also produced a long series of publications that have brilliantly illuminated and integrated the field of law and religion. Two books have been particularly influential: (1) *The Interaction of Law and Religion* (1974), a methodological and historical treatment of the interrelation of legal and religious values, ideas and institutions; and (2) his prize-winning *Law and Revolution: The Formation of the Western Legal Tradition* (1983), an examination of the sources of the Western legal tradition in the revolutionary upheaval of church and state in the late eleventh and twelfth centuries.

II.

Professor Berman's commitment to integrate the study of law and religion is rooted in at least three interrelated concerns.

First, throughout his career Berman has sought to integrate not only law and religion but all legal and liberal education.[1] Since the mid-nineteenth century in America, he argues, legal studies have been "artificially excised"

---

[1]See H. Berman, "Law in the University," *Legal Studies Forum* 10 (1986): 53; H. Berman and W. Greiner, *The Nature and Functions of Law*, 4th ed. (Mineola, NY, 1980), 1–26; H. Berman, "The Secularization of American Legal Education in the Nineteenth and Twentieth Centuries," *Journal of Legal Education* 27 (1975): 382. (A complete bibliography of Professor Berman's writings dealing in whole or in part with the subject of law and religion is provided on pp. 337 ff. herein.)

from the college curriculum, and liberal studies have been banished from the law school curriculum. College students are thus taught the principles and doctrines of sociology, religion, history and other disciplines but receive only a rudimentary understanding of law and legal institutions. Law students are taught the principles and doctrines of law, but receive little exposure to its social, religious, historical and other dimensions.

Legal studies and liberal studies, Berman argues, must be brought together. Law enriches liberal education by (1) offering a unique method of analysis, logic and reasoning; (2) cultivating an informed sense of justice and fairness and a capacity for reasoned discernment and responsible judgment; and (3) demonstrating that legal institutions and doctrines are an integral part of Western thought and action and thus an indispensable subject for such other liberal disciplines as politics, history, sociology, economics and many others. Liberal studies, in turn, enrich legal education by (1) demonstrating that the legal system is a living social process which shapes and is shaped by politics, economics, ethics, religion, history and other subjects; (2) revealing that legal doctrines and concepts have antecedents and analogues in the subject matter of other disciplines—such as the relation between sin and crime, covenant and contract, ritual and procedure; (3) showing that ideas of the origin, nature and purpose of law and authority, of justice and equity, are rooted in deeper philosophical and theological beliefs and values.

Berman has translated many of these pedagogical concerns into practice. Since 1950, he has taught undergraduate courses in law and developed a widely used text, *The Nature and Functions of Law* (1958; 4th ed., 1980). In 1954, he organized a conference devoted to a discussion of the teaching of law in the liberal arts curriculum, which catalyzed the development of several new undergraduate courses, concentrations and colloquia in law at Harvard and elsewhere. In 1960, he organized a series of radio broadcasts to introduce uninitiated listeners to basic legal doctrines and categories; these broadcasts were collected in a volume entitled *Talks on American Law* (1961; rev. ed., 1971). In the early 1960s, he created and (for 25 years thereafter) administered the Liberal Arts Fellowships in Law Program at Harvard Law School designed to provide liberal scholars the opportunity to study law from the perspective of their disciplines. In the early 1970s, he helped to establish Vermont Law School and to develop a law curriculum heavily infused with liberal studies. Since his arrival at Emory, Berman has cultivated new relations between the Law School, Theology School and College and helped to develop new interdisciplinary programs, courses and colloquia.

Second, Berman's commitment to integrate law and religion is part of his critique of prevailing positivist concepts of law and privatist concepts of religion. Throughout much of the West, he argues, law is conceived as a body of rules and statutes designed to govern society; religion is conceived as a body of doctrines and exercises designed to guide private conscience.

Law has no place in the realm of religion; religion has no place in the public square. Such concepts, Berman argues, are far too narrow to recognize the mutual dependence of law and religion: "Law is not only a body of rules; it is people legislating, adjudicating, administering and negotiating—it is a living process of allocating rights and duties and thereby resolving conflicts and creating channels of cooperation. Religion is not only a set of doctrines and exercises; it is people manifesting a collective concern for the ultimate meaning and purpose of life—it is a shared intuition of and commitment to transcendent values. Law helps to give society the structure, the gestalt, it needs to maintain inner cohesion; law fights against anarchy. Religion helps to give society the faith it needs to face the future; religion fights against decadence. These are two dimensions of social relations—as well as of human nature—which are in tension with each other: law through its stability limits the future; religion through its sense of the holy challenges all existing social structures. Yet each is also a dimension of the other. A society's beliefs in an ultimate transcendent purpose will certainly be manifested in its processes of social ordering, and its processes of social ordering will likewise be manifested in its sense of an ultimate purpose. . . . [L]aw and religion . . . need each other—law to give religion its social dimension and religion to give law its spirit and direction as well as the sanctity it needs to command respect. Where they are divorced from each other, law tends to degenerate into legalism and religion into religiosity."[2]

Law and religion, therefore, exist not in dualistic antinomy but in dialectical harmony. They share many elements (such as authority, tradition, ritual, universality), many concepts (such as obligation, fault, justice, atonement) and many methods (such as interpretation, judgment, restitution, reformation). They also balance each other by counterposing justice and mercy, rule and equity, law and love. It is this dialectical harmony that gives law and religion their vitality and strength.

Third, Berman's commitment to the integration of law and religion is part of his response to a foreboding sense of crisis—a crisis both of Western law and of Western religion. In law, he argues, political, economic and social transformations of unprecedented magnitude—the massive growth of government and bureaucracy, the radical centralization and regulation of economic life, the rapid emergence of new social forms and customs—have drastically changed traditional legal doctrines, institutions and concepts. The growing prominence of eastern and southern cultures has led many to question the utility and efficacy of Western law and to consider new alternatives. The skeptical attacks of legal realists, nihilists and deconstructionists have inspired in many a cynical contemptuousness for law and

---

[2]H. Berman, *The Interaction of Law and Religion* (Nashville, TN, 1974), 24–5.

government.[3] Likewise in religion, new philosophies, customs and social movements have challenged traditional religious doctrines and institutions. Many have grown disillusioned with traditional dogma and distrustful of traditional ecclesiastical forms. A range of new sects, both theistic and secular, have emerged, offering radical new teachings and new experiences.[4] Twentieth century Western culture, therefore, Berman writes, is undergoing "an integrity crisis, . . . a deep loss of confidence in fundamental religious and legal values and beliefs, a decline in belief in and commitment to any kind of transcendent reality that gives life meaning, and a decline of belief in and commitment to any structures and processes that provide social order and social justice. Torn by doubt concerning the reality and validity of those values that sustained us in the past, we come fact to face with the prospect of death itself."[5]

Berman does not regard the integration of law and religion, of jurisprudence and theology, as a panacea for this crisis. But by exploring the interaction of law and religion in the past, by retracing the experience through which law and religion have become alienated from themselves and from each other, by summoning the insights and ideas of both disciplines, we shall find signposts to guide us in the future.

III.

Through Professor Berman's efforts, six branches of study have been brought within the purview of law and religion: (1) the legal dimensions of religion; (2) the religious dimensions of law; (3) the institutional interaction of law and religion; (4) the conceptual interaction of law and religion; (5) the methodological interaction of law and religion; and (6) the professional interaction of law and religion. Berman did not invent any of these branches of study, nor did he give equal attention to all of them. He has, however, helped to categorize each of these branches and to adumbrate many of their constitutive themes.

First, religion has a legal dimension, a concern for law, which manifests itself in a variety of forms. Legal structures and legal processes form part of the organization and government of the religious community—such as the Torah and the Talmud in the Jewish community, the canon law in the Roman Catholic community, the Kirchenordnungen in Protestant communities. Laws and legal concepts structure and guide the inner spiritual life

---

[3]See H. Berman, "The Crisis of Legal Education in America," Boston College Law Review 26 (1985): 347; id., Law and Revolution: The Formation of the Western Legal Tradition (Cambridge, MA, 1983), 33–41; id., "The Moral Crisis of the Western Legal Tradition and the Weightier Matters of the Law," Criterion 19 (1980): 15.

[4]Ibid. See also Berman, Interaction, 23, 95–96; H. Berman, "Religious Foundations of Law in the West," "An Historical Perspective," Journal of Law and Religion 1 (1983): 3–5, 37–43.

[5]Berman, Interaction, 23.

and discipline of the believer and of the religious community. Ideas of law, order, justice, restitution, obligation and others are an integral part of theological dogma. Berman writes: "In all religions, even the most mystical, there is a concern for social order and justice, a concern for law. . . . In both Judaism and Christianity law is understood to be a dimension of God's love, faith and grace; both Judaism and Christianity teach that God is gracious *and* just, that he is a merciful judge, a loving legislator, and that these two aspects of his nature are not in contradiction with each other."[6]

Second, law has religious dimensions, attributes that have religious antecedents and analogues.[7] Like religion, law has ritual—ceremonial procedures and actions which reflect and dramatize deeply felt values concerning the objectivity and uniformity of the law, such as the procedures of the court room, the decorum of the legislature, the practices of punishment and many others. Like religion, law has tradition—a continuity of language and practice, a theory of precedent which reflects a belief in the ongoingness of law, its time-tested wisdom, its adaptability to new social issues and ideas. Like religion, law has authority—written or spoken sources of law, texts or oracles, which are considered to be decisive in themselves and which symbolize the bindingness, the obligatory force of law on all subjects. Like religion, law has universality—a claim to embody universally valid precepts and truths. "These four elements," Berman writes, "are present in all legal systems as they are present in all religions. They provide the context in which in every society (though in some, of course, to a lesser extent than in others) legal rules are enunciated and from which they derive their legitimacy. . . . [T]hey symbolize man's effort to reach out to a truth beyond himself. They thus connect the legal order of any given society to that society's beliefs in an ultimate transcendent reality . . . and give sanctity and sustenance to legal values."[8]

Third, law and religion are institutionally related—principally in the relation between church and state, but also in the relation between other religious and political groups. A variety of constitutional and political arrangements have been devised in the past to define the respective jurisdictions and responsibilities of these groups, to protect them from each other, to facilitate their cooperation and to define the liberties and duties of their subjects. A variety of theories have been devised to define the relation

[6]Ibid., 15; see also ibid., 77–106.

[7]See especially Berman, *Law and Revolution*, 165–198 (a discussion of "Theological Sources of the Western Legal Tradition"). See also id., "Law and Religion: An Overview," *Encyclopedia of Religion*, ed. M. Eliade (New York, 1987), 8: 472; id., "Law and Religion in the West," *Encyclopedia of Religion*, 3: 463; id., "The Religious Sources of General Contract Law: An Historical Perspective," *Journal of Law and Religion* 4 (1986): 103; id., "The Religious Foundations of Western Law," *Catholic University Law Review* 24 (1975): 490; id., "Love for Justice: The Influence of Christianity Upon the Development of Law," *Oklahoma Law Review* 12 (1959): 86.

[8]Berman, *Interaction*, 31, 25.

between state and church, between *regnum* and *sacerdotium*—the two powers theory of Gelasius, the two swords theory of the Scholastics, the two kingdoms theory of the Reformers and many others. A variety of concepts and terms of art have been devised to describe these institutional relations—religious accommodation, religious establishment, religious toleration, religious pluralism, caesaropapism, Erastianism, separatism and others. Such arrangements, theories and concepts, Berman writes, can be understood only if viewed in the broader context of the interaction of law and religion. "The interrelationship of church and state is not only a political-legal matter. It is also a religious matter. Analysis of it should begin . . . with a consideration of the interaction between our religious belief . . . and the legal process. It is in the context of the interaction of religion and law, the interaction of our sense of the holy and our sense of the just—it is in that more *general* context that the more *specific* question arises of the proper relation between religious and political *institutions*."[9]

Fourth, law and religion are conceptually intertwined. They share the same fundamental concepts of being and order, man and community, knowledge and truth. They embrace analogous concepts of sin and crime, covenant and contract, grace and equity, righteousness and justice, redemption and rehabilitation and many others. They draw upon each other's concepts in devising their own doctrines. The theological doctrine of man's fallen nature, for example, is rooted in legal concepts of agency, complicity and vicarious liability. The legal doctrine that the punishment must fit the crime rests upon theological concepts of purgation, righteousness and the right order of the universe.

Fifth, law and religion are methodologically interrelated. Both have developed hermeneutical methods, modes of interpreting authoritative texts. Both have developed logical methods, modes of deducing prescriptions from principles, of reasoning from analogy and precedent. Both have developed forensic and rhetorical methods, modes of arranging and presenting arguments and data. Both have developed methods of adducing evidence and adjudicating disputes. Both have developed methods of organizing, systematizing and teaching their subject matter. These legal and religious methods have frequently crossed over and cross-fertilized each other. The scholastic *sic et non* method, for example, was used to systematize

[9]H. Berman, "Religion and Law: The First Amendment in Historical Perspective," *Juris: For Jurisprudence and Legal History* 1 (1987): 1. See also H. Berman and J. Witte, "Church and State," *Encyclopedia of Religion*, ed. M. Eliade (New York, 1987), 3: 489; H. Berman, "Some Reflections on the Differences Between Soviet and American Concepts of the Relations Between Church and State," *Christian Legal Society Quarterly* 5 (1984): 12; id., *Law and Revolution*, 113–115, 206–215.

both theological dogma and legal doctrine. The ordeal method was used to adduce evidence in both religious and legal procedures.[10]

Sixth, law and religion are professionally related. In many earlier societies, and among certain groups still today, the legal profession and the religious profession are undifferentiated. Sacerdotal and legal responsibilities are vested in one office or one person. Even when these professions are differentiated, however, they remain closely related. The professions are similar in form. Both require extensive doctrinal training and maintain stringent admissions requirements. Both have developed codes of ethics and internal structures of authority to enforce them. Both promote collegiality, cooperation and *esprit de corps*. The professions are also parallel in function. There are close affinities between the mediation of the lawyer and the intercession of the pastor, between the adjudication of the court and the arbitration of the consistory, between the beneficence of the bar and the benevolence of the diaconate. Both professions render essential services and reveal essential information to the public. Both seek to exemplify the ideals of community and vocation.[11]

These six branches of study are not the province of jurisprudence and theology alone. They summon the insights and ideas of a variety of other disciplines—anthropology and sociology, politics and government, history and philosophy, linguistics and logic. They require us to move beyond traditional compartments of knowledge and to explore the interaction between them.

IV.

The essays collected in this volume—contributed by students, friends and colleagues in a variety of disciplines—are offered as a tribute to Professor Berman and as a testimony to his path-breaking work in the field of law and religion.

The first group of essays treat various historical aspects of the interaction of law and religion. Brian Tierney offers a critical appraisal of Michel Villey's thesis that the idea of subjective rights was first developed by the fourteenth century nominalist philosopher William Ockham and demonstrates that the idea is already evident in the work of earlier writers, notably Johannes Monachus and John Peter Olivi. Charles Donahue describes a number of plea rolls of the ecclesiastical Court of Canterbury in the later thirteenth

---

[10]Cf. H. Berman, "Legal Reasoning," *International Encyclopedia of the Social Sciences* (New York, 1968), 6: 197; see also Berman, *Law and Revolution*, 120–164, which treats the "Origins of Western Legal Science in the European Universities." Berman has also dealt with some of these matters in two unpublished manuscripts, "Law and Language" and "The Transformation of Legal Science in the Lutheran Reformation."

[11]Cf. H. Berman, "The Prophetic, Pastoral and Priestly Vocation of the Lawyer," *The NICM Journal* 2 (1977); reprinted in *CORAL Newsletter* (July, 1977).

century, analyzes the subject matter and disposition of cases summarized in the rolls and hypothesizes that such rolls were modelled on the rolls of the English royal courts. John Witte describes how the Lutheran reformers displaced the Roman Catholic sacramental concept of marriage with a social concept of marriage and, on that basis, shifted marital jurisdiction from ecclesiastical to civil authorities and transformed the law of marital consent, impediments and divorce. Douglas Sturm analyzes the development of Gerrard Winstanley's unique communal concept of natural law and its influence on the theological beliefs and communitarian practices and proposals of the seventeenth century Diggers. George Williams analyzes the emergence of Harvard College in the revolutionary society of Puritan New England, the influence of biblical concepts of covenant, community and authority on the structure of the university's polity and the influence of the doctrine of the prophethood, priesthood and kingship of believers on the requirements and responsibilities of its teachers. William Butler explores the contributions of V. F. Malinovskii, a prerevolutionary Russian diplomat, pacifist and moralist, to the development of a universally acknowledged law of war and peace.

The second group of essays treat a variety of contemporary aspects of the interaction of law and religion. James Luther Adams compares and contrasts Ernst Troeltsch's and Harold Berman's ideas and assessments of legal history, particularly the history of natural law theory. Cole Durham outlines a method for analyzing the interaction of religion and criminal law, setting forth and illustrating a variety of types and contexts of such interaction. John Orth demonstrates how John Austin's analytical separation of divine law and human law and of moral values and legal doctrines—however well intentioned—laid the foundation for late nineteenth and twentieth century legal positivism. Frank Alexander argues that in devising new theories of law, critics of legal positivism must inquire not into the nature of legal rules and legal systems but into the purposive nature of human individuality and human community, and that the theological doctrines of creation, covenant and redemption offer indispensable insights for this inquiry. Lois Forer demonstrates that judicial cases pose far more trying issues of conscience than is generally assumed and that conventional theories of judicial decision-making offer little guidance to the conscientious judge. Milner Ball argues that the biblical understanding of the Kingdom of God provides a radically different perspective on the interrelation between religion and law and between church and state than is conventionally taught in America. Thomas Shaffer questions the role of law in a secular society for a religious people—a particular people laying claim to a tradition of caution and prophecy.

We have incurred many debts in preparing this volume. The law firm of Kutak Rock & Campbell in Atlanta, Georgia has generously provided its expert word processing and proofreading services in preparing several drafts of this volume. Without this valuable resource and the superb assistance of

Ms. Roberta Robbins and Ms. Teresa Crowder, the task of completing the manuscript in such a short period of time would have been overwhelming. We wish to thank Ms. Linda Emory for preparing the bibliography of Professor Berman's writings and providing her valuable secretarial support. We wish to thank the Emory Law School library staff for helping us complete certain bibliographic items. We are also indebted to Dr. Lawrence Cunningham, Editor-In-Chief of the Studies in Religion series of the American Academy of Religion, for offering his valuable comments and suggestions on an earlier draft of this manuscript and to Dr. Conrad Cherry, President of Scholars Press, for working so assiduously to prepare this volume in time for presentation to Professor Berman on his seventieth birthday.

July, 1987   John Witte, Jr.
                                                                  Frank S. Alexander
                                                                  Emory Law School
                                                                  Atlanta, Georgia

I. Historical Interaction of Law and Religion

VILLEY, OCKHAM AND THE ORIGIN
OF INDIVIDUAL RIGHTS

Brian Tierney

In a long series of studies, published over a period of 40 years, Michel Villey has made notable contributions to our understanding of legal history. His thought is always interesting, sometimes idiosyncratic. In this paper I want to discuss one particular aspect of Villey's work, his account of the origin of Western rights theories.

The concept of individual rights has become central to our political discourse; but, although there is a vast modern literature about the growth of rights theories from the seventeenth century onward,[1] relatively little work has been done on their earlier development, especially during the medieval period. The lack of such work leaves open one of the central problems of modern debate—whether the idea of human rights is something universal, common to all societies or whether it is a distinctive creation of Western culture, which emerged at some specific identifiable point in European history. Villey himself quoted the eminent jurist Gabriel Le Bras as saying that the idea of subjective rights goes back to Adam and Eve.[2] More recently, Alan Gewirth has maintained that rights—defined as "rightful claims or powers had by individuals as subjects of rights"—are recognized in all societies, even when the concept is not formally elucidated.[3] Villey maintains a very different point of view. He is impatient with scholars who introduce modern ideas of subjective rights into their studies on "Roman law, medieval law, and even in their expositions of cuneiform law." For Villey the idea of subjective rights appeared at a particular time and place and in response to a particular set of circumstances. After some hesitation in

---

[1] A bibliography of several hundred recent works is presented in R. Martin and J. Nickel, "A Bibliography on the Nature and Foundations of Rights 1947-1977," *Political Theory* 6 (1978): 395-413. In spite of its length, the list is far from complete. For instance, only one minor paper of Villey is included. The only recent book that attempts a general survey of medieval doctrines is R. Tuck, *Natural Rights Theories: Their Origin and Development* (Cambridge, 1979), but the work is marred by inaccuracies and methodological flaws. For criticism see my "Tuck on Rights. Some Medieval Problems," *History of Political Thought* 4 (1983): 429-441 and M. Villey, "Travaux récents sur les droits de l'homme," *Archives de philosophie du droit* 26 (1981): 411-18. A useful review article with further bibliography is R. Schwartz, "Circa naturam iuris subiectivi," *Periodica de re morali canonica liturgica* 69 (1980): 191-200.

[2] M. Villey, *La formation de la penseé juridique moderne*, 4th ed. (Paris, 1975), 226.

[3] A. Gewirth, *Reason and Morality* (Chicago, 1978), 98-102.

his earlier papers, he defined the occasion of its emergence in a group of studies published in the 1960s, and has since adhered to the position presented there. His argument is set out with clarity and force. The modern idea of subjective rights, Villey asserts, is rooted in the nominalist philosophy of the fourteenth century, and it first saw the light of day in the work of William of Ockham. Ockham inaugurated a "semantic revolution" when he transformed the traditional idea of objective natural right into a new theory of subjective natural rights. His work marked a "Copernican moment" in the history of the science of law.[4]

Such views are quite commonly held nowadays. Ockham is widely regarded as the originator of modern rights theories, at least among scholars who seek an origin for them before the seventeenth century. This is partly because of Villey's work, partly because some of the ideas he uses were developed independently by other well-known scholars. Villey is like Georges de Lagarde, for instance, in treating Ockham as a radical innovator in rights theories, and like Leo Strauss in contrasting an older doctrine of natural right with a newer theory of individual rights—much to the advantage of the former.[5] (Responding to some German jurists who proposed as a slogan "Zurück zu Kant," Villey offered as a counter slogan "Zurück zum Aristoteles."[6]) But Villey is unusual in the exceptionally far-ranging studies on ancient and medieval jurisprudence which he presents as a foundation for his arguments. The whole body of his historical work has never been subjected to a thorough-going appraisal. Yet any scholar who wants to work in this field has to come to terms with his impressive synthesis.[7]

In this paper I shall describe and criticize the various stages of Villey's argument as it developed down to the time of his definitive work on Ockham

[4]La formation, 225 (". . . l'idée du droit subjectif procéde elle aussi du nominalisme et s'explicite avec Occam"), 261 ("Révolution semantique a elle seule riche de conséquences . . . Nous sommes ici-même au moment copernicien de l'histoire de la science du droit").

[5]See G. de Lagarde, La naissance de l'esprit laïque au déclin du moyen âge, 5 vols.; 2d ed. (Paris, 1956–70). (The first edition was published in six volumes, 1934–46.) L. Strauss, Natural Right and History (Chicago, 1950). H. Rommen also presented Ockham as the initiator of modern rights theories in "The Geneology of Natural Rights," Thought 29 (1954): 403–425. Villey's view on Ockham as the originator of rights theories is widely accepted in current American studies. See, e.g., M. Golding, "The Concept of Rights: A Historical Sketch," Bioethics and Human Rights, ed. E. Bandmann (Boston, 1978), 44–49. Golding's discussion of Ockham here was based on Villey. Then Golding, in turn, has been repeatedly cited, e.g., in the papers by J. Pennock and K. Baier in J. Pennock and J. Chapman, eds., Human Rights: Nomos XXII (New York, 1981), 1–28, 201–29.

[6]See below n. 31.

[7]Villey's ideas have been presented in many scattered articles and several works of synthesis. Three volumes of collected essays have appeared: Lecons d'histoire de la philosophie du droit (Paris, 1957); Seize essais de philosophie du droit (Paris, 1969); Critique de la pensée juridique moderne (douze autres essais) (Paris, 1969). Villey's other books (besides La formation cited above) include Le droit et les droits de l'homme (Paris, 1983) and Philosophie du Droit—1, Définitions et fins du droit, 3d ed. (Paris, 1982); 2, Les moyens du droit, 2d ed. (Paris, 1984).

and then, more constructively, indicate some alternative approaches to the problems he has discussed.[8] In particular, I want to suggest that the juridical humanism of the twelfth century might provide a better starting point for our investigations than the nominalist philosophy of the fourteenth.

I. CLASSICAL ROMAN LAW

Villey's distinction between ancient and modern thought about rights was first developed in a series of studies on classical Roman law.[9] A seminal article of 1946 on the concept of *ius* started out from the observation that some early modern jurists radically mispresented classical jurisprudence as a system of individual rights.[10] The seventeenth century lawyer Feltmann, for instance, organized his presentations of Roman law around the categories of rights in persons, rights in things and rights to things (*jura in persona, jura in rebus* and *jura ad res*).[11] But, Villey points out, there is no such classification in classical law. The division of law presented by Gaius was into persons, things and actions. The "things" were again divided into corporeal things and incorporeal things. These latter (*res incorporales*) were legal constructs, legal attributes inhering in external corporeal entities. And, for the classical jurists, *ius* was precisely such a *res incorporalis*. This is Villey's central point. To a modern jurist a right is a power; to a classical jurist a *ius* was a thing. Thus, to a lawyer, a *fundus* was not just a field, a plot of material land, but a field with all its legal attributes. These could include what we might call rights—a right of usufruct, for instance—and the word *"ius"* was used to describe such things in classical law (*ius utendi fruendi*). But the Roman lawyers did not have in mind our modern concept of *ius* as

---

[8]In Villey's writings the same arguments are often reformulated with different nuances in successive publications. I have tried to select for comment a group of works that illustrate the development of his thought from the 1940s to the present.

[9]*Recherches sur la littérature didactique du droit romain* (Paris, 1946); "Du sens de l'expression jus in re en droit romain classique," *Mélanges Fernand de Visscher*, II, *Revue internationale des droits de l'antiquité* 2 (1949): 417–436; "Suum jus cuique tribuere," *Studi in onore di Pietro de Francisci*, 4 vols. (Milan, 1956), 2:361–371.

[10]"L'idée du droit subjectif et les systèms juridiques romains," *Revue historique de droit francais et étranger*, Series 4, 24 (1946): 201–227. The outline of Villey's views on Roman law given above is based mainly on this article. It is often cited in Villey's subsequent works. His most recent restatement of the argument is in *Le droit et les droits*, 55–79.

[11]Ibid., 202. The persistence of this earlier way of thinking can be illustrated from a textbook of 1890. The author rendered Gaius' "De Personis" as "Equal Rights" and "De Rebus" as "Unequal Rights." See E. Poste, *Elements of Roman Law by Gaius* (Oxford, 1890), xv–xvi. By that time though Henry Sumner Maine was arguing that "the Romans had not attained, or had not fully attained, to the concept of a legal Right, which seems to us elementary." *Dissertations on Early Law and Custom* (New York, 1883), 365. The debate about the meaning of "*ius*" in Roman law goes back to the seventeenth century. Villey has an interesting discussion in "Les origines de la notion de droit subjectif," *Archives de philosophie du droit* 2 (1953–54): 163–187.

a subjective right of an individual. For them *ius* was not a power over something; it was a thing itself, specifically an incorporeal thing.[12]

Villey maintains that, although there existed at Rome practical situations that we should discuss in terms of rights, the concept of an individual right was lacking in classical jurisprudence. He defends this interpretation by several lines of argument. For instance, in discussing urban servitudes, Gaius wrote of a *ius altius tollendi*. At first glance, it seems clear enough that Gaius was writing about a right in the modern sense, a "right of building higher." But Gaius went on to mention a *"ius . . . non extollendi."* We cannot possibly translate this as "a right of not building higher." So Gaius's concept of a *ius* is just not congruent with our concept of a right.[13]

It is the same with Ulpian's famous definition of the function of justice—to render to each his right (*suum ius cuique tribuere*). Here again we seem, at first sight, to be dealing with the modern idea of inherent individual rights. But Villey points out that *ius* here has a different meaning. It refers to the just share, the just due, of someone within an established structure of social relationships, varying with each person's status and role. In this sense the word *"ius"* could imply a disadvantage to an individual. Villey observes that the *ius* of parricide was to be sewn up in a sack of vipers and thrown into the Tiber.[14] Again, the meaning of *ius* is not congruent with our idea of a right.

The Romans did have a concept of mastery, power over persons or things, expressed by the word *"dominium."* But, Villey insists, this *dominium* was not defined as a right. A *dominus*, for instance, was not said to have a right of usufruct in his own property. Ulpian wrote, *"dominus . . . utendi fruendi jus separatum non habet."* Gaius also distinguished between the two concepts in the phrase, *"sive dominus sive is qui ius habet."*[15] The point is important for Villey. An owner certainly had the power to use and enjoy his own property. But this power was not a *ius*. Once again, for the classical jurist, a *ius* was not a power but an immaterial thing. Hence it was not a right in our sense. In other works, Villey maintained that *dominium* itself was not a construct of law for the classical jurist but a pre-legal reality, something that law limited.[16]

These arguments are of fundamental importance for Villey's later work on the origin of rights theories, so they need a little further consideration. There are evident criticisms to be made. It may well be that the Romans had

---

[12]M. Villey, "L'idée du droit subjectif," 210, 219–220. Villey persistently indicates that for him the modern idea of a right implies a power. He does not concern himself much with the more elaborate classifications of rights commonly encountered in the Anglo-American literature.

[13]Ibid., 217.

[14]Villey, "Suum jus cuique tribuere," 364.

[15]Villey, "L'idée du droit subjectif," 219; id., "Les origines," 173. Villey returned to these texts of Roman law over and over again in later writings.

[16]E.g., Villey, *La formation*, 235: "La puissance absolue qu' exercise le maître romain sur sa chose, ce n'est point le droit, c'est le silence, ce sont les lacunes du droit."

a highly developed concept of individual rights but used some word other than *"ius"* to express it.[17] It is also possible that Villey was too narrowly selective in the texts he chose to illustrate the meaning of *ius* itself. Alan Gewirth, for instance, pointed out that even modern authors who want to deny the existence of rights in Roman law find it necessary to use the term "a right" (or *"un droit"*) in the modern sense in explicating the relevant texts.[18] Again, the separation between *ius* and *dominium* is crucial for Villey's argument. But, in classical literary Latin, one could certainly refer to *ius* and *dominium* as inhering in the same subject. (Livy mentioned a subordinate king who acknowledged that *ius* and *dominium* over his lands remained with Rome.[19]) In legal Latin, too, from the fourth century onward, the two concepts were commonly confused in phrases like *iure dominii possidere*. Ernest Levy gave many examples and observed that "the former strict contrast of *dominium* and *ius in re aliena* was done for. It did not survive."[20]

One might further argue that, even in Gaius himself, the concepts of *potestas* and *dominium* and *ius* all seem to be interwoven in a passage like this:

> Slaves are in the power (*potestate*) of their masters (*dominorum*) . . . if the cruelty of the masters seems intolerable they are compelled to sell their slaves . . . for we ought not to use our right (*iure*) badly.[21]

It is hard not to see here an assertion of the subjective *right* of the master consisting in his *power* over the slave who was under his *dominium*.

As we are so often told nowadays, all language is context-dependent.[22] A legal term deployed in the cultural context of ancient Rome cannot have exactly the same range of meanings as the same term used nowadays (though the meanings may overlap). But one could make this same point about the language of Ockham or Hobbes or Kant, and Villey does not hesitate to attribute a modern idea of rights to such authors.[23]

---

[17]This was suggested by G. Pugliese, "'Res corporales', 'res incorporales' e il problema del diritto soggetivo'," *Studi in onore di Vincenzo Arangio-Ruiz* (Naples, 1954), 3: 223–60.

[18]*Reason and Morality*, 372. Gewirth mentioned Jolowicz, Buckland and Villey himself.

[19]*Ab urbe condita*, 45.13.15.

[20]E. Levy, *West Roman Vulgar Law* (Philadelphia, 1951), 63. See also ibid., 26, 64–5.

[21]F. de Zulueta, ed., *The Institutes of Gaius* (Oxford, 1946), 1:17 (Inst. 1.52): "In potestate itaque sunt serui dominorum. . . . Si intolerabilis uideatur dominorum saeuitia cogantur seruos suos uendere . . . male enim nostro iure uti non debemus."

[22]Villey, "L'idée du droit subjectif," 225: "Les Romains s'intéressent si peu à l'idée du droit subjectif qu'ils n'ont pas même de terme générique pour l'exprimer." See also id., "Les origines," 170–173.

[23]One may doubt, for instance, whether any author before the twentieth century used the word "right" with precisely the same range of connotations that one finds in the United Nations Universal Declaration on Human Rights. Tuck, *Natural Rights Theories* also raises the issue of

The harshest criticism that could be made of Villey's treatment of Roman law—it could apply also to his later discussion of Thomas Aquinas— is that he selects a few suitable texts, drapes a whole theory of law around them and then refuses to take seriously any texts that do not fit his preferred theory. Responding to such criticisms many years after his original article appeared, Villey has explained that, in discussing classical law, he was not concerned with literary Latin or the language in common use. It would be impossible, he concedes, to prove that the concept of subjective right never existed at all in Rome. Villey even adds that such a negative enquiry would have little interest. The point is that in classical Roman law we have a whole structure of language built around a set of concepts different from the ones we often take for granted.[24] (Although Villey does not write in the jargon of modern French structuralism, his whole mind set seems to be structuralist. For him—as for Saussure, as for Lévi-Strauss—patterns of relationship matter more than particular instances.) Put in this way, Villey's position is defensible. He was, indeed, making a valid point all along. Roman jurists did not conceive of the legal order as essentially a structure of individual rights in the manner of some modern ones.

Still, if we concede that, in some forms of discourse from classical times onward, the word *"ius"* could mean a right, then the case for a "semantic revolution" in the fourteenth century is apparently undermined. Indeed, in some of his earlier work, Villey seemed to favor a more gradual, evolutionary approach. He often used the word *"glissement"* to indicate a "sliding," a "shifting" in the meaning of the term *"ius"* that occurred over a period of several centuries. A paper on the medieval glossators of Roman law (first presented in 1947) is especially valuable for the substantial body of medieval texts collected in a long appendix.[25] Villey repeated here that the idea of subjective right did not exist in classical law, but he found hints of it in the law of the late Empire and a substantial development of the concept in the writings of the medieval glossators.

In this paper, Villey was mainly concerned to argue that, before the early modern period, the technical term *"ius in re"* did not have the full sense of modern property right, the *droit réel* of French law, a power over property enforceable against all other persons. (He mentioned that the accusative form *ius ad rem* could mean a subjective right,[26] but did not explore in detail the intricate development of the canonistic doctrine on *ius ad rem* from 1200 onward.) The author makes his technical point about *ius in re*, though to a

---

language as "theory-dependent" in considering late Roman law but does not pursue the point in considering later texts.

[24]Villey, "Travaux récents," 416. Villey presents a more nuanced discussion on *ius* in Roman law in *Philosophie du droit*, 1:87–96.

[25]Villey, "Le 'jus in re' du droit romain classique au droit moderne," *Conférences faites à l'Institut de Droit Romain en 1947* (Paris, 1950), 187–225.

[26]Ibid., 203.

reader more open to the idea of a twelfth century origin for modern rights theories the "exceptional" texts he cites might seem more striking than the ones that directly support his argument. Villey recognizes in this paper that the medieval glossators created a new terminology, "new notions and, in particular, new words designating subjective rights." They treated the Roman *actio*, for instance, as a subjective *ius*. But their analysis of rights was concerned mainly with the term "*dominium*." They understood the word in non-classical ways, so that *dominium* itself came to be regarded as a *ius*. Setting out from the word "*dominium*," Villey observes, the glossators built a "*grand échafaudage logique de notions de droit subjectifs.*"[27]

All this would, again, seem to suggest a pre-fourteenth century origin for modern rights theories. But Villey resists this conclusion. The glossators' work, he says, was full of hesitations and contradictions and frustrated endeavors. A coherent jurisprudence of individual rights could be created only in a later epoch, in a different climate of thought. In this paper Villey associated the later emergence of such a jurisprudence with "the *cogito ergo sum* of Descartes," "the psychological literature of the seventeenth century" and "Jesuit spirituality."[28] At one point in the paper he described medieval Roman law as marking an era of transition in rights theories—suggesting a process of continuous development. But at another point he asserted that the early modern jurists "broke with history" and adopted "a new language."[29] The reason for this uneasiness becomes clearer in his later work.

II. INDIVIDUAL RIGHTS AND NATURAL RIGHT

An underlying reason for Villey's reluctance to acknowledge a continuity between medieval and early modern thought, even when such continuity was suggested by his own texts, was his prior conviction that major shifts in legal and political ideas could occur only after an appropriate pattern of thought had been created in the sphere of pure philosophy. For Villey, metaphysics always comes before jurisprudence. Aristotelian thought provided a basis for the classical doctrine of objective natural right; Ockham's nominalism made possible the early modern theories of natural rights; Kant's philosophy provided an immediate source for the subjective rights of nineteenth century jurisprudence. Villey's attitude is summed up in an early comment on Ockham: "*La philosophie avait, comme il est ordinaire, précédé les juristes sur la voie révolutionnaire.*"[30]

Villey explored these themes in many articles from the 1950s onward. There was a certain broadening of conceptual horizons in his work. His early papers on Roman law had treated *ius* as something objective but only as a

[27]Ibid., 198–200.
[28]Ibid., 190–91.
[29]Ibid., 204, 191.
[30]Villey, "Les origines," 179.

legal quality inhering in some external entity (as usufruct might inhere in a *fundus*). In his subsequent work he was more concerned with *ius naturale* as an objective right order in relationships between persons. Similarly, when he wrote about subjective rights (or the lack of them), he was at first concerned with legal rights, rights within an established system of human law, specifically Roman law. In later works the emphasis was more on natural rights, rights conceived of as inherent in the human personality. In his "*Abrégé du droit naturel classique*" (1961), Villey wrote, "Subjective rights from their origin and still today are conceived of as natural rights."[31] This emphasis helps to explain why Villey could acknowledge that the word "*ius*" could vaguely mean a right from the time of the late Roman Empire onward and still see a radical change in the fourteenth century. What was lacking before then was the full idea of *subjective* rights, rights inhering in the individual person as such.

The "*Abrégé*" and the first edition of *La formation*, written at about the same time, provide a good introduction to Villey's understanding of the contrast between classical natural right and modern individual rights. These works also make clear his distaste for modern rights doctrines. Villey objects to the subjectivism of contemporary rights theories. He reacts with understandable irony to the vague catalogues of more or less worthy aspirations that are nowadays presented as lists of "human rights"—a "right to leisure," "to work," "to culture," "to health," "to modesty" (invoked against "obscene" films).[32] But Villey is not content to criticize abuses. Rather, he presents the whole modern attempt to base a system of jurisprudence on an affirmation of individual rights as fundamentally misguided. He describes this modern enterprise as utopian, arbitrary and sterile. It is utopian because the supposed absolute rights are fictions; they usually do not exist in actual law or in real life. Rights theories are arbitrary because the rights claimed are ultimately based on subjective whim; they lead on to a debased understanding of justice as "nothing but a label you attach to your own subjective preferences." Modern rights theories are sterile because they cannot form the basis of a coherent jurisprudence.[33] The rights that people assert conflict with one another. Juridical thought begins at the point where one considers the situations that arise as a consequence of this reality. The task of the jurist is to establish just relationships among persons and between persons and property—not to affirm absolute rights, but to determine what is objectively right. Villey does not disdain the values inherent in modern Western society

---

[31]Villey, "Abrégé du droit naturel classique," *Archives de philosophie du droit* 6 (1961): 27–72, at 65. It was in this paper that Villey suggested the slogan "Zurück zum Aristoteles." Ibid., 27.

[32]Ibid., 65. It is as well perhaps that Villey never came upon the work of N. Berger, *Rights: A Handbook for People Under Age* (Harmondsworth, Middlesex, 1974). There he could have found, to add to his list of unlikely rights, a "right to sunshine," "to a tobacco-free job" and "to a sex break."

[33]Villey, "Abrégé," 42–43, 46–47, 68–69.

insofar as they reflect a concern for the human personality, but he thinks those values could be better defended, "in another, more exact language," by an appeal to the classical tradition of natural right.[34] He associates that tradition especially with Aristotle, with the jurisprudence of classical lawyers who took for granted Aristotelian ways of thinking and with the philosophy of Thomas Aquinas who remained faithful to Aristotelian principles. We need to explore a little further Villey's understanding of this tradition before we can consider his attitude toward Ockham and later rights theorists.

A key word for Villey is Aristotle's *"dikaion"*—the just—usually rendered into Latin as *"ius."* Aristotle understood the term in two senses, neither of them equivalent to the modern idea of a subjective right. He distinguished between justice as a moral virtue and justice as an objectively right state of affairs in a particular context, something inherent in the nature of a situation, or "in the nature of the case," we might say. It is this second meaning that especially concerns the jurist. Indeed, by defining it, Aristotle provided the foundation for a whole philosophy of law, according to Villey.[35] In Aristotle's philosophy the universe was a cosmos, informed by a *logos* which gave it order and harmony and purpose. So, too, human society could display a proper harmony and balance, a structure of right relationships. The objective sense of *ius* was well expressed in English by John Finnis—he defined it as "what's fair."[36] For Villey *ius* most often means fair sharing, *juste partage.*

Villey insists—against both Hume and Kant in their different ways—that *ius*, what is right, can be ascertained from observation of external nature.[37] He cites, for instance, an argument from Aristotle and Thomas Aquinas. We can learn from observation that human children, unlike the young of many other species, need a long period of nurture and education; whence one can conclude that a stable marriage between parents is a naturally right relationship.[38] Given this approach, Villey points out, it is not surprising that

[34]Ibid., 66.

[35]See, e.g., Villey, "Bentham et le droit naturel classique," *Archives de philosophie du droit* 17 (1972): 423–31, at 431. After explaining Aristotle's distinction, Villey commented, "Voilà qui est pour nous le fondement d'une philosophie de droit." Villey's understanding of classical natural right explained in the paragraph above is found in many of his works, including "Les origines" and "Abrégé." It was given a systematic presentation in *La formation,* 36–47, in *Philosophie du droit,* 1, and most recently in *Le droit et les droits.*

[36]J. Finnis, *Natural Law and Natural Rights* (Oxford, 1980), 206.

[37]The influence of Kant was especially emphasized (and deplored) in Villey, "Abrégé." For a typical comment on Hume see id., "Bentham et le droit naturel classique," 429. In criticizing Villey, Finnis referred to Hume's law about the impossibility of deriving a moral proposition from factual observation which had, he wrote, "impressed . . . the whole modern anglo-saxon world." Finnis, *Natural Law,* 228. In response Villey referred to " . . . la loi de Hume, si contestable et contestée, à tout le moins sur le continent."

[38]Villey, *La formation,* 126–128.

when Aristotle or Aquinas sought to define *dikaion* or *ius* they did not proclaim the rights and powers of individuals. They were concerned rather with a harmonious structure of relationships, right proportion, *juste partage*.

III. AQUINAS AND THE CANONISTS: *IUS* AND *LEX*

So far we have been concerned mainly with a distinction between *ius* as a subjective right and *ius* as a system of objectively right relationships. In discussing Aristotle and Aquinas in *La formation*, Villey developed another distinction, which became of central importance in his subsequent work. This was a distinction between *ius* understood as an objectively right relationship (what is fair, *juste partage*), and *ius* understood as moral or legal precept, as law binding on individuals, and so equivalent to *lex*.[39]

According to Villey, the first, properly classical meaning was lost, or compromised, in the writings of the Christian Church Fathers. In translating and commenting on the Bible they used the term "*ius*" to mean divine commands, so that, for instance, the Decalogue could be called *ius divinum* or *ius naturale*. This usage was then continued by the medieval canonists. Hence, in the first words of Gratian's *Decretum* (c. 1140), we find "*ius naturale*" defined as the biblical Golden Rule, "by which we are commanded to do unto others what we would have them do unto us. . . ." This development is important for our general theme concerning the origin of rights theories because, in Villey's view, the classical idea of *ius* was undermined by this Christian understanding of the term before the final (disastrous) misinterpretation occurred in the fourteenth century, when *ius* came to be regarded as an individual power or subjective right.

For Villey, one of the great achievements of Thomas Aquinas was to restore for a time the objective, classical meaning of *ius* (a meaning that would be lost again by Ockham and the nominalists). Following the Roman lawyers, Aquinas defined *ius* as "*quod iustum est*," what is just, and again as "*ipsam rem iustam*," the just thing itself.[40] For Aquinas, as for Aristotle, as for Gaius and Ulpian, *ius* was still primarily a "thing" (*rem*), something existing in external nature. After his primary definition, Thomas gave several derivative meanings of *ius* still none of which included any subjective definition of the word. According to Villey, no such meaning was known to him.[41] For Thomas, *ius naturale* was not a power inhering in individuals or

---

[39]Ibid., 127: " . . . la loi morale n'est pas le droit." Among later studies see especially "Torah-Dikaion I" and "Dikaion — Torah II" in id., *Critique de la pensée juridique moderne*, 19–50. The argument is summarized in id., *Philosophie du droit*, 1: 101–112. Finnis complained that "Villey's treatment of *ius* is marred by an exaggerated distinction between *ius* and *lex* . . . which leads him to misplaced distinctions between law and morality. . . . " Finnis, *Natural Law*, 228.

[40]Villey, "Abrégé," 31, referring to T. Aquinas, *Summa theologiae*, 2.2ae.57.1.

[41]H. Hering argued that Aquinas did have a concept of subjective rights, "De iure subjectivo sumpto apud sanctum Thomam," *Angelicum* 16 (1939): 295–97. Villey denied this (below n. 58).

a body of moral precepts but a method, a way of interpreting reality, even an "experimental method."[42] (Perhaps Villey had in mind the secondary definition of *ius* given by Thomas, "The art by which it is known what is just.")

This led Villey to a further point. What is naturally right can change. Thomas clearly insisted on a need for changes in positive human law, and Villey duly emphasizes this. But he goes further. He holds also that, for Thomas, *ius naturale*, too, could change because human beings change—"*natura hominis mutabilis est*," Thomas wrote in the *Summa Theologiae*. Villey observes that justice is a *problem* which always poses itself in new terms and calls for new solutions as circumstances change. What is naturally right—a fair pattern of relationships—will be different in different times and places, not the same, let us say, in a primitive agrarian society as in an advanced commercial one. Villey admires especially the suppleness and flexibility of Thomas's *ius naturale*. It is a vision open to change, open to progress.[43]

Villey was supplying a corrective to modern neo-Thomist doctrines which interpret Aquinas's *ius naturale* too rigidly. But his approach led to a thicket of controversy. The difficulty is that Thomas (following St. Paul) certainly believed in an immutable *lex naturalis*, a moral law inscribed in the hearts and minds of men. Villey had to insist, therefore, that, for Thomas, the meanings of *ius* and *lex* were quite different.[44] And here the problems begin. Thomas did, indeed, distinguish between the two terms in his definition of *ius* at *Summa Theol.* 2.2ae.57.1. But he followed this at once in the next article with a sentence in which the terms seem equated with one another, and in other sections of the *Summa* he often used them interchangeably. Villey insists, in effect, that only the first definition counts. He adds that, where there is an appearance of confusion, it is because Thomas is not using his own language to express his own thought but quoting the language

---

[42]Villey, "Abrégé," 50; id., *La formation* 50, 126: "Le droit naturel est une méthode expérimentale."

[43]Villey, "Abrégé," 35 ("La justice, c'est un probléme qui se pose sous des termes nouveaux . . ."), 50–51 ("[La] vision du juste est relative, ouverte au progrés . . . ").

[44]For further discussion see Villey, "Bible et philosophie gréco-romaine de Saint Thomas au droit moderne," *Archives de philosophie du droit* 18 (1973): 27–57 and, most recently, G. Kalinowski and M. Villey, "La mobilité du droit naturel chez Aristote et Thomas d' Aquin," *Archives de philosophie du droit* 29 (1984): 187–199. Villey might have made a better argument by emphasizing that, for Thomas, *lex naturalis* (as well as *ius naturale*) was a flexible concept that had to be applied differently in different circumstances. See Aquinas, *Summa theologiae*, 1.2ae.95.2: " . . . principia communia legis naturae non eodem mod applicari possunt omnibus, propter multam varietatem rerum humanarum." Harry Jaffa has pointed out that Catholic authors commonly derive, from their understanding of *lex naturalis*, moral principles (especially in the sphere of sexual morality) different from anything that Aristotle taught in his treatment of *ius naturale*. See H. Jaffa, *Thomism and Aristotelianism* (Chicago, 1952). Obviously, Catholic moral doctrine is not identical with Aristotle's. It may be doubted though whether the teachings involved are strictly deducible from Thomas's understanding of *lex naturalis* as "lumen rationis naturalis quo discernimus quid sit bonum et quid malum" (*Summa theologiae*, 1.2ae.91.2).

of the canonists, specifically the terminology of Isidore of Seville incorporated in Gratian's *Decretum*, a terminology that reflected a "decadent
syncretism between Biblical culture and the language of the Roman jurists."
Of course, there is no trace of such an attitude in Thomas himself. He treated
Isidore's texts, like other passages of canon law, as respected authorities. (At
one point, in response to an objection, he wrote simply, "The authority of
Isidore suffices."[45]) Moreover, on one occasion where Thomas equated *ius*
and *lex*, it was Aristotle, not Isidore, who provided the starting point of the
discussion.[46]

It seems to me that Villey's case for a consistent distinction between
droit naturel and *loi naturelle* in Thomas cannot be sustained. In different
contexts, Thomas presented Aristotle's doctrine of natural right and his own
doctrine of natural law. He seems to have regarded the two as complementary. Had he consistently used *"ius naturale"* for the first doctrine and *"lex
naturalis"* for the second, the task of modern commentators might have been
easier. But, in fact, Thomas followed the common usage of his age in which
"ius" and *"lex"* could sometimes be used interchangeably and sometimes
differentiated from one another in their more specialized meanings. One has
only to consult a concordance to see that Thomas used the word *"ius"* (not to
mention *"naturalis"*) in several different senses, sometimes perhaps even in
a subjective sense,[47] without always explaining carefully the various meanings intended in different contexts.

We might expect to find this situation in such a long and far-ranging
work as the *Summa Theologiae*, which drew on sources as diverse as
Aristotle's *Ethics* and Gratian's *Decretum*. But Villey's treatment of the
relationship between Aquinas and the canonists in their understanding of
ius and *lex* is significant for his whole argument. Especially in his more
recent work he has emphasized a conflict—a duel, he says—between the
classical and Thomist concept of *ius* (equivalent to Aristotle's *dikaion* in its
objective sense) and the Judeo-Christian concept of *ius* (equivalent to *lex* or
Torah). In fact, however, the two concepts have coexisted in a reasonably
harmonious fashion since classical times. In Roman law *ius* meant not only
objective right order but also a body of legal or moral precepts, as in *"ius
civile,"* *"ius gentium."* Similarly, the canonists emphasized the meaning of
ius as moral precept, equivalent to *lex*, but they did not lack the meaning of

[45]For Villey on "decadent syncretism" see "Bentham et le droit naturel classique," 429. Cf.
Aquinas, *Summa theologiae*, 1.94.4: "In contrarium auctoritas Isidori sufficiat."
[46]Ibid., 1.95.2. Thomas argued that human law was derived from natural law and then posed as
an objection that natural law was invariable: "Praeterea *lex* naturae est eadem apud omnes; dicit
enim Philosophus quod 'naturale *ius* est quod ubique habet eamdem potentiam'" (emphasis
added). The objection has no point unless Thomas was assuming that Aristotle's *ius* meant the
same as his own *lex*. (He did not distinguish between the two words in his reply to the objection.)
[47]As in phrases like *"ius patriae potestatis"* (Ibid., 2.2ae.12.12) and *"ius dominii"* (ibid.,
2.2ae.62.1).

objective right order. (To anyone familiar with their work, the idea that the canonists were *not* interested in right order in the world will seem startling.) Villey complains that, in the treatise on law that forms the opening section of Gratian's *Decretum*, there is no understanding of justice in the objective sense—as just distribution, *juste partage, ius suum cuique tribuere.* But this precise meaning is presented in the first paragraph of the *Glossa Ordinaria* to the Decretals, a work studied in every canon law school of medieval Europe: " . . . *his (decretalibus) lectis et intellectis sciamus discernere inter aequum et iniquum, et unicuique reddere quod suum est, et in hoc iustitia consistit.*"[48]

A less selective reading of the texts would show that the two meanings of *ius* that Villey contrasts—treating one as truly classical, the other as a sort of Christian aberration—actually existed harmoniously, side by side, in classical philosophy, in Roman law, in medieval jurisprudence, in Thomas Aquinas and in many later natural law philosophers. Moreover, they could coexist in this fashion without undue strain because the two meanings are complementary rather than contradictory. If we observe that it is proper for children to respect their parents, that is an example of an objectively right relationship (*dikaion, ius*). If we say, "Honor thy father and thy mother," that is a precept of natural law (which Gratian would also call *ius*). But we are affirming the same principle in each formulation. Both meanings of *ius* retain the underlying sense of rightness or fairness. A judge cannot establish *ius* (an objectively right relationship, a *juste partage*) unless he has a *ius* (a body of law or moral precepts) to guide his sense of what is considered fair in such a case. We shall have to consider later on how these two meanings of *ius* relate to the third one, of particular interest to us, *ius* considered as subjective right.

Aquinas's use of canon law also raises another problem of central importance for Villey's argument, the relation between philosophical and legal thought. Villey maintained that the development of Thomas's philosophy of law was a prerequisite for the justification of new legislative activity in the church.[49] Thomas envisaged a law open to change and adaptation; but Gratian's *Decretum*, Villey says, did not acknowledge a creative legislative function of the ruler. After the philosophical work of Aquinas, however, papal decretals would no longer present themselves merely as judicial decisions or interpretations of a pre-existing law considered permanently valid but as deliberately creative of new law. Villey points out that Boniface VIII made this assertion in his Preface to the *Liber Sextus* (1298).

But the phrase Boniface actually used to justify new legislation was

[48]Villey, *Critique*, 33. B. Parmensis, *Glossa ordinaria ad Decretales, Proemium in Decretales D. Gregorii Papae IX* (Lyon, 1624), 2.

[49]Villey, *La formation*, 121 ("Il fallait qu'une théologie et une philosophie nouvelles justifiassent le changement de droit"), 133, 174. See also id., "Saint Thomas dans l'histoire des sources," *Études d'histoire du droit canonique dediées à Gabriel le Bras* (Paris, 1965), 1: 355–395.

"humana natura, novas semper deproperans edere formas, lites quotidie invenire conatur. . . ." Villey has overlooked the fact that Honorius III closely paraphrased the same text—it is originally from the Digest—in the letter introducing his decretal collection of 1226,[50] and that it was incorporated in Jacobus de Albenga's commentary on this collection written shortly afterward and also in the *Glossa Ordinaria* to the *Decretals* of Gregory IX (also before Thomas). The canonists did not need to wait for Thomas to tell them that the popes could legislate. For more than a century they had been insisting on the papal *ius condendi canones*. What actually happened is more subtle and more interesting. Thomas did not invent a new theory of legislation. He assimilated the existing doctrine of contemporary Roman and canon lawyers and associated it with his own teachings on *ius naturale* and *lex naturalis*. Then, in turn, Thomas's doctrine of natural law began to react back on the teachings of the academic canonists. (The first time I have found it mentioned in a formal canonistic commentary is in the *Rosarium* of Guido de Baysio from c. 1300.) The process we have to deal with is not simply one of philosophy influencing law but rather of a constant interplay between the two disciplines. It will be useful to keep this in mind as we turn to Ockham.

IV. OCKHAM'S "REVOLUTION"

After mentioning William of Ockham in several of his earlier papers, Villey, in an article first published in 1964, gave a detailed systematic presentation of his argument that Ockham was the inaugurator of modern rights theories.[51] He began by referring again to the abuses of modern rights theories. Then Villey gave two reasons for the rise of such doctrines. The first was simple egotism, the inclination of each person to think of everything in terms of his own self-interest. But since this moral defect is a common human failing it does not in itself explain why the "deviation of language" introduced by theories of individual rights has found wide acceptance among philosophers of law only since the early modern period.

Another influence was needed. So, here again, Villey emphasized the impact of Christianity—not Christian morality as such but a deformed version of Christian ideas (*idées chrétiennes mais déformées*).[52] Christianity always recognized the supreme value of the individual soul and, in the

[50]E. Friedberg, *Quinque compilationes antiquae* (Leipzig, 1882), 152. On the canonistic use of this language see G. Post, *Studies in Medieval Legal Thought* (Princeton, 1964), 534.

[51]M. Villey, "La genèse du droit subjectif chez Guillaume d'Occam," *Archives de philosophie du droit* 9 (1964): 97–127. The article is based on material originally included in Villey, *Cours d'histoire de la philosophie du droit* of 1963. (See *Seize essais*, 141.) The *Cours* was subsequently published as *La formation de la pensée juridique moderne. Cours d'histoire de la philosophie du droit, 1961–1966* (Paris, 1968). Our page references are to the revised edition of this work published in 1975 (see above n. 2). (I have quoted *La formation* in the following discussion when it contains significant phrases not included in "La genèse.")

[52]"La genèse," 97.

cloister, individual mysticism was cultivated as the highest form of life. The mischief arose when these religious attitudes were transplanted to the alien terrain of law. The Franciscan Order was the group that brought about this change and, among the Franciscans, William of Ockham was especially responsible for it. "The cradle of subjective right was the Franciscan Order—William of Ockham, founder of nominalism, an individualist philosophy . . . enemy of the pope and convicted of heresy according to many, may be called the father of subjective rights."[53]

Before turning to Ockham, Villey develops in this paper some of his earlier ideas in order to contrast the newly emerging idea of subjective rights with the older, sounder doctrine. A subjective right, he says, is something that *subiacet*, that underlies or is inherent in a person. It is a quality of the subject, a faculty, a liberty, an ability to act. In a word, "subjective right is a *power* of the individual."[54] This concept, he reminds us, was alien to the thought of Aristotle or Ulpian or Aquinas. For them (in Villey's interpretation) *dikaion* or *ius* meant primarily something objective—what is just. It could not mean a subjective power. Rather, right was something that limited power.[55] Hence the modern concept has combined two ideas that were formerly distinct—right and power. It is precisely in the juncture of these two concepts—*ius* and *potestas*—that Villey will find Ockham most innovative; for, he asserts, the doctrine of classical natural right necessarily excluded the modern idea of subjective rights. "The notion of subjective right is logically incompatible with classical natural right."[56]

Villey acknowledges that, in vulgar usage, even in ancient Rome, some people may have treated the word "*ius*" as a term defining their individual rights—after all they had their share of egotism too. But the *glissement*, the shift in meaning, became much more evident in the practical life of the Middle Ages. After the downfall of Rome, no work of creative jurisprudence was produced for several centuries. The Roman juridical order was forgotten. An anti-juridical attitude (*conception antijuridique*) prevailed. In this juridical void people everywhere began to insist on their "rights"—rights of emperors against popes, rights of kings against subjects, rights of this or that group or class of individuals—and they tended to confuse rights with actual powers.[57]

Here again, as in the paper of 1947 discussed above, Villey seems to be

---

[53]Ibid., 98.

[54]Ibid., 100–102

[55]Ibid., 104: " . . . le pouvoir est au contraire ce que le droit limite . . . ."

[56]Villey, *La formation*, 227: " . . . la notion de droit subjectif est logiquement incompatible avec le droit naturel classique." Similarly, id., "La genèse," 103: " . . . cette philosophie dite du droit naturel classique . . . ait été necessairement exclusive du droit subjectif." On "droit" and "pouvoir," see ibid., 104.

[57]Villey, "La genèse," 110. At this point Villey dismisses the labors of the generations of medieval people who first built a Christian civilization in Western Europe as "le déploiement désordonnée de l'initiative individuelle."

proposing an early medieval origin for theories of subjective rights. But his central argument is quite different. He insists that the shift in meaning of the word "*ius*" was confined to vulgar usage. We cannot define with certainty what "*ius*" meant to people who themselves were not using the word with any philosophic precision, and so there is no basis for holding that the term had acquired the full meaning of subjective right before the fourteenth century. The important point for Villey is that we do not find the subjective meaning in formal academic discourse. The glossators of Roman law and Thomas Aquinas drew up lists of definitions of the word "*ius*" but they did not include the meaning of "power" or any subjective sense of the word.[58] For this meaning to be defined and integrated into a system of jurisprudence, a new philosophy was needed. William of Ockham would provide it.[59]

In approaching Ockham's thought, Villey first sketches out the dispute over Franciscan poverty that led to Ockham's polemical writings from the 1320s onward. (His work in formal logic and philosophy had been accomplished earlier, during his years at Oxford.) The Franciscans had come to teach that, in observing perfect poverty, Christ and the apostles had renounced all property and all right of use in exterior things. For reasons that remain obscure, Pope John XXII denounced this whole position in 1323. He declared that henceforth it would be heresy to hold that Christ and the apostles had no right of use in the things they actually did use. Ockham's response to this was, for Villey, "the decisive moment in the history of subjective right."[60] Ockham was not a jurist by training, but he was obliged by the nature of the controversy to give definitions of legal terms like "*dominium*," "*ususfructus*," "*ius utendi*." The distinctive quality of Ockham's definitions, Villey suggests, is that in them "the concept of *right* is resolutely twisted to the meaning of *power*."[61] For Ockham *ius* meant *potestas*. More specifically, a right for him was a "licit power"—"*ius utendi est potestas licita utendi re extrinseca*." Villey sees these definitions as striking innovations. Ockham, he says, was the first to conceive of subjective right, the first to sanction the conjunction of right and power. His language might perhaps have been suggested in part by some earlier glossator; but, precisely because he was not technically trained as a jurist, Ockham could, in good faith, carry over the meaning that *ius* was acquiring in vulgar discourse into his formal definitions. But, above all, in Villey's view,

[58]Ibid., 107, 111. Here Villey rejected Hering's view that a concept of subjective right can be found in Aquinas (111 n.1). Actually Azo did give *potestas* as one meaning of *ius* but only in relation to the phrase *sui iuris esse* (Villey, "Origines," 271).

[59]Villey, *La formation*, 239: "Pour . . . q'il soit défini, intégré dans un système de pensée juridique moderne, il ne faut pas moins que le concours d'une philosophie . . . je pense que c'est de Guillaume d'Occam que date le tournant décisif."

[60]Villey, "La genèse," 113.

[61]Ibid., 117: "Elles offrent cette particularité . . . simplement que la notion de droit s'y trouve résolument *virer* au sens de *pouvoir*."

Ockham's definitions were derived from his nominalist philosophy, and it was this philosophy that was most important for future rights theories.[62] For Ockham only the individual had real existence; hence there could be no juridical order that did not proceed from the individual will, and no conception of a supra-individual social order.[63]

Villey concludes with a discussion of Ockham's *Brevilogium*.[64] He presents it as a treatise on pure power, which leaves no room for any conception of objective right. At the summit is the absolute power of God. In turn, God confers powers on men, primarily a power of appropriating external goods (after the Fall) and a power of instituting rulers. The ruler then has the power of legislation (*potestas condendi leges*). From human laws come *dominium*, usufruct and right of use—subjective rights guaranteed by state authority. The rights are all absolute. They can be exercised or renounced at will. *There is nothing else.* The subjective rights of individuals have filled the void left by the loss of objective natural right.[65]

So the argument reaches its conclusion. Ockham has achieved his "semantic revolution." "It is the whole philosophy professed by Ockham . . . that is the mother of subjective right."[66]

V. OBJECTIONS TO VILLEY

As I have suggested in presenting the earlier stages of Villey's argument, each phase of it is open to objections on points of detail. Similarly, his presentation of Ockham's views might be criticized as unbalanced. (Ockham's emphasis on individual liberties in the *Brevilogium* was matched by an equal concern for the common good in other contexts.) Yet Villey always has a sound and sensible point to make, even when he seems tempted to press the point to the edge of paradox. (Some early modern jurists did exaggerate the importance of individual rights in Roman law; Aquinas did have a flexible doctrine of *ius naturale*; the Franciscan disputes did focus attention on the problem of natural rights; some modern lists of supposed "human rights" are, indeed, protracted to the point of absurdity.) A more serious objection to Villey's thesis concerns the whole conceptual framework within which it is set. Villey has devised a sort of Manichean universe. There is an Aristotelian thought-world, full of light and sweet reason, and an Ockhamist thought-world, where all is darkness and blind will. The good theory of objective right can flourish only in the first thought-world, the bad theory of subjective rights only in the second. When clear-cut affirmations of

[62]Ibid., 118–120.

[63]Ibid., 121.

[64]Ibid., 123–26.

[65]Ibid., 126: "Et il n'y a rien d'autre . . . Les droits subjectifs des individus ont comblé le vide resultant de la perte du droit naturel."

[66]Id., *La formation*, 253, 261.

individual rights are found in texts before Ockham, they have to be dismissed as exceptions or aberrations or mere misunderstandings of vulgar persons who were too ignorant to attach precise meanings to the terms they used in day-to-day discourse.

There are two main lines of objection to this whole thesis (apart from the historical objection to be discussed below that rights theories did, indeed, exist before Ockham). In the first place, it is not clear that theories of individual rights depend on Ockhamist philosophical premises—even in the work of Ockham himself. In the second place, it is not clear that the ideas Villey contrasts with one another—classical objective right, Judeo-Christian natural moral law and modern subjective rights—are, in fact, inherently inconsistent with one another.

As to the first line of objection, the metaphysical "moderate realism" of Aristotle and Aquinas affirmed the primary existence of individual entities in the external world, in opposition to the Platonic theory of ideal forms. There is no reason why such a metaphysics should be incongruous with an emphasis on individual rights.[67] Similarly, Ockham's more radical criticism of a realist theory of universals did not exclude a concern with right relationships between persons and between persons and things.[68] Ockham's polemical works were, indeed, concerned precisely with such relationships (between empire and papacy, between ruler and subject, between person and property).

Villey simply assumes a dependence of Ockham's legal and political thought on his metaphysical doctrines. "*Avec une cohérence parfaite, Occam-juriste suit la voie d'Occam-philosophe.*" This relationship has, indeed, often been affirmed, especially, before Villey, by Georges de Lagarde; but it has also often been contested.[69] Charles Zuckerman has argued that all modern attempts to relate medieval political theories to metaphysical doctrines involve logical errors.[70] Even if this seems too intransigent, Zuckerman certainly shows that, as a matter of historical fact,

---

[67]The point was made long ago by M. de Wulf, "L'Individu et le groupe dans la scolastique du XIIIe siécle," *Revue néo-Scolastique de philsophie* 22 (1920): 341–357, at 348 and P. Gillet, *La personnalité juridique en droit ecclésiastique* (Malines, 1927). De Wulf especially emphasized the primacy of the individual person in Aquinas.

[68]On Ockham's theory of relations see, e.g., G. Martin, "Ist Ockhams Relationstheorie Nominalismus?" *Franziskanische Studien* 32 (1950): 31–49, at 49: "Ockham steht hier in einem unauflöslichen Zusammenhang mit Aristoteles, Thomas und Duns Scotus."

[69]Villey, *La formation*, 224. Some of the criticisms directed against de Lagarde's work (above n. 5) would apply also to Villey's interpretation. See, e.g., J. Morrall, "Some Notes on a Recent Interpretation of William of Ockham's Political Philosophy," *Franciscan Studies* 9 (1949): 335–69; W. Kölmel, *Wilhelm Ockham und sein kirchenpolitischen Schriften* (Essen, 1942) and id., "Das Naturrecht bei Wilhelm Ockham," *Franziskanische Studien* 35 (1953): 39–85.

[70]C. Zuckerman, "The Relationship of Theories of Universals to Theories of Church Government in the Middle Ages: A Critique of Previous Views," *Journal of the History of Ideas* 35 (1973): 579–594.

there is no correlation between the two spheres of thought in the positions of many medieval thinkers. We can find Thomists and realists and nominalists at every point on the political spectrum. (For instance, Wyclif and Huss, like Ockham, upheld the rights of Christian subjects against the pope; but, unlike Ockham, they were metaphysical realists in philosophy.) There is, indeed, no incongruity between Ockham's philosophy and his political theory, but there is no necessary connection between them either.

Ockham's own emphasis on a distinction between philosophical demonstration and knowledge of religious truth would argue against such a connection. For Ockham's so-called "political theory" was a political theology; its whole purpose was to convince the Catholic world that Pope John XXII was a heretic. Ockham could hardly achieve this by appealing to his own suspect innovations in philosophy (even if they had seemed relevant). Instead, his works are filled with appeals to canonistic and biblical authorities.

By the time Villey wrote on Ockham in the 1960s a substantial literature had grown up (which Villey simply ignores) asserting that Ockham was not radically destructive in his philosophy nor radically innovative in his political theory and, further, that there was no close connection between these two spheres of his activity. John Morrall called Ockham "an interpreter and defender of the achievements of the past." Philotheus Boehner, after a lifetime's study of Ockham's work, maintained that "Ockham's political ideas . . . could have been developed, so far as we can see, from any of the classical metaphysics of the 13th century."[71] Villey has emphasized that it was not only Ockham's own rights theories that were important for the future but his whole nominalist philosophy. And yet the great Spanish scholastics of the sixteenth century, the Jesuits and Dominicans who provided the essential link between medieval rights theories and modern ones, were not Ockhamists. Most of them considered themselves Thomists (though Villey, of course, sees them as, at best, erring disciples).

The fact that rights theories can be upheld by philosophers of different persuasions—including eminent natural law theorists—leads to our second

---

[71]J. Morrall, "Some Notes," 369; P. Boehner, "Ockham's Political Ideas," *Collected Articles on Ockham*, ed. E. Buytaert (St. Bonaventure, NY, 1958), 442–468, at 446. A bibliography of the "revisionist" work on Ockham and a sympathetic discussion of it is provided by H. Junghans, *Ockham im Lichte der neueren Forschung* (Berlin, 1968). See also J. Miethke, *Ockhams Weg zur Sozialphilosophie* (Berlin, 1969) and H. Oberman, *The Harvest of Late Medieval Theology: Gabriel Biel and Late Medieval Nominalism* (Cambridge, MA, 1963). On Ockham as a "constructive" political thinker, see A. McGrade, *The Political Thought of William of Ockham: Personal and Institutional Principles* (Cambridge, 1974). For changing views on the cultural significance of nominalism see W. Courtenay, "Nominalism and Late Medieval Religion," *The Pursuit of Holiness*, eds. C. Trinkhaus and H. Oberman (Leiden, 1974), 26–59. An overview of contemporary views on Ockham is presented in the papers of the Ockham Centennial Congress held at St. Bonaventure's University, October 10–12, 1985, to be published in a forthcoming volume of *Franciscan Studies*.

major line of objection to Villey's thesis. The various senses of *ius* that he discusses are not contradictory concepts. Rather, they are correlative. In considering Aquinas and the canonists we suggested that the concepts of *ius* as objective right order and as moral or legal precept are not intrinsically incompatible with one another. Now we can add that both concepts are compatible with the idea of individual rights. (We can define the relationship of parents and children in terms of an objectively right order. Or we can define it in terms of moral precept—"Honor thy father and thy mother." But we could also define the same relationship by saying that parents have a right to the respect of their children.)

As for individual rights and *ius naturale* considered as meaning what is objectively right: to affirm a right ordering of human relationships is to imply a structure of rights and duties. In propounding a system of jurisprudence one can emphasize either the objective pattern of relationships or the implied rights and duties of persons to one another—and, then again, one can focus on either the rights or the duties. The emphasis can fall in different ways depending on social, economic and political circumstances and on the temperament of a particular author. (It will probably have little to do with his abstract metaphysics.) The resulting works may be very different in tone and spirit, but the different emphases do not necessarily imply logical contradictions. Despite the assertion of Villey (and similar assertions by some disciples of Leo Strauss in America), it is just not true that "[t]he notion of subjective right is logically incompatible with classical natural right."

It is the same with *ius* understood as a body of moral or legal precepts. Villey noted that some modern jurists regard rights as merely the advantages to individuals implied by general laws; but he added that this could not explain the existence of natural rights.[72] He saw an association only in that traditional natural law theories allowed for "permissive laws" as well as precepts or prohibitions, and he held that rights theories grew up in this area of permissiveness.[73] But one can go further than this. The precepts and prohibitions also imply rights. To say that "Thou shalt not steal" is a command of natural law is to imply that others have a natural right to acquire property, a point that medieval jurists clearly grasped.[74] In fact, one finds

[72]Villey, "La genèse," 99.

[73]Villey, *Le droit et les droits*, 123: "En outre, il n'est pas que des lois *préceptives* . . . ou *interdictives* . . . mais aussi des lois *permissive* . . . Ainsi naît le droit subjectif. . . . "

[74]For some examples of this in canonistic thought see R. Weigand, *Die Naturrechtslehre der Legisten und Dekretisten von Irnerius bis Accursius und von Gratian bis Johannes Teutonicus* (Munich, 1967), 357–59. The view that natural law and natural rights are contradictory concepts is often found in current American literature. See, e.g., W. Berns, "The Constitution as Bill of Rights," *How Does the Constitution Secure Rights?*, eds. R. Goldwin and W. Schambra (Washington, 1985), 50–73, at 55: " . . . natural rights and traditional natural law are, to put it simply yet altogether accurately, incompatible . . . . " Such views seem based on a mistaken idea that modern rights theories are derived entirely from Hobbes and on simple ignorance of the history of the concept of *ius naturale* before the seventeenth century.

natural rights regarded as derivative from natural law at every stage in the history of the doctrine—in the twelfth century renaissance of law, in the eighteenth century Enlightenment and still in twentieth century discourse. A modern thinker like Jacques Maritain, steeped in the Thomistic tradition of natural law, has defended natural rights as an aspect of that tradition, essential to the dignity of human personality.[75] More recently, John Finnis, arguing in the language of contemporary analytic jurisprudence, has also treated the concept of rights as a "valuable addition ... to the tradition of 'natural law doctrine'."[76]

VI. ALTERNATIVE APPROACHES

Once we realize that the assertion of rights doctrine is not necessarily dependent on a prior acceptance of a nominalist philosophy and that claims for individual rights have commonly existed in a symbiotic relationship, one might say, with theories of objective natural right and natural moral law, rather than in opposition to them, then the whole problem of the origin of Western rights theories can be approached in ways different from Villey's. In suggesting some alternative approaches I am not concerned primarily to contest Villey's understanding of Aristotelian natural right as an ideal to which modern civilization should return—that is another whole question— but rather to argue that his commitment to a particular philosophical stance has led him to present a distorted version of the course of medieval intellectual history. We can agree that the concept of individual rights was not prominent (to say the least) in classical law and that Ockham was an important transmitter of rights theories to the modern world. But if we realize further that Ockham's own theory of rights was not a radical innovation based on a transposition of his novel philosophical concepts into juridical language (which seems an unwarranted assumption), then an obvious approach to the origin of Western rights theories is to investigate the earlier medieval development of such doctrines, especially in the sources that contributed to Ockham's thought in this area.

A natural starting point is the "renaissance" or "revolution" of the twelfth century, which saw so many new beginnings in Western life and thought. Villey himself, as we have seen, emphasized the concern for individual rights in the everyday, secular life of the age, and many recent writers have discussed the new personalist or humanist forms of religious devotion that grew up then. Villey appreciated the importance of Christianity for the growth of rights theories, and he saw, too, that Ockham's philosophy was not mere "cobweb of the brain" spun out of his own

---

[75]J. Maritain, *Les droits de l'homme et la loi naturelle* (Paris, 1945).

[76]Finnis, *Natural Law*, 221. The traditional interdependence of natural law and natural rights theories was also emphasized by J. Dabin in a criticism of Villey. See J. Dabin, "Droit subjectif et subjectivisme juridique," *Archives de philosophie du droit* 9 (1964): 17–35.

subjective consciousness but, rather, a reflection of the real-life circumstances of the Middle Ages.[77] Yet Villey still supposed that social and
religious realities could shape a new system of jurisprudence only after they
had passed through the filter of Ockham's nominalist thought. In fact
though—as Harold Berman most recently and notably has pointed out—
already by the twelfth century the writings of the canonists were permeated
by doctrines based on individual intention and individual will in areas like
the law of tort, the law of contract and the law of marriage.[78] It would seem
not unreasonable to look for a concern with individual rights also in such a
juristic culture. Moreover, the political writings of Ockham himself are
saturated with canonistic references. He could hardly have avoided them.
Before he ever became involved in the Franciscan poverty dispute, the
issues had already been formulated in juridical terms by two formidable
lawyers, Pope John XXII and his Franciscan adversary, Bonagratia of
Bergamo.

The earlier literature of the Franciscan controversies provides another
rich body of source material, along with the writings of the canonists, for the
investigation of medieval rights theories. Villey was correct to see the
Franciscan Order as a "cradle" of rights doctrines even though he exaggerated the importance of Ockham as an innovator.[79] If we go back to the early
days of the Order, the whole Franciscan movement can be seen as a
culmination in the religious sphere of the personalism or individualism that
also influenced twelfth century law. From the beginning, there was a special
kind of individualism in Francis's attitude to the world around him; he did
not love mankind in the abstract, but particular men and women.[80] He
attracted an extraordinary group of vividly diverse personalities as his first
followers. Francis laid down in his Rule that all the brothers were to obey
their superiors, but then added "in everything that is not against their
conscience. . . . " A little later, from the 1250s onward, the conflicts of
mendicants and seculars stimulated a more legalistic concern with individual rights in the writings of Franciscan masters.

Two streams of thought, then, flowed together in Ockham's polemical
works. One had its source in canonistic writings, the other in the early
literature of the Franciscan disputes. For the rest of this paper, I would like
to suggest some ways in which the further investigation of these sources

---

[77]Villey, La formation, 236, 266.

[78]H. Berman, Law and Revolution: The Formation of the Western Legal Tradition (Cambridge, MA, 1983).

[79]Villey also calls attention to the voluntarism of Scotus but still finds the decisive break-
through in Ockham. See, e.g., La formation, 179–189. Villey's treatment of Scotus would require
another paper. But the remarks above about the pervasiveness of will and intention that one finds
already in twelfth century law are relevant here too.

[80]As Chesterton wrote: "He did not call nature his mother: he called a particular donkey his
brother, or a particular sparrow his sister."

might advance our understanding of pre-modern rights theories. There is an almost embarrassing profusion of topics that led, long before Ockham, to the discussion of *ius* in subjective terms and also to the identification of *ius* with *potestas*—I can do little more than mention some of them here.

Among the canonistic writings of the twelfth century perhaps the most interesting texts belong to a group in which the precise terminology that Villey considers distinctively modern is used to define *ius naturale* as a "power," "force," "faculty" or "ability" of the human personality, related to man's free will and moral intuition. As Sicard of Cremona wrote, "*Ius naturale . . . est quedam vis et potentia naturaliter insita. . . .*"[81] The meaning of the canonists' language is not identical with that of early modern rights theorists (although they sometimes used the same words). The twelfth century writers were thinking of *ius naturale* primarily as a power of the soul, but they certainly used the term in a subjective sense. Their texts, it seems to me, provide a crucial link between Stoic theories of a natural law in man and later theories of inherent natural rights. They stand at a mid-point between Cicero's *vis naturae* and Suarez's *facultas moralis*. (I hope to return to this question in a more detailed study.)

On a less abstract level, Huguccio initiated a major debate on the rights of the poor with an argument that, *iure naturali*, the poor had a just claim to the surplus property of the rich.[82] A little later Innocent IV defended the claims of infidels to property and jurisdiction in terms of natural right.[83] These controversies about the rights of the poor and of infidels continued all through the Middle Ages and beyond, and both themes found a place in Ockham's work.[84]

Canonistic corporation theory is also relevant for the history of individual rights. The influential "fiction theory"—the definition of a corporation as a *persona ficta*, a fiction of law—was developed precisely because the canonists insisted that real personality belonged only to individual human

---

[81]Weigand, *Naturrechtslehre*, 184. See also ibid., 197 [". . . dicitur ius naturale facultas discernendi . . . et hoc est liberum arbitrium" (from the *Summa Lipsiensis*)], 216 ["Ius ergo naturale dicitur ratio, scilicet naturalis vis animi . . ." (from Huguccio)]. Huguccio also gave a permissive definition: ". . . scilicet omne licitum et approbatum, ita quod nec precipitur nec prohibetur . . ." ibid., 217. See also ibid., 144, 203, 208, 213. Villey occasionally mentions such texts (*La formation*, 115; *Critique*, 33–34), but does not seem to see their significance.

[82]On this see my *Medieval Poor Law* (Berkeley/Los Angeles, 1959), 33. The whole question of the rights of the poor is discussed, with numerous medieval texts, in G. Couvreur, *Les pauvres, Ont-ils des droits?* (Rome, 1961). In reading these discussions it is often hard to know whether *iure naturali* should be translated as "by natural law" or "by natural right." Both meanings can be present at once. But sometimes the subjective sense is clearly intended.

[83]On Innocent's doctrine and its repercussions in later controversies, see J. Muldoon, *Popes, Lawyers, and Infidels: The Church and the Non-Christian World* (Philadelphia, 1979) and, most recently, A. Garcia y Garcia, *Iglesia, Sociedad y Derecho* (Salamanca, 1985).

[84]Ockham, however, attributed to Innocent IV a position opposite to the one the pope actually held. On this see A. Melloni, "William of Ockham's Critique of Innocent IV," *Franciscan Studies* (forthcoming).

beings.[85] (Again, this was based on a religious insight—only individual persons had immortal souls.) The canonists also displayed an unusual concern for the rights of individuals within corporate structures, as Maitland long ago pointed out.[86] Another related topic is what we might call the "right of association," the right of individuals to form corporate bodies. Classical Roman law had been very restrictive about this, but medieval canon law became more and more permissive until Innocent IV laid down that corporate status was acquired automatically if at least three members joined together and if the aim was "to preserve for each his justice." As Anthony Black has recently observed, "*Justitia* in this context may just as well be translated as 'rights'."[87]

Many medieval discussions of *ius* were concerned, not with natural rights, but with rights derived from positive law; however, they led to detailed analyses of the subjective sense of *ius* that could subsequently be absorbed into natural rights theories. One important topic concerned the status of a prelate after his election to a bishopric but before his confirmation and consecration.[88] To borrow Gewirth's modern language, the election gave the bishop a "rightful claim" to his see but not a "rightful power" over it. Shortly after 1200 the canonists devised the technical terms *"ius ad rem"* and *"ius in re"* to describe the two kinds of right. In the refined discussions on this question the canonists were sometimes led to identify *ius* with *potestas*. They also made careful distinctions between having a right and exercising a right (a distinction that persists in modern canonistic literature). These themes can be found woven together in a few lines from Huguccio:

> Before confirmation they have the power (*potestas*) of administering, that is the right (*ius*) of administering, but they do not have the exercise of that right.[89]

Besides discussing the acquisition of office, the canonists were also concerned with problems about voluntary renunciation of rights or forced deprivation of them. (Johannes Teutonicus wrote, in the ordinary gloss to the

[85]P. Michaud-Quantin, *Universitas. Expressions du mouvement communautaire dans le moyen-âge latin* (Paris, 1970) provides an overview of the extensive modern discussions on the "fiction theory."

[86]F. Pollock and F. Maitland, *The History of English Law*, 2 vols., 2d ed. (Cambridge, 1898), 1: 506–7.

[87]A. Black, *Guilds and Society in European Political Thought* (Ithaca, NY, 1984), 17.

[88]The best modern discussion is in R. Benson, *The Bishop-Elect: A Study in Medieval Ecclesiastical Office* (Princeton, 1968).

[89]T. Lenherr, "Der Begriff 'executio' in der Summa Decretorum des Huguccio," *Archiv für katholisches Kirchenrecht* 150 (1981): 5–45, 361–420, at 392: "Ante habent potestatem administrandi, id est ius administrandi, set non habent executionem illius iuris in actu." For "use" of rights in modern canon law, see M. Wegan, "La distinction 'Ius et Usus Iuris'," *Revue de droit canonique* 29 (1979): 93–113.

Decretum, "No one is to be deprived of his right except for a very grave offense."[90])

A final group of texts, where the canonists used *ius* in a subjective sense, and also identified it with the idea of power, concerned the rights of the papacy. (Here we are dealing with a kind of divine right.) The papal election decree of Nicholas II, included in Gratian's *Decretum,* attributed to the electors "the right of the power to elect" (*ius potestatis . . . eligere*).[91] Gratian himself attributed to the Roman church a *ius condendi canones,* and the phrase was taken up by later canonists as a proof-text to demonstrate that the word "*ius*" could, indeed, mean *potestas.* Another text of Nicholas II, also incorporated into the *Decretum,* claimed for the pope "rights (*iura*) over a heavenly and earthly empire."[92] This gave rise to a considerable body of comment and controversy about the temporal power of the pope and the meaning of the term "*ius*" in this context. One of the first commentators on the *Decretum* made an important distinction here between "right of authority" and "right of administration"; others identified the papal *ius* specifically as a power in referring to the "power of the sword."[93]

An extensive technical literature has grown up around each of the canonistic themes mentioned above, but it is not addressed to our particular problem—the origin of rights theories and, specifically, the juristic understanding of the term "*ius*" before Ockham.[94] It is the same when we turn to Franciscan history. In this area, too, there is a huge body of modern writing on the early history of the Franciscan Order and especially on the Franciscan poverty disputes.[95] But it is only when we come to Ockham that historians of rights theories seem to regard the subject as relevant to their inquiries. In fact, the mass of controversial Franciscan literature before 1300 is relevant too.

If we had to choose one pre-eminent philosopher as the first who transplanted Franciscan religious concepts to the alien field of legal theory it might well be Bonaventure rather than Ockham (though no one has accused Bonaventure of being a nominalist). Writing in 1269, Bonaventure distinguished four forms of common ownership associated with four categories of

---

[90]*Decretum Gratiani . . . una cum glossis* (Venice, 1600), gloss *ad Dist.* 56.c.7: "Non enim privandus est quis iure suo nisi pro gravissimo delicto."

[91]*Dist.* 23. c.1.

[92]*Dist.* 22. c.1: " . . . terreni simul et celestis imperii iura. . . ."

[93]Many canonistic comments on *Dist.* 22 c.1 were published in A. Stickler, "Imperator Vicarius Pape," *Mitteilungen des Instituts für Oesterreichische Geschichtsforschung* 62 (1954): 165–212.

[94]On Ockham's use of canonistic sources see my "Ockham, the Conciliar Theory, and the Canonists," *Journal of the History of Ideas* 15 (1954): 40–70 and "Natural Law and Canon Law in Ockham's Dialogus" in *Aspects of Late Medieval Government and Society. Essays Presented to J. R. Lander* (Toronto, 1986), 3–24.

[95]M. Lambert, *Franciscan Poverty* (London, 1961) provides a convenient introduction. For a more detailed study of Ockham's involvement, see M. Damiata, *Guglelmo d'Ockham: Povertà e potere,* 2 vols. (Florence, 1978–79).

rights—those derived from necessity of nature, from fraternal charity, from the civil law of the world and from ecclesiastical endowments. The first two could not be renounced; the second two had to be renounced by anyone seeking the highest form of evangelical perfection.[96] Bonaventure (like Ockham) claimed for the Franciscans a right of use separate from ownership but not a right based on secular law. The friars had a right to material support by virtue of the law of mercy and by virtue of the law of justice, he wrote (but Bonaventure meant natural or divine justice here). Villey has suggested that, in Roman law, *ius utendi* was essentially a legal attribute of the thing used; but such a position cannot be sustained in relation to Franciscan uses of the term in the century before Ockham. The friars and their adversaries were constantly concerned with the inner intention and inner disposition of the user. Bonaventure wrote, "They must claim their right with humility . . . that they may be humiliated in receiving" (and it was a natural right that he was discussing).[97] We have seen that a dispute exists as to whether Thomas Aquinas had any idea of subjective right. But what of Bonaventure? Was his concept of *ius* more subjective than Thomas's? Any serious study of medieval rights theories would need to address the question.

In such a study we should also need to consider not only the writings of the Franciscans but also those of their adversaries among the secular theologians—William of St. Amour, Gerard of Abbeville, Henry of Ghent, Godfrey of Fontaines, John of Pouilly.[98] Here again, there is a vast terrain that needs to be explored before we can hope to make an adequate map of medieval rights theories. Besides denouncing the Franciscan doctrine of poverty, the secular masters also attacked the papal privileges that enabled the friars to preach throughout the church. Such privileges, they maintained, undermined the traditional status of bishops and priests in their dioceses and parishes. To a modern mind it is clear that the issue could have been stated in terms of the rights of subjects (bishops and priests) against their ruler (the pope). But could the mind of a medieval theologian (before Ockham) have conceived of the issue in those terms? Godfrey of Fontaines, writing in the 1280s, in fact did so. The question he posed was, "Whether a superior prelate can take away from his subjects what belongs to them by right." Arguing for the superior, he pointed out that popes often did take away powers of their subordinates—for example, a chapter's power of electing or the right (*ius*) that an electee had acquired. On the other side, he quoted a

---

[96]*Apologia pauperum* in *S. Bonaventurae . . . Opera omnia* (Quaracchi, 1898), 8: 233–330, at 309.

[97]Ibid., 329. Bonaventure wrote here that the friars were entitled to receive alms, not *iure fori* but *iure poli*. (Ockham would later use the same distinction.) " . . . iure poli eam exigere possunt et debent per modum humilitatis . . . ut ipsi humilientur recipiendo."

[98]On this literature see especially Y. Congar, "Aspects ecclésiologiques de la querelle entre mendiants et séculiers dans la seconde moitié du XIIIe siécle et le debut du XIVe," *Archives d'histoire doctrinale et littéraire du moyen âge* 36 (1961): 35–151.

text of Gregory the Great, included in the *Decretum*, where the pope said that he wished to maintain the rights (*iura*) of all other churches. Godfrey concluded that the ruler could take away the rights of subordinates only in exceptional cases when such action was necessary for the common good. If he tried to act otherwise he could be resisted.

> ... Good rulers, especially ecclesiastical ones ... ought to rule as is fitting in the best polity, one in which the ruler does not intend his own good but the good of his subjects, who are not slaves but free men, having the power to oppose their ruler if he wishes to tyrannize over them.[99]

Of course, we encounter a feudal right of resistance in innumerable medieval documents. But here we have an academic philosopher, in formal philosophical discourse, using Aristotle's theory of government—which Villey regarded as incompatible with subjective rights—precisely in order to defend a right of resistance to papal tyranny. The same issue will recur in Ockham's work, but Godfrey was not a nominalist or even a Franciscan.

In discussing the problems of evangelical poverty also, the opponents of the Franciscans—just as much as the friars themselves—were led to consider questions concerning property rights. The Dominican Hervaeus Natalis, a Thomist and adviser to Pope John XXII, wrote that the words *"dominium," "ius"* and *"proprietas"* all implied the meaning of *potestas*. Some scholars have suggested that John XXII, the adversary of Ockham, contributed as much to rights theories as Ockham himself.[100] Sometimes questions arose about natural law and, specifically, about natural rights as in these lines, also from Godfrey of Fontaines:

> On account of this, that each one is bound by the law of nature to sustain his life, which cannot be done without exterior goods, therefore also by the law of nature (*iure naturae*) each has dominion and a certain right (*ius*) in the common exterior goods of this world which right also cannot be renounced.[101]

[99]*Les Quodlibets onze-quartorze de Godefroid de Fontaines*, ed. J. Hoffmans, vol. 5 of *Les philosophes Belges* (Louvain, 1932), 94 (Quodl. 12. q.3).

[100]H. Natalis, *De paupertate Christi et apostolorum*, ed. J. Sykes, in *Archives d'histoire doctrinale et littéraire du moyen âge* 12–13 (1937–38): 209–297, at 235–6: "... Sciendum quod ista nomina, 'dominium', 'ius', et 'proprietas' idem dicunt in re. Nihil enim aliud dicunt quam habere potestatem in aliqua re per quam possit licite re aliqua uti vel rem aliquam alienare ..." On the role of John XXII, see A. McGrade, "Ockham and the Birth of Individual Rights," in *Authority and Power. Studies on Medieval Law and Government Presented to Walter Ullmann*, eds. B. Tierney and P. Lineham (Cambridge, 1980), 149–165, at 152.

[101]*Philosophes Belges* 4 (1924): 105 (Quodl. 8. q.11): "Immo etiam propter hoc quod unusquisque tenetur iure naturae vitam suam sustentare, quod non contingit nisi de bonis exterioribus, ideo etiam iure naturae quilibet habet dominium et quoddam ius in bonis communibus exterioribus huius mundi, cui etiam iuri renuntiare non potest licite."

Here the meaning of the word *"ius"* shifted from objective natural law to subjective natural right in the course of a single sentence. Here again, the argument about an inalienable right to use what is needed to sustain life is one that recurred in Ockham. Indeed, it seems evident that we cannot write meaningfully about Ockham's distinctive contribution to rights theories—or even determine whether he made any such distinctive contribution—until his work has been brought into relationship with the great body of writing by earlier participants in the Franciscan controversies.

The fullest and most interesting discussion of *ius* as a subjective right in a Franciscan source before Ockham is found in a *Quaestio* of John Peter Olivi. Here, once more, *ius* was identified with *potestas*. The question Olivi posed was whether the possession of a *ius*—he mentioned specifically the "right of royal power" and the "right of property"—added anything real to the person of the right-holder.[102] Pervading the whole discussion was an awareness of the correlativity of rights and duties. (Olivi also asked whether the obligation by which a subject was bound to his king or a monk to his abbot added something real to the subject or the monk.) Moreover, the whole argument turned on Olivi's acceptance of a doctrine common to earlier scholastic philosophers, including Aquinas—the divine governance of the universe through rational natural law and divine positive law.

> There is a certain order so absolutely fixed . . . by reason of virtue and justice that God cannot and ought not to will the opposite . . . and this order is commonly called the order of natural right (*ordo iuris naturalis*). There is another order proceeding from the command of the divine will, such that God can will or will the opposite . . . as he pleases.[103]

Olivi did not regard subjective rights as somehow contrary to this overarching structure of law but as implicit in it. Rights of rulership and rights of property were a part of the divine scheme of things; that was why transgression of these rights by disobedience or theft was considered a mortal sin.[104] Such considerations favored the argument that acquiring a *ius* did add something real to the personality of the right-holder. But there were arguments on the other side too. A person could sell his rights, which meant that the purchaser received the same rights the other had formerly held, and this could not be if the rights were something real, informing the person of

---

[102]The text is edited in F. Delorme, "Question de P. J. Olivi 'Quid ponat ius vel dominium' ou encore 'De signis voluntariis'," *Antonianum* 20 (1945): 309–330. Olivi regarded his question about rights as analogous to the questions of whether a sacrament (e.g., baptism or ordination) conferred a real character on the recipient, and whether the attribution of meaning added something real to a word or sign.

[103]Ibid., 324: " . . . est ordo sic absolute prefixus . . . ratione virtutis et iustitie, que est quod Deus non potest nec debet oppositum eius velle . . . et hic ordo communiter vocatur ordo iuris naturalis. Alius autem est ordo sic a dominativo imperio divine voluntatis procedens, quod Deus ipsum et eius oppositum . . . pro libitu protest velle."

[104]Ibid., 317.

the first right-holder. Again, a right could not be said to inhere in the body of a right-holder or any part of it, or in the intellect or in the will. And rights could be acquired or taken away without any real change in the subject (as a seal could lose its validity without any real change in the seal).[105] These are only a few points from a very complex scholastic discussion, but they give some idea of how much sophistication could be brought to bear on a consideration of rights concepts before the end of the thirteenth century. (Olivi eventually concluded that a right did add something to the person of the right-holder, but not of such a nature as to change his real essence.)

Let us turn back to the canonists for one final text. Villey observed that the lists of definitions of the word *"ius"* given by the Roman lawyers and by Thomas Aquinas did not include the subjective meaning of the term as a power inhering in individuals. But around 1310, 20 years before Ockham wrote his first polemical works, the canonist Johannes Monachus made a more ample list, ending with a mnemonic verse to help his students remember a score of different meanings.[106] Johannes set out from a decretal of Nicholas III stating that, when an election required papal confirmation, the electee had to appear at Rome *"cum omnibus actis, iuribus et muni-mentis suis"* ("with all his acts, rights, and documents"). This reminded Johannes of another canonistic text, borrowed from Roman law, which affirmed that the pope had *"omnia iura in scrinio pectoris sui"* ("all laws in the shrine of his breast"). How could the electee bring his *iura* when the pope already had all *iura*? The word *"ius"* was obviously being used in different senses, and this consideration launched Johannes into a list of all the possible meanings he could think of. There is a note of heavy-handed playfulness in some of his definitions. He began with the entirely non-legal meaning of *"ius"* as a rich liquid (*aqua pinguis*), a broth or juice, and proceeded with some word-play on *mando* as meaning either to eat or to command. (Then he solemnly explained the pun to his students, *"Mando* of the first conjugation, has two different meanings . . .") His mnemonic verse began,

> *Ius* is water, *ius* is right, *ius* is called a power,
> An art, a form, the rigor of law, a bond, a nature, a place . . .

and continued with many more explanations. Johannes' second definition shows a kind of overlapping of objective and subjective right. *"Ius* means the right and just, as when we say so-and-so has or does not have a *ius.*"[107] Another definition identified *ius* with *dominium*. The most important dis-cussion for us, however, was on the third definition, which treated *ius* as

---

[105]Ibid., 326.

[106]J. Monachus, *Glossa Aurea* (Paris, 1535), fol. xcir, Gloss *ad Sext.* 1.6.16.

[107]See also ibid., n. 108: "Secundo ius dicitur rectum seu iustum ut cum dicimus iste habet vel non habet ius. . . . "

meaning *potestas*. *"Tertio idem est quod potestas . . ."* Johannes first cited in support of this the text of Gratian we have mentioned which claimed for the Roman church a right of making laws (*ius condendi canones*).[108] Johannes assumed that this evidently referred to a power of making laws. Johannes next gave an example from the Roman law of tutors. One text of the Digest defined a guardianship as a *ius*; another defined it as a *potestas*. So again, it seemed that the two words could be used interchangeably. But at this point the argument took a new and interesting turn. Accursius, in the ordinary gloss to the Digest, had suggested that guardianship might be called a "violent power" since it could be imposed upon a person against his will. But Johannes would not accept that a *ius* could be based on violence, which was normally culpable. Rather, *ius* was a power introduced by right, or by law, *a iure introducta*. Still not satisfied with his definition, Johannes introduced some more verbal equivocation, this time in connection with the word *"virtus"* as meaning either "force" or "virtue." He thought *"virtus"* was derived from *vis intus*. But one common definition of *ius naturale* called it a *vis* implanted in all creatures and hence, Johannes suggested, a *virtus*. This innate *virtus* was a natural power. But, the author continued, "Art imitates nature," and so the *ius* of the lawyers was a *virtus* too. But here the meaning of *"virtus"* shifted and led Johannes to his final definition. *Ius* was not a violent power but a "virtuous power."[109]

The argument involved word-play and a sort of web of free association of juridical ideas. It was not a philosophical argument; it had nothing to do with nominalism. Still, it led Johannes to a definition of *ius* as a subjective power, a "virtuous power" which was very similar to Ockham's "licit power" and, indeed, to Gewirth's modern definition, "a rightful power." The definition acquired a broad currency in the later Middle Ages because it was incorporated into the standard commentary on the *Liber Sextus* of Johannes Andreae. Then, in the sixteenth century, Johannes Andreae, in turn, was quoted in the widely-read *Summa* of the Dominican, Sylvester Prieras.[110]

---

[108]Ibid.: "Tertio idem est quod potestas, xxv q. prima § his ita . . ." (i.e., C.25 q.1 *dictum post* c.16, where Gratian referred to the *ius condendi canones*).

[109]Ibid. The gloss is so compressed and allusive as to resist literal translation: "Alio modo legitur illa littera ius cum dicat glossa ibidem ius et potestas, i.e., violenta potestas. Sed hec glossa videtur mala. Nam omne violentum est reprobum . . . sed accipitur (ius) pro potestate a iure introducta. Sic dicitur quod nature virtus i.e. vis intus id est vis insita rebus naturalibus in quibus est vis generativa. Sed trahitur a simili in artificiatis, cum ars imitetur naturam in quantum posset, ff de adopt. si pater, 1, in fine, et sic dicitur ius et potestas, i.e. virtus potestativa seu virtuosa potestas. . . ."

[110]Johannes Andreae reproduced the definitions of Johannes Monachus in slightly abbreviated form in his *In titulum de Regulis iuris novella commentaria* (Venice, 1581), fol. 2v (Gloss *ad Sext.* 5.12). Cf. S. Prieras, *Summae Sylvestrinae* (Venice, 1584), 79r. Johannes Andreae added a significant comment in another context, *In quintum Decretalium librum novella commentaria* (Venice, 1581), fol. 151v. The text of the Decretals (X.5.40.12) stated (quoting Isidore of Seville): "Ius est a iure possidendo." Johannes commented, "Non loquitur hic Isidorus de iure generali quod legibus vel moribus constat . . . sed sumitur pro iure quod competit privato in re aliqua." It

When Peter Olivi and Johannes Monachus discussed *ius* as subjective right, they were not just casually or carelessly borrowing a usage from vulgar discourse. Rather each was providing a detailed analysis (philosophical or juridical) of a concept whose importance was fully apparent to them. When Ockham, in turn, came to write on subjective rights there was no need for him to inaugurate a "semantic revolution." A rich language already existed in which rights theories could be articulated. The doctrine of individual rights was not a late medieval aberration from an earlier tradition of objective right or of natural moral law. Still less was it a seventeenth century invention of Suarez or Hobbes or Locke. Rather, it was a characteristic product of the great age of creative jurisprudence that, in the twelfth and thirteenth centuries, established the foundations of the Western legal tradition. Villey is justified in calling attention to the abuses of rights language by many modern theorists. But, in an age like ours, so fertile in the invention of new forms of tyranny, the underlying concept may still prove of value in our political discourse. As to the history of the doctrine, there is still a great deal of work to be done. Villey may not have been correct in all of his conclusions, but he certainly stated the problem perceptively. *"Si toutes les notions juridiques modernes ... nées de l'idée de droit subjectif, n'existaient pas encore a Rome, quel vaste champ d'études que l'examen de leur véritable origine!"*[111]

---

is just the distinction between *ius* as general law and *ius* as private right that one finds in Suarez and other seventeenth century authors.

[111]Villey, "L'idée du droit subjectif," 226.

INSTITUTIONAL HISTORY FROM ARCHIVAL HISTORY: THE COURT OF CANTERBURY ROLLS*

Charles Donahue, Jr.

Hal Berman has emphasized the importance of the system of canon law in the development of Western legal thought; he has also emphasized the fundamental unity of the Western legal tradition. This paper, dedicated to him in friendship, touches on both themes. It concerns not the precocious development of canon law as an intellectual system, but rather the much slower development of a working system of ecclesiastical courts in which the intellectual system could be tested and implemented. My suggestion is that the Court of Canterbury (later called the Court of Arches), the provincial court of the archbishop of Canterbury, was influenced in its development as an institution by the English central royal courts. The evidence for this proposition is the fact that in the middle of the second half of the thirteenth century the Court of Canterbury was maintaining plea rolls, or something quite like plea rolls.[1] I would like to take this opportunity to describe them briefly, to suggest what kind of information can be drawn from them and to close by speculating upon why it is that the English courts Christian did not continue to maintain such rolls.[2]

I. THE COURT OF CANTERBURY ROLLS

The rolls in question, presently housed in the Cathedral Archives and Library in Canterbury, are the rolls of the Court of Canterbury *sede vacante*, the vacancy being that between the death of Archbishop Boniface of Savoy

---

*An earlier version of this paper was given at the Conference on British Legal Manuscripts at the Newberry Library, April 4, 1986, and I benefited greatly from the discussion that followed. Material from the Cathedral Archives and Library, Canterbury [hereafter CALC] is used with the kind permission of the Dean and Chapter of Canterbury. This paper is part of a larger undertaking, a cooperative venture surveying medieval church court records in England and on the Continent, to be published in the series *Comparative Studies in Continental and Anglo-American Legal History (Vergleichende Untersuchungen zur kontinentaleuropäischen und anglo-amerikanischen Rechtsgeschichte)*. The project is described in the first vol. of the series: H. Coing and K. Nörr, eds., *Englische und kontinentale Rechtsgeschichte: ein Forschungsprojekt* (Berlin, 1985), 63–71.

[1]The most accessible description of plea rolls is probably C. Flower, *Introduction to the Curia Regis Rolls, 1199–1230*, Selden Society, no. 62 (London, 1944).

[2]The only printed description of these rolls is in N. Adams and C. Donahue, eds., *Select Cases from the Ecclesiastical Courts of the Province of Canterbury, c.1200–1301*, Selden Society, no. 95 (London, 1981) [hereafter SCC], 16–18. SCC also contains an edition of three of the rolls at 49–95. This paper will serve, inter alia, to expand and to correct that description.

in July of 1270 and the assumption of administration by Archbishop Robert Kilwardby in December of 1272.[3] There are eight rolls, containing from one to six membranes, 27 membranes in all, and the entries on them bear dates from September 22, 1270 to December 5, 1272.[4] The patterns of dates on the rolls and on other related documents suggest that what we have is close to complete for the period from September of 1271 to December of 1272, and only fragments remain of what may have been ten membranes dating from November 1270 through July 1271.[5]

The membranes are of good quality; if not the very back of the beast, at least a long strip from the side. They are sewn foot-to-head, and that is clearly the way in which they were sewn originally. The longer rolls have a rod at each end so that they can be read like a Roman scroll, but these are of modern origin, and it is not clear that they replaced anything medieval.[6] By and large, the dorse of the rolls is blank. Only a few membranes have entries on the dorse, and there are never more than two or three such entries.[7]

The most notable physical feature of the rolls is the large number of documents sewn to the left-hand sides. The number of such documents on each membrane varies from none to 11.[8] Sewing holes on the sides of the membranes indicate that many more documents were once attached, and sewing holes on the sides of documents still found in the archives indicate that they were once attached to these rolls or to ones like them.[9]

---

[3]While the See of Canterbury was vacant, the prior and chapter administered the spiritualities of the See, including the ecclesiastical courts. Kilwardby was provided on October 11, 1272, at which point, from a legal point of view, he received the spiritualities of the diocese. See R. Benson, *The Bishop Elect* (Princeton, 1968), 350; I. Churchill, *Canterbury Administration* (London, 1933), 1:567. His temporalities were restored on December 12, 1272; he was not consecrated until February 23, 1273. The rolls tell us that the court was sitting under the authority of the prior and chapter until at least December 5, 1272, and it may have sat later than that, since it is quite possible that the final rolls were brought back to London for use of the court *sede plena*.

[4]CALC, Ecclesiastical Suit Roll [hereafter ESR] 14 (2 mm.), 18 (1 m.), 20 (6 mm.) (the fragment needed to complete the last membrane may be found in CALC, Sede Vacante Scrapbook [hereafter SVSB] III: 105), 21 (2 mm.), 23 (1 m.), 30 (4 mm.), 39 (3 mm.), 208 (2 mm.), 222 (6 mm.).

[5]There are four fragments from January and February, 1271 in ESR 370i–iv. The conjecture both of the virtual completeness of the court year 1271–2 and of the number of missing membranes from 1270–1 is based on the facts that relatively few cases that can be dated to 1271–2 do not have entries on the surviving membranes and that many cases can be traced throughout the year. The year is not quite complete because ESR 21 begins with the end of an entry that had obviously started on a previous membrane, now missing, and there may be one more membrane missing at the end of the court year. See further n. 44 below. The estimate of missing membranes of the previous year was calculated by extrapolation.

[6]E.g., ESR 222.

[7]E.g., ESR 23 (1 entry), ESR 30 m.1 [hereafter ESR 30/1] (3 entries), ESR 39/1 (1 entry).

[8]E.g., from the court year 1271–2: ESR 20 (3 on mm. 1–2), 20/3 (3), 20/4 (1), 21/1 (1), 21/2 (4), 23/1 (2), 30/3 (1), 39/1 (2), 39/2 (11), 208/1 (6), 208/2 (4).

[9]E.g., SVSB III:362 (dilatory exception with sewing holes on the left-hand side); ESR 30/2 (an entire membrane of the rolls with no attached documents but with many sewing holes on the left-hand side).

Only one membrane has a heading. The first in chronological order has written on the dorse: "*Acta* and libels of divers processes from 21 September, 1270, to 10 July, 1271,"[10] suggesting both that the court calendar was an annual one and that only certain types of material will be found here. We will have to return to this latter suggestion.

With one exception,[11] each of the membranes has from six to 12 entries of court *acta* for a given case, which follow, when extended, a relatively fixed form:[12]

Acta in Christ Church, Canterbury, on the Tuesday after the feast of Blessed Hilary, continued from the preceding Monday, in the year of Our Lord 1271, before us, Master Henry de Stanton, commissary of the lord official of the Court of Canterbury, appointed by the prior and chapter of Christ Church, Canterbury, *sede vacante*, in a case of appeal which is pending between Emma de Eworth, appellant, appearing by William de Boys, clerk, substituted by her proctor, Walter le Govene, who has a special mandate of substitution, on one side, and Simon de Partinges, appellee, appearing by his legally appointed proctor, Martin de Brampton, clerk, on the other, to wit:

There follows a recitation of what had been set to happen at the session according to the previous *acta*. In this case the appellee had been given a day to consider the libel supplied to him and to reply to it. Next comes what happened at the session. In this case, the appellee conceded the validity of the appeal; the commissary pronounced in favor of the appeal, and ordered the *processus* held before the judge *a quo*, the dean of Chichester, sent to Canterbury for further proceedings. Finally, a day was set for the next session, in this case, 8 February, 1271/2, to do what the *ordo juris* should demand in the principal case.

A few of the entries do not follow this format. There are memoranda, which differ slightly from *acta* in that they frequently refer to *ex parte* proceedings (though this is not invariable) or to a given act of the judge, such as rendering a sentence, without giving a description of all the other

---

[10]ESR 18/d: "Acta et libelli diversorum processuum a festo Sancti Matthei apostoli, anno domini M°CC°lxx°, usque ad diem veneris proximo post festum translacionis Sancti Thome martiris, anno domini M° CC°lxx° primo." Head [margin]: "In nomine patris et filii et spiritus sancti. Amen." Dorse [further down]: "Originale actorum." Ed. in *SCC*, 49.

[11]ESR 21/2; see below text at n. 17.

[12]ESR 20/2/11. (I.e., the 11th entry on the second membrane of ESR 20. The entries are numbered in this paper membrane by membrane. An "a" following the membrane number indicates that the entry is attached to the roll, a "d" that it is found on the dorse of the roll. All numbers, other than the initial ESR number and an occasional number on an attached document, have been supplied; the archive uses only the ESR number.) This is entry "B.3.s" in *SCC*, 79, whence the translation with some modifications.

ings at the session.[13] Further away in format from the *acta* are the entries that simply quote a document submitted by one of the parties to the court, a libel, for example, or an exception, or a sentence rendered by the court.[14] In the attached documents this last sort of material predominates, although some of the attached documents are themselves court *acta* indistinguishable from the entries on the rolls.[15]

The entries bear dates not in strictly chronological order but within relatively close proximity to each other. Thus the first membrane of one roll bears dates from October 2 through October 22, 1271, but the entry with the earliest date is the sixth of ten entries on the membrane, and the entry with the latest date is the ninth.[16] An exceptional membrane has 15 entries with dates from January 16 through July 9, 1272, in strictly chronological order. This was probably intended to be the "clean-up" membrane for that court year, since it is the second membrane of a roll, the first membrane of which contains entries dating from July 9 to August 6, 1272, after which date the court went on a holiday of roughly two months.[17]

There are at least two hands at work in the composition of these rolls, and the overlapping of dates on different membranes suggests that in some periods two membranes were deliberately being maintained.[18] It is tempting to think that there was notionally one membrane for each clerk, but there

---

[13]E.g., ESR 20/1/3 (*SCC*, B3c) (memorandum that the commissary dismissed a case for refusal of the appellant to proceed with the principal); ESR 30/1/4 (*acta* in memorandum form in which the *actor, ex parte*, asks instance); ESR 21/la/A (*SCC*, C6/2) (*acta* in memorandum form at a time when the case is proceeding in the absence of the *rea*); ESR 222/5/2 (memorandum that the official gave copies of the documents in the case to the advocate of the *reus*).

[14]E.g., ESR 18/11 (*SCC*, Blk) (quoted libel, interlocutory sentence and *litis contestatio* within *acta*); ESR 14/1/3 (*SCC*, B2c) (quoted proxy preceding *acta*); ESR 14/1/5 (*SCC*, B2e) (substitution proxy independent of *acta*).

[15]E.g., ESR 20/la/2 (*SCC*, B3g); ESR 21/2a/C (*acta* with memorandum of dismissal for non-appearance of *actor*); ESR 30/3a; ESR 30/3a/1 (*SCC*, C2/3).

[16]ESR 30/1. The dates given are the last date of session. I chose the ending date because the entry could not have been written before the ending date, but a tedious listing of the starting dates, the first date mentioned and the dates set for further proceedings shows that there is no strictly chronological order to these entries. Dates in *acta* are normally given in one of two forms: one in which the first date stated is the last day of session, as in the example quoted above, and one in which the first date stated is the first date of session, e.g., "*Acta* in Christ Church, Canterbury, on the Monday after the feast of Blessed Hilary, continued and prorogued until the Tuesday next following." Although the second form seems to be used more often when the hearing stretched over several days, the choice between the two forms seems to have been largely a matter of the momentary preference of the clerk.

[17]ESR 21. The "clean-up" was not complete. ESR 222/1 contains two entries from June, 1272 (ESR 222/1/1–2) and an attached document that probably dates from April, 1272 (ESR 222/la/la). There may have been another "clean-up" membrane that is now missing. See below n. 44. For the court's calendar, see below text at n. 65.

[18]E.g., there is an almost complete overlap in the dates on ESR 23 and those on ESR 20/1–2, on ESR 20/6 and ESR 208/1, and on ESR 39/1–2 and ESR 21/1.

are too many membranes on which both clerks have worked for us to be confident that this was even notionally the case.

There are some personal variations in style. One of the clerks frequently puts the names of the parties and their proctors in the margin; the other does not. The second clerk's system is preferable from the point of view of the twentieth century reader, and I suspect from that of the thirteenth century reader, because the first clerk seems to have put in his marginalia before he filled in the entries, and when he guessed wrong as to how much space he was going to need he had to squeeze in the entry by writing smaller and abbreviating with reckless abandon.[19] There are also some variations in style across time, the entries on the first two rolls being less fixed in form than those on the last six. For example, one of the early rolls contains notes of the days set for hearing cases of tuitorial appeal in which inhibition and citation mandates had been issued.[20] Such entries are not found on the later rolls. Apparently, the mandates and their returns were kept in separate files, perhaps similar to the writ files of the central royal courts.[21] There are also differences in the style of the *acta* that seem to vary with the judge rather than with the clerk or with the date of composition. For example, the entries written in the name of Brother John de Bocton, commissary for a brief period in the autumn of 1270, seem fuller and more personal than those of either Geoffrey de Romney, the official, or Henry de Stanton, the commissary for most of the vacancy.[22]

The pattern of dates indicates that the rolls were not compiled on the spot by clerks attending the sessions of the court. Brief minutes were probably taken at each session, perhaps dictated by the presiding judge. These were later entered on the rolls in the extended form in which we have them. The multiplicity of hands evident on the attached documents suggests that some of them are probably the originals submitted to the court. The *acta* and sentences found in the attached documents are probably not the first drafts but, rather, copies that were made for some other purpose (such as giving them to one of the parties who never came back to pay for them), but then used in lieu of entering the matter separately on the roll.[23] Why some

---

[19]ESR 208/1 is a particularly good example of the first clerk's system.

[20]ESR 18/1/6–8 (*SCC*, Blg–Bli).

[21]For examples, see SVSB III: 316, 328–30; for the practice in the vacancy of 1292–4, see *SCC*, 32–3, 60–1; for writ files, see M. Clanchy, ed., *The Roll and Writ File of the Berkshire Eyre of 1248*, Selden Society, no. 90 (London, 1973), lx–lxv, xci–xcii; see also n. 29 below.

[22]See ESR 14/1/2–4 (*SCC*, B2b–B2d).

[23]For examples of what seem to be first drafts of *acta*, see the *sessio acta* in the Stratford audience court book of 1340–3: CALC, Chartae Antiquae A.36.IV, noted in C. Donahue and J. Gordus, "A Case from Archbishop Stratford's Audience Act Book and Some Comments on the Book and its Value," *Bulletin of Medieval Canon Law* n.s. 2 (1972): 45–59. One of the party-produced documents from the 1270 vacancy, ESR 348, a replication to exceptions, has notes on the dorse that seem to be a draft of *acta*. At some periods in the fourteenth century the libels of the York cause papers regularly have the *acta* on the dorse. E.g., York, Borthwick Institute [hereafter YBI], CP.E. 79/10 (1357); CP.E. 95/1 (1368); CP.F. 1/1 (1402).

of the libels and exceptions were entered onto the roll while others were attached to the roll is a puzzle. It is possible that libels and exceptions were entered on the roll if the document had been acted upon and that phase of the case concluded but attached if the clerk thought that further proceedings concerning them might be necessary. But this is just a guess because there is little apparent consistency in the practice.

A knowledge of how these rolls were composed gives us some clue as to why they were composed. The Romano-canonical procedure used in the Court of Canterbury involved multiple hearings of the same case. Such a procedural system needs some kind of record of what happened at the last session and when the next session will be held. The *acta* recorded on the Canterbury rolls give us this information, but the system for recording it makes it difficult to find. A strictly chronological record, like that found in some of the fourteenth and fifteenth century English and Continental church court act books, is far more effective for these purposes.[24] Since there are no strictly chronological English church court records that antedate these rolls, it is possible that the Court of Canterbury clerks did not keep a strictly chronological record because the idea had not occurred to them. Michael Clanchy has taught us that the ability to make records and the ability to find things in them do not necessarily go together (a disjunction that is not confined to the thirteenth century, as my biographer will discover to his dismay).[25]

Furthermore, there is far more information on the rolls than is needed to be able to determine what should happen at a given session and when the next one would be held. For example, the rolls contain definitive sentences, and, once a definitive sentence is rendered, there are normally no further proceedings.[26] Some of the party-documents are necessary for managing a session—the exceptions, for example, allow us to determine what is being debated at a given session—but not all of them are necessary.[27] The libel, for example, is the most frequently found document, but Court of Canterbury appeal libels, particularly in tuitorial appeals, rarely tell us much about a case.[28] They almost always refer to another document, the *suggestio*, and *suggestiones* are never found attached to the rolls.[29]

---

[24]E.g., Hereford, Hereford and Worcester County Record Office, Acts of Office, Box 1, 0/2 (1442–3); Instance Acts, Box 1, I/1 (1491–9); YBI, Cons.AB 1 (1417–20); Cons.AB 2 (1424–7), etc. See also Appendix II.

[25]M. Clanchy, *From Memory to Written Record in England, 1066–1307* (Cambridge, MA, 1979), 120–5, 138–46.

[26]A hearing on the award of costs could take place after the definitive sentence, but no such hearings are recorded on the rolls, and they do not seem to have been usual.

[27]For exceptions, see *SCC, 41–3, 50–2*.

[28]For appeal libels, see *SCC, 62*.

[29]A large number of *suggestiones* from the 1292–4 vacancy survive at Canterbury. See *SCC, 32–3, 60–1*. None from the 1270–2 vacancy seem to have survived, however, although there are a few returns of inhibition and citation mandates (the document that followed upon and was modeled after the suggestion). These usually recite the mandate. E.g., SVSB III: 315 (*SCC,*

The *suggestio* is not the only document that we know was used in Canterbury litigation in this period but that is never found on the rolls. The heart of most cases was the proof, and proof generated four types of documents: (1) positions (questions put by one party to the other); (2) articles (matters about which witnesses were to be questioned); (3) interrogatories (cross-examination questions to be put to witnesses); and (4) depositions (records of the witnesses' testimony). All four types of documents survive from the 1270–2 vacancy, including a rather large number of depositions, but none is ever found attached to the rolls.[30]

It seems clear from the foregoing that a case could not proceed with only the information that is on the rolls. Not only are the rolls set up in such a way as to make it difficult to find a record on the basis of a date, but, once found, only certain types of documents are found associated with it, and even these types of documents are not found invariably. In many instances the court would need more. The rolls, then, were put together somewhat after the fact, probably not so much to aid in processing a case as it was going along but more to keep a record of what had happened.

There are a number of reasons for the court to have kept such a record, among others, that the law of the Church required it to do so. But the canon of the Fourth Lateran Council that required the keeping of such records is not confined to records of *acta* and libels.[31] The canon required that all the steps of the *ordo*, including the depositions, be put in writing. Another reason for keeping a record would be that a *processus*, a record on appeal, would have to be prepared if a case were appealed to Rome. But, again, such *processus* (and a number of them have survived from cases that were appealed to Canterbury)[32] would contain all of the material concerning a case, including the depositions and the documents surrounding them. The rolls of *acta* and their attached documents would certainly be helpful in fulfilling the requirements of the law and in preparing *processus*, but if this were the sole purpose of the rolls, we would expect to find more.

The Court of Canterbury rolls, then, are curious documents. They contain more than one would need simply to find out what was going to happen next in a case but less than one would need to be fully informed at the session and far less than one would need if one were going to compile a

---

C3/1); SVSB III: 121 (*SCC*, C4/1); SVSB III: 328–30. It may be significant that all of these are returns from judges sitting in Lincoln diocese. The returns of the mandates may have been kept in files organized by diocese, somewhat in the way that the writ files of the central royal courts were organized by county. For further speculation, see *SCC*, 35–7.

[30]For positions, articles, interrogatories and depositions, see *SCC*, 33–5, 47–50; for a list of printed examples from the 1270–2 vacancy, see *SCC*, 118.

[31]Lateran IV (1215) c. 38, in A. Garcia y Garcia, ed., *Constitutiones Concilii quarti Lateranensis una cum Commentariis glossatorum*, Monumenta Iuris Canonici, Series A: Corpus Glossatorum, vol. 2 (Vatican City, 1981), 80–1.

[32]For a list of printed examples, see *SCC*, 118–19.

full record of the case. But despite their curious nature, these rolls, and similar collections of *acta*, can be used by the modern researcher to answer a number of different types of questions.

II. WHAT CAN BE LEARNED FROM *ACTA*: THE COURT YEAR 1271–2

Let us focus our attention on one court year, that from September 1, 1271 through August 31, 1272, the rolls for which, as we suggested above, are almost complete. There are a total of 286 separate documents and entries on rolls that can be identified to that year. Three of them cannot be assigned to cases.[33] The remaining 283 concern 97 cases.[34] Those cases are also the topic of 104 other documents and roll entries found at Canterbury that either date from outside our year or that concern proceedings in a different court, normally the court from which appeal was taken to the Court of Canterbury. A table of these cases is given in Appendix I.

Ninety-seven cases is not very many. Even if we dismember the cases that we consolidated for numbering purposes,[35] assume that each of the unassignable documents refers to a new case,[36] and take an expansive view of what has been lost, the number of cases heard by the court during this year could hardly have reached 150. While the case load of the central royal courts in this period has not been studied statistically, it is clearly of a different order of magnitude. The plea rolls of the central royal courts in the late thirteenth century number in the hundreds of membranes for each term.[37] Ninety-seven cases is also a small number compared to the number of cases heard by the Court of Canterbury in the next vacancy for which we have records, that of 1292–4. The official of the court issued inhibition and citation mandates in at least 90 appeals over the course of just eight weeks in 1294.[38]

Where other documents connected with the case have survived, the *acta* can be combined with those documents to give us a quite full picture of how the substantive law, the procedure and the facts interacted in a given case. This is particularly true if documents concerning the proof have survived. Examples of such reconstructed *processus* may be found in *Select Canterbury Cases*, edited for the Selden Society a few years ago.[39]

---

[33]More careful work at the archives would probably allow at least some of these documents to be assigned to cases.

[34]As Appendix I shows, I have defined "cases" in such a way as to reduce somewhat the total number. Even if the parties are different, a document or entry is assigned to a given case if it certainly or probably concerns the same substantive issues (e.g., the tithes of a particular church). If we define a "case" as encompassing only those proceedings in which both the parties were the same, then there are 111 cases.

[35]See n. 34 above.

[36]See n. 33 above.

[37]I owe this information to the kindness of Dr. Paul Brand.

[38]*SCC*, 32–3.

[39]*SCC*, C2–C5, C6–C7, C9, C12–C18, all have one or more documents or roll entries dating from this year.

Even where the surrounding documents have not survived, the rolls themselves can be used to form an overall picture of the business of the court, and in some cases they will cast light on patterns of litigation before the court. For example, the rolls for the court year 1271–2 show us 86 separate cases in 162 separate sessions. Although the average number of sessions per case is 1.88, the modal number is one (39 cases). Twelve cases have no recorded sessions, even though they left documents that were or could have been entered onto or attached to rolls,[40] and 14 had two sessions. What brings up the average number of sessions per case is a few cases, almost all of which concern church property or rights in benefices and which frequently involve multiple parties. These cases take up a disproportionate amount of the court's time. The *Letheringsett* case, for example, a complicated benefice case from Norwich diocese involving four sets of parties, required ten sessions, and the *Hambye* case, probably also a benefice case, involving an alien priory, the bishop of Norwich and five sets of parties, required nine sessions.

What happened in these 86 cases may be summarized as follows:

Table 1

RESULT	SS[41]	NS[42]	TOT
Continued in next year	14		14
Tuition granted/denied	11	1	12
Dismissed	6		6
Definitive sentence	5	1	6
Prohibited	2		2
Recognizance of debt	1		1
Compromise	3	1	4
Postponed *sub spe pacis*	3		3
Disappear	28	6	34
Peter out	13	2	15
Total	86	11	97

The striking thing about these data are the number of cases that either "disappear" (are set for a given date for which no entry has been found) or "peter out" (no further session set and no conclusion reached). Four cases

[40]In creating this subsample, I included all entries on the rolls, all documents attached to the rolls and all documents, such as libels, *acta* and exceptions, that could have been attached to the rolls, even though they are now separate. I did this because some of the separate documents clearly were, at one time, attached to the rolls (see n. 9 above), and in many cases it is not possible to tell whether they were or not. Granted the uncertainty it seemed better to err on the side of over-inclusion.

[41]Cases with one or more documents or entries that were or could have been recorded on the rolls.

[42]Cases from the court year for which there are no documents or entries that were or could have been recorded on the rolls (added for completeness).

result in recorded compromises; the recognizance of the debt may be a compromise of an otherwise unrecorded piece of litigation;[43] cases are expressly postponed "in the hope of peace." We may surmise that some sort of agreement was reached in many, if not all, of the cases that seem to end in midstream. The Court of Canterbury rolls never record a session if neither party appears, and there seems to have been no penalty for default if both parties fail to appear. We cannot exclude the possibility that there were entries that were never recorded on the rolls or that were recorded on rolls now lost, but the evidence for lost rolls is not of this magnitude,[44] nor am I prepared to believe in clerical ineptitude on this scale. There is also no evidence that a fee was owed for enrolling the *acta* (failure to pay the fee being another possible explanation of the disappearance of a case). The legal obligation to keep a record existed independent of fees, and all the evidence points to the rolls as a means of preservation for the sake of the court, not for that of the parties.

The rolls also allow us to trace the jurisdictional pattern of the court in the 1270s. Our sample of 86 cases from the court year 1271–2 reveals the following pattern: In 16 cases the *acta* do not tell us the substance of the case. Fifty-seven percent (40) of the remaining 70 deal with some form of ecclesiastical property: benefice, tithes, pension and miscellaneous.[45] There are 16 marriage cases, 12 testament cases, one recognizance of a debt and one case of allegedly unjust excommunication of a layman.

These patterns can be used to show the shifting nature of ecclesiastical court jurisdiction across time and place. For example, the consistory court of York in the fourteenth century reveals similar kinds of jurisdiction, but the proportions are markedly different: ecclesiastical cases comprise about three-eighths of the total; marriage occupies about three-eighths, and a miscellaneous category, comprised of approximately equal portions of testament, breach of faith, defamation and *ex officio* matters, accounts for the final quarter. The difference in proportions probably relates more to the differences in courts than it does to differences in time. The York consistory was a diocesan court as well as the appellate court for the province.[46]

---

[43]The Court of Canterbury in the thirteenth century did not regularly serve as a registry for recording debts.

[44]As noted above in n. 5, there is evidence of a missing membrane prior to ESR 21/1. This evidence is confirmed by the number of cases that are set for dates in May–July, 1272 and which have no follow-up entry. The number is sufficiently large that two membranes may be involved. See n. 17 above.

[45]The last category includes both genuinely miscellaneous cases, such as one case between the parishioners of two churches concerning contributions to the repair of the nave of one of them, and cases that clearly deal with some form of ecclesiastical property but that cannot be delineated more precisely.

[46]See C. Donahue, "Roman Canon Law in the Medieval English Church: Stubbs vs. Maitland Revisited after 75 Years in the Light of Some Records from the Church Courts," *Michigan Law Review* 72 (1972): 659–60 and n. 63. Since that article was written, the CP.E. series at York has

We may tabulate these results as follows:

Table 2

TYPES OF CASES[47]	C/C	71-2[48]	%	C/Y	s14[49]	%
Uncertain		16	19		2	1
Ecclesiastical Property						
Benefice	16			27		
Tithes	13			36		
Pension	3			4		
Miscellaneous	3			18		
Total		40	47		85	37
Marriage		16	19		85	37
Testament		12	14		18	8
Debt (breach of faith)		1	1		13	6
Defamation		0	0		15	6
Ex officio[50]		1	1		15	6
Total		86	100		233	100

A third pattern that emerges from the rolls is a pattern of appeals. Where are the cases coming from? Six of our 86 cases do not yield up their diocese of origin while the remaining 80 show the pattern indicated in Table 3 (next page).

A few things stand out both by their presence and by their absence. Canterbury and Rochester are notable by their absence. They are both small dioceses, but in the case of Canterbury it may still have been uncertain whether appeal lay from the diocesan court to the Court of Canterbury. The large number of appeals from Lincoln is not surprising considering the size and wealth of the diocese. What the appeals show, however, is how well the court structure in this diocese was developed at this relatively early date. We have appeals from the officials of the archdeacons of Buckingham, Huntingdon, Oxford and Northampton, as well as from the Lincoln consistory, the bishop of Lincoln's audience and the chancellor of Oxford. The large number of appeals from Exeter and Chichester, on the other hand, seems to show something different. Six out of seven appeals from Exeter and

been given a splendid new calendar by Dr. David Smith, the director of the Borthwick. I have taken the opportunity to recalculate the statistics given in the article in Table 2.

[47]Caution: the categories are broad, and questionable cases have been included without comment.

[48]I.e., Court of Canterbury 1271–2. The 11 cases that did not leave documents or entries of the type suitable for the rolls reveal the following substantive pattern: benefice, 3; tithes, 2; marriage, 4; testamentary, 2.

[49]I.e., Court of York 1300–99.

[50]Includes cases raising issues of correctional jurisdiction, and, in the case of York, one instance case concerning an assault on a prioress. The occasional ex officio marriage case is classified with marriage. (In contrast to many English ecclesiastical courts, neither the Court of York nor the Court of Canterbury did much ex officio business.)

Table 3

PLACE OF ORIGIN	SS	NS	TOT
Uncertain	6		6
Arches deanery[51]	1		1
Bath and Wells	4	1	5
Chichester	6		6
Coventry and Lichfield	4		4
Ely	1		1
Exeter	6	1	7
Hereford	6	1	7
Lincoln	24	8	32
London	6		6
Norwich	12		12
Original	1		1
Salisbury	5		5
St. Davids	2		2
Winchester	1		1
Worcester	1		1
	86	11	93

five out of six from Chichester involve the judge *a quo* personally, Walter de Gloucester, the dean of Chichester, in one case, and John de Esse, the official of Exeter, in the other. Walter was serving as custodian of the diocese while the bishop was in exile, and it may be that he simply did not have the power to make his judgments stick. In the case of John, the problem seems to have been different. If even half of the allegations against him were true, he simply was not a very good judge.

I have spent some time on what can be gleaned from records of *acta* because such records are the dominant record that we have from the English medieval church courts. The subsequent history of church court record-keeping in England, however, reveals that shortly after the compilation of the Court of Canterbury rolls, perhaps by the end of the century, the courts kept their records differently. *Acta* are found in books, parchment or paper quires bound together, usually in strictly chronological order. Libels, depositions, proxies and sentences, however, are usually kept separately in files of what have come to be called cause papers. The two were combined for purposes of compiling a *processus*.[52]

The act books themselves vary in comprehensiveness. Sometimes quite a bit can be found out about a piece of litigation from the entries. Sometimes

---

[51]This was an exempt deanery in London subject to the direct jurisdiction of the archbishop.

[52]The best source for *processus* are the appellate courts. Canterbury has many of them for the thirteenth century; York has some for the fourteenth and fifteenth. There may be some to be found in cartularies. Books of *processus* exist on the Continent (e.g., Marseille, Archives départementales [hereafter AD] des Bouches du Rhône, 5 G 771 to 5 G 776 (1396–1410)), but the closest that the English seem to come is in the audience books of Winchelsey and Stratford. See Appendix II.

the entries are terse in the extreme, telling us in highly abbreviated form that a given case had been heard on a given day, a stage of the proceedings took place and the case was set down for the next stage. The more procedural the act book the more we suspect that separate files of cause papers (or, in some cases, separate books of sentences, depositions, etc.) were being kept.[53] This suspicion is confirmed by the example of York which has singularly uninformative act books and a magnificent surviving set of cause papers.[54] Occasionally, one can find act books that have cause papers stuck into the binding. One suspects, however, that these inserts are not part of the original record as they are in the case of the Court of Canterbury rolls, but rather a chance occurrence—someone put the two sets of material from a case together, and the cause papers, fortunately for us, were never returned to their proper file.[55]

III. ORIGINS OF THE ROLLS

We now have two puzzles to explain: (1) why are the Court of Canterbury rolls set up the way they are; and (2) why did the practice of making such rolls not continue? We have already suggested that the Court of Canterbury rolls are a curious hybrid, too much for a record of *acta* and not enough for a *processus*. Hybrid records, however, are by no means uncommon in the Middle Ages, and medieval bureaucracies did not welcome change any more than do modern bureaucracies. The catalyst of change was probably the introduction of Italian notarial practices into the English church courts, during the pontificate of Archbishop John Pecham (1278–92), when the Italian notary John of Bologna wrote his elementary handbook for English church court notaries.[56]

After Pecham's time court *acta* seem to have been recorded in books. There are very few rolls after this time, and what few rolls there are come from lower courts.[57] The model for the English church court act book is probably the Italian *imbreviatura*, examples of which, recording court *acta*,

---

[53]E.g., CALC, X/10/1 (Canterbury diocesan court deposition book, 1410–21). For sentence books we have to go to the Continent [e.g., Lille, AD du Nord, 5 G 148 to 5 G 149 (1438–55)], although there are some sentences mixed into the Canterbury diocesan act books of the fourteenth century [e.g., CALC, Y/1/1 (1372–5)].

[54]YBI, CP.E (14th c., 233 cases); CP.F (15th c., over 300 cases).

[55]See B. Woodcock, *Medieval Ecclesiastical Courts in the Diocese of Canterbury* (Oxford, 1952), 140.

[56]See C. Cheney, *Notaries Public in England in the Thirteenth and Fourteenth Centuries* (Oxford, 1972), 26–8; *SCC*, 21 and n. 10.

[57]E.g., the rolls of the prior and chapter's peculiar court at Norwich: Norwich, Norfolk and Norwich Record Office, DCN/65/1 to DCN/65/13 (1416–52).

can be found from as early as the 1230s.[58] The earliest known English act book is the act book of Archbishop Winchelsey's audience court (1304–8), which at least archival tradition associates with his register.[59]

That fact suggests another model for the court act book: the bishop's register. While registers in book form do exist from before John of Bologna's time, some bishops, such as the bishop of Lincoln, were still keeping their records on rolls. After John's time all extant registers are in book form.[60] The connection of the court act book with the bishop's register is also suggested by the fact that the earliest known English diocesan court act book (1347–8) is found bound in the register of Hamo Hethe, bishop of Rochester, and pieces of judicial *acta* are found in bishops' registers throughout the Middle Ages.[61] It is not until 1374 that we get an act book of a diocesan consistory court that is in something like its original form, and its style suggests that it is the product of a long course of development.[62]

If the influence of Italian notarial practice is what put the shape on the church court act book for the rest of the Middle Ages, what is it that shaped the Court of Canterbury rolls? As we have seen, the logic of the procedure being employed does not dictate their form nor do the possible purposes for which they might be used. Could it be that the model for the Court of Canterbury rolls is the plea rolls of the central royal courts?

We now know that the Court of Canterbury was established in London during the pontificate of Archbishop Boniface of Savoy in the 1250s.[63] At that time the court was just beginning to be a separate institution, and it probably did not bring with it a fixed tradition for maintenance of records. Indeed, probably no church court outside of Italy had a fixed tradition for maintaining records at this time. The oldest church court book that survives in France is contemporary with the Court of Canterbury rolls. It comes from the diocese of Mende and is highly experimental in nature.[64] At the same time, however, the central royal courts at Westminster, with a case load far heavier

---

[58]See G. Dolezalek, ed., *Das Imbreviaturbuch des erzbischöflichen Gerichtsnotars Hubaldus aus Pisa, Mai bis August 1230*, Forschungen zur neueren Privatrechtsgeschichte, no. 13 (Cologne, 1969).

[59]London, Lambeth Palace MS 244 (121 fols.).

[60]For royal influence on the earlier form of bishops' registers, see D. Smith, *Guide to Bishops' Registers of England and Wales* (London, 1981), ix–x; Clanchy, *Memory to Written Record*, 53–5.

[61]The act book from the audience court of Archbishop Stratford is a curious composite that seems to have acquired its present form when its owners, the monks of Canterbury, dismembered a more regular act book in order to make a formulary. See Donahue and Gordus, "Stratford's Audience Act Book," 47–50. Appendix II lists all the fourteenth century act books known to me.

[62]The York fragments listed in Appendix II may also be in their original form, unbound quires.

[63]See *SCC, 14–16*; Hereford, Dean and Chapter Muniments 1946–70 (407–22), 2918–22 (420, 419, 414) (documents in case heard in Court of Canterbury, 1256–8).

[64]Mende, AD de la Lozère, G 963 (186 fols., 1268–72).

than that of the Court of Canterbury, had been keeping records for almost a century.

To be sure, there are many characteristics of common law procedure and record keeping that cannot be carried over into Romano-canonical procedure. For example, the Court of Canterbury in the 1270s does not have fixed terms. Each case has its own rhythm, and the judge can and does set down a case for virtually any time outside of Sundays, great saints' days and three ill-defined periods around Christmas, Easter and harvest time.[65] If the rolls of the central royal courts were to be taken as a model, they could not be arranged by terms. Further, the diplomatic for recording the *acta* shows little or no influence of the royal plea rolls. The style of writing *acta* was already well fixed by 1270. Examples quite like the one given above can be found as far back as Hubert Walter's time.[66]

Certain other characteristics of the royal court plea rolls would not be adopted simply because there was no reason to do so. When an entire year's business can be kept on 16 or 17 membranes, there is no particular reason to use the dorse of the rolls, and no particular reason to sew all the membranes together at the top so that they will lie flat. Storage space can be saved by sewing them end-to-end and rolling them up.

Where the possible influence of the royal court rolls can be seen, however, is in the division of subject matter. Romano-canonical procedure, unlike common law procedure, does not make a sharp distinction between pleading and proof. At common law, the distinction is necessitated both by the widespread use of juries, and by what Professor Milsom has called the "ancient pattern of law-suit."[67] Romano-canonical procedure knows neither; yet the Court of Canterbury rolls make the same distinction. *Acta* before the judge, libels, exceptions and some proxies are found on the Court of Canterbury rolls. Proceedings before the examiners, positions (which were presented before the judge), articles (which were frequently debated before the judge) and depositions are no place to be found.[68]

If I am right in my suggestion that the Court of Canterbury rolls were modeled, in part, on the rolls of the central royal courts, that suggests a couple of things about the development of canon law and common law in the great formative period of the thirteenth century: the two systems ended up being markedly different; they did not start out that way, however, and

---

[65]See *SCC*, 17–18, 34.

[66]See *SCC*, 10–11.

[67]S. Milsom, *Historical Foundations of the Common Law*, 2d ed. (Toronto, 1981), 38–9.

[68]It seems reasonably clear that the examiners had a separate clerical staff, at least for recording the depositions. They may also have had separate files. These facts do not, however, completely explain the total exclusion of such material from the rolls. ESR 208/2a/B4, an exception of excommunication against witnesses, is the closest we come to having this type of material on the rolls. It may have found its way onto the rolls because it was presented to the judge when the witnesses were first produced in court.

habits of thought that survived from a period in which they were not that different continued to influence development.[69] Further, though the two systems ended up being quite different, they were both in the control of a relatively small group of men who, at least in the area around London, probably knew one another. Cross-fertilization was possible even if it was, as in the case of the Court of Canterbury rolls, fertilization of a plant that grew up to be quite different.

[69]See C. Donahue, "Proof by Witnesses in the Church Courts of Medieval England: An Imperfect Reception of the Learned Law," *On the Laws and Customs of England: Essays in Honor of Samuel E. Thorne*, eds. M. Arnold et al. (Chapel Hill, NC, 1981), 127–58.

SUMMARY OF CASES IN THE COURT OF CANTERBURY, SEPTEMBER 1271—AUGUST 1272

[Abbreviations: A = abbot; adn = the official of the named archdeacon; bp = bishop (normally the bp personally and not his off); chanc = chancellor; comm = commissary; cons = consistory court (i.e, the court of the bishop's official); cont'd = case continued in the next court year (further results, if available, given following the semicolon); excomm = excommunication; Glouc & H = Gloucester and Hertford; off = official; J & W = all that is legible of the names; set beyond = set beyond the vacancy or so close to the end that one cannot be sure that it did not continue; U = university; vg = vicar general.]

[Sources: CALC: Chartae Antiquae, Christ Church Letters I-III, Eastry Correspondence I-VI, ESR, Scrapbooks A-C, SVSB I-III.]

CASE NAME	ORIGIN	TYPE	RESULT	DOCUMENT[70]		
				EN	EX	OT
Unidentified				3		
Alexander & Sarra c John & Constance	Norwich cons	Marriage ?	Dismissed	1		
Algarkirk c Champeneys	Lincoln (dean of Holland)	Testamentary	Disappears		1	
Arthur c Ydemeston	Bath & Wells cons	Benefice	Cont'd; disappears	3		1
Attebury c de la Leye	Lincoln (adn Huntingdon)	Marriage	Disappears		3	1
Atterburn c Hapeneye	?	Testamentary	Tuition granted	1		
Audenard c Bermondsey	Winchester (comm A st Albans)	Benefice ?	Tuition granted	2		
Avenbury c Aigueblanche	Hereford bp	Benefice	Sentence definitive	9		
B—tre c Marber	Norwich cons	Marriage ?	Disappears	2		
B—tre c Hingeringham						
Baudeser & Garsum	Chichester dioc	Debt	Recognizance	1		
Baumfeld c Esse	Exeter off	?	Disappears	1		
Beauchamp c Cov & L	Cov & L bp	Unjust excomm	Disappears	2		
Beaupel c Esse	Exeter off	Adultery	Peters out	2		1
Bedford c Whiteside	Lincoln adn	Marriage	Disappears		2	

[70]Gives first (EN) the number of entries on the rolls [including attached documents and those that may have been attached (see above n. 40)], then (EX) Court of Canterbury documents that date from this period but that never were attached to the rolls, then (OT) documents or entries found in the archives that either date from outside our period or that concern proceedings in a different court (normally the court of origin).

CASE NAME	ORIGIN	TYPE	RESULT	EN	EX	OT
Bekwell c Denarston	Norwich dioc	Ecclesiastical	Postponed sub spe	3		
Bernham c Kimbolton	Lincoln (adn Huntingdon)	Marriage	Disappears		2	1
Blund c Bramber	Chichester custodian	Tithes	Disappears	5	1	
Blund c Lega	Lincoln vg	Benefice	Compromise	2		1
Bona Villa c Cotel	Bath & Wells cons & Wells adn	Tithes	Peters out	2	2	2
Bosbury c Langone	Hereford dioc	Benefice	Disappears	4		
Burnham c Boche	Norwich dioc	Marriage ?	Disappears	2		
Burton c Griffin	Salisbury bp's comm	Testamentary	Tuition granted	7	4	
Burton c Wimborne			Disappears			
Capella c Huntingdon	Lincoln (adn Huntingdon)	?; tuitorial appeal ?	Disappears	1		
Cleseby c Newerk	Lincoln (comm of papal legate)	Benefice	Dismissed	1		3
Clifford c Maidstone	Lincoln custodian	Benefice	Peters out	1		
Corscombe c Powerstock	Salisbury dioc	Tithes	Peters out	1	1	
Cotel c Parton	Lincoln (chanc Oxford U)	?	Compromise, enforced	1		
Debanford c Esse	Exeter off	?	Peters out ?	1		
Deneswell c Colchester	London (adn Colchester)	?; tuitorial appeal	Peters out	1		
Denis c Wellington	Norwich dioc	Tithes ?	Disappears	5		
Donton c Gogh	London ?	?; tuitorial appeal	Disappears	1		
Eastry c Saint-Evroult	Lincoln bp	Tithes	Cont'd; rei withdraw contumaciously	9		3
Eastry c Marlborough						
Essex c Insula	Lincoln dioc	?; tuitorial appeal	Disappears	1		
Eya c Hornel	Lincoln dioc	?; tuitorial appeal	Disappears	1		
Ghent & Vescy c Stonesby	Lincoln dioc	Benefice	Disappears	10		1
Gousel c Maidstone			Disappears			
Gousel c Stonesby			Disappears			
Giffard c Drayton	Arches deanery ?	Marriage	Disappears	4		
Gip c Starling	Norwich cons	Testamentary	Disappears	1		
Glastonbury c Branston	Bath & Wells dioc ?	Ecclesiastical	Cont'd; both dismissed	2		4
Glastonbury c Branston						
Glouc & H c Fanencourt	Original jd ?	Testamentary	Postponed sub spe	3		2
Gospel c Lincoln	Lincoln cons	Marriage; ex officio separation for consanguinity	Disappears		1	
Guestling c Battle	Chichester custodian	Tithes	Dismissed	3	4	7

Parties	Forum	Subject	Action		
Halton c Aigueblanche	Hereford cons	?	Postponed sub spe	1	
Hambye c Shouldham	Norwich bp	Testamentary	Tuition granted	19	2
Hambye c Norwich		Benefice	Peters out		
Norwich c Shouldham			Tuition denied		
Wincote c Hambye			Tuition granted		
Shouldham c Norwich			Disappears		
			Tuition denied		
Haselbech c Bronescombe	Exeter bp	Benefice	Compromise[71]		1
Haughmond c Pykerell	Cov & L dioc ?	Benefice ?	Tuition granted	2	
Hawkley c Cor	Hereford dioc	Benefice	Compromise ?[72]	5	
Hawkley c Hereford					
Heggestorp c Bardney	Lincoln dioc	Ecclesiastical ?	Cont'd; dismissed	2	3
Wyllinby c Bardney			Peters out		
Herleston c Clifton	Cov & L cons & Stafford adn	Ecclesiastical; repair of ch nave	Cont'd	2	2
J & W					
Lada c Maidstone	?	?	Disappears ?	1	
Lada c Nes	Lincoln dioc	Sequestration	Tuition granted ?	2	
			Tuition granted		
Leghe c Chichester	Chichester custodian	Benefice	Disappears	2	2
Letheringsett c Norwich	Norwich bp	Benefice	Disappears	13	
Langley c Norwich			Cont'd; disappears		
Letheringsett c Rudham			Disappears		
Rudham c Langley			Disappears		
Leukenor c Archenton	?	?	Cont'd; postponed sub spe	2	2
Linecot c Cesterton	Lincoln bp	Testamentary ?	Disappears	3	1
Lockere c Young & Lox	?	Marriage	Peters out	2	1
Loose c Brandon	Norwich cons	Pension	Sentence definitive	3	1
Ludlow c Hereford	Hereford off	Sequestration	Tuition granted	1	1
Mare c—venal	Lincoln (chanc Oxford U)	?; tuitorial appeal	Dismissed	1	
Martin c Martin	St Davids cons	Testamentary	Cont'd; set beyond	1	
Michilham c Pollingesand	Chichester custodian	Tithes ?	Tuition granted	1	
Mobant c Hinton	Salisbury (dean of Wymborne)	Marriage ?	Tuition granted	2	5
Morteyn c Wald	Lincoln dioc	Testamentary	Disappears	2	
Murie c Milneford	Lincoln dioc	Tithes ?	Disappears	2	
Newbury c Crips	Lincoln dioc ?	Marriage ?	Disappears	1	
Newbury c Hereford	Hereford dioc	?; appeal	Dismissed	1	

[71] See SCC, 232–3.
[72] See ESR 39/1/6 (third party resigns from the benefice at issue; no further date set).

CASE NAME	ORIGIN	TYPE	RESULT	DOCUMENT		
				EN	EX	OT
Nicholas c Lunes	?	Testamentary	Peters out	1		1
Norman c Prudfot	Lincoln (adn Buckingham)	Marriage	Disappears	5		
Overe c Kenebant	Ely dioc	Tithes ?	Disappears	3		
Partinges c Eworth	Chichester custodian	Marriage	Disappears	7		
Pevensey c Giffard Meriden c Giffard	Worcester bp	Benefice	Sentence definitive	1	5	5
Picheford c Nevill	Lincoln (delegate of papal legate)	Benefice	Sentence definitive		1	24
Povere c Runwalle	Lincoln dioc	Marriage ?	Peters out	1		
Radenore c Aubres	Hereford (adn Salop)	?	Peters out	1		
Raveningham c Mortimer	Lincoln (adn Huntingdon)	Benefice ?	Prohibited	2		
Roseya c Bokelond	Norwich (adn Norfolk)	Tithes ?	Cont'd; tuition granted	1		4[73]
Rouen c Exeter	Exeter off	Ecclesiastical	Tuition granted	3		
Roughton c Kyrkeby	Lincoln bp	Tithes	Disappears	1	1	
Royata c Lacy	Lincoln dioc	?; tuitorial appeal	Peters out	1		
Rydel c Fetcham	St Davids vg	Benefice	Cont'd; set beyond	2		4
St Frideswide c Borewald	Lincoln (adn Oxford)	Testamentary	Disappears	1		
St Leofard c Bath & Wells	Bath & Wells bp	Benefice ?	Tuition granted	2		

[73] A parallel case with two more entries develops in the next court year, it is set beyond the vacancy.

Salisbury c Falconer	Salisbury dioc	Tithes	Cont'd; dismissed and prohibited	5	1	2
Smith c Dolling	Salisbury cons	Marriage	Cont'd; sentence definitive	1		4
Stanere c Castleacre	Norwich dioc	Tithes ?	Tuition granted	6		
Tilney c Castleacre			Tuition granted			
Stogursey c Over Stowey	Bath & Wells cons	Tithes	Prohibited; dismissed	4	4	7
Stow c Selby	Lincoln cons	Pension	Dismissed	1		2[74]
Summerton c Gros	Norwich bp's comm	?; tuitorial appeal	Disappears	2		
Summerby c Badde	Lincoln dioc	Testament	Cont'd; dismissed	1		
Thorald c Christian	Lincoln (adn Northampton)	Marriage	Sentence confirmatory	4	1	1
Thurlaston c Branston	Lincoln bp's comm	Tithes ?	Dismissed	5		
Thurlaston c Shirley			Dismissed			
Trebarcha c Trewrgy	Exeter off	Marriage ?	Peters out	2		
Tristram c Wacton	Norwich ?	Marriage	Disappears	2		
Vienna c Luvel	London vg	Sequestration	Disappears	2	1	
Wengeham c Erlintone	Lincoln dioc	Testament	Peters out	1		
Wingfield c Bartholomei	Lincoln (adn Huntingdon)	Marriage	Sentence definitive	1		2
Woccesdon c Stratford	?	Pension ?	Cont'd	6		6
Totals				244	42	104

[74] A parallel case with two entries develops in the next court year; it "disappears."

APPENDIX II

FOURTEENTH-CENTURY ECCLESIASTICAL COURT BOOKS

[In the interest of saving space, references are radically abbreviated. For full references, see Smith, *Bishop's Registers*. Aud. = Audience Court; C&YS = Canterbury and York Society (followed by vol. number); cal. = calendared; CALC = Canterbury, Cathedral Archives and Library; Cons. = Consistory Court; D&C = Dean and Chapter; n.c. = no classification number; RO = Record Office; UL = University Library; WHS = Worcestershire Historical Society (followed by vol. number); YBI = York, Borthwick Institute. In the case of bishops' audience courts, the name of the bishop is given first, followed by the diocese; in the case of consistory courts, the order is reversed.]

Independent Quires or Books:

1304–1308 Winchelsey (Canterbury) Aud., Lambeth MS 244, 121 fols.

1316–1329 York (D&C) Aud., York D&C MS M2(1)a, 62 fols.

1316–1330 Martival (Salisbury) Aud., ed. Owen, C&YS 68, 4:1–136

1323–1330 Hethe (Rochester) Aud., ed. Johnson, C&YS 48, 1:190–256

1324–1328 Stratford (Winchester) Aud., Hampshire RO, A1/5, fols. 160r-168r

1325–1328 Reynolds (Canterbury) Aud., CALC, Chartae Antiquae A36.I, 18 fols.

1328–1330 Meopham (Canterbury) Aud., CALC, Chartae Antiquae A36.II, 20 fols.

1330 Dalderby (Lincoln) ?Aud., Lincolnshire RO, Episcopal Register II, fols. 356r-v

1334–1337 Montacute (Worcester) ?Aud., Hereford/Worcester RO, b 16.093–BA.2648 (iii), pp. 191–4 (inhibitions from the Court of Canterbury)

1340–1343, 1347–1348 Stratford (Canterbury) Aud., CALC, Chartae Antiquae A36.III, 3 fols.; A36.IV, 117 fols.

1347–1348 Rochester (Hethe) Cons., ed. Johnson, C&YS 49, 2:911–1043

1342–1352 Zouche (York) ?Aud., YBI, Reg 10, fols. 347r-356r (register of criminous clerks)

1357–1420 York (D&C) Aud., York D&C MS M2(1)f, 75 fols.

1364 Canterbury (Whittlesey) Cons., CALC, X/1/19 (fragment)

1371 York (Thoresby) Cons., York, D&C MS M2(1)b

1371–1375 York (Thoresby, Neville) Cons., York, D&C MS M2(1)c

1372–1375 Canterbury (Whittlesey) Cons., CALC, Y/1/1, 111 fols.

1374–1382 Ely (Arundel) Cons., Cambridge UL, Ely Diocesan Records D2(1), 142 fols.

1376–1386 York (D&C) Aud., York D&C MS M2(1)h, 68 fols.

1387–1394 York (D&C) Aud., York D&C MS M2(1)g, 98 fols.

1387–1494 York (D&C) Aud., YBI D/C.AB/1

1389–1395 Waltham (Salibury) ?Aud., Wiltshire RO, n.c., fols. 228r-230v

1393–1436 York (D&C) Aud., York D&C MS M2(1)d, 104 fols.

1395–1410 Canterbury (Courtenay, Arundel, Walden) Cons., CALC X/8/1, 67 fols.

1396–1399 Canterbury (Arundel, Walden) Cons., CALC Y/1/2, 169 fols.

Legal Proceedings Mixed into Bishops' Registers:

1294–1313 Winchelsey (Canterbury), ed. Graham, C&YS 51–2

1303–1307 Gainesborough (Worcester), ed. Bund, WHS 22

1319–1352 Hethe (Rochester), ed. Johnson, C&YS 48–9

1339–1349 Bransford (Worcester), cal. Haines, WHS n.s. 4

1389–1404 Trefnant (Worcester), Hereford/Worcester RO, n.c., fols. 64–132 *passim*

Processus in Bishops' Registers:

1370–1371 Hatfield (Durham), Durham, Prior's Kitchen, n.c., fols. 69r-75v (proceedings re archdeacon of Northumberland accused of homicide)

1375 Burghill (Lincoln), Lincolnshire RO, B/A/1/7, fols. 128r-139v (rector of Mancetter c. Prior and Convent of Atherstone)

1397–1399 Braybrooke (London), Greater London RO, MS 9531/3, fols. 485r-495v (jurisdiction dispute re probate and visitation between bishop and archbishop of Canterbury)

THE TRANSFORMATION OF MARRIAGE LAW IN THE LUTHERAN REFORMATION*

John Witte, Jr.

"[T]he estate of marriage has fallen into awful disrepute," Martin Luther declared in 1522.

> There are many pagan books which treat of nothing but the depravity of womankind and the unhappiness of the estate of marriage. . . . Every day one encounters parents who forget their former misery because, like the mouse, they have now had their fill. They deter their children from marriage and entice them into priesthood and nunnery, citing the trials and troubles of married life. Thus do they bring their own children home to the devil, as we daily observe; they provide them with ease for the body and hell for the soul. . . . [Furthermore,] the shameful confusion wrought by the accursed papal law has occasioned so much distress, and the lax authority of both the spiritual and the temporal swords has given rise to so many dreadful abuses and false situations that I would much prefer neither to look into the matter nor to hear of it. But timidity is no help in an emergency.[1]

According to many contemporary observers, Luther's alarm over the decrepit estate of marriage and marriage law was not unfounded. Germany had suffered through decades of indiscipline and immorality in the late fifteenth and early sixteenth centuries. Prostitution and homosexuality were rampant. High clerics and officials of government regularly kept concubines and visited the numerous brothels in German cities. The small fines incurred for such activity discouraged few. Drunken orgies were commonplace. Women were raped and ravaged, particularly by robber bands and soldiers. Lewd pamphlets and books exalting sexual liberty and license were published often with impunity. Writings by some Roman Catholics extolling celibacy and deprecating marriage and sex dissuaded many couples from marriage and persuaded many parents to send their children to monasteries and cloisters. The numbers of single men and women, of monasteries and cloisters, of monks and nuns reached new heights in the years shortly before the Reformation. Within the estate of marriage itself, instances of bigamy, incest and polygamy appeared with alarming frequency. The canon laws

---

*Another version of this paper appeared in *The Journal of Law and Religion* 4(2) (1987): 1.
[1]M. Luther, *Works*, J. Pelikan, et al., eds. (Philadelphia, 1955-) [hereinafter *LW*], 45:36, 17.

governing the formation and dissolution of marriages were flouted or arbitrarily enforced in several parts of Germany. Laws prescribing care and education of children as well as laws proscribing abortion, abuse of family members, adultery and desertion were regularly violated.[2] Calls such as Luther's for the reformation of marriage and marriage law and for the reinforcement of public morality were, therefore, received sympathetically by Roman Catholics and Protestants alike.

Unlike many Roman Catholics, however, Luther and other German Protestant reformers attributed much of the decay of marriage not only to the negligence and arbitrariness of authority and the moral laxness of society but also to the canon laws of marriage and the Roman Catholic theological concepts of marriage underlying these laws. For the reformers the canon law of marriage yielded paradoxical results. It discouraged and prevented mature persons from marrying by its celebration of celibacy, its proscriptions against the breach of vows to celibacy, its permission to breach oaths of betrothal and its numerous impediments. Yet it encouraged marriages between the immature by declaring valid secret unions consummated without parental permission as well as oaths of betrothal followed by sexual intercourse. It highlighted the sanctity and solemnity of marriage by deeming it a sacrament. Yet it permitted a couple to enter this holy union without clerical or parental witness, instruction or participation. Celibate and impeded persons were thus driven by their sinful passion to incontinence and all manner of sexual deviance. Married couples, not properly taught the scriptural norms for marriage, adopted numerous immoral practices.

Such paradoxical results, the reformers averred, were rooted in tensions within the Roman Catholic theology of marriage. Although Roman Catholic theologians emphasized the sanctity and sanctifying purpose of the marriage sacrament, they, nevertheless, subordinated it to celibacy and monasticism. Although they taught that marriage is a duty mandated for all persons by divine natural law, they excused many from this duty through the restrictions of canon law. Both the Roman Catholic theology and the canon law of marriage thus met with sharp criticism on the part of the reformers.

This criticism was motivated by more than a concern for public morality and sexual propriety, more than a desire to remove arbitrariness and abuses in the law. The reformers deliberately focused on traditional marriage doctrine and the traditional canon law of marriage for two additional reasons.

First, many of the cardinal issues of the Lutheran Reformation were implicated by this doctrine and law. The Roman Catholic Church's exclusive legal authority over marriage was, for the reformers, a particularly flagrant example of the church's usurpation of civil legal authority. The Roman

[2]See, generally, S. Ozment, *When Fathers Ruled: Family Life in Reformation Europe* (Cambridge, MA, 1983), 1–49; B. Gottlieb, *Getting Married in Pre-Reformation Europe* (Ph.D. Diss., Columbia, 1974); W. Kawerau, *Die Reformation und die Ehe* (Halle, 1892), 67ff.

Catholic sacramental concept of marriage, on which the church had founded this authority, raised questions of sacramental theology and scriptural interpretation. The numerous canon law impediments to marriage and prohibitions against complete divorce were in tension with the reformers' understanding of scriptural norms for marriage. That a child could enter marriage without instruction or permission raised questions about the responsibilities of the family, church and state to children. Issues of marriage doctrine and law implicated and epitomized the broader theological, political and social issues of the Reformation. It is thus not at all surprising that such a large number of German reformers—Luther, Melanchthon, Bucer, Brenz, Osiander and numerous other theologians as well as Schürpf, Monner, Kling, Lagus, von Beust, Schneidewin and many other jurists[3]—debated these questions with such vigor.

Second, the reformers viewed the family as an independent model of authority and rule and a vital instrument for the reform of the church and society. "[T]he Christian household ... [was] the source of evangelical impulses in society .... The families of Lutheran [believers] were to serve as wholesome examples of wedded life, and it is clear that Luther regarded his own household as a model of conjugal and parental conduct in both its private and its public aspects."[4] The family was seen as an indispensable social unit alongside church and state, with its own sphere of authority and responsibility and its own moral and pedagogical tasks within society. Because, in the reformers' view, traditional marriage law and doctrine did not adequately respect and protect the integrity and autonomy of the family or facilitate its social tasks, its reform was an urgent priority.

Acting on these criticisms, the Lutheran reformers transformed many traditional concepts and laws of marriage. They rejected the sacramental concept of marriage and the subordination of marriage to celibacy and removed numerous marriage laws that were developed on these assumptions. They introduced a social concept of marriage and the family, defining a variety of distinctive social tasks and uses for the family. They shifted jurisdiction over marriage from the church to the state and substantially revised the role of parents, priests and peers in the process of marriage formation and dissolution.

The German Lutheran reformers did not, however, entirely eclipse the marriage doctrine and law of the Roman Catholic tradition. Several cities and

---

[3]Martin Luther (1483–1546); Philip Melanchthon (1497–1560); Martin Bucer (1491–1551); Johannes Brenz (1498–1570); Andreas Osiander (1498–1552); Hieronymous Schürpf (1481–1554); Basilius Monner (c. 1501–1566); Melchior Kling (1504–1571); Konrad Lagus (d. 1546); Joachim von Beust (1522–1597); and Johannes Schneidewin (1519–1568). See generally *Allgemeine Deutsche Biographie* (1875–1910); see also below, n. 45 for a list of some of their writings on marriage law.

[4]G. Strauss, *Luther's House of Learning: Indoctrination of the Young in the German Reformation* (Baltimore, 1978), 112.

territories in Germany remained avowedly Roman Catholic, preserved the traditional theology of marriage and continued to administer the canon law in ecclesiastical courts. These Roman Catholic polities were ultimately protected in their faith and law by the Peace of Augsburg (1555). Even in many Lutheran cities and territories, the break with the Roman Catholic tradition was ultimately not nearly so radical as the early reformers had envisioned. The new theology of marriage, though filled with bold revisions, preserved much of the teaching of the Roman Catholic tradition. The new marriage courts were frequently comprised of both church consistories and civil judges with both civil and ecclesiastical authority. Much of the new civil marriage law was heavily indebted to the canon law which it replaced.

This article analyzes the Lutheran reformers' transformation of the Roman Catholic theology and law of marriage. Part I provides a very brief overview of the Roman Catholic theology and law of marriage in the early sixteenth century. Part II provides a more detailed analysis of the reformers' theological doctrines of marriage and marriage law. Part III outlines the reforms of marriage law posed by Lutheran theologians and jurists and accepted by various German polities.[5]

I. Concepts and Laws of Marriage in the Roman Catholic Tradition

The doctrine and law of marriage was an important concern to the Western Christian Church from its very beginnings. Several early Christians wrote commentaries on Biblical passages on marriage. The Church Fathers, most notably St. Ambrose (c. 339–397) and St. Augustine (354–430), discussed the sacramental character of marriage, the problems of divorce and remarriage and the propriety of sex and contraception. The Church urged Roman and Germanic rulers to adopt laws proscribing polygamy, adultery and oppression of women and prescribing education and proper care for children. By the later ninth century, Church councils began insisting on these reforms in a number of decrees. But the doctrine and law of marriage in the Western Church of the first millennium remained primitive and under the shadow of pagan folkways and folklaw.[6]

It was not until what Professor Berman has called the "Papal Revolu-

---

[5]This article will not analyze the impact of the Lutheran Reformation on Germanic customary marriage law or on Romanist marital jurisprudence, nor will it treat the influence of the new humanists on marriage doctrine and law. Responsible analysis of these intricate topics requires another article.

[6]See J. Noonan, *Contraception: A History of Its Treatment by the Catholic Theologians and Canonists* (New York, 1967), 119ff. R. Huebner, *A History of Germanic Private Law*, trans. F. Philbrick (Boston, 1918); M. Glendon, *State, Law, and Family: Family Law in Transition in the United States and Western Europe* (Boston, 1977), 304–308; H. Berman, *Law and Revolution: The Formation of the Western Legal Tradition* (Cambridge, MA, 1983), 226.

tion" of the late eleventh through thirteenth centuries that a systematic theology and canon law of marriage emerged. For the first time theological doctrines, including the doctrine of marriage, were categorized, systematized and refined, initially in the discourses of St. Anselm (1033–1109) and Peter Abelard (1079–1142), then in the great *Summae* of Peter Lombard (1100–1160), Albert the Great (c. 1200–1250) and Thomas Aquinas (1225–1274). For the first time a systematic body of canon law, including marriage law, was formed by Gratian (c. 1095–1150) and his commentators and then elaborated by papal and conciliar legislation. For the first time the external forum of the Church began to exercise autonomous jurisdiction over numerous subjects, including marriage, and to apply the new canon law.[7]

The doctrine of marriage taught by the Roman Catholic Church at the time of the Protestant Reformation was built directly upon the teach: of this earlier revolutionary period. Generations of commentators from the thirteenth to the sixteenth centuries had, to be sure, refined and amended these earlier teachings and sought to resolve the tensions among them. Much new ecclesiastical legislation was promulgated. But the cardinal doctrines of the origin, nature and function of marriage and its laws, set out in this early period, were preserved with relatively few changes.[8]

[7]This is the provocative thesis of ibid., 226–230. Some important primary sources on marriage and marriage law in this period are collected in C. von Schwerin, ed., *Quellen zur Geschichte der Eheschliessung* (Bonn, 1925), 10ff.; R. Weigand, *Die Naturrechtslehre der Legisten und Dekretisten von Irnerius bis Accursius und von Gratian bis Johannes Teutonicus* (München, 1967), 283ff.; H. Schroeder, *Disciplinary Decrees of the General Councils: Text, Translation and Commentary* (St. Louis/London, 1937). See also P. Lombardus, *Quatuor Libri Sententiarum*, 4: Dist. 26–42, partly translated in E. Rogers, *Peter Lombard and the Sacramental System* (New York, 1917; repr. Merritt, NY, 1976) [hereinafter Lombard, *Sentences*]; *The Summa Theologica of St. Thomas Aquinas*, trans. Fathers of the English Dominican Province (London, 1922), Part III (Supp.), QQ. 41–68; Hugh of St. Victor, *On the Sacraments of the Christian Faith*, trans. R. Deferrari, (Cambridge, MA, 1951), Part 11. Authoritative secondary accounts, in addition to Berman, include G. Duby, *Medieval Marriage: Two Models From Twelfth-Century France* (Baltimore, 1978); H. Zeimentz, *Ehe nach der Lehre der Frühscholastik* (Dusseldorf, 1973); D. Schwab, *Grundlagen und Gestalt der staatlichen Ehegesetzgebung in der Neuzeit bis zum Beginn des 19. Jahrhunderts* (Bielefeld, 1967), 15–40; J. Ziegler, *Die Ehelehre der Ponitentialsummen von 1200–1350* (Regensburg, 1956); J. Friesen, *Geschichte des kanonischen Eherechts bis zum Verfall der Glossenliteratur* (Paderborn, 1963; repr. of 1893 ed.); R. Sohm, *Das Recht der Eheschliessung aus dem deutschen und kanonischen Recht geschichtlich entwickelt* (Aalen, 1966; repr. of 1875 ed.) 107–186; A. Esmein, *Etudes sur l'histoire du droit canonique privé. Le mariage en droit canonique*, 2 vols. (New York, 1963).

[8]There are three major groups of writings on marriage and marriage law in the period from the late thirteenth to the early sixteenth centuries that were influential in Germany: (1) commentaries on Lombard's discussion of the marriage sacrament in the *Sentences*, most notably those of John Duns Scotus (c. 1265–1308), William of Paris (d. 1314), Petrus Aureolus (d. 1322), William of Ockham (1280–1349), Thomas of Straussburg (d. 1357), Gabriel Biel (1425–1495) and John Major (1469–1550); (2) tracts on marriage and marriage law, including commentaries on Gratian's *Decretum* and subsequent decretal collections, most notably those of Thomas Aquinas (1225–1274), Joannes Andreae (1270–1348), Johannes Gerson (1363–1429), Jacobus de Zocchis (d. 1457), Antonius de Rosellis (d. c. 1469), Jacobus Almainus (d. 1515), Johann von Breitenbach

Three broad perspectives on marriage can be found in the Roman Catholic tradition of the late eleventh through fifteenth centuries. Marriage was seen (1) as a created natural institution, subject to the laws of nature; (2) as a sacrament of faith, subject to the laws of Scripture; and (3) as a contract, subject to the general canon laws of contract formation, maintenance and dissolution. These three prespectives were, in an important sense, complementary, each emphasizing one aspect of marriage: its divine origin, its symbolic function and its legal form respectively. There was, nevertheless, a certain tension among these three perspectives as well, which manifested itself in the laws of marriage.

Marriage was regarded, first, as a created natural institution which serves both as "a duty for the sound and a remedy for the sick."[9] Already in Paradise, God had commanded man and woman to "be fruitful and multiply."[10] He had created man and woman as social beings, naturally inclined to one another. He had endowed them with the physical capacity to join together and beget children. He had commanded the man and the woman to help and nurture each other and to inculcate within their children the highest virtue and love of God. These qualities and duties continued after the Fall into sin. But, after the Fall, marriage also came to serve as a remedy for the individual sinner to allay his lustful passion, to heal his incontinence and to substitute a bodily union with a spouse for the lost spiritual union with the Father in Paradise. Rather than allow sinful man to burn with lust, God provided the institution of marriage wherein man could direct his natural drives and desires toward the service of the human community.

A number of theologians and canonists, however, subordinated the duty

---

(d. 1507) and William Hay (c. 1470–1542); and (3) various confessional manuals, principally the *Summa Raymundi de Peniafort de poenitentia et matrimonio* (c. 1280), the *Summa confessorum Joannes Friburgensis* (c. 1294), the *Summa Pisana casuum conscientiae* (c. 1338), the *Summa Baptiniana* (c. 1483; after 1489 called the *Summa Rosella*) and the *Summa Angelica de casibus conscientiae* (1486). See, generally, R. von Stintzing, *Geschichte der populären Literatur des römischen-kanonischen Rechts in Deutschland am Ende des 15. und im Anfang des 16. Jahrhundert* (Leipzig, 1867), 514ff.; J. von Schulte, *Die Geschichte der Quellen und Literatur des kanonischen Rechts* (Graz, 1956; repr. of 1875 ed.); R. Weigand, *Die bedingte Eheschliessung im kanonischen Recht* (München, 1980), 6ff; H. Coing, ed., *Handbuch der Quellen und Literatur der neueren europäischen Privatrechtsgeschichte*, 2 vols. (München, 1973–76), 2: Part I, 1002ff.; and W. Trusen, "Forum internum und gelehrten Rechts im Spätmittelalter; Summae Confessorum und Traktate als Wegsbereiter der Rezeption," *Zeitschrift der Savigny-Stiftung (Kan. Ab.)* [hereinafter ZSS (K.A.)] 57 (1971): 83.

[9]The phrase is from St. Augustine and is repeated in numerous Roman Catholic tracts on marriage.

[10]Genesis 1:28. For discussions of the duty and remedy of marriage see Lombard, *Sentences*, 4: Dist. 26.2; Aquinas, *Summa*, Part III, Q. 41, Art. 1; Angelus de Clavassio, *Summa Angelica de casibus conscientiae* (Clavassio, 1486), first page of topic 'Matrimonio' (the ms. is unpaginated and folio numbers are indecipherable); W. Hay, *Lectures on Marriage (1533–35)*, trans. J. Barry (Edinburgh, 1967), 19, 39–41.

of propagation to that of celibate contemplation, the natural drive for sexual union to the spiritual drive for communion with the Father.[11] For, as Peter Lombard put it,

> The first institution [of marriage in Paradise] was commanded, the second permitted . . . to the human race for the purpose of preventing fornication. But this permission, because it does not select better things, is a remedy not a reward; if anyone rejects it, he will deserve judgment of death. An act which is allowed by permission, however, is voluntary, not necessary.[12]

After the Fall, marriage remains a duty, but only for those tempted by sexual sin. For those not so tempted, marriage is only an inferior option. It is better and more conducive to virtue to remain celibate and to contemplate. For marriage is an institution of the natural sphere, not the supernatural sphere. Though ordained by God and good, it serves primarily for the perfection of the human community, not for the perfection of the individual. Participation in it simply keeps man free from sin and vice; it does not directly contribute to his virtue. The celibate, contemplative life, by contrast, is a calling of the supernatural sphere. Participation in it increases man's virtue and aids him in the pursuit of beatitude. To this pursuit, "marriage is a very great obstacle," for it forces man to dwell on the carnal and natural rather than the spiritual and supernatural aspects of life.[13]

As a created natural institution, marriage is subject to the laws of nature and natural reason. These natural laws, the Church taught, communicate God's will that persons marry, beget children and teach them to fear the Lord. It prescribes monogamous, indissoluble unions. It proscribes bigamy, incest and other unnatural relations. It dictates that all true promises, including marriage promises, be binding.

Marriage is not only a natural institution created by God and governed by natural law; it is also raised by Christ to the dignity of a sacrament and thus subject to ecclesiastical law.[14] It is a visible sign of the invisible

[11]Lombard, *Sentences*, 4: Dist. 26.3–4; Aquinas, *Summa*, Part III, Q. 41, Art. 2; J. Gerson, *Oeuvres completés*, ed. P. Glorieux (Paris, 1960–70), 7:416ff. See Friesen, *Geschichte*, 25ff; J. Yost, "The Value of Married Life for the Social Order in the Early English Renaissance," *Societas* 6 (1976): 36. Cf. the reaffirmation of this teaching by the Council of Trent (1563): "If any one saith that the marriage state is to be placed above the state of virginity, or celibacy, and that it is not better and more blessed to remain in virginity, or in celibacy, than to be united in matrimony: let him be anathema." P. Schaff, *The Creeds of Christendom with a History and Critical Notes* (New York, 1882), 2: 97.

[12]Lombard, *Sentences*, 4: Dist. 26.3.

[13]Aquinas, *Summa*, Part III, Q. 41, Art. 2.

[14]Roman Catholic writers were divided on the question of whether the sacrament of marriage was already instituted in Paradise or had been first created by Christ. For an analysis of this debate and its significance see J. Pelikan, *Reformation of Church and Dogma (1300–1700)*

covenantal union of Christ with His Church. Both the physical and the spiritual union of the married couple are symbolic. The harmony of their wills and minds reflects the concordance of the Church with the will and mind of Christ. Their physical and spiritual union in love symbolizes the gracious union of spirit and flesh in the manhood of Christ. The marriage bond, like the covenant bond, is a voluntary union by both parties based on mutual consent, love and desire, is consummated by the union of the parties and, once consummated, becomes indissoluble and eternally binding.

Unlike the other six sacraments, marriage required no formalities and no clerical or lay instruction, witness or participation. The two parties were themselves "ministers of the sacrament" whose consciences instructed them and whose own testimony was sufficient witness to validate their marriage. Although from the thirteenth century on, the Church strongly encouraged the couple to solemnify their union with the blessing of the priest, to invite witnesses to the marriage and to comply with the marital customs of their domicile, these were not requirements. For, as an early sixteenth century theologian wrote, "it is not of the essence of marriage to contract it in the presence of the church and according to the custom of the country, but a matter of propriety. The fitness of the parties [and the consent between them] is of the essence of marriage."[15]

Like the other sacraments, marriage was conceived to be an instrument of sanctification which, when contracted between Christians, conferred grace on those who put no obstacle in its way.[16] Marriage sanctified the Christian couple by allowing them to comply with God's law for marriage and by reminding them that Christ, the bridegroom, took the Church as His bride and accorded it His highest love and devotion, even to death. It sanctified the Christian community by enlarging the church and by educating its children as people of God. The natural marital functions of propagation and education were thus given spiritual significance when performed by Christians within the extended Christian *ecclesia*.

Because marriage was a Christian sacrament it was subject to the authority and law of the Church. As the Church sought to regulate marriage formation and dissolution, marriage was increasingly conceived as a legal relationship. Marriages could not be formed and dissolved spontaneously by anyone. Specific rules—arising from the moral laws of the internal forum and

---

(Chicago, 1984), 61ff. and R. Lawrence, *The Sacramental Interpretation of Eph. 5:32 from Peter Lombard to the Council of Trent* (Washington, 1963).

[15]Hay, *Lectures*, 31. See Canon 51 of the Fourth Lateran Council (1215) in Schroeder, *Disciplinary Decrees*, 280–281.

[16]On the purpose of sacraments, see Lombard, *Sentences*, 4: Dist. 1; Aquinas, *Summa*, Part III, QQ. 60–65. Cf. A. von Harnack, *History of Dogma*, trans. W. Gilchrist (New York, 1958), 6: 200–226; Friesen, *Geschichte*, 29–44; and J. Martos, *Doors to the Sacred: A Historical Introduction to Sacraments in the Catholic Church*, (Garden City, NY, 1981), 63ff., 397ff.

the canon laws of the external forum—were required to define which unions were properly sanctioned and which could be properly dissolved.[17]

The canon law of marriage was built on this tripartite conceptual foundation. Through these positive laws, the Church protected natural monogamous unions and prohibited polygamy, bigamy, homosexuality and other unnatural unions. It encouraged the natural marital functions of propagation and child rearing and forbad contraception, abortion and child abuse. It ensured that a couple entered this union freely without mistake or compulsion and without physical ties to another person or spiritual ties to the clergy or cloister. It ensured that the sanctification conferred by the marriage sacrament was not obstructed by spiritual, familial or blood ties between the couple, by criminal, adulterous, heretical or pagan acts by one party or by impotence or physical abuse by either party. It ordered that all valid marriage promises, freely made and accepted, be indissoluble.

A man and woman could form a marriage bond only through voluntary consensual agreement, and numerous treatises were devoted to defining "consent" and "agreement."[18] Most of the canonists distinguished between: (1) the betrothal or promise to marry in the future ("I, Martin, promise to take you, Mary, to be my wife"); (2) the promise to be married in the present which constitutes a true and valid union, even without sexual intercourse ("I, Martin, now take you, Mary, as my wife"); and (3) consummation of the marriage by voluntary sexual intercourse.[19] Each stage of consent or promise was governed by a number of canon law rules.[20]

By the early sixteenth century, the church courts recognized a variety of lawful impediments to betrothal, that is, conditions under which either of the parties could break off their engagement without sin. A faithful party could (but need not) reject a fiancé who had become a heretic or pagan, had abducted another (particularly a relative of a fiancé), had been raped, had become impotent, severely deformed or deranged after betrothal, had deserted him or her for more than two years or had failed to make a present

---

[17]The three perspectives of marriage are set out by Aquinas in *Summa*, Part III, Q. 42, Art. 2. Cf. discussion in Schwab, *Grundlagen*, 34–40.

[18]See, generally, J. Noonan, "Power to Choose," *Viator* 4 (1973): 419 and ibid., "Marital Affection in the Canonists," *Studia Gratiana* 12 (1967): 489.

[19]On the origin of this three-fold doctrine of consent, see C. Donahue, "The Policy of Alexander the Third's Consent Theory of Marriage," *Proceedings of the Fourth International Congress of Medieval Canon Law, Monumenta Iuris Canonici*, Series C: Subsidia 5 (1976): 251ff.; Sohm, *Das Recht der Eheschliessung*, 110–144.

[20]The following overview of the canon law of marriage is derived largely from Hay, *Lectures*, 47–355; Angelus, *Summa Angelica*, 3–23 of the section 'Matrimonio'; the *Summa confessorum Joannes Freiburgensis von Latein in Teutsch gemacht durch Berthold von Freiburg* (1472) which is also summarized in R. Stanka, *Die Summa des Berthold von Freiburg. Eine rechtsgeschichtliche Untersuchung* (Wien, 1937), 83–100; Stintzing, *Geschichte der populären Literatur*, 151ff.; Aquinas, *Summa*, Part III, QQ. 50–68; Lombard, *Sentences*, 4: Dist. 30–42; and Gratian, *Decretum*, J. Noonan, trans. (unpubl., 1978), Part II. An exhaustive summary of the discussion of marriage law among earlier Roman Catholic writers is provided by Friesen, *Geschichte*, 227ff.

promise within the time of engagement agreed upon by the parties. In all these cases, the innocent party was required to petition an ecclesiastical judge to annul the betrothal. A religious vow or entry by either party into a religious order automatically nullified the betrothal; the other party, in such instance, had no discretion to continue the relationship. A betrothal could also be dissolved by mutual consent of the parties.

A future promise to marry, followed by sexual intercourse, was a consummated marriage at canon law. The sex act after betrothal raised the presumption that the parties had impliedly consented to be truly married and to consummate their marriage. This presumption could be defeated if one of the parties testified that he or she had been beguiled or forcibly abducted by the other.

The canon law also recognized several other impediments to the present promise to marry. These were of two types: (1) prohibitive impediments which rendered the contracting of marriage unlawful and sinful, but whose violation did not render the marriage invalid; (2) diriment (or absolute) impediments which proscribed the contracting of marriage, and, if it was contracted, nullified and dissolved it completely; such a putative marriage, contracted in violation of such impediments, could never be considered a true and valid marriage.

The prohibitive impediments dealt largely with cases of remarriage. A married person who had abducted a relative of his or her spouse or another married or betrothed person could not marry that person after his or her own spouse's death. For those who murdered their spouses, murdered a cleric, married a nun or monk or had done public penance for a particularly egregious sin, marriage was proscribed altogether.

Far more important were the diriment impediments used by the ecclesiastical courts to nullify even fully consummated putative marriages. One group of these impediments sought to preserve the freedom of consent of both parties. Thus a mistake about the identity of the other party nullified the marriage. (Mistakes about the social, financial or civil status of the other generally were no longer considered to be grounds for nullification after the early fourteenth century.) Extreme duress, fear, compulsion or fraud (by parents, spouses or third parties) also impinged on consent and invalidated the marriage contract.

The canon law not only defined free consent but also specified which parties were free to give their mutual consent. Those who had made religious vows of celibacy or chastity in one of the sacred orders of the Church were eternally bound to God and thus could not bind themselves to another in marriage. Christians could not contract marriage with infidels, Jews or pagans since the sacrament of baptism was a prerequisite for marriage. Furthermore, such marriages could not symbolize the union of Christ with his faithful Church. Thus if a party departed from the faith after consummation and remained incorrigible, the marriage could be declared void. Persons related up to the fourth degree either to a common ancestor or to a couple (whether or not married) who had engaged in sexual relations were prohibited from marrying. These were called the impediments of consanguinity and affinity. Parents could not marry their adopted children or grandchildren, nor the spouses of their adopted children. One who had baptized or confirmed a party or who had become a godparent could not marry him or her; for these persons were considered to be the "spiritual fathers or mothers" of the party who received the sacrament.

The canon law also developed a group of impediments to protect the ultimate sanctity and function of the sacrament of marriage. First, conditions attached to marriage promises which were illegal or which were repugnant to the sacrament or harmful to the offspring automatically rendered the marriage contract void. Thus a promise with the condition "that we abstain for a season" was valid, but a condition "that we abort our offspring" or "that we permit each other sexual liberty with others" nullified the marriage contract. Such conditions vitiated the divine purpose of marriage: to unite together in love and to raise children in the service of God. Second, permanent impotence, insanity or bewitchment of either party were generally grounds for nullification as well, provided that such a condition was latent before marriage; if the parties knew of the condition before marriage, they generally had no action for nullification. Third, the Church annulled all bigamous and polygamous relations as contrary to the Gospel and to the divine purpose of marriage. Fourth, an unconsummated marriage could be annulled if one party severely abused or consistently threatened the other with death, contracted a permanent contagious disease or committed adultery. Where the marriage was consummated, however, the church permitted only a divorce, that is, a judicial separation from bed and board. Divorce in the modern sense was not permitted. The sacramental bond, once consummated, remained indissoluble till the physical or civil death of one of the parties.

This intricate array of sacramental marriage laws remained in constant tension with the concept of marriage as a created natural institution. Though God had created marriage as a duty and a remedy for sinful man, the Church had foreclosed this option to many through its numerous impediments. Though God had provided the Church with His natural law and Scripture to govern marriage, the church had added numerous canon laws not prefigured in natural law or Scripture. The tension between the natural and sacramental concepts of marriage manifested itself, for example, in papal policy. The pope could in certain cases authorize marriage by remitting the canon law impediments of affinity and consanguinity and adopting the far less restrictive impediments set by Scripture. In other cases of hardship, inequity or incompatability, he was free to dissolve unconsummated marriages on grounds specified neither in canon law nor in Scripture.

More important was the tension between the concept of marriage as a sacrament governed by the moral authority of the internal forum and the concept of marriage as a contract governed by the legal authority of the external forum. This tension, writes Harold Berman,

> was reflected in the questions which the ecclesiastical courts had to answer, such as whether a marriage is invalid because of mistake, fraud or duress; whether a husband may abandon an adulterous wife; whether a wife who marries another, thinking her first husband dead, must return to the first man when he reappears; and whether a clandestine marriage, contracted with no third party present, is valid. The tension was also reflected in many of the answers which the ecclesiastical courts gave to such questions. It came out clearly in the resolution of the question of the validity of clandestine marriages. On the one hand, as Gratian stated, 'marriages secretly contracted are prohibited by all the authorities' and are unlawful. On the other hand, such marriages are valid if they can be proved by the confession of both spouses. But if the will of one of the parties had changed, the judge is not to give credence to the confession of the other. Thus the strong policy of social betrothals and of external obligations was affirmed, while the sanctity of sacramental consent was also maintained. Yet the solution—resting as it does on a fiction in the law of evidence—though 'systematic', was hardly perfect.[21]

II. THE TRANSFORMATION OF THE THEOLOGICAL CONCEPT OF MARRIAGE IN THE LUTHERAN REFORMATION

The Lutheran reformers, like the Roman Catholics, viewed marriage as a duty and a remedy established at creation. The duty of marriage stems from God's command that man and woman unite, help each other, beget children and raise them as God's servants. It is also a gift which remedies and restrains man's lust and incontinence.[22]

Unlike many Roman Catholics, however, the reformers taught that all persons should heed the duty and accept the gift of marriage. By stressing God's moral and pedagogical functions for the family in society, alongside its

---

[21]Berman, *Law and Revolution*, 229–30.

[22]*LW*, 28: 9–15; 45:17ff.; 46: 265ff.; P. Melanchthon, *De Coniurio* (1551), in *Corpus Reformatorum*, eds. G. Bretschneider, et al. (Brunsvigae, 1843), 21: 1072ff. See the discussions of these writings as well as those of numerous other Lutheran theologians and jurists in H. Dietrich, *Das protestantische Eherecht* (München, 1970); H. Liermann, "Evangelisches Kirchenrecht und staatliches Eherecht in Deutschland, ein Rechtsgeschichtliches-Gegenwartsprobleme," *Existenz und Ordnung: Festschrift für Erik Wolf* (Frankfurt/Main, 1962), 43ff.; E. Friedberg, *Das Eheschliessung in seiner geschichtlichen Entwicklung* (Leipzig, 1865), 153–240; W. Köhler, "Luther als Eherichter," *Beiträge zur sachsischen Kirchengeschichte* 47 (1947): 18; R. Seeberg, "Luthers Anschauung von dem Geschlechtsleben und der Ehe ihre geschichtliche Stellung," *Luther-Jahrbuch* 7 (1925): 77; K. Michealis, "Über Luthers eherechtliche Anschauungen und deren Verhältnis zum mittelalterlichen und neuzeitlichen Eherecht," *Festschrift für Erich Ruppel zum 65. Geburtstag* (Hannover, 1968), 43.

procreational function, and by defining for the family its own created sphere of authority and responsibility, alongside that of the church and the state, the reformers accorded great importance to the institution. The married couple, the family, was seen as an important, independent institution of creation. It was as indispensable an agent in God's plan of redemption as the church had been for the Roman Catholics. It, too, was in Luther's words, "a divine and holy estate of life," a "blessed holy calling," an institution with created social tasks. The family was to teach all persons, particularly children, Christian values, morals and mores. It was to exemplify for a sinful society a community of love and cooperation, meditation and discussion, song and prayer. It was to hold out for the church and the state an example of firm but benign parental discipline, rule and authority. It was to take in and care for wayfarers, widows and destitute persons—a responsibility previously assumed largely by monasteries and cloisters.[23] The family thus no longer stood beneath the church in the created order, but alongside it. The tasks to which its members were called were as vital and virtuous as the tasks of the church officials. Marriage was thus not to be viewed as an inferior option, but, rather, as a divine calling and a social status desirable for all people.

The Lutheran emphasis on man's total depravity provided a further argument for accepting the remedial gift of marriage. Since the Fall, lust has pervaded the conscience of every person. Marriage has thus become an absolute necessity. Without it, man's distorted sexuality becomes a force capable of overthrowing the most devout conscience. He is enticed by his own nature to prostitution, masturbation and homosexuality. The gift of marriage, Luther wrote, should be declined only by those who have received God's gift of continence. Such persons are "rare, not one in a thousand, for they are a special miracle of God." The Apostle Paul has identified this group as the permanently impotent and the eunuchs; few others can claim such a unique gift.[24]

This understanding of the created origin and purpose of marriage undergirded the reformers' bitter attack on celibacy and monasticism. To require celibacy of clerics, monks and nuns was beyond the authority of the church and ultimately a source of great sin. Celibacy was for God to give, not for the church to require. It was for each individual, not for the church, to decide whether he had received the gift. By institutionalizing and encouraging celibacy, the reformers charged, the church preyed on the immature

---

[23]See *D. Martin Luthers Werke kritische Gesamtausgabe* (Weimar, 1883), 73: 341; *The Book of Concord*, trans. and eds. T. Tappert et al. (Philadelphia, 1959), 393; P. Althaus, *The Ethics of Martin Luther*, trans. R. Schultz (Philadelphia, 1965), 86ff; Strauss, *Luthers House of Learning*, 115; R. Bainton, *Here I Stand: A Life of Martin Luther* (New York, 1963), 221–37. Cf. the even broader perspective on the worldly orders in P. Melanchthon, *Loci communes* (1555), in *Melanchthon on Christian Doctrine*, trans. and ed. C. Manschreck (Oxford, 1965), 323–24.

[24]*LW*, 28: 9–12, 27–31; 45: 18–22. See the discussion of views of other theologians in Dietrich, *Eherecht*, 78–80.

and the uncertain; by holding out food, shelter and security, the monasteries enticed poor and needy parents to "condemn" their children to celibate monasticism. Celibacy, Luther taught, was hardly a prerequisite to true service of God. Instead it led to "great whoredom and all manner of fleshly impurity and . . . hearts filled with thoughts of women day and night,"[25] for the consciences of Christians and non-Christians alike are infused with lust.

Furthermore, to impute to the celibate contemplative life superior spirituality and holier virtue was, for the reformers, contradicted by Scripture. Scripture teaches that each person must perform his or her calling with the gifts that God provides. The gifts of continence and contemplation are but two among many and are by no means superior to the gifts of marriage and child-rearing. Each calling plays an equally important, holy and virtuous role in the drama of redemption, and its fulfillment is a service to God. Luther concurs with the Apostle Paul that the celibate person "may better be able to preach and care for God's Word." But, he immediately adds, "it is God's Word and preaching which makes celibacy—such as that of Christ or of Paul—better than the estate of marriage. In itself, however, the celibate life is far inferior."[26]

The reformers' lengthy arguments for marriage as a created natural institution were also arguments against the Roman Catholic sacramental concept of marriage. For, in the context of Luther's two kingdoms theory,[27] to place marriage in the natural order of creation was to deny it a place in the spiritual order of redemption. Marriage was seen as an earthly natural institution. Though divinely instituted to serve a holy purpose it remains in Luther's words, "an outward, physical and worldly station."[28] The sacraments, by contrast, are part of the heavenly kingdom of faith and salvation. They are spiritual instruments of salvation and sanctification.

As part of the earthly kingdom, the reformers argued, marriage is a gift of

---

[25]*LW*, 28: 10; cf. Luther's other epigrams assembled in Seeberg, "Luthers Anschauung," 94ff. See also the long diatribe against clerical celibacy in *LW*, 44: 251–400 and "The Apology of the Augsburg Confession," in *Concordia Triglotta Libri Symbolici Ecclesiae Lutheranae* (St. Louis, MO, 1921), 363–381. For a discussion of the breadth and intensity of the reformers' attack on celibacy and monasticism, and the Roman Catholic reaction, see Ozment, *When Fathers Ruled*, 3–24; Strauss, *Luther's House of Learning*, 111ff.; A. Franzen, *Zölibat und Priesterehe in der Auseinandersetzung der Reformationszeit und der katholisches Reform des 16. Jahrhundert* (Münster, 1969).

[26]*LW*, 45: 47.

[27]The Lutheran two kingdoms theory is described in, inter alia, Althaus, *Ethics*, 43–82; H. Bornkamm, *Luther's Doctrine of the Two Kingdoms in the Context of His Theology*, trans. K. Hertz (Philadelphia, 1966); Seeberg, "Luthers Anschauung," 88–92; and W. Thompson, *The Political Thought of Martin Luther* (New York, 1984), 36–61.

[28]*LW*, 21: 93; 46: 265; 63: 111–112; see also, Althaus, *Ethics*, 89; Dietrich, *Eherecht*, 34ff. This view was shared by several other Lutheran theologians, particularly M. Bucer, *De Regno Christi*, ed. and trans. W. Pauck (Philadelphia, 1969), chap. 15 and Melanchthon, *De Conjurio*, 1074; see also Dietrich, supra, 80ff. and W. Köhler, *Das Ehe- und Zurcher Ehegericht und Genfer Konsistorium*, 2 vols. (Leipzig, 1932–42), 2: 427ff.

God for all persons, Christians and non-Christians alike. It functions in the earthly kingdom much like law: it has a number of distinctive uses in the life of the person and of society as a whole.[29] Marriage reminds man of his lustful nature and his need for God's soothing remedy of marriage, just as law reveals to man his sin and impels him to grace; this is its theological use. Marriage restrains man from yielding to sins of prostitution, incontinence and promiscuity, just as civil law restrains him from destructive cheating, feuding and stealing; this is its civil use. Marriage teaches man the virtues of love, patient cooperation and altruism, just as law teaches him restraint, sharing and respect for another's person and property; this is its pedagogical use. Marriage, therefore, not only has its own created tasks, it also has distinctive social uses.

Marriage can, to be sure, symbolize for all men the union of Christ and His Church, but that does not make it a sacrament. Sacraments are gifts and signs of grace ensuring Christians of the promise of redemption which is available only to those who have faith.[30] Marriage carries no such promise and demands no such faith. "Nowhere in the Scripture," writes Luther, "do we read that anyone would receive the grace of God by getting married; nor does the rite of matrimony contain any hint that this ceremony is of divine institution."[31] Scripture teaches that only baptism and the eucharist confer this promise of grace. All other so-called sacraments are "mere human artifices" created by Roman Catholics through false interpretations of Scripture for the purpose of augmenting the church's legal powers and filling its coffers with court fees and fines.[32]

Like the Roman Catholics, the Lutherans taught that marriage could not be formed and dissolved spontaneously by anyone. Specific rules were needed to define which unions were proper and which could be dissolved. But, because marriage is an institution of the earthly kingdom, not a sacrament of the heavenly kingdom, it is subject to civil law and civil

---

[29]For a discussion of the Lutheran doctrine of the uses of the law see F. Cranz, *An Essay on the Development of Luther's Thought on Justice, Law, and Society* (Cambridge, MA, 1959), 94–112 and F. Alexander, "Validity and Function of Law: The Reformation Doctrine of Usus Legis," *Mercer Law Review* 31 (1980): 509. The reformers themselves never spoke of the "uses of marriage," but there is remarkable unanimity in their description of the functions of marriage and of the uses of law. See, especially, *LW*, 45: 38–49 and the discussion of the writings of Bugenhagen, Colerus, Brenz, and other Lutheran writers in Ozment, *When Fathers Ruled*, 8–9 and Dietrich, *Eherecht*, 81–82.

[30]See Luther, *The Babylonian Captivity of the Church* (1520), *LW*, 36: 11ff. and *The Smalcald Articles* (1537), in *The Book of Concord*, 310ff. (Other reformers, in addition to Luther, helped to draft these articles.) For a comparison of the sacramental doctrine in these two works and in the works of other Lutheran writers, see J. Pelikan, *Scripture Versus Structure: Luther and the Institutions of the Church* (New York, 1968), 17–31, 113–138.

[31]M. Luther, *Selections From His Writings*, ed. J. Dillenberger (New York, 1961), 326.

[32]Ibid., 331. Early in his career Luther had tentatively accepted penance as a third sacrament, but he later rejected this position.

authority, not canon law and ecclesiastical authority. Marital questions are to be brought before civil courts, not ecclesiastical courts.

This does not mean that marriage is beyond the pale of God's authority and law, nor that it should be beyond the influence and concern of the church.[33] The civil ruler holds his authority of God. His will is to appropriate God's desire. His law is to reflect God's law. His rule is to respect God's creation ordinances and institutions and to implement His purposes. His civil calling is no less spiritual than that of the church. Marriage is thus still completely subject to godly law, but this law is now to be administered by a civil ruler.[34] Because marriage is an important social institution, its formation, maintenance and dissolution are public concerns, particularly to church officials and members. The church, the reformers argued, retained a fourfold responsibility in marriage. First, through its preaching of the Word and the teaching of its theologians, the church had to communicate to the civil authorities and their subjects God's law and will for marriage and the family. Second, it was incumbent upon church members as priests to quiet, through instruction and prayer, the consciences of those troubled by marriage problems and to hold out a model of spiritual freedom, love, care and equality in their own married lives. Third, to aid church members in their instruction and care and to give notice to all members of society of a couple's marriage, the church was to develop a publicly available marriage registry which all married couples would be required to sign. Fourth, the pastor and consistory of the church were to instruct and discipline the marriages of church members by blessing and instructing the couple at their public church wedding ceremony and by punishing sexual turpitude or egregious violations of marriage law with the ban or excommunication.[35]

III. The Influence of the Lutheran Reformation on Sixteenth Century German Marriage Law

This new Lutheran social concept of marriage not only revolutionized the theology of marriage but also helped to transform the law of marriage in Germany. For the concept was a self-executing program of action. It required

---

[33]Throughout his life, Luther rejected the suggestions of many writers that, by placing marriage in the earthly kingdom, he and his followers had totally secularized marriage, i.e., removed it from the pale of God's authority and law. "It is sheer folly," Luther opined, to treat marriage as "nothing more than a purely human and secular state, with which God has nothing to do." *LW*, 21: 95. This misunderstanding of Luther's doctrine of marriage—still much in evidence today—stems from a failure to view it in the context of his two kingdoms theory and a failure to recognize his multiple definitions of the terms "worldly," "earthly," and "secular." Cf. Althaus, *Ethics*, 49–50; Dietrich, *Eherecht*, 32.

[34]See Ibid., 44ff., 81ff.; Seebaas, "Luthers Anschauung," 93ff.

[35]See Dietrich, *Eherecht*, 47, 86; R. Kirstein, *Die Entwicklung der Sponsalienlehre und der Lehre vom Eheschluss in der deutschen Protestantischen bis zu J. H. Bohmer* (Bonn, 1966), 39ff.; W. Köhler, "Die Anfänge des protestanischen Eherechtes," *ZSS (K.A.)* 74 (1941): 271, 278ff.

civil authorities to divest the Roman Catholic Church of its marital jurisdiction and ensured them that this was a mandate of Scripture, not a sin against the church. It called for new civil marriage laws that were consonant with God's Word but required that the church (and thus the reformers themselves) advise the civil authorities on what God's Word commands. Both the princes' seizure of power and the reformers' active development of marriage laws were thus seen as biblical tasks. The transformation of German marriage law followed this program: new civil marriage courts emerged first; new civil marriage laws followed.

A. The Development of Civil Marriage Courts

The reformers catalyzed the development of civil marriage courts throughout Germany. Prior to the sixteenth century, most marriage and family cases had been heard in ecclesiastical courts. Local priests or clerical bodies usually had primary jurisdiction over marital disputes between their parishioners and had authority to dispose of minor issues. More serious cases, particularly those involving divorce or annulment, were referred to the court of the cathedral dean. Parties could, in most cases, appeal judgments of the dean's court to the territorial archbishops, and, in certain instances, to the papal curia in Rome.[36] In the 1520s and 1530s, reformers throughout Germany sharply attacked the church courts in a welter of published sermons, pamphlets and confessional writings. These courts, they charged, had illegitimately usurped the judicial authority of the prince. They were repositories of corruption and arbitrariness, prone to bribery and gross inconsistency of judgment. They were too distant from Rome to be adequately supervised and too insulated by canon law to be adequately disciplined by the prince or city council. Their procedures were cumbersome and costly, their fines and punishments frequently excessive. The requirement that serious cases be brought before the cathedral dean foreclosed action to those who could not afford or risk to travel to the cathedral city.

With these criticisms the reformers molded public and official opinion against the church courts and successfully petitioned numerous city and territorial councils to develop local civil marriage courts. The first such court was established in 1525 in Zurich at the insistence of Ulrich Zwingli and his followers. Within a decade, similar courts had been established in Nürnberg on the strength of Andreas Osiander's proposal, in Konstanz under the influence of Ambrosius Blarer, in Schwabisch-Hall under the direction of Johannes Brenz, in Strassburg under Martin Bucer's influence, and in Basel

---

[36]On ecclesiastical courts and their procedure, see Weigand, *Die bedingte Eheschliessung*, 48–54, 64–67; R. Helmholtz, *Marriage Litigation in Medieval England* (London, 1974); B. Hashagen, "Zur Charakteristik der geistlichen Gerichtsbarkeit vornehmlich im späteren Mittelalter," *ZSS (K.A.)* 6 (1916): 205; J. Harvey, *The Influence of the Reformation on Nuremberg Marriage Laws* (Ph.D. Diss., Ohio State University, 1972), 74–90.

based on the proposals of Johannes Oekolampadus.[37] In the following two decades, dozens of cities and territories followed these early examples. In a few Lutheran territories the princes retained the church courts, but replaced church officials with civil judges.

This process of removing marital jurisdiction from the church also had a momentum independent of the Reformation. The territorial princes had long envied the church's lucrative and powerful control over marriage and had decried the corruption and delinquency of certain church courts and bishoprics. Already in the late fourteenth and fifteenth centuries, therefore, certain civil rulers had gained a measure of control over marital questions. In a 1440 statute passed in Ulm, for example, the local civil court (*Gerichtshof*) was given authority (1) to order a man who had seduced a virgin either to marry her or to pay her dower; (2) to fine a secretly betrothed couple and order them to publicize their marriage and to gain parental or clerical approval; and (3) to enforce the canon law impediments of affinity and consanguinity. Civil courts in several other territories and cities assumed authority to fine, imprison or banish parties guilty of concubinage, prostitution, adultery, desertion, bigamy and wife or child abuse—though such cases had traditionally been under ecclesiastical jurisdiction.[38] Such scattered instances of civil jurisdiction, however, did not change the reality of a predominant ecclesiastical authority over marriage. Church courts were systematically divested of their marital jurisdiction only with the outbreak of the Lutheran Reformation.

The secularization of marriage courts in Germany, however, was neither

---

[37]See, generally, Dietrich, *Eherecht*, 150–152 and Köhler, "Die Anfänge," 272–275. For separate treatments of the development of the procedure and law of marriage courts in various territories and cities of Germany, see W. Seebaas, *Das reformatorische Werk des Andreas Osiander* (Nürnberg, 1967), 184ff.; Harvey, *The Influence*, 90–114; K. Koch, *Studium Pietatis. Martin Bucer als Ethiker* (Neukirchen, 1962), 135ff.; F. Wendel, *Le mariage a Strausbourg a l'epoque de la Reforme 1520–1692* (Straussburg, 1928), 77ff.; Köhler, *Das Ehe*, 33ff.; P. Vogt, *Kirchen- und Eherecht der katholischen und evangelischen in der konigl. preussischen Staaten* (Breslau, 1875), 147ff.; F. Hauber, *Württembergisches Eherecht des Evangelischen* (Württemberg, 1956); B. Gesschen, *Zur ältesten Geschichte und ehegerichtlichen Praxis des Leipziger Konsistorium* (Straussburg, 1894).

Many of the Church Ordinances (*Kirchenordnungen*) [hereinafter KO] and Policy Ordinances (*Polizeiordnungen*) [hereinafter PO] which established these courts and defined their jurisdiction, procedure and membership are collected and discussed in E. Sehling, *Die evangelischen Kirchenordnungen des XVI. Jahrhunderts*, 16 vols. (Leipzig, 1902–1978); A. Richter, *Die evangelischen Kirchenordungen des sechszehnten Jahrhunderts*, 2 vols. (Nieuwkoop, 1967; repr. of 1846 ed.); W. Kunkel, et al., eds., *Quellen zur neueren Privatrechtsgeschichte*, 2; and G. Schmelzeisen, *Polizeiordnungen und Privatrecht* (München/Köln, 1955), 21–67.

[38]See Köhler, "Die Anfänge," 277ff. for a discussion of civil marital jurisdiction in Ulm and in a number of other German cities and territories in the fifteenth and early sixteenth centuries. See also the marriage provisions in the *Nürnberg Reformation* (1479), Arts. 12–13 and the *Freiburg Reformation* (1520), Art. 2. in Kunkel, et al., eds., *Quellen*, 1: 6ff., 265ff. These latter provisions, however, are extremely laconic and deal only with discrete problems such as the age of consent or the timing of parental consent.

as universal nor as radical as Luther and his early followers had envisioned. A number of cities and territories, particularly in southern Germany, remained devoutly Roman Catholic and retained the canon law and ecclesiastical courts. These courts and their laws were later protected by the Peace of Augsburg of 1555.[39] Even in strong Lutheran cities and territories, few purely civil marriage courts emerged. Nürnberg (1526) and Straussburg (c. 1535) did develop civil courts under the exclusive control of the city councils and without church officials as judges or staff members—but these were exceptions.[40] The Wittenberg court, developed ultimately in 1545 by Melanchthon, Schürpf and others, was a more typical example. Theologians and jurists were appointed to the court by the city council. It was given authority to hear and adjudicate all marriage cases using formal written procedures in court or the informal inquisitions of the pastor with his parishioner. The court could use either the visitation process of pastors and other church superintendents or the inspections of city police to discover or investigate violations of marriage law. In cases raising particularly difficult moral or legal questions, the court could also seek the advice of the theology and law faculties of the local university. The court would then render a judgment, which was to be enforced by the city council but was subject to its revision. In cases where the theologians of the court determined that the parties had violated the laws of Scripture, morality or conscience, the court would recommend that the church exercise spiritual discipline against the parties, such as the ban or excommuncation.[41] Similar "mixed courts" appeared in numerous other cities and territories of Germany.[42] In a few territories, the princes simply ordered local church consistories to adjudicate all marital disputes and sent them superintendents, conversant with the marriage law of

[39]See a translation of the Peace of Augsburg (Arts. 2, 3, 7, 10) in S. Ehler and J. Morrall, *Church and State Through the Centuries: A Collection of Historic Documents with Commentaries* (London, 1954), 164ff.

[40]See Seebaas, *Das reformatorischen Werk*, 194; Harvey, *The Influence*, 98–100; Koch, *Studium Pietatis*, 136.

[41]See the Constitution of the Wittenberg consistory (1542) and the Wittenberg KO (1545) in Sehling, *Kirchenordnungen*, 1: 200ff. Cf. the similar adjudicatory structure in Württemberg and several southern German cities as described in Hauber, *Württembergischen Eherecht*, 31–41 and T. Safley, *Let No Man Put Asunder; The Control of Marriage in the German Southwest: A Comparative Study* (Kirksville, MS, 1984), 41–180. On Luther's bitter invective against the lawyers and jurists who urged that ecclesiastics should retain a prominent place in marital adjudication, see H. Liermann, "Der unjuristische Luther," *Luther-Jahrbuch* 24 (1957): 69; K. Köhler, *Luther and die Juristen. Zur Frage nach dem Gegenseitigen Verhältnis des Rechts und der Sittlichkeit* (Gotha, 1873), 3–4, 39–49; T. Muther, *Aus dem Universitäts- und Gelehrtenleben im Zeitalter der Reformation* (Erlangen, 1866), 206–16.

[42]Dietrich, *Eherecht*, 151ff. See the statutes of Schwabisch-Hall (1525), Hamburg (1529), Lübeck (1531), Hannover (1535), Mecklenberg (1573), and Prussia (1584) in Richter, *Kirchenordnung*, 1: 40ff., 127ff., 149ff., 154ff., 273ff.; Sehling, *Kirchenordnungen*, 5: 233ff.; 4: 30ff. See also discussion in H. Dietrich, *Evangelisches Ehescheidungsrecht nach den Bestimmungen der deutschen Kirchenordnungen des 16. Jahrhundert* (Erlangen, 1892), 43ff.

the territory, to aid them in their task. The consistories had to judge each case in accordance with princely marriage law, and their activity was closely supervised. Each group of congregations formed a circuit (*Kreis*); this circuit was headed by a superintendent, appointed by the prince to oversee the activities of the churches. A number of circuits formed a district (*Sprengel*) with its own supervisor. Each district was, in turn, part of the territorial church (*Landeskirche*) under the direct supervision of the prince, his council and his court.[43]

The continued involvement of ecclesiastics in civil marriage courts throughout the sixteenth century was a matter both of necessity and of doctrine. Ecclesiastics were often drawn onto these courts, or ordered to form their own courts, because they were respected community leaders, were educated and well-connected and were often among the few to have the necessary financial resources. As the territorial princes and city councils grew in power, and the number of legal professionals grew, the role of ecclesiastics and consistories in marriage law diminished quickly. A number of reformers themselves, however, in opposition to Luther, insisted on active participation in the civil marriage courts. The presence of learned theologians and pastors on the court, they argued, was the institutional means whereby the advisory function of the church in matters of marriage law could best be implemented.[44]

B. The New Learned and Statutory Law of Marriage

As the marriage law courts were reformed, so, too, was the law applied by them. This transformation the reformers also helped to catalyze, for they were instrumental both in developing a new body of learned marriage law and in promoting a new body of marital legislation.

The local university became the chief forum of reform. Lutheran theologians throughout Germany, many themselves trained in law, joined with university jurists to debate detailed questions of marriage law raised by Scripture, Roman law, canon law and local custom. At the University of Wittenberg, for example, Luther, Melanchthon, Bugenhagen, Cruciger, Jonas and numerous other theologians gave courses and public lectures on marriage law along with such renowned jurists as Kling, Lagus, Apel, Schürpf, Monner, Pauli and Schneidewin. By 1560, the Wittenberg theology and law professors had together published more than 80 tracts on marriage law questions, disseminating their ideas throughout Germany and beyond.[45]

[43]On the "established" territorial church system in Germany, see generally, K. Holl, "Luther und das landesherrliche Kirchenregiment," *Gesammelte Aufsätze zur Kirchengeschichte* (Tubingen, 1921) 1: 279ff. and E. Sehling, *Kirchenrecht* (Leipzig, 1908), 29–45.

[44]See Dietrich, *Eherecht*, 44.

[45]Among the most important of these writings on marriage law by Wittenberg reformers as well as others are the following: M. Luther, *A Sermon on the Estate of Marriage* (1519), *LW*, 44: 5; id., *The Estate of Marriage* (1522), *LW*, 45: 17; id., *The Order of Marriage for Common Pastors*

Professors at other German universities, particularly in Freiburg, Basel, Marburg and Greifswald, were equally active in developing a learned civil law of marriage.

This learned law did not remain confined to the academy or to books. Four channels allowed it to penetrate directly into the law of the courts and the councils. First, both the theology and the law faculties of local universities were regularly consulted by courts throughout the sixteenth century by use of what was called the *Aktenversendung* procedure. Files of marital cases raising difficult legal and moral issues were sent by the courts to the faculties who would discuss a case and submit separate or joint judgments. These judgments were frequently accepted by (and, in certain territories, were made binding on) the courts.[46] Studies of marriage law in Strassburg, Nürnberg, Goslar and elsewhere have shown the important influence of this *Aktenversendung* procedure on substantive marriage law.[47] Second, and closely related, courts, councils and litigating parties solicited opinions (*consilia*) from prominent individual jurists—a practice which thrived in sixteenth century Germany, as it had thrived in previous centuries in Italy.[48]

(1529), *LW*, 53: 111; id., *On Marriage Matters* (1530), *LW*, 46: 265; Melanchthon, *De Conjurio*; id., *De arbore consanguinitatis et affinitatis* (Wittenberg, 1541); J. Bugenhagen, *Vom Ehebruch und Weglauffen* (1539), in Sarcerius, *Corpus juris matrimonia* (Frankfurt/Main, 1569), folio 171; J. Brenz, *Wie in Ehesachen* (Wittenberg, 1529), in id., folio 184; J. Apel, *Defensio Johannis Apelli ad Episcopum Herbipolensem pro suo conjugio* (Wittenberg, 1523, 1524); M. Kling, *Tractatus matrimonialium causarum, methodico ordine scriptus* (Frankfurt/Main, 1553); Sarcerius, *Buch vom heiligen Ehestand* (Leipzig, 1556); B. Monner, *Tractatus de matrimonio in genere, de clandestinis conjugiis et explicatus quaestionis* (Frankfurt, 1561); id., *De clandestine conjugio libellus* (Jena, 1594); J. Schneidewein, *In Institutio imperialium titulum X, de nuptiis primi commentarii* (Venice, 1571); N. Hemming, *Libellus de conjugio* (Leipzig, 1578); K. Mauser, *Explicatio erudita et utilis X. tituli Instituti de nuptiis* (Wittenberg, 1569); J. von Beust, *De jure connubiorum et dotium tractatus* (Frankfurt, 1591). Several tracts on marriage by jurists from Wittenberg and other cities in Germany were apparently collected in *Tractatus connubiorum praestantis, juris consultorum* (Frankfurt, 1618; Jena, 1742), though I have not located this source.

[46]On the *Aktenversendung* process in general, see J. Dawson, *The Oracles of the Law* (Ann Arbor, 1968), 198–213, 240–41; W. Ebel *Studie über ein Goslarer Ratsurteilsbuch des 16. Jahrhundert* (Göttingen, 1961), 30ff.

[47]See Harvey, *The Influence*, 96–112 on Nürnberg; Koch, *Studium Pietatis*, 139ff. on Strassbourg; J. Haalk, "Die rostocker Juristenfakultat als Spruchskollegium," *Wissenschaftliche Zeitschrift der Universität Rostock* 3 (1958): 401, 414ff. on Rostock; Ebel, *Studie*, 37ff., 53ff. on Goslar. Cf. also the function of Schoppenstuhle on marital adjudication as described briefly by A. Stölzel, *Der Brandenburger Schoppenstuhl* (Berlin, 1901), 388ff.

[48]A list of the most important *consilia* by German jurists is provided in G. Kisch, *Consilia: Eine Bibliographie der juristischen Konsiliensammlungen* (Basel, 1970). On the history of the *consilia* practice in Europe see, generally, H. Gehrke, "Die privatrechtliche Entscheidungsliteratur Deutschlands. Charakteristik und Bibliographie der Rechtssprechungs- und Konsiliensammlungen vom. 16 bis 19. Jahrhundert," *Ius Commune* 3 (1974): 53; F. Wieacker, *Privatrechtsgeschichte der Neuzeit* rev. ed. (Göttingen, 1967), 80ff.; Stintzing, *Geschichte der populären Literatur*, 527ff.; R. von Stintzing, *Geschichte der deutschen Rechtswissenschaft* (München/Leipzig, 1880), Erste Abth., 16ff.

Particularly the opinions of the new authorities on marriage law were eagerly sought after, for they were frequently dispositive of issues raised in court. Hieronymous Schürpf, for example, the Lutheran jurist at Wittenberg, was famous throughout Germany for his learned *consilia* on difficult marriage questions. When not teaching at the University of Wittenberg, he travelled extensively to dispense his opinions. His published *consilia*, along with those of many of his colleagues, were frequently reprinted and disseminated throughout Germany.[49] Third, this body of marriage law was passed on to students who ultimately became lawyers, judges and government officials. Fourth, from the 1520s on, there was an enormous growth of civil legislation on marriage. Detailed marriage laws were set forth in a large group of church ordinances (*Kirchenordnungen*), visitation ordinances, moral and sumptuary laws, criminal laws, public policy laws (*Polizeiordnungen*) and other statutes promulgated by urban, territorial and imperial authorities. University jurists and theologians (and their students) were often directly involved in this legislative activity as advisors, administrators and draftsmen. Because the same jurists and theologians participated in drafting statutes, the provisions of early statutes often were repeated in subsequent ones. This is particularly true of the church ordinances. The Wittenberg theologian and jurist Johannes Bugenhagen, for example, helped to draft the Church Ordinances of Hamburg (1529), Lübeck (1531), Ulm (1533–34), Pommern (1535), Hannover (1536), and Wittenberg (1545) and these statutes, accordingly, have markedly similar marriage provisions. Bugenhagen also strongly influenced Martin Bucer and Johannes Brenz, and the statutes under their influence contain many similar marriage provisions.[50]

The new professorial law thus became part of the statutory law, and both types of law became the primary marriage law of the courts.

This new civil marriage law introduced three groups of changes in the traditional canon law of marriage, which shall be explored in turn. The new law: (1) modified the traditional doctrine of consent and required the

---

[49]See Muther, *Aus dem Universitäts*, 186–189. Schürpf's *consilia* on marriage are collected in H. Shurffi, *Consilia seu responsa* (Frankfurt, 1556) and are discussed in O. Mejer, "Zur Geschichte des ältesten protestantischen Eherechts, inbesondere der Ehescheidungsfrage," *Zeitschrift für Kirchenrecht* 16 (1881): 35ff. Schürpf was a close friend of Luther and served as the "best man" at his wedding. He rediscovered with Luther the important doctrine of justification by faith alone, stood by when Luther burnt the canon law books in 1520, accompanied Luther to the Diet of Worms in 1525 and spoke on his behalf and remained an eloquent spokesman in Germany for the new Lutheran theology. It was Schürpf's example most of all, Luther wrote later in his life, "that inspired me [in 1517] to write of the great error of the Catholic Church." See Muther, supra, 190–203 and Stintzing, *Geschichte der deutschen Rechtswissenschaft*, 267–8, as well as Melanchthon's panegyric, "Oratio de vita clarissimiviri Hieronymi Schurffi," *Corpus Reformatorum*, eds. G. Bretschneider, et al. (Brunsvigae, 1843), 12: 86. See also W. Schaich-Klose, *D. Hieronymous Schürpf. Leben und Werk des Wittenberger Reformationsjuristen, 1481–1554* (Tübingen, 1967).

[50] Sehling, *Kirchenordnungen*, ix and A. Sprengler-Ruppenthal, "Zur Rezeption des römischen Rechts in Eherecht der Reformation, *ZSS (K.A.)* 112 (1978): 363, 392ff.

participation of others in the process of marriage formation; (2) sharply curtailed the number of impediments; and (3) introduced a new doctrine of divorce and remarriage. Such changes, taken together, simplified the laws of marriage formation and dissolution, provided for public participation in this marriage process and protected the social functions of marriage and the family.

C. The Law of Consent to Marriage

As in canon law so in the new civil law, the marriage bond was formed by free consensual union between the parties. Many of the reformers, however, accepted the traditional consent doctrine only after: (1) modifying the canonists' three-fold distinction between the betrothal or future promise to marry (*sponsalia de futuro*), the present promise to marry (*sponsalia de praesentia*) and the consent to consummate the marriage through sexual intercourse; (2) requiring that parents and witnesses participate in the process of marriage formation; and (3) enlarging the task of the church in the process of marriage formation.

Luther was the most ardent initial advocate for these reforms. For Luther, the three forms of consent were scripturally unwarranted, semantically confusing and a source of grave public mischief. Scripture, Luther averred, makes no distinction between the present and future promise. Any promise to marry freely given in good faith creates a valid, indissoluble marriage before God and the world. This marriage is consummated through the physical act. Even before consummation, however, Scripture makes clear that breach of this promise through sexual relations with, or a subsequent marriage promise to, another is adultery. Furthermore, the distinction between the present and future promises depends upon "a scoundrelly game" (*ein lauter Narrenspiel*) in Latin words that have no equivalent in German and thus confuse the uneducated. The ecclesiastical courts had usually interpreted the promise "*Ich will Dich zum Weibe haben*" or "*Ich will Dich nehmen, ich will Dich haben, Du sollst mein sein*," as a future promise, though, in common German parlance, these were usually intended to be present promises.[51] A present promise, the ecclesiastical courts insisted, must use the terms "*Accipio te in uxorem*" or "*Ich nehme Dich zu meinem Wiebe*" though neither phrase was familiar outside academic circles. Such a post hoc interpretation of promises, Luther charged, preyed on the ignorance of the common people, disregarded the intent of the couple and betrayed the presumption of the ecclesiastical courts against marriage. By interpreting many promises to be betrothals, the ecclesiastical judges had availed themselves of the much more liberal rules for dissolving betrothals

---

[51]*LW*, 44: 11ff.; 46: 274ff. See discussion of Sohm, *Das Recht Der Eheschleissung*, 138–39, 197–198; Friedberg, *Das Eheschliessung*, 203–207; Kirstein, *Die Entwicklung*, 28ff. The promises are ambiguous because the verbs "will" and "sollst," though commonly understood to be in the present tense, could be interpreted as future verbs.

and thus had been able to dissolve numerous marriages. Through their combined practices of construing marriage promises as betrothals and of permitting religious vows to dissolve betrothals, the canon lawyers had covertly subsidized celibacy and monasticism. To allay the confusion and reverse the presumption against marriage, Luther proposed that all promises to marry be viewed as true binding marriage vows (*sponsalia de praesentia*) unless either party had expressly stipulated some future condition or event. A promise in any language with a verb in the future tense was not enough to defeat the presumption. An expressly-stated condition was required.

Luther and his followers did not attach such solemnity and finality to the marriage promise without safeguards. First, they insisted that, before any such promises, the couple seek the consent of their parents, or, if they were dead or missing, of their next of kin or guardian. To the reformers, the parents played an essential role in the process of marriage formation. They judged the maturity of the couple and the harmony and legality of their prospective relationship. More importantly, their will was to reflect the will of God for the couple. Like the priest and like the prince, the parent had been given authority as God's agent to perform a specific calling in the institution of marriage. Parents, Luther wrote, are "apostles, bishops, and priests to their children." By giving their consent to the couple, parents were giving God's consent. Where parents withheld their consent unreasonably, ordered their child to lead a celibate life or used their authority to coerce a child to enter marriage unwillingly, they no longer performed a godly task. In such cases, Luther urged the child to petition a church or government official for his consent and protection; the official would thus surrogately represent God's will. If the official, too, was unreasonable or coercive, Luther urged the child to seek refuge in another place. Marriages contracted without such parental or surrogate parental consent were, in Luther's view, void altogether; other theologians deemed these unions valid if the parents gave their consent post hoc.[52]

Second, Luther insisted that the promise to marry be made publicly, in the presence of at least "two good and honorable witnesses." These witnesses could, if necessary, attest to the event of the marriage or to the intent of the parties and could also help instruct the couple of the solemnity and responsibility of their relationship—a function tied to Luther's doctrine of the priesthood of all believers.[53]

Third, Luther and his followers insisted that, before consummating their marriage, the couple repeat their vows publicly in the church, seek the blessing and instruction of the pastor and register in the public marriage directory kept in the church. The further publicizing of marriage was seen as

---

[52]*LW*, 46: 205ff.; id., *Letters of Spiritual Counsel* trans. and ed. T. Tappert (Philadelphia, 1955), 263ff. Cf. discussion in Kirstein, *Die Entwicklung*, 32–35 and Dietrich, *Eherecht*, 54–59, 93–96.

[53]*LW*, 46: 268ff. See discussion in Althaus, *The Ethics*, 91.

an invitation for others to aid and support the couple, a warning for them to avoid sexual relations with either party and a further safeguard against false or insincere marriage promises made for the purpose of seducing the other party. Just as the parental consent was to reflect God's will that the couple be married, so the priest's blessing and instruction was to reflect God's will for the marriage—that it remain an indissoluble bond of love and mutual service.[54]

With these requirements of parental consent, witnesses and church registration and solemnization, Luther had deliberately discouraged the secret marriages that had always been recognized (though not encouraged) by canon law. He had made marriage "a public institution," advocating the involvement of specific third parties throughout the process of marriage formation. Luther did, however, concede that private vows followed by sexual intercourse could constitute a valid marriage but only if the woman was impregnated or if the intercourse became publicly known. This was not, however, because of the validity of the private promise. Luther's concern was rather to protect the child and to prevent the woman from falling victim to "the strong prejudice [against] marrying a despoiled woman."[55]

Luther's broad reform of the doctrine of marriage promises found support only among later jurists. Earlier jurists, such as Kling, Schürpf and Lagus retained the traditional canonist distinction between present and future promises to marry and insisted on a separate group of impediments for each promise. Though they did urge courts to interpret promises in accordance with the common German language, they silently rejected Luther's other recommendations.[56] Only in the second half of the sixteenth century were Luther's teachings made, in Rudolph Sohm's words, "the general Protestant doctrine and praxis which lasted into the eighteenth century."[57] Later Lutheran jurists rejected or severely diminished the distinction between the present promise to marry and the public unconditioned betrothal. Like Luther, they inveighed against the secret marriage, and many affirmed, for the same reason as Luther, the exception for private marriages whose consummation became publicly known or resulted in pregnancy.[58]

Luther's doctrine of consent also found a place in marriage statutes of the sixteenth century. In many statutes, the terms 'betrothal' ('*Verlöbnis*') and 'marriage' ('*Ehe*') were used interchangeably, and the public betrothal

---

[54]*LW*, 53: 11ff. See discussion in Kirstein, *Die Entwicklung*, 39–45; Kawerau, *Die Reformation*, 734; Köhler, "Die Anfänge," 292.

[55]*LW*, 45: 384. On the Lutheran reformers' heavy emphasis on the requisite public character of marriage, and the relation of this emphasis to Lutheran theological beliefs, see Michealis, "Über Luthers eherechtliche Anschauungen," 51–56.

[56]Dietrich, *Eherecht*, 121.

[57]Sohm, *Das Recht der Eheschliessung*, 198; see also Friedberg, *Das Eheschliessung*, 210.

[58]See ibid., 233ff. and the primary sources cited therein.

was deemed a completed (*geschlossen*) marriage.[59] Several other statutes, while retaining the traditional distinction between promises of betrothal and marriage, attached far greater importance and finality to public unconditioned betrothals, providing (1) that these promises take precedence over all secret betrothals (even those made subsequently); (2) that promiscuity by either betrothed party is punishable as adultery; and (3) that these promises can be dissolved only on grounds also permitted for divorce.[60] The functional distinction between future and present promises was thus considerably narrowed by these statutes.

The requirements of parental consent won virtually unanimous acceptance in the sixteenth century among jurists and legislative draftsmen alike. It was a particularly prominent topic of discussion among the jurists. Several early jurists, like Kling and Schürpf, regarded parental consent as recommendable but not absolutely necessary; couples who married without parental consent should be fined by the state and disciplined by the church, but neither the parents nor one of the parties should be able to annul the marriage because of this. Several later jurists, most notably Monner, Mauser and Schneidewin, argued that such clandestine marriages should be annulled, unless the parties had consummated their private vows, and that post hoc consent by the parents should have no effect. Virtually all the jurists urged that the couple seek the approval of both fathers and mothers. For cases in which the parents were dead or missing, they assiduously listed in the order of priority the next of kin, tutors, curators and others whose consent should be sought. Finally, the jurists discussed in detail the conditions which parents could attach to their consent. Reasonable conditions of time, place or support were generally accepted by the jurists, but they carefully denied parents the opportunity to use the consent doctrine to place coercive demands or unreasonable restrictions on the couple. Monner and Mauser, in fact, argued that parents or guardians who abused their consensual authority be stiffly fined or imprisoned.[61]

Given the prominent attention to parental consent by theologians and jurists, it is not surprising that such consent was required by the majority of jurisdictions in Lutheran Germany. Very few statutes, however, ordered that all marriages contracted without parental consent be nullified.[62] The presence of witnesses or the public declaration of betrothal in a church was

[59]See the Zurich KO (1529), Brandenburg-Nürnberg KO (1533), Württemberg KO (1536), Kassel KO (1539), Schwabisch-Hall KO (1543), Cologne KO (1543) and Tecklenberg KO (1573), Richter, *Kirchenordnungen*, 1: 135ff., 209ff., 270ff., 304ff.; 2: 16ff., 47ff., 381ff. and 476ff.

[60]See the Goslar Consistory Ordinance (1555) and the Declaration of the Synod of Emden (1571), ibid., 2: 166ff. and 340. See also the Opinion of the Wittenberg Court quoted by Sohm, *Das Recht der Eheschliessung*, 199–200.

[61]Dietrich, *Eherecht*, 123–127 and the primary sources cited therein.

[62]The Marriage Ordinance of Württemberg (1537), Richter, *Kirchenordnungen*, 1: 280. The Wittenberg marriage court apparently also took this rigid stance, though absolute parental consent was not prescribed in the Wittenberg statute. See Dietrich, *Eherecht*, 156–157.

usually accepted as an adequate substitute—though several statutes ordered stern civil and ecclesiastical penalties for parties who failed to gain parental consent.[63] The ambit of the parents' authority in the marriage process was also often carefully defined. Parents were prohibited from entering their unwilling children into cloisters or monasteries or from obstructing children who wished to leave their sacred orders. Children saddled with severe conditions or restrictions on their prospective marriages were granted rights of appeal to the local court; where the court found for the child, the parents (or guardians) were subject to penalty.[64] In most jurisdictions, parental consent was no longer required once the child reached the age of majority.[65]

The requirement of at least two good and honorable witnesses to the marriage promise was accepted by virtually all jurists and legislative draftsmen. A few early statutes denied outright the validity of an unwitnessed marriage promise, but, in most jurisdictions, the validity of these promises was left to the discretion of the court.[66] At first, unwitnessed marriages were rarely dissolved. But as the scandal of pre-marital sex and pregnancy grew, and courts were faced with time consuming evidentiary inquiries into the relationship of litigating couples, these private promises were increasingly struck down. Parties who had consummated their private promises were fined, imprisoned and, in some areas, banished. In the later sixteenth century, a number of territories also began to require either that the couple invite a government official as one witness to their promises or that they announce their promises before the city hall or other specified civic building.[67]

In many territories, the church was assigned an indispensable role in the marriage process. Couples were required, on pain of stiff penalty, to register

---

[63]See, e.g., the Basel KO (1529) and Brandenburg KO (1573) and the Declarations of the Synod of Emden (1571), Richter, *Kirchenordnungen*, 1: 125; 2: 376, 340. See also the Reformation Ordinance of Hessen (1526), Württemberg Ordinance (1553) and the Schauenburg PO (1615), described by Schmelzeisen, *Polizeiordnungen*, 33–34.

[64]See the Constitution of the Wittenberg Consistory Ordinance (1542), the Cellische KO (1545), the Marriage Ordinance of Dresden (1556), the Territorial Ordinance of Prussia (1577), the Marriage Ordinance of Kürpf (1582) and the Schauenburg PO (1615), Sehling, *Kirchenordnungen*, 1: 20ff., 292ff.; 343ff. and Schmelzeisen, *Polizeiordnungen*, 36. See also Dietrich, *Eherecht*, 155; Ozment, *When Fathers Ruled*, 24, 194.

[65]See, e.g., the Goslar KO (1555), Richter, *Kirchenordnungen*, 2: 165. The age of majority in that jurisdiction was 20 for men, 18 for women; in some jurisdictions, the age of majority was as high as 27 for men and 25 for women; see Schmelzeisen, *Polizeiordnungen*, 35.

[66]The Marriage Ordinance of Zurich (1525)—copied in several south German cities—was, apparently, the first to declare void *ab initio* all unwitnessed marriages. See Köhler, *Das Ehe- und Zurcher Ehegericht*, 74ff. More typical early statutes are the Ulm KO (1531) and the Marriage Ordinance of Württemberg (1537), Richter, *Kirchenordnungen*, 1: 158, 280; see discussion in Köhler, "Die Anfänge," 291; Dietrich, *Eherecht*, 122–23, 154; Schmelzeisen, *Polizeiordnungen*, 37–38.

[67]Marriage Ordinance of Württemberg (1553) and Goslar KO (1555), Richter, *Kirchenordnungen*, 2: 129, 165. See discussion in Köhler, "Die Anfänge," 292.

their marriage in the church.[68] The public church celebration of the marriage and the pastor's instruction and blessing were made mandatory even for couples who had already publicly announced their betrothal and received parental consent.[69] Several ordinances explicitly ordered punishment for betrothed couples who consummated their marriages prior to the church ceremony.[70] By the 1550s, this "anticipatory sex" was grounds for imprisonment or banishment from the community as well as excommunication from the church.[71]

These four interrelated reforms—the equation of unconditioned future and present promises to marry along with the requirements of parental consent, of witnesses and of church registration and celebration—remained standard provisions in the marriage law of the next three centuries, not only in Germany but also in many other Western European nations.[72] The reforms also found a place in the canon law of the Roman Catholic Church. In 1563 the Council of Trent decreed that (1) to contract a valid marriage, parties had to exchange present promises in the company of a priest and witnesses; (2) all betrothals had to be announced publicly three times before celebration of the marriage; and (3) each parish was required to keep an updated public registry of marriage. The Council further encouraged (but did not require) parents to counsel their children in choosing compatible spouses.[73]

D. The Law of Impediments

Lutheran theologians and jurists strove with equal vigor to reform the canon law of impediments. For the reformers, a number of these impediments were scripturally unwarranted; several others, though properly mandated, had become a source of corruption and confusion.

According to Scripture, marriage is a duty prescribed by the law of

[68]See, e.g., Ulm KO (1531) in Richter, *Kirchenordnungen*, 1: 159 and discussion in Köhler, "Die Anfänge," 292.

[69]See the Zurich Chorgericht Ordinance (1525), Basel KO (1530), Kassel KO (1530), Ulm KO (1531), Straussburg KO (1534) and the numerous later statutes quoted and discussed by Friedberg, *Das Eheschliessung*, 213–217, Schmelzeisen, *Polizeiordnungen*, 45–46.

[70]See the Statutes of Nürnberg (1537), Augsburg (1553) and Ulm (1557) described in O ment, *When Fathers Ruled*, 36; Harvey, *The Influence*, 221ff.; and Köhler "Die Anfänge," 296ff. respectively.

[71]See the Marriage Ordinance of Württemberg (1553), Richter, *Kirchenordnungen*, 2: 128, the Geneva KO (1561) and Palatine of the Rhine KO (1563) described in Gottlieb, *Getting Married*, 124ff.

[72]See H. Coing, *Europäischen Privatrecht* (München, 1985), 1: 224–60; Glendon, *State, Law, and Family*, 313ff.

[73]Decree Tametsi (1563) in H. Deuzinger and A. Schonmetzer, *Enchiridion Symbolorum*, 36th ed. (Freiburg/Breslau, 1976), 415. For an account of the effects of the Decree, see H. Conrad, "Das tridentinische Konzil und die Entwicklung des kirchlichen und weltlichen Eherechts," *Das Weltkonzil von Trent. Sein Werden und Werken*, 2 vols., ed. G. Schneider (Freiburg, 1951), 1: 297–324.

creation and a right of man protected by the law of Christ. No human law could impinge on this godly duty or infringe on this God-given right without the warrant of divine law. No human authority could obstruct or annul a marriage without divine authorization.[74] "It is contrary to faith as well as to love," wrote one reformer, "when man puts asunder, without God's command, what God has brought together."[75] Impediments, therefore, that were not commands of God could not be countenanced. Thus the impediments protecting the sanctity of the marriage sacrament were untenable, for Scripture (as the reformers understood it) does not teach that marriage is a sacrament. Impediments protecting religious vows of celibacy or chastity were unnecessary, for Scripture subordinates such vows to the vows of marriage.

Even the biblically based impediments of the canon law had, in the reformers' view, become sources of corruption and confusion. It had long been the official practice of the Roman Catholic Church to relax certain impediments (such as consanguinity and affinity) where they worked injustice to the parties or to their children. Parties could pay a dispensation and be excused from the legal strictures. This "equitable" practice met with little criticism. The reformers' concern was with the abuse of this practice in certain bishoprics. Corrupt clerics had turned their "equitable" authority to their own financial gain by relaxing any number of impediments if the dispensation payment was high enough. This clerical bribery and trafficking in impediments evoked caustic attacks from the reformers. "There is no impediment nowadays," Luther charged, "that the church cannot legitimize for money. These man-made regulations seem to have come into existence for no other reason than raking in money and netting in souls."[76] Such abuses not only desecrated the priestly office but also resulted in a liberal law of impediments for the rich and a constrictive law of impediments for the poor. Furthermore, the reformers averred, the impediments had become so intricate that they were confusing to the common man. The confession manuals were filled with ornate legalistic discussions of the impediments incomprehensible to the uninitiated and frequently not in the language of the common people.[77]

Acting on these criticisms of canon law, the reformers developed a simplified and, in their view, more biblical law of impediments. They (1) accepted, with some qualification, the impediments protecting the parties' consent; (2) adopted a severely truncated law of personal impediments;

---

[74]See Luther's radical criticisms of this body of law in *LW*, 45: 22; Luther, *Selections*, 330–331.

[75]A. Osiander, *Gutachten über die Zeremonien* (1526), 69, quoted by Harvey, *The Influence*, 232; see also Seebaas, *Das reformatorische Werk*, 191ff. for further discussion of Osiander's views.

[76]Luther, *Selections*, 330–331.

[77]Ibid., 330. Cf. *LW*, 45: 22–30; Bucer, *De Regno Christi*, chap. 17 and discussion of the views of other theologians by Dietrich, *Eherecht*, 97–8.

(3) discarded the impediments protecting the sanctity of the sacrament; and
(4) adopted most of the physical impediments.

(1) In accepting the consensual theory of marriage the reformers also
accepted the traditional impediments that guaranteed free consent. Thus a
man and a woman who had been joined under duress, coercion or fear were
seen as "unmarried before God" and thus free to dissolve their union. Both
the theologians and jurists, however, unlike their canonist contemporaries,
required that the pressure exerted on the couple be particularly pervasive
and malicious—a requirement which they based on patristic authority.[78] The
reformers, like the canonists, accepted errors of person as ground for
annulment. Luther, Bucer and Brenz, however, urged Christian couples to
accept such unions as a challenge placed before them by God—a recommendation which is repeated in some of the statutes.[79] A number of
reformers also permitted annulment of marriages based on errors of quality—
that is, the mistaken assumption that one's spouse was a virgin. For, as the
Mosaic and Pauline law made clear, one's prior commitment to marriage,
whether through a promise or through sexual intercourse, prevents one from
entering any true marriage thereafter. Thus the second putative marriage is
void from the start.[80]

(2) In developing the civil law of personal impediments the reformers
were far less faithful to the canon law tradition. They rejected several of
these impediments and liberalized others in an attempt to remove as many
obstacles to marriage and as many obfuscations of Scripture as possible.
First, impediments designed to protect the celibate and the chaste were
largely rejected by Lutheran theologians and later jurists. The canon laws
prohibiting marriage to committed clerics, monks and nuns were unanimously rejected as unscriptural.[81] Several statutes explicitly permitted clerics to marry and enjoined subjects to accept their offspring as legitimate
children and heirs.[82] Canon laws forbidding remarriage to those who had

[78]Ibid., 66, 102, 129–30. Luther concurred in this position only after 1530.

[79]Ibid., 54ff., 93ff., 122ff., 153ff.; Friedberg, *Das Eheschliessung*, 212ff.; Köhler, "Die Anfänge,"
375; and Kirstein, *Die Entwicklung*, 28ff., 57ff. See, e.g., the Consistory Ordinances of Brandenburg (1573) and Prussia (1584) in Richter, *Kirchenordnungen*, 2:383ff., 466ff.

[80]For the views of jurists and theologians, see Dietrich, *Eherecht*, 65–66, 102, 128–29 and W.
Köhler, "Gutachten der Juristen Nürnberg über die Ehesachen erstattet an Markgraf Georg zu
Brandenberg, *Archiv für Reformationsgeschichte* 11 (1914): 254, 266ff. The error of quality is
cited as a ground for annulment in the Kurbrandenburg KO (1540), Richter, *Kirchenordnungen*,
1: 323ff. Although the statutes of the sixteenth century make little mention of these impediments,
studies of the case law of a number of cities show that these impediments protecting consent
were enforced. See Dietrich supra, 157–58.

[81]See *LW*, 35: 138; 45: 28; M. Bucer, *Commonplaces of Martin Bucer*, trans. and ed. D. Wright,
(Appleford, 1971), 406ff. and discussion of other reformers' views in Dietrich, *Eherecht*, 78ff.,
110ff.

[82]Northeim KO (1539), Kurbrandenburg KO (1540), Braunschweig-Wolfenbuttel KO (1543) as
well as the Consistory Ordinance of Wittenberg (1542), Richter, *Kirchenordnungen*, 1: 287ff.,
323ff., 367ff.; 2: 56ff.

initially married a cleric, monk or nun had no parallel in the new civil law. The traditional assumption that vows to chastity and celibacy automatically dissolved betrothals and unconsummated marriages was rejected by virtually all Lutheran writers.[83] Second, the reformers rejected or simplified the intricate restrictions on those related by blood, familial, spiritual and legal ties. The canon law impediment of consanguinity—which permitted annulment of marriages between parties related by blood to the fourth degree—was accepted, in qualified form, only by early jurists and legislative draftsmen.[84] Several other theologians permitted restrictions on parties related by blood only to the third or to the second degree. Both positions found statutory expression.[85] Luther's repeated arguments for adopting the slender group of impediments of consanguinity set forth in Leviticus met with little sympathy.[86] Similarly, the canon law impediments of affinity and public decorum—which proscribed marriage between a person and the blood relatives of his or her deceased spouse or fiance to the fourth degree—were accepted in qualified form only by the early jurists and draftsmen.[87] The arguments by theologians to reduce the restrictions to "in-laws" to the third, second or even first degrees all came to legislative expression.[88] Third, the spiritual impediments, prohibiting marriages between godparents and their children, were rejected by virtually all the reformers and legislative draftsmen.[89] Fourth, legal impediments, proscribing marriages between a variety of parties related by adoption, were liberalized.[90] Fifth, a number of jurisdictions that had accepted Luther's reform of the doctrine of consent rejected the canon law impediment of multiple relationships. The canonists had maintained that any betrothal was dissolved if one of the parties made a subsequent marriage promise to, or had sexual relations with, another. This rule was adopted by the reformers only for conditioned betrothal promises. Unconditioned public promises of betrothal were regarded as indissoluble

---

[83]Luther, *Selections*, 335. For the views of the early jurists, see Dietrich, *Eherecht*, 128–9.

[84]Ibid., 134–5.

[85]Ibid., 99; Harvey, *The Influence*, 250. Impediments of consanguinity to the third degree were accepted by the Württemberg Marriage Ordinance (1537), Cellisches Ehebedenken (1545), Mecklenburg KO (1557) Hessen Reformation Ordinance (1572), Mecklenburg PO (1572) and the Lübeck Ordinance (1581) in Richter, *Kirchenordnungen*, 1: 280; Sehling, *Kirchenordnungen*, 1: Part 1, 296; 5: 212; Schmelzeisen, *Polizeiordnungen*, 50ff. Impediments of consanguinity to the second degree were accepted by the Saxon General Articles (1557) in Richter, supra, 2: 178ff.

[86]See LW, 45: 23; Bucer, *Commonplaces*, 410. The Levitical law of impediments of consanguinity was adopted by later statutes, e.g., the Brandenburg Ordinance (1694) and the Prussian Cabinet Order (1740), discussed in Schmelzeisen, *Polizeiordnungen*, 51–52.

[87]Dietrich, *Eherecht*, 135–36.

[88]Ibid., 100, 161.

[89]Ibid., 100, 136. Though most statutes silently ignore the spiritual impediments, a few statutes explicitly deny their validity, e.g., the Lower Saxony KO (1585) and the Braunschweiger PO (1618).

[90]Dietrich, *Eherecht*, 101, 137 and the Württemberg Marriage Ordinance (1537) in Richter, *Kirchenordnungen*, 1: 279ff.

and thus superior to any subsequent physical or verbal commitments to marriage.[91]

(3) The reformers rejected the impediments of nonbelief and crime which had been designed to protect the sanctity of the marriage sacrament. The canonists had prohibited marriage between Christians and non-Christians and permitted annulment where one party had permanently left the church. Only those couples who had been sanctified by baptism and who remained true to the faith could symbolize the union of Christ and His Church. To the reformers, marriage had no such symbolic Christian function and thus no prerequisites of baptism or unanimity of faith.[92] The canonists had also prohibited marriage to the person who had done public penance or who was guilty of certain sexual crimes. For his or her marital union would be constantly perverted by this former grave sin, and thus neither he nor his spouse could receive the sanctifying grace of the sacrament. To the reformers, marriage imparted no such sanctifying grace and thus required no such prerequisite purity.[93]

(4) Given the importance attached by the reformers to the physical union, they were understandably receptive to the canonists' physical impediments. Thus the impediment of permanent impotence and prohibitions against polygamy and bigamy were unanimously accepted.[94]

E. The Law of Divorce and Remarriage

The reformers' attack on the canon law of impediments was closely allied with their attack on the canon law of divorce. Just as they discarded many impediments as infringements on the right to enter marriage, they rejected the canon law of divorce as an abridgement of the right to end one marriage and to enter another.

The Roman Catholic Church had, for centuries, taught that (1) divorce meant only separation of the couple from bed and board; (2) such separation had to be ordered by an ecclesiastical court on proof that one party had committed adultery, brutalized the other or contracted a contagious disease; and (3) despite the divorce, the sacramental bond between the parties remained intact, and thus neither party was free to remarry. This stern law of divorce was partly mitigated by the law of impediments, which permitted many parties to dissolve putative marriages and enter others. The declaration of annulment, however, simply meant that the marriage had never existed because it had been contracted improperly. It often also meant that

---

[91]See the Cellisches Ehebedenken (1545), the Consistory Ordinance of Goslar (1555) and the Marriage Ordinance or Dresden (1556) in Sehling, *Kirchenordnungen*, 1: Part 1, 295; Richter, *Kirchenordnungen*, 2: 166 and Sehling, supra, 1: Part 1, 343.

[92]Dietrich, *Eherecht*, 68, 102.

[93]*LW*, 45: 26.

[94]These physical factors, however, were more frequently regarded by the reformers as grounds for divorce rather than for annulment.

the parties had sinned gravely in joining together and were su
penitential discipline. Annulments did not dissolve valid consu
marriages. Once properly established, the marriage bond could never be
severed, even if the parties became bitter enemies. This traditional doctrine
the reformers rejected with arguments from Scripture, history and utility.

In the reformers' view of Scripture, marriage was a natural institution of
the earthly kingdom, not a sacramental institution of the heavenly kingdom.
The essence of marriage was the cleavage and community of husband and
wife in this life, not their sacramental union in the life to come.[95] For a
couple to establish "a true marriage" in this earthly life, wrote one reformer,
"God requires of them to live together and be united in body and mind . . . .
The proper end of marriage is . . . the communicating of all duties, both
divine and humane, each to the other with the utmost benevolence and
affection."[96] Irreconcilable separation of the parties was tantamount to
dissolution of the marriage, for the requisite benevolent communion between the parties had been destroyed. Furthermore, the social tasks of
marriage could no longer be carried out. The Roman Catholic teaching that
permanently separated couples were still bound in marriage rested on the
nonbiblical assumption that marriage is an eternally binding sacrament.

Furthermore, the reformers charged, for the Roman Catholic Church to
equate divorce with judicial separation and to prohibit divorcees from
remarrying had no basis in Scripture. The term "*divortium*," as used in
Scripture, means dissolution of marriage, not simply separation. No philo-
logical evidence from biblical or early patristic times suggests otherwise.
The Roman Catholics had improperly introduced their interpretation of the
term in order to support their sacramental concept of marriage.[97] Where
Scripture permits divorce, it also permits remarriage. "In the case of adultery
[for example]," Luther writes, "Christ permits divorce of husband and wife
so that the innocent person may remarry."[98] Other reformers considered the

---

[95]The reformers set forth their views on divorce and remarriage in a variety of tracts. See, e.g.,
LW, 46: 276ff.; Melanchthon, *De Conjurio*, 1076ff.; Bugenhagen, *Vom Ehebruch*, folio 171ff.;
Brenz, *Wie in Ehesachen*, folio 185ff.; Schneidewin; *In institutio imperialum*, 484ff.; Mauser,
Explicatio erudita, 335ff.; Monner, *Tractatus matrimonio*, 203ff. For general discussions, see H.
Hesse *Evangelisches Ehescheidungsrecht in Deutschland* (Bonn, 1960); F. Albrecht, *Verbrechen
and Strafen als Ehescheidungsgrund nach evangelischen Kirchenrecht* (Stuttgart, 1903); J.
Gräbner, *Ueber Desertion und Quasi-desertion als Scheidungsgrund nach dem evangelischen
Kirchenrecht* (Stuttgart, 1882); A. Richter, *Beiträge zur Geschichte des Ehescheidungsrecht in
der evangelischen Kirche* (Bonn, 1858); R. Hauber, "Ehescheidung im Reformationsjahrhun-
dert," *Jahrbuch für deutsche Theologie* 2 (1857): 209.

[96]M. Bucer, "The Judgement of Martin Bucer Touching Divorce taken out of the second book
entitled The Kingdom of Christ," *The Complete Prose Works of John Milton (1643–1648)*, repr.
ed. (New Haven, 1959), 465.

[97]Bucer, *De Regno Christi*, 416–7; *LW*, 46: 275–281. Cf. J. Greve, *Die Ehescheidung nach der
Lehre des neuen Testament* (Leipzig, 1873), 225ff.

[98]*LW*, 45: 30–31.

sentence of divorce and the right of remarriage to be "one and the same."[99]
For the divorcee, like any single person, had to heed God's duty to form
families and to accept God's remedy against incontinence and other sexual
sins. To deprive the divorcee of the spiritual and physical benefits of
marriage, as the Roman Catholic Church had done, was unbiblical and led to
all manner of sexual sin.

A number of reformers bolstered these scriptural arguments for divorce
and remarriage with arguments from history. They adduced support for their
biblical exegesis from the commentaries of the Church Fathers. They found
a wealth of precedent for laws of divorce and remarriage in the Mosaic law,
the ordinances of the early Church and the decrees of the Christian Roman
emperors.[100]

These historical laws of divorce, however, were hardly commensurate
with the teachings of the Gospel. Christ had permitted divorce only on
grounds of adultery and only as a special exception to the general command
"what God has joined together let not man put asunder."[101] The laws of
Moses, of the early Church and of the Roman Empire, however, had put
marriages asunder for many reasons other than adultery. The Mosaic law had
permitted divorce for indecency and incompatability of all kinds. At Roman
law, a person could divorce a spouse who was guilty of treason or icono-
clasm, who had committed one of many felonies or fraudulent acts against
third parties, or who had abused, deserted, threatened or, in other ways,
maltreated members of their family. Divorce was also permitted if a husband
wrongly accused his wife of adultery or if a wife was guilty of shameful or
immoral acts (such as abortion, bigamy or exhibitionism), became delinquent, insolent or impotent or persistently refused to have sexual relations.
In the later Roman Empire, divorce was even permitted by mutual consent
of the parties. The innocent party was, in most instances, permitted to
remarry. The early church had not only acquiesced in this liberal law of
divorce but had been the first to advocate the adoption of many of its
provisions.[102] Such liberal laws remained in constant tension with Christ's
command that all but the unchaste must remain indissolubly bound.

The reformers resolved this tension by distinguishing between moral
laws designed for Christians and civil laws designed for the sinful earthly

[99]Bucer, quoted and discussed by Ozment, *When Fathers Ruled*, 84.

[100]See, e.g., Bucer, *The Judgment*, 447ff.; id., *Commonplaces*, 407ff. For the historical
arguments of other reformers, see Dietrich, *Eherecht*, 103ff., 142ff.

[101]Mark 10:2–12; Luke 16:18; Matt. 5:31–32, 19:3–19.

[102]*Theodosian Code* 3.16.1,2, trans. and ed. C. Pharr (Princeton, 1959); Justinian Code
5.17.8,9,10, *The Civil Law*, trans. and ed. S. Scott, (Indianapolis, 1932). Divorce by mutual
consent, permitted by Emperor Anastasius in 497, was rejected some 40 years later in Justinian's
Novella 117. 8–14. See further, P. Corbett, *The Roman Law of Marriage* (Oxford, 1930), 218ff. For
a discussion of the influence of early Christian Church on the Roman laws of divorce, see E.
Jonkers, *Het Invloed van het Christendom op de romanische Wetsgeving betreffende het
Concubinaat en de Echtscheiding* (Ph.D. Diss. Amsterdam, 1938).

kingdom. Christ's command, the reformers taught, is an absolute moral standard for Christians. It demands of them love, patience, forgiveness and a conciliatory spirit. It sets out what is absolutely right, what the true law would be if the earthly kingdom were free from sin. The earthly kingdom, however, is fallen, and many of its sinful citizens disregard the moral law. Thus it becomes necessary for civil authorities to promulgate laws that both facilitate and protect marriage and its social functions as well as maintain peace and order in sinful society. The positive laws of the German princes, like those of Moses and the Roman emperors, therefore, must inevitably compromise moral ideals for marriage. They must allow for divorce and remarriage.[103]

> It might be advisable nowadays, that certain queer, stubborn, and obstinate people, who have no capacity for toleration and are not suited for married life at all, should be permitted to get a divorce. Since people are as evil as they are, any other way of governing is impossible. Frequently something must be tolerated, even though it is not a good thing to do, to prevent something even worse from happening.[104]

Laws of divorce and remarriage, like other positive laws, must thus be inspired by norms of Scripture and morality as well as by concerns of utility and good governance.

By conjoining these arguments from Scripture, history and utility, the reformers established that (1) divorce in the modern sense had been instituted by Christ; (2) the expansion of divorce was a result of sin and a remedy against greater sin; and (3) God had revealed the expanded grounds for divorce in history. On this basis, the reformers successfully advocated a new civil law of divorce and remarriage. They specified the proper grounds for divorce and the procedures which estranged couples had to follow.

The theologians and legislative draftsmen unanimously accepted adultery as a ground for divorce on the authority of Scripture and frequently also of Roman law and early canon law.[105] Several theologians, such as Luther

[103]*LW*, 21: 94ff.; Bucer, *Commonplaces*, 411ff.; and the views of Brenz and Bugenhagen discussed in Ozment, *When Fathers Ruled*, 89; Sprengler-Ruppenthal, "Zur Rezeption," 395ff.

[104]*LW*, 21: 94. See similar sentiments in J. Brenz, *Wie in Ehesachen* (1531), quoted by Ozment, *When Fathers Ruled*, 89, and Bucer, *Commonplaces*, 411–412. See also the similar views of Melanchthon and Bugenhagen discussed in Richter, *Beiträge zur Geschichte*, 32ff. and Albrecht, *Verbrechen und Strafen*, 12ff.

[105]See the numerous church ordinances and other statutes quoted and discussed by Dietrich, *Evangelisches Ehescheidungsrecht*, 12–14; Dietrich, *Eherecht*, 164; Hesse, *Evangelisches Ehescheidungsrecht*, 31–33; Albrecht, *Verbrechen und Strafen*, 43–46. The Lübeck KO (1531) and Marriage Ordinance of Württemberg (1537), drafted by Brenz, as well as the Marriage Ordinance of Pfalz (1563) and Huttenberg KO (1555) cite Roman law prominently alongside Scripture in support of this ground for divorce. Sehling, *Kirchenordnungen*, 5: 356; Richter, *Kirchenordnungen*, 1: 180; 2: 163, 157. Melanchthon and Kling refer several times to earlier canonical and patristic writings in their discussions of adultery. Melanchthon, *De Conjurio*, 1075 and Kling, *Tractatus matrimonialum*, folio 101v.

and Bugenhagen, however, advocated that a couple first be given time to resolve the matter privately. They instructed adulterers to seek forgiveness and innocent spouses to be forgiving. They further urged pastors and friends to sponsor the mending of a torn marriage in any way. These recommendations found ample statutory support. A number of marriage ordinances repeated the reformers' prescriptions.[106] Moreover, criminal statutes provided that punishment of the adulterer could not commence until the innocent party sued for divorce. Absent such suits, a judge could begin criminal proceedings against an adulterer only if his or her violation was "open, undoubted and scandalous."[107] Even in such cases, authorities preferred less severe penalties (not banishment or imprisonment) that would still allow the couple to rejoin. Where efforts toward private reconciliation failed and continued cohabitation of the parties yielded only misery and threats to the safety of the parties and their children, the innocent spouse could sue for divorce. He or she was then permitted to remarry, after a time of healing. The adulterer faced stern criminal sanctions scaled to the egregiousness of the offense. These ranged from fines and short imprisonment for the first offenders to exile and execution in the case of repeat adulterers. The call of many reformers to execute all divorced adulterers found little acceptance among the authorities, though many jurisdictions, in response, stiffened their penalties for adultery. Only the egregious repeat offender was subject to execution.[108]

Though a few theologians and legislative draftsmen accepted adultery as the only ground for divorce,[109] many others defended a far more expansive divorce law.

Desertion or abandonment was a widely accepted ground for divorce among the reformers. A party who deserted his or her spouse and family destroyed the bond of communal love, service and support needed for the marriage to survive and for children to be properly nourished and reared. Not every absence of a spouse, however, could be considered an abandon-

---

[106]LW, 45: 32; Ozment, When Fathers Ruled, 85ff.; Hesse, Evangelisches Ehescheidungsrecht, 32.

[107]Bambergischen Halsgerichts und rechtliche Ordnung (1507), Art. 145 and Constitutio Criminalis Carolina (1532), Art. 120 quoted and described by Harvey, The Influence, 117–118. Both criminal statutes were drafted by Johann von Schwarzenberg, a friend and protegé of Luther and other Lutheran reformers. On Schwarzenberg, see H. Berman, "Law and Belief in Three Revolutions," Valparaiso Law Review 18 (1984): 569, 582–85; W. Scheel, Johann Freiherr zu Schwarzenberg (Berlin, 1905). On the marriage provisions in the Bambergensis and Carolina, see E. Schmidt, "Sinn und Bedeutung der Constitutio Criminalis Carolina als Ordnung des materiallen und prozessuallen Rechts," ZSS (G.A.) 83 (1966): 239; R. His, Geschichte der deutschen Strafrechts bis zur Karolina (München/Berlin, 1928), 140ff.

[108]For the view of the reformers on capital punishment of adulterers, and the responses of civil authorities to these views, see LW, 45: 32–33; Bucer, Commonplaces, 410–11; Dietrich, Eherecht, 105ff.; Harvey, The Influence, 113ff.; Koch, Studium Pietatis, 141ff.; Kühler, Das Ehe, 109ffSee Köhler, "Die Anfänge," 302; Hesse, Evangelischen Ehescheidungsrecht, 32–33; Albrecht, Verbrechen und Strafen, 14–16; Schmelzeisen, Polizeiordnungen, 61.

ment. Jurists, such as Schneidewin and Bugenhagen, insisted that the abandonment be willfull and malicious; this requirement was repeated in several statutes.[110] No divorce was thus permitted if the absent partner was serving the prince's army, engaged in study or business abroad or was visiting a foreign place. Divorce for desertion was permitted only where the partner's absence was completely inexcusable and inequitable, left the spouse and family in grave danger or was so unreasonably prolonged that the party had presumably died or fallen into deliquency or adultery. The deserted spouse was in such cases free to marry. The desertor was regarded and punished as an adulterer.[111] Where the desertor never returned, the spouse could, after a designated period of time, petition for divorce and for the right to marry another.

Quasi-desertion, the unjustifiable abstention from sexual intercourse, found limited acceptance as a ground for divorce. Luther, Brenz and Bucer and the jurist Clammer argued that voluntary abandonment of such an essential aspect of marriage was tantamount to abandonment of the marriage itself. Furthermore, it violated the Apostle Paul's injunction that spouses abstain from sex only by mutual consent. Luther counselled the deprived spouse to warn the other of his of her discontent and to invite the pastor or friends to speak with the spouse. If the spouse remained abstinent, he permitted divorce.[112] A few statutes repeated this teaching and permitted remarriage to the deprived spouse.[113]

At the urging of several liberal Lutherans, most notably Bucer and Sacerius, numerous other grounds for divorce sporadically gained acceptance in Lutheran territories. Already in the 1520s Zurich and Basel recognized alongside adultery and desertion, impotence, grave incompatability, sexually incapacitating illnesses, felonies, deception and serious threats against the life of a spouse as grounds for divorce.[114] By the 1550s, confessional differences between the couple, defamation of a spouse's moral character, abuse and maltreatment, conspiracies or plots against a spouse,

[110]Among the numerous statutes quoted and discussed by Hesse, *Evangelischen Ehescheidungsrecht*, 33–35, Dietrich, *Evangelischen Ehescheidungsrecht*, 17–25, Grabner, *Ueber Desertion*, 63ff., and Schmelzeisen, *Polizeiordnungen*, 60–61, see especially the Pommern KO (1535) and Lippische KO (1538), Richter, *Kirchenordnungen*, 1: 250ff. 2: 499ff. For a general historical overview of divorce based on desertion, see P. Hinschius, "Beiträge zur Geschichte des Desertionsprozesses," *Zeitschrift für Kirchenrecht* 2 (1857): 28.

[111]See, e.g., the Goslar KO (1531), Cellische KO (1545) and Consistory Ordinance of Mecklenberg (1571) in Richter, *Kirchenordnungen*, 1: 156; Sehling, *Kirchenordnungen*, 1: 295ff.; 5:239ff.

[112]*LW*, 45: 33–34; Dietrich, *Eherecht*, 105–106, 145; Dietrich, *Evangelischen Ehescheidungsrecht*, 25–31.

[113]Lippische KO (1538), Gottingen KO (1542), Mecklenberg KO (1552), Württemberg Marriage Ordinance (1553) and the Consistory Ordinance of Prussia (1584) in Richter, *Kirchenordnungen*, 1: 365; 2: 120, 130, 446, 499.

[114]Ozment, *When Fathers Ruled*, 93.

acts of incest and bigamy, delinquent frequenting of "public games" or places of ill repute and acts of treason or sacrilege all came to legislative expression as grounds for divorce.[115] A few statutes permitted divorce "on any grounds recognized by Scripture and the Roman law of Justinian,"[116] though it is unclear whether courts in these territories actually enforced the expansive Roman law of divorce.

The reformers insisted that divorce, like marriage, be a public act. Just as a couple could not form the marriage bond in secret, so they could not sever it in secret. They had to inform the community and church of their intention and petition a civil judge to order the divorce.[117] This requirement of publicity was a formidable obstacle to divorce. Couples who publicized their intent to divorce invited not only the counsel and comfort of friends and pastors but frequently also the derision of the community and the discipline of the church. Furthermore, judges had great discretion to deny or delay petitions for divorce and to grant interim remedies short of this irreversible remedy. Particularly in conservative courts, the petitioner had a heavy burden of proof to show that the divorce was mandated by statute, that all efforts at reconciliation had proved fruitless and that no alternative remedy was available.[118]

IV. SUMMARY AND CONCLUSIONS

For more than three centuries before the Lutheran Reformation, Roman Catholic concepts and laws of marriage had dominated Germany. Marriage, the Church had taught, was at once an institution of creation, a sacrament of the Church, and a legal relation between two fit parties. Marriage was instituted at creation to permit man to beget and raise children and to direct his passion to the service of the community. Yet marriage was subordinated to celibacy; propagation was made less virtuous than contemplation. Marriage was also raised to the dignity of a sacrament. It symbolized the indissoluble union between Christ and His Church and thereby conferred sanctifying grace upon the couple and community. Couples could perform the sacrament in private, provided they were capable of marriage and complied with rules for marriage formation. As a legal relation, properly contracted, marriage prescribed an indissoluble relation of love, service and

---

[115]See the statutory provisions listed in Dietrich, *Evangelischen Ehescheidungsrecht*, 31ff.; Köhler, "Die Anfänge," 303ff.

[116]See the Hannover KO (1536), Huttenberg KO (1555), and Marriage Ordinance of Pfalz (1563) quoted by Dietrich, *Evangelischen Ehescheidungsrecht*, 31–32. A similar provision is recommended by Sacerius, *Corpus juris matrimonium*, folio 216.

[117]See, e.g., *LW*, 36: 102ff.; 45: 30ff; 46: 311ff.

[118]Witness the conservative practices of the courts of Nürnberg, Zurich and Basel as described in Harvey, *The Influence*, 153ff.; Ozment, *When Fathers Ruled*, 93ff. and A. Staehelin, *Die Einführung der Ehescheidung in Basel zur Zeit der Reformation* (Basel, 1957), 101ff.

devotion and proscribed unwarranted recision or disregard for one's obligations and covenants under the marriage contract.

The Church built an intricate body of marriage law upon this conceptual foundation. Because marriage was a holy sacrament, the Church had jurisdiction over it, appropriating and expanding the laws of nature, Scripture and morality. The canon law punished contraception, abortion and child abuse as violations of the created marital functions of propagation and childrearing. It proscribed unnatural relations, such as homosexuality, bigamy and polygamy. It protected the sanctity and sanctifying purpose of the marriage sacrament by deeming valid bonds indissoluble and by impeding or dissolving numerous invalid unions such as those between Christians and non-Christians, between parties related by legal, spiritual, blood or familial ties or between parties who could not or would not perform their connubial duties. It supported celibacy by dissolving unconsummated vows to marriage if one party made a vow to chastity, by prohibiting remarriage to those who had married a priest or monastic and by punishing clerics or monastics who contracted marriage. It ensured free consensual union by dissolving marriages contracted by mistake or under duress, fear, fraud or coercion.

The Lutheran Reformation gave birth to a new social concept of marriage, and, on that basis, transformed the marriage law of Germany. The reformers, like the Roman Catholics, taught that marriage is a natural, created institution, but they rejected the subordination of marriage to celibacy. Man was too tempted by his sinful passion to forgo marriage. The family was too vital a social institution in God's plan of redemption to be hindered. The celibate life had no superior virtue and no inherent attractiveness vis-à-vis marriage and was no prerequisite for ecclesiastical service. The reformers replaced the sacramental concept of marriage with a social concept. Marriage, they taught, was part of the earthly kingdom, not the heavenly kingdom of faith, redemption and sanctification. Though a holy institution of God, marriage required no prerequisite faith or purity and conferred no sanctifying grace, as did true sacraments. Rather, it had distinctive uses in the life of the individual and of society. It revealed to man his sin and his need for God's marital gift. It restricted prostitution, promiscuity and other public sexual sins. It taught love, restraint and other public virtues and morals. Any fit man and woman were free to enter such unions, provided they complied with laws of marriage formation. As part of the earthly kingdom, marriage was subject to the prince, not the pope. Civil law, not canon law, was to govern marriage. Marital disputes were to be brought before civil courts, not ecclesiastical courts. Marriage was still subject to God's law, but this law was now to be administered by the civil authorities who had been called as God's vice-regents to govern the earthly kingdom. Church officials were required to counsel the prince about God's law and to cooperate with him in publicizing and disciplining marriage. All church members, as priests, were required to counsel those who contemplated

marriage and to admonish those who sought annulment or divorce. But the
church no longer had legal authority over marriage.

The reforms of marriage law introduced in Lutheran Germany gave
expression to this reconceptualization of marriage. Civil marriage courts
replaced ecclesiastical courts in numerous Lutheran territories, frequently at
the instigation of Lutheran reformers. A welter of new civil marriage statutes
were promulgated, many replete with Lutheran marriage doctrine and
scriptural marriage laws. Lutheran jurists throughout Germany published
treatises on marriage law, affirming and embellishing the basic marriage
doctrine set forth by the theologians. The new statutory and learned
marriage law, like the new marriage doctrine, remained indebted to the
tradition. Traditional marriage laws like prohibitions against unnatural
relations and against infringement of marital functions remained in effect.
Impediments that protected free consent, that implemented scriptural prohibitions against marriage of relatives and that governed a couple's physical
relations were largely retained. Such laws were as consistent with Roman
Catholic as with Lutheran concepts of marriage. Changes in marriage
doctrine, however, also yielded changes in marriage law. Because the
reformers rejected the subordination of marriage to celibacy, they rejected
laws that forbad clerical and monastic marriage, that denied remarriage to
those who had married a cleric or monastic and that permitted vows of
chastity to annul vows of marriage. Because they rejected the sacramental
nature of marriage, the reformers rejected impediments of crime and heresy
and prohibitions against divorce in the modern sense. Marriage was for them
the community of the couple in the present, not their sacramental union in
the life to come. Where that community was broken, for one of a number of
specific reasons (such as adultery or desertion), the couple could sue for
divorce. Because man by his lustful nature was in need of God's remedy of
marriage, the reformers removed numerous legal, spiritual and consanguin-
eous impediments to marriage which were not countenanced by Scripture.
Because of their emphasis on the godly responsibility of the prince, the
pedagogical role of the church and the family and the priestly calling of all
believers, the reformers insisted that both marriage and divorce be public.
To be valid, marriage promises required parental consent, witnesses, church
consecration and registration and priestly instruction. Couples who wished
to divorce had to announce their intention in the church and community and
petition a civil judge to dissolve the bond. In the process of marriage
formation and dissolution, therefore, the couple was subject to God's law, as
appropriated in the civil law, and to God's will, as revealed in the admoni-
tions of parents, peers and pastors.

Many of these legal changes, to be sure, had other causes. The shift in
marriage jurisdiction, for example, resulted as much from German princes
who sought to expand their jurisdiction as from the reforms introduced by
Lutherans. The new laws of divorce resulted as much from jurists newly

enamoured of the Roman law of divorce as from the reforms of theologians who had denied the sacramental nature of marriage. It was the new concept of marriage introduced by the Lutheran Reformation, however, that provided both the new paradigm and the revolutionary situation needed to stimulate and justify these legal reforms.

WINSTANLEY, SEVENTEENTH CENTURY RADICAL: FROM THE MYSTERY OF GOD TO THE LAW OF FREEDOM

Douglas E. Sturm

> This great Leveller, Christ our King of righteousness in us, shall cause men to beat their swords into plowshares, and spears into pruning hooks, and . . . every one shall delight to let each other enjoy the pleasures of the earth, and shall hold each other no more in bondage.
>
> G. Winstanley, *A New-Years Gift* (1650)

From 1648 until 1652, Gerrard Winstanley published a wide range of works, from poetry to political broadside, out of an intense religious passion. The times were grim, yet hopeful. Many people were living in dire poverty. But the Civil Wars in England, hardly welcome by all, nonetheless signified to both gentry and peasant the prospects of radical change and a better time. Winstanley gave voice to both the suffering and at least one version of the expectation. He spoke on behalf of the poor of the land, yet, by intention, for the benefit of all humankind, if not of all creation.

In a sense, Winstanley's was a minor voice. He was not a systematic theorist. He held no high post. His following was minuscule. His influence on subsequent events and thought was negligible. Yet, to Eduard Bernstein, he "represents the most advanced ideas of his time."[1] To Perez Zagorin, he is "one of the pre-eminent political thinkers of his time," a remarkable judgment placing Winstanley in the company of Thomas Hobbes and John Locke.[2] To T. Wilson Hayes, given Winstanley's use of religious symbolization, he "ranks . . . among the most important poet-prophets in the English language."[3] To Fenner Brockway, "Winstanley was the father of British socialism, action wedded to theory, 200 years before Robert Owen, William Morris or Karl Marx."[4]

Though the thought of Gerrard Winstanley is almost wholly neglected in

---

[1] E. Bernstein, *Cromwell and Communism: Socialism and Democracy in the Great English Revolution*, trans. H. Stenning (New York, 1963), 131. Original publication in German, 1895.

[2] P. Zagorin, *A History of Political Thought in the English Revolution* (London, 1954), 56.

[3] T. Hayes, *Winstanley the Digger: A Literary Analysis of Radical Ideas in the English Revolution* (Cambridge, 1979), 1.

[4] F. Brockway, *Britain's First Socialists: The Levellers, Agitators and Diggers of the English Revolution* (New York, 1980), 150.

historical studies of legal theory, I would contend that he occupies a significant place in the development of reflection about natural law. As Hayes remarks, "The identification of God with reason and reason with natural law is a key to Winstanley's philosophy."[5] Winstanley's version of natural law, however, while not without precedent and not totally unique in the seventeenth century, stands in stark contrast to that of his contemporaries, Thomas Hobbes and John Locke.

Hobbes' *Leviathan* of 1651 was an apology for absolute sovereignty, albeit an apology grounded in a new and significantly non-traditional cosmology. The laws of nature are integral to his argument. They provide maxims of rational advice to those who would effectively sustain their right to preserve their individual lives and persist in the pursuit of their individual desires. Self-preservation, in effect, requires absolute political authority, the formation of a centralized body politic. Although suspicious of the new philosophy underlying the doctrine, royalists viewed it as supportive of their cause.

Locke's *Second Treatise*, first published in 1689, was written, in part at least, to support the cause of the Whigs against the king. Therein he announced that the law of nature, grounded in a religiously informed reason, mandates that we avoid harming anyone in life, liberty or estate—or, in sum, property. Although controversy continues to swirl about how to interpret Locke's doctrine of property as a natural right of humankind, propertied classes from his time to the present have invoked his doctrine as a justification for their interests, economic and political.

Winstanley, by contrast, would have nothing to do with the cause of either the royalists or the propertied classes. Nor would he have anything to do with the new philosophy or mainline Puritanism. His people were the poor, particularly peasants in rural areas, but, more generally, the entire class of people later called "the mob." His were the people living at or below the poverty line, moving from place to place in search of a viable life, neglected, if not scorned, by those in power.[6] Thus he, together with others, shortly after they had begun "to dig up, manure, and sow corn on George Hill" declared that, "In the beginning of time, the great creator Reason made the earth to be a common treasury, to preserve beasts, birds, fishes and man, the lord that was to govern this creation . . . but not one word was spoken in the beginning, that one branch of mankind should rule over another."[7]

Respect for the law of nature and for nature's God compels a restoration of this pristine condition of the "beginning of time," a condition antithetical to principles of both private property and monarchy. Winstanley, in short, as most interpreters assert, was a "communist." As such, Winstanley's perspec-

[5]Hayes, *Winstanley the Digger*, 93, n.3.

[6]See C. Hill, *The World Upside Down* (New York, 1975), esp. chap. 3: "Masterless Men."

[7]*The True Levellers' Standard Advanced*, C. Hill, ed., *Winstanley: 'The Law of Freedom' and other Writings* (Cambridge, 1983), 77.

tive, according to George Sabine, was unique in his time: "Winstanley's communism stood quite by itself in the political philosophy of the seventeenth century. It spoke with the authentic voice of proletarian utopianism, giving expression to the first stirring of political aspiration in the inarticulate masses and setting up the well-being of the common man as the goal of a just society."[8]

The new social union of Winstanley and his group, the Diggers, inspired, in Christopher Hill's words, a "revolt within the [English] Revolution," which was countenanced by neither royalists nor Parliamentarians.[9] The English Revolution itself succeeded and brought sweeping legal and political changes. The revolt of Winstanley and the Diggers failed. Had it succeeded, it "might have established communal property, a far wider democracy in political and legal institutions, might have disestablished the state church and rejected the protestant ethic."[10]

While the Diggers were not alone in pressing for this far-reaching vision of the good society, they were among the most consistent in living it out as far as they were able and in insisting on its profoundly religious roots. The Diggers were as uncompromising as they were gentle, as committed to what they discerned to be the inner intention of creation as they were prepared to subject their cause to principles of reason.

The natural law doctrine expressed through Winstanley's writings originated in a mystical vision with millennarian overtones, was enacted in a year-long ritualistic event of cultivating common land and culminated in the design of a platform offered to Oliver Cromwell for the radical reformation of English society. The doctrine thus closely conjoins the sacred and the secular, theory and praxis, faith and reason, mystical visions and political policy.

Winstanley's natural law doctrine has been subjected to various interpretations. Hill discerns a maturation within Winstanley's writings from religious commitment to materialistic philosophy leading to secularism.[11] Hayes bemoans the loss of "linguistic intensity and nuance" as Winstanley developed his more immediately political program.[12] I would contend that all Winstanley's work is of a piece, from his earlier, more mystical and strictly theological, writing to his final published piece, his proposal to Oliver Cromwell. From beginning to end, Winstanley's work is informed by a communal principle which is, in effect and by his own affirmation, a kind of

[8]G. Sabine, A History of Political Theory, rev. 4th ed. (Hinsdale, IL, 1973), 256.

[9]Hill, The World Upside Down, 14.

[10]Ibid., 15.

[11]Ibid., 139, 142, 150. It is not insignificant that in his edited collection of Winstanley's writings, Hill includes none of Winstanley's earlier publications. See Hill, ed., Winstanley.

[12]Hayes, Winstanley the Digger, 211. Hayes, in fact, devotes very little space in his otherwise brilliant interpretation of Winstanley's literary style to his final, longest and best known book, the platform for the reformation of English life addressed to Oliver Cromwell.

natural law. It is a "law" in that it functions as the supreme canon of action for the construction of forms of social intercommunication. It is "natural" in a two-fold sense: ontological and epistemological. Ontologically, the communal principle expresses the intention of the Creator, the essential structure of the universe, the true nature of being human. Epistemologically, the communal principle is a discovery of the "inner light," a power of knowledge available to everyone, peasant, professor and prince.

I. MYSTICISM AND THE "MYSTERY OF GOD" IN WINSTANLEY'S EARLY WRITINGS

Relatively little is known about Winstanley's early years. He was born, apparently, in 1609 in Lancashire in the town of Wigan. His family was of notable prestige. His father was a mercer, a dealer in fabrics, and a dissenter. It is unlikely that Winstanley attended university. By 1630, he had gone to London where he was apprenticed to the widow of a Merchant Taylor. After seven years, he had become a freeman and a full-fledged member of the Merchant Taylors' Company.

In 1640, the year that Charles called the Long Parliament into session, Winstanley married Susan King. The times were not auspicious for one in his profession, partly because of actions by more wealthy merchants against small dealers, partly because of the turmoil of and the heavy financial obligations imposed by the Civil War which broke out in 1642. By 1643, Winstanley had gone bankrupt. As noted in a later court case in which he was the defendant, "in the year of the Lord 1643 when the late unhappie wars in England were violent, your oratour left off his trading with . . . all . . . persons by reason of the badness of the tymes."[13] Hence Winstanley moved outside London to Cobham in Surrey where his father-in-law had property.[14] Throughout the remainder of the 1640s, he worked as a hired cow herder, learning firsthand about life among the peasants and about the impact of the enclosure movement on the landless and the poor.

Following the famed Putney Debates within the New Model Army, the dramatic escape of Charles from his imprisonment and the outbreak of the Second Civil War, Winstanley burst into his brief career as writer and public advocate of a new, but, in his own judgment, ancient mode of understanding and enacting life. In 1648 he published four pamphlets, all of which manifest his radicalism.[15] Of the first two, David Petegorsky remarks that they are

---

[13]Quoted in D. Petegorsky, *Left-Wing Democracy in the English Civil War: A Study of the Social Philosophy of Gerrard Winstanley* (London, 1940), 123. See also Hayes, *Winstanley the Digger*, 7.

[14]Hill, ed., *Winstanley*, 12.

[15]Abstracts of the first three and the full text of the fourth are included in G. Sabine, ed., *The Works of Gerrard Winstanley*, (Ithaca, NY, 1941). Lengthy passages are included in Hayes' detailed and scholarly discussions of all four texts in his study, *Winstanley the Digger*, chaps. 1–3.

"typical products of the mystical theology of the period."[16] I would extend the judgment. All four tracts published during 1648 possess the quality of mysticism, assuming that mysticism bears in a two-fold way—as a matter of understanding and a matter of being—on the relation between the divine and the human.

As a matter of understanding, mysticism declares that knowledge of God derives from immediate insight, from an intense experience of the depths of one's own inner being which constitutes a point of contact between the divine and the human. Significantly, Winstanley's pamphlets and books are devoid of direct quotations or references to any writings, save to Scripture. Repeatedly, he excoriates scholars and learned ministers for their imaginary constructs. By contrast, he praises "mechanic preachers" whose understanding is "experimental." Thus, as an apology for his own first writing, he asserts that God "does not always take the wise, the learned, the rich of the world to manifest Himself in, and through them to others, but He chooses the despised, the unlearned, the poor, the nothings of the world, and fils them with the good tidings of Himself, whereas, He sends the others empty away."[17] The inner experience of the divine presence is readily available to the most humble and inconspicuous of persons.

Winstanley's use of Scripture must be cast within the same context. His knowledge of the scriptural text was extensive and detailed. He was, in his own estimation, capable of demonstrating the validity of his judgments more thoroughly and soundly than were his opponents. Yet *sola Scriptura* is not his final appeal, for Scripture is but a manifestation of something else, the living Spirit. Thus in opposition to university scholars and learned clergy, he insists:

> The *Gospel* is the *Spirit* that ruled in the *Prophets* and *Apostles*, which testified to them, that in the later daies the same *Spirit* should be poured out upon all *flesh*. . . . then their writings is [sic] not the *Spirit*; but a report or declaration of that law and testimony which was within them. Now the Spirit spreading it selfe from East to West, from North to South in sonnes and daughters, is everlasting, and never dies; but is still everlasting, and rising higher and higher in manifesting himself in and to mankinde.[18]

Hayes properly stresses that Winstanley's mode of interpreting Scripture is complicated and sophisticated; he identifies it as a typological method, unfolding several layers of meaning from the text—literal, moral,

---

[16]Petegorsky, *Left-Wing Democracy*, 125.

[17]*The Mysterie of God*, as quoted in L. Berens, *The Digger Movement in the Days of the Commonwealth as Revealed in the Writings of Gerrard Winstanley, the Digger: Mystic and Rationalist, Communist and Social Reformer* (London, 1906), 52.

[18]*Truth Lifting up its Head above Scandals*, Sabine, ed., *Works*, 101.

allegorical, anagogical—the most determinative of which is the last.[19] In the final analysis, Scripture is but a secondary report of a primary source, the inner testimony of the Spirit, and that Spirit is everywhere present: "The Spirit, or Father, which as he made the Globe, and every creature, dwels in every creature, but supreamly in Man . . . and there is no man or woman can say that the Father doth not dwell in him, for he is everywhere."[20]

Winstanley identifies the Spirit, that is, God, with Reason. He remarks that "Though men esteeme this word Reason to be too meane a name to set forth the Father by, yet it is the highest name that can be given him."[21] Winstanley elaborates this point in his defense of William Everard against a charge of blasphemy:

> But if you demand of mee, why I say Reason did make, and doth governe and preserve all things: I answer, Reason is that living power of light that is in all things; it is the salt that savours all things; it is the fire that burns up all drosse, and so restores what is corrupted; and preserves what is pure; he is the Lord of our righteousness. It lies at the bottom of love, of justice, of wisdome; for if the Spirit Reason did not uphold and moderate these, they would be madnesse.[22]

The mysticism represented in Winstanley's work is, I have asserted, both a matter of understanding and a matter of being. In its latter aspect, the *unio mystica* is a principle of communal interdependency articulating both how the universe is constituted and how humans ought to conduct themselves in their relations with it.

> The spirit of the Father is pure Reason: which as he made, so he knits the whole creation together into a one-nesse of life and moderation; every creature sweetly singing in love lending their hands to preserve each other, and so uphold the whole fabrique.
> The clouds send downe raine, and there is great undeniable reason in it, for otherwise the earth could not bring forth grasse and fruit. The earth sends forth grasse, or else the cattle could not be preserved. The cattle feed upon the grasse, and there is Reason in it, for else man could not be preserved. The Sunne gives his light and heate, or else the creation could not subsist. So that the mighty power, Reason, hath made these to give life and preservation one to another.

---

[19]Hayes, *Winstanley the Digger*, 13.

[20]*The Saints Paradise*, as quoted by ibid., 49.

[21]*The Saints Paradise*, as quoted by Petegorsky, *Left-Wing Democracy*, 133. Petegorsky declares that this stress on the primacy and priority of reason constitutes a "remarkable development [in Winstanley] within a few months from a mystical to a rational theology." Ibid., 134. I would conjecture that the development is not remarkable at all; it is rather a deepening of the meaning of Winstanley's mystical principle. Petegorsky, I suspect, betrays an unwarranted assumption, namely, that matters spiritual and rational are, ultimately, antithetical.

[22]*Truth Lifting up its Head*, Sabine, ed., *Works*, 104.

[N]ow the Spirit Reason . . . is that spirituall power, that guids all mens reasoning in right order, and to a right end: for the Spirit Reason, doth not preserve one creature and destroy another; as many times mens reasoning doth, being blind by the imagination of the flesh; but it hath regard to the whole creation; and knits every creature together into a onenesse; making every creature to be an upholder of his fellows; and so every one is an assistant to be an upholder of his fellow; and so every one is an assistant to preserve the whole: and the neerer that mans reasoning comes to this, the more spirituall they are; the farther off they be, the more selfish and fleshy they be.[23]

In sharp contrast to Hobbes' rendition of reason as an instrument of mathematical and utilitarian calculation, Winstanley presents reason as both ontological and moral. Its imperatives mandate a life of moderation and mutuality: "if Reason be King in a man, then he moderates the man both within and without, so that he may be truly said to be a reasonable man. . . . Reason tels him, is thy neighbour hungry, and naked today, do thou feed him, and cloath him, it may be thy case tomorrow, and then he will bee ready to helpe thee."[24] As Hayes comments, this is not an ethic of the middle class; it manifests the ethical sensibilities of the lower class, the dispossessed of the land. Yet it affirms a moral vision that extends beyond any and all class, a vision of solidarity and unity. The poor and despised are the children of light who can see life as it is meant to be, perhaps because they have suffered so excruciatingly life in its anguish.

From his first pamphlet on *The Mystery of God* to his final offering to Cromwell, Winstanley is cognizant of life in its anguish, that is, of the tragic dimension of human experience. The powers of darkness struggle mightily with the powers of light. The Genesis story of the Fall and of the bondage of the Serpent is more than a story; it is indicative of the actual conditions of human life, psychological and political.

The story of the Fall, however, is not the final word. Winstanley casts his version of relations between the divine and the human in dynamic and dramatic form as a matter of both the internal experience of the individual and the historical experience of the human species. The classical theological schema of Creation, Fall and Redemption constitutes the narrative structure of both autobiography and political development. As we shall have occasion to note again, covetousness and private property comprise, respectively, the internal and external qualities of the Fall of humankind away from the intention that informs and defines the creation. But, in keeping with his principles of interpretation, Winstanley insists that the Fall is not (simply) an event that occurred in some hoary past. It is, if you will, an existential event,

---

[23]Ibid., 105, 108, 109.
[24]*Saints Paradise*, quoted by Hayes, *Winstanley the Digger*, 86–87.

an event that stands as an ever-present temptation to every man, woman and child. (Moreover, the effects of the Fall, initiated by humankind, have a destructive effect on the entire creation.) In a statement that smacks of modern ecological sophistication, Winstanley asserts: "For the curse being first falen upon mankinde, through man it fell upon the other creatures, and the Earth was cursed for his sake; and the poyson of mans unrighteous body, dunging the Earth, filled the grasse and herbs with strong unsavory spirits, that flowed from him whereby the cattell feeding, comes to be made bitter spirited, and mad one against another. For the Ayre and Earth is all poysoned, and the curse dwels in both, through mans unrighteousness."[25]

But, as noted, the Fall is not the final moment in the dynamic interplay between the divine and the human. As insistent as Winstanley is about the pervasiveness and depth of unrighteousness, he is equally insistent about the possibility of redemption. From his first pamphlet on, he strikes a note of universal salvation (a doctrine, incidentally, condemned by the Blasphemy Act of 1648!): "Jesus Christ . . . will dwell in the whole creation, that is, in every man and woman without exception."[26] Winstanley's conviction in this regard emerges from both his own inner biography as well as from his reading of history. At numerous points throughout his writings, he indulges in millennarian designs about the unfolding of events—through seven dispensations or three ages—culminating in a final communion of all with all under the aegis of the Spirit.

The "mystery of God" is precisely this promise of restoration, of a moment of perfection in which Reason and Righteousness will prevail. In what appears to be a commentary on the turmoil of the Civil Wars in England, Winstanley strikes an apocalyptic note of hope. Addressing directly "the despised Sons and Daughters of Zion, scattered up and down the Kingdome of England," he declares: "Rejoyce in the midst of this cloud of nationall troubles, for your redemption drawes near. God is working out an inward and outward peace and liberty for you all."[27]

Thus in its ontological aspect, Winstanley's mysticism provides him with a framework for ethical reflection, historical understanding and political action, all grounded, by claim, on the illumination of the inner light that resides, in principle at least, in everyone.

II. WINSTANLEY'S PROGRAM FOR SOCIAL REFORM IN ENGLAND

During the next two years, 1649 and 1650, the Diggers made a valiant effort to demonstrate to the world the wisdom of their convictions by direct action. Winstanley was their primary advocate. In various locations through-

---

[25]*Truth Lifting up its Head*, Sabine, ed., *Works*, 114.

[26]*The Mysterie of God*, quoted by Petegorsky, *Left-Wing Democracy*, 128.

[27]*The Breaking of the Day of God*, quoted by ibid., 129–130. The opening address is quoted by Hayes, *Winstanley the Digger*, 24.

out England, most prominently at St. George's Hill and later at Cobham Heath, the Diggers sought to establish a series of agricultural communes on common land. The digging and manuring at St. George's Hill commenced on April, 1649. Two months before that date, Winstanley announced his intention to go beyond declaration to action in a text whose title betrays the import of his vision: *The New Law of RIGHTEOUSNES Budding forth, in restoring the whole Creation from the bondage of the curse: A Glimpse of the new Heaven, and new Earth, wherein dwels Righteousnes.*

The *New Law of Righteousness* was published four days before Charles was beheaded following his trial. The Second Civil War had come to an end. Kingship, presumably, was a thing of the past. A new time was dawning. Yet many classes and groups of citizens were not so sure what sort of time it might be. Whether Cromwell and his compatriots were to be trusted to act on behalf of the common good was doubtful. But what should be done for the common good was dramatically envisioned by Winstanley. It had come to him in a moment of inspiration: "As I was in a trance not long since . . . I heard these words, *Worke together. Eat bread together*; declare this all abroad."[28] Publication of his treatise was the first step of his response to this mandate: "I have now obeyed the command of the Spirit that bid me declare this all abroad . . . I have now declared it by my pen. And when the Lord doth shew unto me the place and manner, how he wil have us that are called common people, to manure and work upon the common Lands, I wil then go forth and declare it in my action."[29] As he commented some months later, reflecting back upon his trance, the composition of his book and his engagement in the digging on St. George's Hill, "action is the life of all, and if thou dost not act, thou dost nothing."[30]

Petegorsky expresses some surprise at this development, assuming that it constituted a radical shift in Winstanley's mind: "Within a period of six or seven months Winstanley had traversed a path that led from a chiliastic mysticism through a progressive rationalism to a practical communism."[31] But the development was merely an unfolding of the impulse implicit in his earlier tracts. Winstanley's was not a mysticism of the cloister, but of the land. It was not contemplative, but active. It was not dualistic, but incarnational. In his mysticism, Winstanley joined together spirit and matter, eternity and time, religion and politics, myth and history. His communism was a direct expression of his mystical vision.

To work together and to eat bread together was for Winstanley far more than a mere ritual. It constituted an act of cosmic significance, a transformative moment in the history of humankind and the universe. It marked the transition from the first Adam to the second Adam which, in institutional

---

[28]*The New Law of Righteousness*, Sabine, ed., *Works*, 190.
[29]Ibid., 194.
[30]*A Watch-Word to the City of London and the Army*, Hill, ed., *Winstanley*, 127–128.
[31]Petegorsky, *Left-Wing Democracy*, 148.

form, meant a transition from private to communal property and thus a return
to the original intention of creation:

> The first *Adam* is the wisdome and power of flesh broke out and sate
> down in the chair of rule and dominion, in one part of man-kind over
> another. And this is the beginner of particular interest, buying and
> selling the earth from one particular hand to another, saying, *This is
> mine*, upholding this particular propriety by a law of government of his
> own making, and thereby restraining other fellow creatures from seek-
> ing nourishment from their mother earth. But when the earth becomes
> a common treasury as it was in the beginning, and the King of Righ-
> teousness comes to rule in every ones heart, then he kils the first *Adam*;
> for covetousnesse thereby is killed. A man shall have meat, and drinke
> and clothes by his labour in freedome, and what can be desired more in
> earth . . . .
> And so this second *Adam* Christ, the restorer, stops or dammes up the
> runnings of those stinking waters of self-interest, and causes the waters
> of life and liberty to run plentifully in and through the Creation, making
> the earth one store-house, and every man and woman to live in the law
> of Righteousnesse and peace as members of one household.[32]

The transformation envisioned in the Christian story and intended as a
principle for enactment is, to Winstanley, a requisite for the maturation of
humanity. In effect, we are commanded to become what we are, which
command is the epitome of natural law theory. In one of Winstanley's
renditions: "none can call himself a man, till the man Christ or Spirit rules in
him, for til then; the greatest Lord of all, is but a Beast and one Beast kils
another; for a man will never kill a man."[33] But the command extends
beyond the first taking of life to the taking of those things that sustain life:

> When this universall law of equity rises up in every man and woman,
> then none shall lay claim to any creature, and say, *This is mine, and that
> is yours, This is my work, that is yours*; but every one shall put to their
> hands to till the earth, and bring up cattle, and the blessing of the earth
> shall be common to all; when a man hath need of any corn for cattle, take
> from the next storehouse he meets with.
> There shall be no buying nor selling, no fairs nor markets, but the whole
> earth shall be a common treasury for every man, for the earth is the Lords.
> And man kind thus drawn up to live and act in the Law of love, equity and
> onenesse, is but the great house wherein the Lord himself dwels.[34]

The restoration of the original communal life of creation, however,
cannot be attained without struggle or without pain. Winstanley warns his

---

[32]*The New Law of Righteousness*, Sabine, ed., *Works*, 158–159.
[33]Ibid., 193.
[34]Ibid., 184.

readers to anticipate resistance. The Civil Wars may be over, but the more critical battle is not: "Therefore count it no strange thing to see wars and rumours of wars, to see men that are put in trust to act for publike good, to prove fals . . . ; To see Kings storm against the people [did Winstanley have a premonition of what was to come?]; To see rich men and gentry most violent against the poor, oppressing them and treading them like mire in the street."[35]

Nonetheless, Winstanley's vision was conceived to be realistic, at least in the sense that he discerned the central social problem confronting England at the time and a means of resolving the problem. The problem? How life might be sustained by and for all the citizens of the land. "Divide *England* into three parts, scarce one part is manured: So that here is land enough to maintain all her children, and many die for want, or live under a heavy burden of povertie all their daies." Unfortunately, this condition is, in part, perpetuated because of the poor themselves. They have submitted to a social system that immiserates them: "And this miserie the poor people have brought upon themselves, by lifting up particular interest, by their labours." They are subject, in brief, to cultural hegemony.

In response, Winstanley proposed "three doors of hope for *England* to escape destroying plagues." The first: "let every one leave off running after others for knowledge and comfort, and wait upon the spirit Reason." The second: "[l]et every one open his bags and barns, that al may feed upon the crops of the earth, that the burden of povertie may be removed: Leave of this buying and selling of Land, or of the fruites of the earth; and as it was in the light of Reason first made, so let it be in action, amongst all a common Treasurie; none inclosing or hedging in any part of earth, saying, this is mine; which is rebellion and high treason against the King of Righteousness." And third: "[l]eave off dominion and Lordship one over another, for the whole bulk of man-kinde are but one living earth."[36]

Reliance on the inner spirit, establishment of communal property and the formation of a radical democracy: these were the marks of Winstanley's program for England in the midst of the country's revolutionary period. In comparison with other alternatives proferred at the time, the program has a ring of plausibility.[37]

III. Winstanley and the Revolt of the Diggers

Winstanley did not wait for Parliament to consider his program. No doubt he suspected the existing Parliament, even following Pride's Purge, would find it wholly unacceptable. Instead, Winstanley joined with his compeers, the Diggers, to enact the program themselves. On April 1, 1649,

[35]Ibid., 208.
[36]Ibid., 200–201.
[37]Hill, *The World Upside Down*, 129–131.

they gathered on St. George's Hill and, in breaking ground together, they broke through an encrusted social order to reveal the possibility of a new heaven and a new earth: "I took my spade and went and broke the ground upon George Hill in Surrey, thereby declaring freedom to the creation, and that the earth must be set free from entanglements of lords and landlords, and that it shall become a common treasury to all, as it was first made and given to the sons of men."[38]

Throughout the next year, Winstanley published an extensive range of declarations, letters, broadsides and appeals, all pertaining to the actions of the Diggers at St. George's Hill and Cobham Heath. The documents contained explanations of and justifications for their actions, complaints about the responses of officials and local lords, requests for assistance and statements of intention. Almost invariably, the fundamental framework of these documents was theological, usually explicitly stated, but always present.

Winstanley made frequent use of the biblical motif of Creation, Fall and Redemption as, in Hayes's words, "a mythopoeic exposition of human history."[39] Winstanley writes, "the Scriptures consist of Three Parts. First, they declare the righteous Law of Creation . . . Secondly, they declare the fall of Mankind from this righteous Law . . . Thirdly, they declare the restoration of Mankind to his creation-righteousness."[40] History moves, Winstanley believed, from a moment of belonging to a moment of alienation and from thence to a return, a moment of reconciliation.

At the first moment, love is incarnate.

In the beginning of time, the spirit of universal love appeared to be the father of all things. The creation of fire, water, earth and air came out of him and is his clothing. Love is the Word.

The creation is the house or garden in which this one spirit hath taken up his seat, and in which he manifests himself. . . . There are two earths in which the spirit of love declares himself. First the living earth, called mankind. . . . Secondly, in the great body of earth, in which all creatures subsist, the spirit of universal love appears to preserve his creation in peace: for universal love unites not only mankind into an oneness, but unites all other creatures into a sweet harmony of willingness to preserve mankind.[41]

At the second moment, the house is rent asunder, and darkness covers the earth. "But when covetousness or particular love began to work, then not only mankind was divided amongst themselves but all creatures were divided, and enmity rose up amongst them, setting one against another; and

---

[38]A Watch-Word to the City of London and the Army, Hill, ed., Winstanley, 128.
[39]Hayes, Winstanley the Digger, 167.
[40]An Humble Request, Sabine, ed., Works, 423.
[41]A New-Years Gift for the Parliament and the Army, Hill, ed., Winstanley, 186.

this power is the wicked man."[42] Within human life, this moment consists in two sides: internally, covetousness and, externally, private property. "[W]hen he consented to that serpent covetousnesse, then he fell from righteousness, was cursed, and was sent into the earth to eat his bread in sorrow: And from that time began particular propriety to grow in one man over another; and the sword brought in propriety, and holds it up, which is no other but the power of angry covetousness."[43]

Hill oversimplifies this moment when he quips that "Winstanley reversed the traditional formula: it was not the Fall that caused property, but property that caused the Fall."[44] But Hill is correct to identify the Fall with the social institution of private property. In Winstanley's judgment, private property resides at the basis of many of the world's ills; it "is the cause of all wars, bloodshed, theft and enslaving laws, that hold the people under misery."[45] This theme recurs repeatedly throughout Winstanley's writings:

> wherefore is it that there is such wars and rumours of wars in the nations of the earth? And wherefore are men so made to destroy one another? but only to uphold civil property of honour, dominion and riches over another, which is the curse the creation groans under, waiting for deliverance.[46]

The enclosure movement of the sixteenth and seventeenth centuries— whereby landlords, sometimes with the sanction of official authority but ofttimes without, appropriated common lands to their exclusive use—was the most immediate institutionalized expression of the dynamics of the Fall in English society. In Winstanley's judgment, enclosures run contrary to the principle of righteousness, for they take land away from the poor and exacerbate divisions between the classes. They "dishonor the work of creation." As a form of private property, they contradict the maxims of the law of nature. In particular, they violate the seventh and eighth commandments of God, those against stealing and against killing. Landlords are guilty of such illegalities in a three-fold way:

> First by their oppression: they have by their subtle imaginary and covetous wit got the plain-hearted poor . . . to work for them for small wages . . . ; or else by their covetous wit they have outreached the plain-hearted in buying and selling, and thereby enriched themselves but impoverished others: or else . . . having been lifted up into places of trust, have enforced people to pay money for a public use, but have divided much of it into their private purses. . . .

---

[42]Ibid., 186–187.

[43]A Letter to the Lord Fairfax, Sabine, ed., Works, 289–290.

[44]Hill, The World Upside Down, 163.

[45]A Declaration from the Poor Oppressed People of England, Hill, ed., Winstanley, 107.

[46]The True Levellers' Standard Advanced, ibid., 79–80.

Then secondly for murder: they have by subtle wit and power pretended to preserve a people in safety by the power of the sword; and
what by large pay, much free-quarter and other booties ... they get
much monies, and with this they buy land and become landlords; and if
once landlords, then they rise to be justices, rulers and state
governors....

And likewise thirdly a breach of the eighth commandment, *Thou shalt
not steal*; but these landlords have thus stolen the earth from their
fellow-creatures, that have an equal share with them by the law of reason
and creation, as well as they.[47]

Thus also landlords violate the fifth commandment to which Winstanley
lends a novel interpretation. Customarily construed as a mandate to obey
higher authorities, including lords and ladies, the commandment becomes,
in Winstanley's reading, a maxim of mutuality, a rule for communal living
and sharing. "And hereby thou wilt *Honour thy father and thy mother*: thy
father, which is the spirit of the community, that made all and that dwells in
all; thy mother, which is the earth, that brought us forth: that as a true mother
loves all her children. Therefore do not thou hinder the mother earth from
giving all her children suck, by thy enclosing it into particular hands, and
holding up that cursed bondage of enclosure by thy power."[48]

Most fundamentally, civil or private property is a violation of the first
commandment, for the God who alone should be honored is "the King of
righteousness, ruling and dwelling in every one and in the whole."[49] Private
property is, in effect, idolatry. It is a distortion of creation and a perversion of
true religion which Winstanley defines with provocative originality: "True
religion and undefiled is this, to make restitution of the earth, which hath
been taken and held from the common people by the power of conquests
formerly and so *set the oppressed free*."[50] As such, true religion is the way to
true freedom which to Winstanley "lies in the community of spirit, and
community in the earthly treasury; and this is Christ the true man-child
spread abroad in the creation, restoring all things into himself."[51]

Restoration is the third moment in the dynamic of the world, the
moment beyond the Fall, the moment in which the entire creation might,
once again, become whole. Winstanley challenges England to inaugurate
the moment of restoration. Yet to have that honor, England "must cheerfully
(and dally no longer) cast out kingly covetous property, and set the crown
upon Christ's head, who is the universal love or free community, and so be
the leader of that happy restoration to all the nations of the world." Should

[47]Ibid., 85–86.
[48]Ibid., 93.
[49]Ibid.
[50]*A New-Years Gift for the Parliament and the Army*, ibid., 185. See also *An Humble Request*,
Sabine, ed., *Works*, 428.
[51]*A Watch-Word to the City of London and the Army*, Hill, ed., *Winstanley*, 129.

England refuse, another nation will be chosen for the task, although the ultimate power effecting the reunion is Christ, the supreme Leveller. However accomplished, the restoration consists in a two-fold reunion: of humankind and of the earth.

> First community of mankind, which is comprised in the unity of spirit of love, which is called Christ in you or the law written in the heart, leading mankind into all truth and to be of one heart and one mind;
> The second is community of the earth, for the quiet livelihood in food and raiment without using force or restraining one another. These two communities, or rather one in two branches, is that true levelling which Christ will work at his more glorious appearance, for Jesus Christ the saviour of all men is the greatest, first and truest Leveller that ever was spoke of in the world.[52]

The work of restoration, however, must not be accomplished by conquest or the sword, for it was by these means that private property was attained initially. That successive generations inherit property in a lawful and peaceable way does not legitimize private property. There is blood on the hands of all landlords: "though you did not kill and thieve, yet you hold that cursed thing in your hand by the power of the sword."[53] The work of true freedom, therefore, cannot resort to the sword. "We abhor fighting for freedom, it is acting of the curse . . . ; and do thou uphold it by the sword, we will not: we will conquer by love and patience, or else we count it no freedom. Freedom gotten by the sword is an established bondage to some part or other of the creation."[54] Though there is no conclusive evidence that the Diggers adopted a policy of absolute non-violence and though Winstanley himself, in his final proposal to Cromwell, countenanced political institutions to enforce the law, in this period he repeatedly affirmed a method of peaceful revolution. Perhaps his insistence on the presence of the spirit of life in all creatures, but especially in humankind, led him to affirm the ultimate efficacy of moral suasion by word and by exemplary action. The law of love and righteousness is thus both a substantive and a procedural morality, both an ultimate intention and a way of proceeding through life.

The intended significance of the action by Winstanley and the Diggers on April 1, 1649 is found in the context of the three moments of Creation, Fall and Restoration: "The work we are going about is this, to dig up George Hill and the waste ground thereabouts and to sow corn, and to eat our bread together by the sweat of our brows. And the first reason is this, that we may work in righteousness and lay the foundation of making the earth a common treasury for all, both rich and poor, that everyone that is born in the land may

---

[52]A New-Years Gift for the Parliament and the Army, ibid., 198–199.
[53]A Declaration from the Poor Oppressed People of England, ibid., 99.
[54]A New-Years Gift for the Parliament and the Army, ibid., 190.

be fed by the earth his mother that brought him forth, according to the reason that rules in creation."[55]

The digging and manuring, on one level, was merely the effort of a group of the poor to sustain their lives in a time of dire need. But, in the judgment of Winstanley, it was far more than that. It was an act of moral propriety, of political significance, of legal meaning, of cosmic dimension. Morally, the poor were in the right to use the land in the manner for which it was intended. Politically, they were leaders in bringing England to acknowledge her proper role in a world in desperate need of transformation. Legally, they were acting through the authority of the law of creation which supersedes all other laws and all lesser authorities. And, on the cosmic level, they were enacting the third moment in the dynamics of the world order. In acting for themselves, they were acting on behalf of all creation. In their digging, they were engaged in a revolutionary liturgy, a liturgy fraught with apocalyptic meaning.

IV. THE LAW OF FREEDOM

However profound the intended significance of their action on St. George's Hill and Cobham Heath, the Diggers encountered constant opposition, often violent, to their efforts. Winstanley details their sufferings in several works.[56] They persisted as well and as long as they could, but by the spring of 1650, the Digger movement had collapsed.

Shortly before the collapse, Winstanley published one of his major works, *Fire in the Bush*. Over a year later, he published his final work, a detailed proposal for the political reformation of English life, *The Law of Freedom in a Platform*. The former is addressed to the churches, the latter to Cromwell. The former, on the surface, focuses primarily on the dynamics of the self; the latter focuses primarily on institutional forms. Both unfold in greater detail the communal vision provoking Winstanley into his brief career as writer and activist.

Of *Fire in the Bush*, Petegorsky has written, "Only on one subsequent occasion did he [Winstanley] again cast his ideas wholly in a theological mould; and that tract seems to have been writen [sic] during a period of profound disappointment at the failure of his practical venture."[57] Petegorsky's deprecation of the work, given his anti-theological bias, blinds him to its significance. Its style is metaphoric. Its central images are religious. But its import is thoroughly political, albeit in a broad sense of that term. The images of the Garden of Eden and of the apocalyptic battle between

[55]*The True Levellers' Standard Advanced*, ibid., 84.

[56]See, e.g., "A bill of account of the most remarkable sufferings that the diggers have met with" attached to *A New-Years Gift for the Parliament and the Army*, published on January 1, 1650, ibid., 205–206.

[57]Petegorsky, *Left-Wing Democracy*, 148.

"Michael the Seed of Life, and the great red Dragon" are construed as directly applicable to the inner dynamics of the human spirit, to movements throughout the history of humankind, and to prospects for a new world. While in no way slighting the seeming ineluctability of the forces of darkness, the text, far from a statement of disappointment, is a reaffirmation of hope for the future.

To know oneself, declares Winstanley, is to know "three particulars": the living soul, the mystery of iniquity and the life of God.[58] The living soul is the aboriginal image of God which, nonetheless, may move in either of two directions—toward righteousness and universal love or toward unrighteousness and the life of covetousness. This condition of innocence (or "plainheartedness") was "not an estate 6000 years ago only; but every branch of mankind passes through it."[59] The mystery of iniquity is the curse of darkness, the temptation of self-seeking, the move toward divisiveness and separation, a move engendered by giving consent to the attractiveness of outer objects.[60] The life of God is the prospect of "the righteous spirit rising up in the living soul . . . bringing mankind into peace."[61] Hayes avers that this theory of the "three particulars" is Winstanley's "most complex theological point"; it applies equally to "the microcosmic body of each individual" and to the "macrocosmic body of mankind."[62] The tensions marked by these three particulars are both internal and external, psychological and political, existential and historical.

Thus the initial step of the Fall—consent—"breaks forth into outward action" in sundry ways which Winstanley details: private property, commercial enterprise, murder and mayhem, legal structures, war and conquest.[63] The Fall gives rise to a "four-fold power" which Winstanley associates with the four beasts in Daniel, but whose concrete visage is clearly the seventeenth century English social elite: clerics, lords, jurists and merchants. These are the four "imaginary powers . . . to be shaken to pieces at the resurrection of Christ."[64] They are the cause of "the greatest sins in the world," namely, (1) "to lock up the treasuries of the earth in chests and houses, and suffer it to rust or moulder while others starve for want"; and (2) "to take the earth by the power of the murdering sword from others, and then by the laws of their own making do hang or put to death any who takes the fruits of the earth to supply his necessaries."[65] Winstanley is keenly aware of the structural collaboration effected by these four classes, engaged through

[58]*Fire in the Bush*, Hill, ed., *Winstanley*, 248–249. Winstanley expands on these "three particulars" throughout the final chapters of the text on 248–272.

[59]Ibid., 254.

[60]Ibid., 263–264.

[61]Ibid., 249.

[62]Hayes, *Winstanley the Digger*, 195.

[63]*Fire in the Bush*, Hill, ed., *Winstanley*, 264–268.

[64]Ibid., 234. See, generally, 233–242.

[65]Ibid., 271.

their institutional interconnections in conspiring to sustain a social system of oppression.

All the complex conflicts that constitute human history are reduced by Winstanley to one simple concern: whose is the earth? "And all the strivings that is [sic] in mankind is for the earth, who shall have it; whether some particular persons shall have it and the rest have none, or whether the earth shall be a common treasury to all without respect of persons. And this is the battle that if fought between the two powers, which is property on the one hand, called the devil or covetousness, or community on the other hand, called Christ or universal love."[66]

At this point in the text Winstanley alludes, seemingly, to Hobbes' version of the state of nature, rejecting it in favor of his rendering of the basic nature of life: "Now this same power in man, that causes divisions and war, is called by some men that state of nature. . . . But this law of darkness in the members is not the state of nature; for nature or the living soul is in bondage to it, and groans under it, waiting to be delivered from it."[67] And that is the burden to which Winstanley calls the churches: to acknowledge the law of creation and to join in the task of deliverance—"if any of you will truly acknowledge Christ . . . come join hands and hearts together and set the earth free; nothing now stands in the way of Englishmen but inward covetousness."[68]

At about the same time that Winstanley addressed the churches to join the revolution, he initiated a proposal to Oliver Cromwell for radical political reform. For a time he set it aside but completed it in November, 1651 and published it the next year as *The Law of Freedom in a Platform: or, True Magistracy Restored*. It is a long, detailed text of variable quality. As Petegorsky remarks, it is "marked by many flashes of profound insight," yet large portions "are conceived in far too simple and, frequently, naive terms."[69] The foundation of the platform is "the rule of righteousness, which is God's Word." In that sense, Winstanley conceives the political philosophy of the text as an expression of natural law. On the other hand, the details of the platform are presented as suggestive, not as preemptive of alternative possibilities. Thus, for example, Winstanley enjoins Cromwell to "be as the industrious bee, suck out the honey and cast away the weed."[70]

The charge to Cromwell is of serious import. Displaying all the justifiable suspicions the radical sectarians had of Cromwell, Winstanley reminds him of the more encompassing history of which he is a part: "The spirit of the whole creation (who is God) is about the reformation of the world, and he will go forward in his work. For if he would not spare kings who have sat so

[66]Ibid., 268.
[67]Ibid., 268–269.
[68]Ibid., 216.
[69]Petegorsky, *Left-Wing Democracy*, 213.
[70]*The Law of Freedom*, Hill, ed., *Winstanley*, 285.

long at his right hand governing the world, neither will he regard you, unless your ways be found more righteous than the King's."[71]

The *leitmotiv* of the text is the idea of true freedom. The substance of true freedom is not to be found in free trade, freedom of worship, free love or private property; it lies rather in "the free enjoyment of the earth":

> True freedom lies where a man receives his nourishment and preservation, and that is in the use of the earth. For as man is compounded of the four materials of the creation, fire, water, earth and air; so is he preserved by the compounded bodies of these four . . . and he cannot live without them. For take away the free use of these and the body languishes, the spirit is brought into bondage and at length departs, and ceaseth his motional action in the body.[72]

Winstanley's definition of government is derived directly from his concept of true freedom: "Government is a wise and free ordering of the earth and the manners of mankind by observation of particular laws or rules, so that all the inhabitants may live peaceably in plenty and freedom in the land where they are born and bred."[73] In a simplified typology, Winstanley distinguishes but two kinds of government: perverse (monarchy) and true (commonwealth). A commonwealth is "the ancient of days," for it is the archetypal pattern of government. A commonwealth "makes provision for the oppressed, the weak and the simple, as well as for the rich, the wise and the strong."[74] Noting that Parliament had declared England to be a commonwealth, Winstanley summons Cromwell to make the name a reality.

Positive laws spring from two possible roots: common preservation and self-preservation. The latter is an expression of covetousness. The former is an expression of the fundamental law of creation: "The first root you see is common preservation, when there is a principle in everyone to seek the good of others as himself, without respecting persons: and this is the root of the true magistracy, and the law of righteousness and peace: and all particular laws found out by experience, necessary to be practised for common preservation, are the boughs and branches of that tree."[75] Thus Winstanley defines law, most basically, as "a rule whereby man and other creatures are governed in their actions, for the preservation of the common

---

[71]Ibid., 276. Despite their alliance with Cromwell during the First Civil War, the more radical sects were harassed and suppressed in diverse ways by the new establishment. The Agitators in the New Model Army and, more generally, the Levellers were cast aside once the Parliamentarians were in control. Later, in 1653, Cromwell became Lord Protector which, in the lexicon of Winstanley, constituted the restoration of kingly government.

[72]Ibid., 295.

[73]Ibid., 305. Given Winstanley's persistent stress on the internal light as ultimate authority, it is tempting to consider him a political anarchist. But that distorts the dialectic he espouses between internal and external, psychological and political realities, the inner spirit and institutional forms.

[74]Ibid., 311.

[75]Ibid., 315–316.

peace."[76] As such, the power of law may be distorted through the interven-tion of self-love, but it cannot be destroyed. It is, in effect, a primordial reality, a law of God and a law of the inner self:

> . . . the true ancient law of God is a covenant of peace to whole mankind; this sets the earth free to all; this unites both Jew and Gentile into one brotherhood, and rejects none: this makes Christ's garment whole again, and makes the kingdoms of the world to become commonwealths again. It is the inward power of right understanding, which is the true law that teaches people, in action as well as in words, to do as they would be done unto.[77]

In its particular laws, a commonwealth must provide for a whole array of officers to do its work. Winstanley designates appropriate officers for family, town, county and the entire land. His general prescriptions for office are radically democratic. All officers are elected. Terms are no longer than a year ("if water stands long, it corrupts"[78]). Eligibility for office is a matter of age and moral character, not religious affiliation or technical expertise. Officers include peacemakers, overseers, soldiers and taskmasters. Judges are also included among the officers, but they are required to apply the law strictly, without interpretation, lest they lift themselves "above the Parliament, above the law, and above the people of the land."[79]

Among the more innovative offices in Winstanley's scheme are those of postmaster and minister. Winstanley provides for an extensive network of postmasters throughout the country for purposes of intercommunication of two sorts. Local postmasters are required, once a month, to survey conditions of life in their territory. Their surveys are sent to a central office and published for everyone to know: "The benefit lies here, that if any part of the land be visited with plague, famine, invasion or insurrection, or any casual-ties, the other parts of the land may have speedy knowledge, and send relief."[80] Secondly, whenever anyone uncovers "any secret in nature" or makes a useful invention of any kind, that information is similarly to be made available to the entire population that all may benefit therefrom, finally, "to the beauty of our commonwealth."[81]

Winstanley calls for one day each week to be set aside for friendship, rest and instruction. The minister's role is instruction. Ministers, elected each year like other officers, are to make three presentations on this special day: (1) to review the affairs of the whole land (as gathered by postmasters);

[76]Ibid., 374.
[77]Ibid., 377.
[78]Ibid., 318. Winstanley sketches out several reasons for annual elections, most of them showing his sensitivity to the temptations of office. The inner light, he knew, is often dimmed. One's eyes are easily blinded, he notes, by the pride of political power.
[79]Ibid., 336.
[80]Ibid., 355.
[81]Ibid., 355–356.

(2) to read the law of the commonwealth; and (3) to sponsor speeches on such topics as history and government, arts and sciences or the nature and destiny of humankind. Winstanley encourages that speeches be made in several languages to promote a broadened wisdom and love among the denizens of the entire world. In Winstanley's version of the sabbath, all these presentations are ways of knowing God, for God dwells in and lives through all things of the world. As Winstanley put it in what one commentator calls "the finest passage in all his works":[82]

> To know the secrets of nature is to know the works of God; and to know the works of God within the creation is to know God himself, for God dwells in every visible work or body. And indeed if you would know spiritual things, it is to know how the spirit or power of wisdom and life, causing motion or growth, dwells within and governs both the several bodies of the stars and planets in the heavens above, and the several bodies of the earth below, as grass, plants, fishes, beasts, birds and mankind; for to reach God beyond the creation, or to know what he will be to a man after the man is dead, if any otherwise than to scatter him into his essences of fire, water, earth and air of which he is compounded, is a knowledge beyond the line or capacity of man to attain to while he lives in his compounded body.[83]

Winstanley's platform calls for the education of all youth, boys and girls. Their initial education includes the arts, languages and sciences. But it must include practical learning as well—trades and household arts.[84] Everyone in

---

[82]Quoted from J. Patrick by Hayes, *Winstanley the Digger*, 215.

[83]*The Law of Freedom*, Hill, ed., *Winstanley*, 348. Given what appears to be the import of this and other passages throughout Winstanley's works, virtually all interpreters consider Winstanley a pantheist. However, I suspect, these interpreters are not as knowledgeable of the classical or neoclassical theological tradition as they should be to make that judgment. Indeed, in a passage in which Winstanley depicts the character of the "living soul (Man)," he constructs a careful distinction between the human and the divine: "this innocent estate is the image of God, but not the strength and life of God. It is wise, but not wisdom itself; it is just but not justice; it is loving, but not love itself. It rejoices, but it is not joy itself; it is patient, but not patience itself; it is chaste, yet not chastity; it is plain-hearted without guile, yet not sincerity itself" (*Fire in the Bush*, ibid., 254). To be sure, in the "third estate," redeemed humanity will be drawn into the unity of the Godhead. Within the dynamics of this theological framework, however, the term "pantheism" is far from appropriate. Using a more modern lexicon, I would venture that Winstanley sounds more like a panentheist than like a pantheist.

[84]Throughout his writings, Winstanley is careful to include both male and female as co-equals. At times when he uses the generic term, "man," he adds as an appositive, sons and daughters or men and women. On that level, Winstanley deliberately adopts a principle of equality between the sexes. However, he also makes distinctions. Thus, for example, boys are trained in the trades; girls, on the other hand, in "reading, sewing, knitting, spinning of linen and woollen, music and all other easy neat works" (*The Law of Freedom*, ibid., 365). Moreover, only fathers, not mothers, are listed among the officers of a commonwealth. Again, when he warns against the temptations of sexuality, he addresses only men. Finally, there are some more metaphysical passages in which he distinguishes masculine and feminine principles, but he does not seem, in those contexts, to identify the principles as such with males and females.

the envisioned commonwealth must be trained to work and must be engaged in productive activity. Winstanley provides for a method of disciplining those who shirk such responsibilities.

However, "there shall be no buying and selling in the commonwealth, neither shall any one hire his brother to work for him."[85] Indeed, except for purposes of international trade, money is excluded from the society. In its stead, Winstanley outlines a plan for stockhouses of raw materials and of finished products to which everyone shall have free access. While the plan is not delineated in minute detail, Winstanley has considered the problem of free riders and has every anticipation that the arrangement is feasible. The stockhouses are the institutional means of distributing common resources to the community. Each family, Winstanley insists, retains its own integrity and distinctiveness. Once the family has taken what it needs, those things belong to it for its use. That is the one moment of "private" property: property for immediate use. But otherwise land and its products, materials both gross and fabricated, constitute a common treasury available on a principle of need.

Winstanley concludes the platform with a poem, "his finest" in Hayes' judgment.[86] It demonstrates that he is not sanguine about the prospects of the platform's enactment, however true it might be in affirming the law of creation:

> Here is the righteous law; man, wilt thou it maintain?
> It may be, is, as hath still, in the world been slain.
> Truth appears in light, falsehood rules in power;
> To see these things to be is cause of grief each hour.

After the manner of the Hebraic prophets, Winstanley seems almost bitter about the grief that has accompanied his vocation during this period:

> Knowledge, why didst thou come, to wound and not to cure?
> I sent not for thee, thou didst me inlure.
> Where knowledge does increase, there sorrows multiply,
> To see the great deceit which in the world doth lie:
> Man saying one thing now, unsaying it anon,
> Breaking all's engagements, when deeds for him are done.

He concludes with a note a resignation, yet peace, awaiting his own demise, but with the anticipation of ultimate reunion and reconciliation:

> O death where art thou? Wilt thou not tiding send?
> I fear thee not, thou art my loving friend.
> Come take this body, and scatter it in the four,
> That I may dwell in one, and rest in peace once more.[87]

---

[85]*The Law of Freedom*, ibid., 367.
[86]Hayes, *Winstanley the Digger*, 217.
[87]*The Law of Freedom*, Hill, ed., *Winstanley*, 387.

These poetic lines, so far as we know, concluded Winstanley's vocation as writer and advocate for radical reform. There is evidence that, subsequent to this period of his life, Winstanley became an established farmer, occupied several local political posts, remarried following the death of his first wife and, shortly before his own death in 1676, joined with the Quakers. But, for four years, his was a prophetic voice, calling all his compatriots to the law of creation, the principle of community, the intention of God, the fundamental meaning of reason and nature.

Winstanley and the Diggers were not the only group representing the lower classes and the need for radical reform during the time of the English revolution, but they were distinctive. The Ranters (Laurence Claxton, *et al.*), like the Diggers, rejected the principle of private property but, against the Diggers, promoted a life free from all customary moral restraints on eating, drinking and sexuality.[88] The Levellers (John Lilburne, *et al.*) were in agreement with the Diggers on the need for a government by and for the people but repudiated the Diggers' insistence on communal property.[89]

The Diggers were perhaps closest in spirit to the Quakers. Indeed, interpreters of these movements—both at the time and in the twentieth century—have suggested that the Diggers were the inspiration for the formation of the early Quaker community.[90] But the Quakers, the only sectarian group of the set to survive beyond the seventeenth century, lost their radical edge by adapting to the changing times. As Christopher Hill remarks, almost sardonically, "In the last resort, perhaps, Quakers did not want to overturn the world, any more than constitutional Levellers wanted to overthrow the sanctity of private property."[91]

---

[88]See Winstanley's strong and detailed opposition to the Ranters in *A Vindication of Those, Whose Endeavors is only to make the Earth a Common Treasury, called Diggers*, Sabine, ed., *Works*, 399–403. According to Hayes, Claxton (Clarkson) and others made an effort to infiltrate the Diggers, but were expelled because of their libertinism. See Hayes, *Winstanley the Digger*, 171–172.

[89]Thus Winstanley coined the label "true levellers" for the Diggers. See Hill, ed., *Winstanley*, 75–95. Sabine's comparison of the ideologies of Levellers and Diggers, while neglecting variations within each group, is instructive: "The common ground between the Leveller and the communist lay in the fact that both claimed the law of nature as their justification, as any radical in the seventeenth century was certain to do. The Leveller turned the law of nature into a doctrine of individual rights, of which the right to property was inevitably one of the most important. The Digger interpreted the law of nature as a communal right to the means of subsistence, of which land was the most important, and gave to the individual only the right to share in the produce of the common land and the common labor. The land was given by God or nature to be 'the common treasury' from which all are entitled to draw their sustenance." Sabine, *A History of Political Theory*, 453.

[90]See Berens, *The Digger Movement*, 49–51. Berens' book is dedicated to "The Society of Friends (The Children of Light)" in a seeming effort to bring that society back to its roots. See also B. Reay, *The Quakers and the English Revolution* (New York, 1985), chap. 1: "Birth of a Movement," esp. 13–14, 19–20.

[91]Hill, *The World Upside Down*, 374.

If nothing else, the case of Gerrard Winstanley is a reminder of the need, in each generation, to probe the difficult question of ultimate foundations in matters of law and religion. But it is also a reminder of a truth too often perverted by prevailing legal and religious institutions. Our lives are so deeply entangled with each other and with the entire world of being that we are under a heavy burden to seek out constructive ways to encourage and to enhance the life of all lest we all perish in a night of utter darkness and oblivion. In bearing that burden, we must give paramount attention to that resource—that common treasury—that sustains us all: the earth. That is the sense of Winstanley's neglected contribution to the venerable tradition of natural law.

RELIGION, LAW AND REVOLUTION IN THE SHAPING OF HARVARD COLLEGE, 1636–1708*

George Huntston Williams

Harold Berman in his book *Law and Revolution* views law as having been of pluralistic origin in Western civilization (Latin Christendom and its extension overseas), an organic development of various codes and some measure of tolerated concurrent jurisdictions. He states that this organic development has been punctuated by a succession of revolutions but that each revolutionary generation has "eventually made peace with the legal tradition that they or some of their leaders had set out to destroy."[1] Berman

---

*This essay represents an adapted and expanded portion of a Lecture, *"Religio et Veritas,"* delivered in Harvard Hall during the symposia celebrative of the 350th anniversary of Harvard University, September 4, 1986. It was published in a variant form in *Harvard Divinity Bulletin* 17:2 (November/December, 1986). The present essay substantially amplifies, corrects and interrelates certain themes dealt with in my *"Translatio Studii*: The Puritans' Conception of Their First University in New England, 1636," *Archiv für Reformationsgeschichte* 57 (1966): 152–181.

[1]*Law and Revolution: The Formation of the Western Legal Tradition* (Cambridge, MA, 1983), 5. For the English or Puritan Revolution, see ibid., 15, 21, 24. Growing out of this work and anticipating its publication, Professor Berman wrote "Religious Foundations of Law in the West: An Historical Perspective," in five parts, *Journal of Law and Religion* 1 (1983): 3–43, parts 2 and 3 being on the Lutheran and the Calvinist impact on the law. These parts were expanded and conjoined with material on the French Revolution and the Napoleonic Code, in Berman's "Law and Belief in Three Revolutions," *Valparaiso Law Review* 18 (1984): 569–629. He reflects on the impact of Luther on German law and particularly on the *Carolina* of 1532, the comprehensive criminal code for the Empire, that shows the influence of Luther's thought about the three uses of the law as grasped by its chief drafter, the Baron Johann von Schwarzenberg, a Lutheran who knew Luther. (Luther himself was acquainted with discussions at the Wittenberg court on updating the *Sachsenspiegel*.) Closer to the present essay is the section on the impact of Puritanism on the law in England and New England. Observing that Puritanism harked back to the common law "before the Tudor-Stuart monarchy had assumed supremacy over the church," he notes that in Calvinism "in effect, a new Two Swords doctrine [was] added to [Luther's] Two Kingdoms doctrine," that it in contrast to Lutheranism "transferred to the local community of the faithful [notably in New England] the concept of a visible, corporate, political-legal body." As in the present essay, he stresses "the Calvinist emphasis on voluntary action, the act of the will, in the service of God" in Puritan covenantalism and written constitutions. With his clarification of "the reformation of the world" in the sense of the temporal order under biblical and common law, Berman has occasion to quote the famous sermon of Governor John Winthrop on the Arabella in 1630 with his vision of "a City upon a Hill." What follows in my essay is presumably congenial and familiar to the Honorand, even my suggestion that the college corporation of Harvard recovered under Puritan auspices something of the pre-Tudor-Stuart, medieval idea of the relative independence of the university, wherein professorship eventually gains a status as an order next to magistracy and ministry.

recognizes five such revolutions of modern times that engendered demonstrable accommodations after the initial pitch of revolutionary fervor to rid society of vestiges of the old and oppressive order.

Puritan Independent New England, and the College it brought forth from its matrix, was related to two of these revolutions. Indirect heir of the Reformation/Revolution of 1517, the College was created just before 1640, the beginning of what Berman calls the English or the Puritan Revolution. Although Berman does not list as decisive the Glorious Revolution of 1688–89, which, nevertheless, had a strong impact on the Massachusetts Bay Colony, on their law and on their Academy in the reorganized royal Province, the institutional history of Harvard in the seventeenth century can be brought into the perspective opened up by Professor Berman.

Berman's whole study pivots on the Papal Revolution of Gregory VII Hildebrand (1073–85) and his successors into the twelfth century, under whom the Church of Rome, from being a local corporation in the terms of the Roman law of Justinian (that is, a *prima inter pares* among such other ecclesiastical corporations as bishoprics, abbeys and parishes), evolved swiftly as a supranational corporation. By accommodating ancient conciliar canons, papal letters, Roman law, Germanic law and local church law and usage, the reformed papacy fashioned the universal "new canon law," which, in turn, clarified and universalized other legal systems—royal, feudal, manorial, urban and mercantile.

Although Berman does not deal directly with academic law in the sense of the charters, statutes and customs modeled on those of urban guilds and cathedral chapters by which the academic *universitas* was governed, he does treat the universality of the Western Christian *studium generale* as an institutional consequence of the Papal Revolution. It is, therefore, appropriate to bring his thought swiftly forward to the Tudor and Stuart period not handled in his work and to the transit of what was by then the partly nationalized university across the Atlantic to New England.[2] In so doing, this study joins Professor Berman in deploring "the separation of law and history" and, with his encouragement, sees law and religion in the larger setting of sustaining the metaphors that bind society together over time.

Professor Berman's perspective invites us to view Harvard's institutional history as an integral part of the theocratic society of the Bay Colony, in which all was placed under the authority of scriptural law. The Bay Colony theocracy, in which Harvard College replicated academically what was familiar and beloved in old England, anticipated the form of society and government later produced by the English Revolution. To be sure, this

[2]Edward Eggleston dealt thematically with the transfer of law, religion and education in *The Transit of Civilization from England to America in the Seventeenth Century*, 2d ed. (Boston, 1959; first published in 1900). See also N. Pettit, "The English in New England: Their Reluctance to Become Americans," *The Transit of Culture Across the North Atlantic, Essays in Honor of Hans Galinsky*, eds. W. Herget and K. Ortseifen (Tübingen, 1986), 45–51.

religiously revolutionary society was grounded in an ecclesiology at the other extreme from that of the Papal Revolution; it understood the true church, in appeal to New Testament precedent, to be precisely the *local* church. It was a local *societas*, although its fellows (*socii*) were, in fact, called *membra* only at that moment when the spiritually qualified, eternally elect saints partook of communion and thus constituted a fleeting *corpus mysticum*. In contrast to the uniquely surviving corporation of President and Fellows (*socii*) of Harvard College, these local churches were not incorporated until after the period here under consideration.

The local Congregational churches, each a plenary church under Christ, were covenantal, that is, voluntary societies. Each prospective member depended upon the eternal will of the triune Godhead for election to salvation and the experiential gift of the sealing covenant of grace along with the obligation to recount the qualifying experience of the covenantal gift to the congregation, when the converted adult subscribed to the church covenant, the words of which differed slightly from one local church to another.

While the Bay Colony thought of its non-Separating Congregational churches each as a plenary *ecclesia*, the College brought forth from this congeries of covenantal towns and covenantal churches was not in any sense a gathered church. It was not held together by covenant or by an academic oath, nor did it even meet corporately on the Sabbath in its own chapel for the administration of the Word and sacraments. It was, instead, a higher school, the creation of the legislature of the Colony through an emerging Board of Overseers (1636) and by the incorporation of the President and Fellows (1650). As a quasi-independent and self-perpetuating body academic, it was also, by the words of its charter, a body politic, a corporation at law, with immunities from military service and taxation and the capacity as a legal person to sue and to be sued.

In short, the incorporation of Harvard College, coming about as it did in an environment of intense religiosity, set it apart not only institutionally, but also as a distinctive component of the larger theocratic society. The story of Harvard College, which granted its first degrees in 1642, has been magisterially recounted several times, especially for the seventeenth century.[3]

---

[3]The first was that of the Librarian B. Pierce, *A History of Harvard University, From its Foundation, in the Year 1636, to the Period of the American Revolution*, posthumously edited by J. Pickering (Cambridge, MA, 1833). It was used, along with the surviving archival material, by President J. Quincy, *The History of Harvard University*, 2 vols. (with many documents) (Cambridge, MA, 1840). It was in his research that he discovered the *Veritas* seal of 1642. The father of the future President Samuel Atkins Eliot summarized Quincy's *History* in *A Sketch of the History of Harvard College and of its Present State* (Boston, 1848), which is of special interest in regard to his own period. Samuel Eliot Morison prepared four books on Harvard: *The Founding of Harvard College* (Cambridge, MA, 1935, 1968); *Harvard College in the Seventeenth Century* (Cambridge, MA, 1936); *Three Centuries of Harvard, 1636–1936* (Cambridge, MA, 1936). Morison also edited the collective *The Development of Harvard University Since the*

Illumined by rays from an earlier age of revolution as explored by Professor Berman, part of that story can here be retold to supply the context for new particulars in the interface of law and religion.

I. The Voluntarist Society Out of Which the College Emerged

Recollection of the unusual character of New England in the colonial and provincial periods brings the emergence of Harvard College into better focus. Any colonial settlement involves both the transmission of old institutions and procedures from the mother country and the improvisation of new ones. The New England colonies, however, were extraordinarily innovative. They gave unusual prominence to covenants and thus, in theory, to a voluntarist social and institutional motif. This voluntarist motif contrasts with an organic motif in transplanting culture wherein emphasis is placed on reconstituting what is remembered from the motherland. The latter motif has led many later generations of American immigrants to embalm their religious institutions in the language and culture of the old world.

New England covenants were ever subject to renewal, and the new society was to this degree both more precarious and more self-consciously willed and sustained than the organic societies of village, borough and parish from which the colonists seceded. Although the divine covenant of grace received as a personal experience within each believer was deemed to be based upon the eternal decree of the Godhead and, therefore, irrevocable, the town covenant and within it the church covenant were always potentially dissoluble. They were subject to repeated renewals and even reformulations, each modeled on the covenant renewals of ancient Israel.

A new local church of visible saints could gather only by permission of

---

Inauguration of President Eliot, 1869–1969 (Cambridge, MA, 1930). He projected in his retirement a volume on the eighteenth century. Among treatments of the whole history, the most recent is B. Bailyn, et al., *Glimpses of the Harvard Past* (Cambridge, MA, 1986). A major work on the Corporation and the Board of Overseers is that of J. Hoffmann, *Commonwealth College: The Governance of Harvard in the Puritan Period* (Ph.D. Diss., Harvard, 1972). Hoffmann deals in several long footnotes with my earlier writings on University themes, but he finds them non-functional for his purposes, however interesting.

Though not the subject of a major monograph, the role of the Board of Overseers has been intermittently examined, most recently by [R. Shenton], *Report from the Committee on the Structure and Function of the Board of Overseers (The Gilbert Committee) Concerning Harvard's Governmental Structure* (Cambridge, MA, 1978). Hoffmann, *Commonwealth College*, 145–209, deals with the Board of Overseers and asserts broader powers than now obtained for the Board, an observation substantiated by the present study. See, in general, D. Tewksbury, *The Founding of American Colleges and Universities Before the Civil War With Particular Reference to the Religious Influences Bearing Upon the College Movement* (New York, 1932) and L. Cronin, *American Education: The Colonial Experience, 1607–1783* (New York, 1940).

the colonial government and the abutting churches. It had to be constituted by seven or more men of expressed and approved saving experience, just as ten Jewish men were required to constitute the *minyan* for the establishment of a synagogue. (The colonists appealed to this precedent or analogue and, indeed, occasionally referred to their churches as synagogues.) Women, though members, were not constituent members of the church; if all the communicant men were to perish by Indian assault or plague, a church composed only of communicant women and their children would *ipso facto* dissolve.

The Congregationalist planters of the Bay Colony regarded themselves as constitutive of reforming churches, that is, societies of experiential believers who had hitherto worshiped *within* the mixed spiritual company of the parish of the Anglican establishment. They had shed a chrysalis inclusive of all nominal Christians (except for notorious sinners) to gather, as they put it, into disciplined churches of visible saints formed by a church covenant. The church in all New England was, henceforth, to mean the chosen people of God gathered locally in a meetinghouse that initially might serve purposes other than worship. Such churches did not regard themselves as separating from fellow Puritans within the parishes of the Church of England—in contrast to the Pilgrims of Plymouth Colony who were avowed Congregational Separatists. The Bay Colonists have, therefore, been referred to in the scholarly literature as non-Separating Congregationalists.[4]

As Congregationalists or Independents, the Bay Colonists held that every local company of visible saints is a plenary church, whose pastor is the counterpart of a bishop or presiding presbyter in the New Testament or apostolic church. They deemed themselves under no decisive ecclesiastical authority above the level of the elected officers of the local church. They elected teaching elders of two kinds, ruling elders and deacons, adapting as scripturally sanctioned John Calvin's understanding of the fourfold ministry.[5] They eliminated the offices of especially inspired prophets and apostles, generally regarding them, as did Calvin, as functional for the apostolic age only. Thus, although teaching and ruling elders might meet in an occasional synod, the disciplinary or theological findings of any such synod had the status only of reasoned recommendations; they did not have for them the same authority as in Presbyterian or Episcopal polities.

So consistent were the founders of the Bay Colony as Congregationalists that they believed that their ministers—whether priests ordained by bishops in England or ministers ordained in New England by their own congrega-

---

[4]A term given wide acceptance by Perry Miller in contrast to Separatist Congregationalists of Plymouth Colony.

[5]See J. Calvin, *Ordonnances ecclésiastiques* (Geneva, 1541).

tions—lost their ministerial character and were suspended from the ministerial office when in transit between two congregations. Hence, the call and installation of a minister (or, according to Anglican nomenclature, the "institution") by a new congregation was tantamount to a new ordination, performed by the laying on of hands of the congregants or their chosen representatives.[6]

To speak of the Bay Colonists as non-Separating Congregationalists can, nevertheless, avert the eye and mind from the still profoundly "anglican" character of the Bay Colony. The Bay Colonists considered themselves not only as planters of a new society but also as perhaps only temporary exiles from the motherland. Itself in part voluntarist in character, the government of the Bay Colony was a royally chartered company of corporation stockholders and planters. Twelve signatories of the company took their charter with them to their plantation as arranged by the Cambridge Agreement of 1629, an arrangement unique on the whole Atlantic seaboard. This commercial company rapidly evolved into a nearly autonomous society, its court serving as a miniature local parliament in all but name.

Yet, in the context of continuing to acknowledge the English monarch, the Bay Colonists conceived their ecclesial and civil institutions as serving ideally as models for the "reformation of the Reformation." Had this reformation developed along *their* lines, it would have resulted in Congregational anglicanism as distinguished from an episcopal (or, in Scotland, a presbyterian) establishment. Had the "non-Separating Congregationalist anglicans" had their way during the Protectorate, the congeries of scripturally reformed cathedral chapters, parish churches and universities would have still collectively been the *Ecclesia Anglicana*—disciplined, locally autonomous, "non-Separating" churches within the hull of the dismantled institutions of a much simplified national fragment of the old *corpus Christianum*.

It was partly in an attempt to accomplish this "reformation of the Reformation" that the non-Separating Congregationalists sought so insistently to implement in New England those ideas that had remained inchoate and untested while they yet lived in England or sojourned in the Netherlands. Finding warrant for their congregational polity in the New Testament, the Bay Colonists modeled their vision of a scripturally reformed *Ecclesia Anglicana* on the covenantal reformation of Judah carried out by King Josiah in the seventh century B.C. (2 Kings 22:1–20; the code of Deuteronomy). Having adopted this monarchical model, the non-Separating Congregationalists were not, therefore, wholly opposed to Erastianism, that policy artic-

---

[6]By the end of the seventeenth century, the clerical status was being acknowledged and a once-for-all ordination was distinguished from any subsequent installation. The laying on of hands of the congregation receded.

ulated by Thomas Erastus of resisting the imposition of church discipline by ministers and elders on princes and magistrates.[7]

At issue in designating the Bay Colony as "semi-Erastian," however, would be their own eschewal of the term. Quite plausibly, the Congregational Puritans would have taken umbrage at a label associated with such High Church Erastians as Archbishop William Laud, whose Arminian views on predestination they rejected.[8] Furthermore, interwoven with the term "Erastian" was the issue of the qualifications for admission to the sacraments of baptism and the eucharist. Pedobaptism was fiercely, if perhaps inconsistently, retained as a *right of parents*, a New Covenant counterpart of circumcision. The Bay Colony moved swiftly to separate the experientially elect from the only nominally Christian at the Lord's Supper. Even prior to colonization, there existed a practice of assembling apart from their parish in eucharistic piety, waiting for the vestiges of popery, as they called them, to be scoured away.

The first Puritan to have used the key phrase "converting ordinance" for a sacrament and particularly for the Lord's Supper was the Parliamentarian William Prynne, an avowed Erastian. Prynne later resisted the experientialists in his party in 1645 and sought to deprive ministers of any authority to restrict communion to the regenerate or the experiential. As he wrote, the Lord's Supper is a "converting ordinance," and, therefore, must be open to ordinary sinners as well as to the experiential saints.[9] Against this concept, the New England colonists consistently held that the two sacraments, being for them seals of the covenant of a grace already received by the predestined elect, could not be open to all inhabitants.

The Bay Colonists have not been generally known in the scholarly literature as "semi-Erastian," both because (1) the local churches stressed their disciplinary autonomy, particularly in limiting access to the "ordinances of the converted"; and (2) they eschewed the prelatical Arminian connotation of the term "Erastian." There was, however, an Erastian component in the New England mind as in the Laudian mind. While not seeking to control the inner life of the local church, the Colony was Erastian in exempting public officials or elected representatives from the disciplinary effects of the local church of which a public figure was a member.

In recognition of the Erastian stance of the Colony, the use herein of the unfamiliar term "Congregational anglicanism"[10] is intended to enhance our

---

[7]See T. Erastus, *Treatise on Excommunication* (c. 1568; first published in Latin, London, 1589). By 1659 the work was published in English as *The Nullity of Church Censures*.

[8]E. Holifield, *The Covenant Sealed: The Development of Puritan Sacramental Theology in Old and New England, 1570–1720* (New Haven, CT, 1974), 113.

[9]This in the anonymous *Vindication of foure Questions* (against George Gillespie of Edinburgh), quoted by ibid.

[10]Dean Willard L. Sperry of the Harvard Divinity School, himself a Congregationalist, aware of the scholarly idiom, nevertheless wrote instinctively and validly: "Massachusetts Bay, which

understanding of the religious character of the theocratic civil society shaped by these Puritan Congregationalists. Indeed, the traditional term "Congregationalism" does not alone sufficiently bring out the covenantal (hence, religious but still voluntarist) character of the civil carapace in the formative theocracies of New England and the distinctive role in the divine economy filled by their first colleges, Harvard and Yale. As a product of a Congregational anglicanism, rather than of a disaggregated congregationalism, the emergence of Harvard College highlights the integral nature of this carapace.

By calling the ambient society of the colonial College "Congregational anglicanism," we rightly keep within our purview the extent to which the government of the Colony, town and county discharged functions bearing directly on the contours and character of churches within their jurisdiction. The government took over a number of religious functions lodged in England with the parish, with select vestrymen ("selectmen" as simplified in New England) or with the ecclesiastical courts—for example, the registry of births, marriages and deaths, the care of burial grounds and of the poor and the sick, the calling of synods, the adjudication and punishment of cases of heresy and other infringements of the Decalogue. In the early period, temporal officials were often also called upon to solemnize marriage.

The General Court, as empowered by the law of 1631, gave church members the franchise. By a law of 1636, it required the central colonial magistracy, along with the elders of the majority of the churches, to authorize every new gathering of a church of visible saints or the orderly division of a settled congregation in the separated precincts of a growing town. By a law of 1637, the Court set the precedent for requiring towns to supplement weekly or monthly freewill offerings through taxation. This support of the local meetinghouse and ministry led at length to Congregational anglicanism becoming a "Standing Order" in New England, just as the Episcopal Church was the established church in England.

Thus in this study "Congregational anglicanism" refers not only to duly constituted, experiential churches non-Separating from the Church of England but, with expanded settlement, also to their non-separating from each other except through an orderly fission and diffusion process governed jointly by the ecclesiastical and civil leadership.

The overarching theocratic community created a body of colonial law combining common, statutory and biblical (or revealed) law and expressly excluding equity. As early as March, 1635 the deputies conceived of the

---

had originally been *Puritan-Anglican* in its English origins, soon became a community of Congregational (Independent) Churches. Why the theoretical obligation to the Church of England should have worn thin so soon, and finally given way altogether, is something of a riddle. The Bay people had not intended to become Independents as the Plymouth people were." W. Sperry, *Religion in America* (Cambridge/New York, 1946), 32ff.

necessity of framing a body of laws—"in resemblance of the Magna Charta"—that would facilitate the conversion of a commercial corporation into a body politic of the whole Colony of émigré. A committee consisting of five magistrates and three ministers produced a draft, entitled *Moses his Judicialls*, composed largely by the Reverend John Cotton of First Church, Boston. This proposal, however, was not in the end accepted by the Court. It was regarded as too severe in its reliance primarily on the Old Testament, with an extensive list of crimes punishable by death,[11] and as too aristocratic, as exemplified in calling for councilors with life tenure, much like the House of Lords. Rejected, the document lay at hand as another body of law was drafted by legally-trained Nathaniel Ward, pastor in Ipswich.

Ward's work was adopted provisionally in 1641. It received its definitive form as the *Book of the Laws and Liberties Concerning the Inhabitants of Massachusetts* in 1648,[12] constituting the civil counterpart of the *Cambridge Platform of Church Discipline* adopted the same year. As the latter work had much to say about the role of the magistracy, so the *Book of the Laws and Liberties* was replete with references to the proper relation of town government and local church and of the commonwealth and the aggregation of representatives of the churches in clerical associations and non-binding synods.

Under its 16 general "ecclesiasticals" there were substantial safeguards of the right of the churches to proceed with self-discipline and with the election and dismissal of ministers and other members. Each town government was also required to support the church and its minister. The law further provided that government "hath the power to see the peace, ordinance, and rules of Christ be observed in every [local] church according to His word"; this meant for magistrates and ministers that the sacraments or ordinances of baptism and the Lord's Supper were not to be considered converting ordinances. At the same time, in a semi-Erastian tone, the *Book of the Laws and Liberties* refused to acknowledge that any church censure could "degrade or depose any man [in a church] from any civil dignity, office or authority . . . in commonwealth" or "otherwise allow the intrusion of the ministry in the affairs of state."[13]

Having introduced the voluntarist character of the Bay Colony society in the seventeenth century, we are better able to focus on the distinctive character of Harvard College in relation to law and religion as it emerged as a distinct entity. Its distinction is derived in part from the sense of its being

---

[11]Even in the authorized *Laws and Liberties* (discussed below, n. 12), in the list of 15 capital laws, all sanctioned by passages in the Pentateuch, there was still included the execution of any child over 16 who had cursed or smitten a parent and also of any stubborn or rebellious son, of anyone of deviant worship or blasphemous of God or the Holy Trinity.

[12]*Laws and Liberties*, 1648, in A. Vaughan, ed., *The Puritan Tradition in America (1620–1730)* (Columbia, SC, 1972).

[13]*Laws and Liberties*, 1648, quoted by ibid., 171.

a body politic with roots separate from the other institutional components in the bibliocratic theocracy.

II. THE HARVARD OVERSEERS, THE CORPORATION AND THE COLLEGE WITHIN THE COVENANTAL THEOCRACY

In the midst of a semi-Erastian non-Separating Congregational anglicanism, Harvard College emerged with unusual swiftness. The focus here will be on certain theological and constitutional presuppositions evident in selected strands of the history of Harvard.

A. Synopsis of the Earliest Years of the College

To make clear the rise and development of these distinctive institutional features of America's first university in its earliest stages, we may recall the rapid succession of events that brought the College into being. On October 28, 1636 the Court agreed to raise from the general levy 400 pounds toward "a school or college," 200 pounds over each of two years, the first installment amounting to one half the total tax receipts from the whole Colony of the following year. On November 2, 1637, the General Court, sitting in Newtown, condemned for sedition Anne Hutchinson, the strong-minded follower of John Cotton of First Church, Boston, on the covenant of grace. She, carrying her assault against sanctification ("works righteousness") as no evidence of election and justification and as not qualifying one for communicant membership, scoffed at a hireling and learned ministry; she was banished. On November 15, 1637 the magistrates and deputies of the Court ordered that the college be at Newtown—partly in recognition of the stalwart and decisive role of its pastor, Thomas Shepard, in checking the threat of Antinomianism, embodied in Mistress Hutchinson and her considerable following, not excluding a few educated ministers and an ousted Governor (Henry Vane).[14] On November 20 of the same year, the Court committed the erection of College Hall to a committee of Twelve, six magistrates and six elders, who were not yet called "overseers."[15] On May 2, 1638 the Court ordered that Newtown be henceforward called Cambridge.[16] On March 13, 1639 (old calendar 1638) the Court ordered that the College of Cambridge be called Harvard College in grateful recognition of the nuncupative will of John Harvard of Charlestown, who had left his substantial library and one half of his estate (of about 1700 pounds) to the College.[17] Thereafter, the

---

[14]See, generally, D. Itall, *The Antinomian Controversy, 1636–1638: A Documentary History* (Middeltown, CT, 1968).

[15]*Massachusetts Bay Colony Records*, I, 217; see Morison, *The Founding of Harvard College,* 179, 325.

[16]*Massachusetts Bay Colony Records*, I, 208, 217, 228.

[17]Ibid., I, 253. John Harvard died on September 14, 1638 at the age of 31.

Court, except through its role *ex officio* on the Board of Overseers, claimed for itself only an indirect role in the life of the College.[18]

Harvard College was governed ultimately by two boards, one long since known as the Reverend the Honorable the Board of Overseers, tracing its beginnings to 1636, the other, the Corporation, going back to the charter of 1650. Originally, the senior Board of Overseers—which represented the interests of the whole Bay Colony and, to some extent, eventually the whole United Colonies—reflected in some ways the distinctively scriptural sanctions and theories of what the College was for the Bay Colony theocracy. The Corporation also embodied vestiges of the medieval and the Tudor conception of the College corporation as a body politic as well as related conceptions of a society of fellows (*socii*). The legal fictions of a perpetual society and a body politic, the *corpus mysticum*, also were rooted in Christian legal thought.

The Board of Overseers discharged some of the functions traditionally assumed by a university visitor (in Europe usually a prelate and his suite, or a cleric in the service of the territorial prince). But, in some ways, the Board was in itself the overall institution of university authority, for example, in its implicit sanction of degree-granting by this one-college *academia/universitas*. Until 1708, the senior Board was actually dominant and more decisive than the Corporation of the then youthful and transient fellows and tutors. The President of the Corporation, in any case, the senior tutor, also took a place *ex officio* on the Board of Overseers, ranking third after the Governor and the Deputy-Governor.

B. The Board of Overseers

On August 27, 1640, an ad hoc committee of ten magistrates and 16 teaching elders invited the Reverend Henry Dunster, but recently arrived from England, a Hebraist of some note, to serve as first President of the College (1640–54).[19] Attending at first to the reorganization of the College and the instruction of its students, Dunster presided at the first commencement on September 23, 1642, with nine commencers (graduates). Their graduation theses, together with an account of the College, were printed as

[18]Most English colleges were private endowments within universities and not foundations of the state, although indeed of the sovereign in some instances.

[19]Dunster was invited to serve as President after an initial disaster (academic and parietal) with the first master, also called "professor," Nathaniel Eaton. In his Memorandum of 1653, prepared when he was later defending himself for having come to espouse believers' baptism (see below text at nn. 101ff.), Dunster refers to the overseers not by any particular name, simply as "About ten magistrates and sixteen elders," whom he elsewhere styles "Honorable and Reverend." Morison, *The Founding of Harvard College*, Appendix E, 448ff. Dunster says he was called to instruct, not specifically to be President. Thomas Danforth says that he was invited to be President, *College Book III*, Colonial Society of Massachusetts, 15, 173. Morison surmises that the perhaps indecisive if not indolent Twelve were augmented to give resonance to the call to Dunster. Morison, *The Founding of Harvard College*, 241, n. 2.

New England's First Fruits, part one on the Indian mission, part two on the College.[20] In the main account of this work, the members of the committee of Twelve were, for the first time, called "overseers," the first recorded usage in this sense in English.[21] In the Latin theses, the sitting committee succeeding to the Twelve (which had largely dispersed before the accession of Dunster in 1640) was addressed, among other magistrates and ministers, as *"fidelissmi inspectores."*[22] Neither the English nor the Latin has an academic precedent for this title.

Dunster may have known that the first use of the word "overseer" was by William Tyndale, translator of the Bible into English, who remarked in 1530: "Those ouerseers which we now call Byshops after the Greek, were always bidyng in one place to governe the congregation."[23] The Puritans, like Dunster, almost by definition opposed by bishops in England, would have been impatient with even low-church bishops.

Use of the term "overseers" in the plural to denote elders with oversight and governance, however, had a special scriptural sanction in Acts 20:28 where the term *"episkopoi"* was rendered "overseers" in both the Geneva Bible of 1557 and the King James Version of 1611. The passage occurs within Paul's farewell address to the ruling and teaching elders of Ephesus (20:17–38).[24] The Geneva Bible reads: "Take hede ... to all the flocke, whereof the holy Gost hath made you *Ouersears*, to *governe* the Church of God." The King James version used "rule" instead of "govern"; this may, in part, explain the alternative term used by the Overseers of themselves as Governors. In the Latinization of the office Dunster naturally eschewed the Vulgate *"episcopi"* and contrived to use *"inspectores"* to obviate further any suggestion of ecclesiastical oversight that would unduly enter into the internal matters of the College apart from finances and discipline.[25] The passage in Acts sanctions the term "overseer" in a new academic sense (in place of visitor/*visitator* with its prelatical, canonical and princely connotation).

Among the Overseers was Governor John Winthrop, who recorded the

[20]The text, first published in 1643, is reprinted in full by Morison, *The Founding of Harvard College*, Appendix D.

[21]*The Oxford English Dictionary*, 12 vols. with supplement in 4 numbered vols., Supplement (Oxford, 1982), 3: 175.

[22]Morison, *The Founding of Harvard College*, Appendix D, 438.

[23]*The Oxford English Dictionary*, 7: 322, citing *An Answere to Sir Thomas More's Dialogue* (1530) in William Tyndale, *Works* (London, 1572), 1: 252.

[24]Dunster would not have tolerated the idea of presbyterial oversight of a local gathered church but would have construed the "Flock" to be the whole Puritan colony and its central College to be the training ground of its future shepherds and guardians. Dunster was seeking for a new English and Latin equivalent of "university visitor." Cambridge's *colleges*, however, did not usually have visitors. Oxford's did.

[25]His chosen Latin term is found only once in Scripture as the *inspector* of the heart, Proverbs 24:12.

commencement with satisfaction. On petition of President Dunster, the Court ordered, on September 27, 1642, that the new overseers be granted quasi-corporate powers. The Board was to consist of all the magistrates of the Colony (that is, the assistants annually elected by church members) and the "teaching elders" (pastors and teachers) of the six towns. Nine clerics thus served on the Board along with the Governor, the Deputy-Governor and 11 magistrates. Provisions were made for the replacement of each such member. The President of the College was also *ex officio* a member of the Board.[26] This senior Board of the Reverend the Honorable Overseers of varying composition and authority has had a virtually continuous history to the present.[27] That the name "overseers" for members of this Board was not at once fixed is suggested by its only record before the College Charter, namely, that of December 27, 1643, wherein they call themselves "Governours of Harvard College."[28] (It was this meeting that authorized the *Veritas* seal, hence called the Overseers' Seal.)

The use of the word "overseers" to describe the body that was, at times in the seventeenth century, much more authoritative than the College Corporation of the President, Fellows and tutors was perhaps inspired by a law of Elizabeth in 1601 that made provision for "overseers of the poor" in each parish.[29] (The College in the wilderness was relatively poor compared to those in the motherland.)

That 12 magistrates and ministers served from 1636 to 1642 surely suggests a conscious attempt to reach for an old covenantal and apostolic number, although the immediate task of "the committee"[30] was simply to oversee the building of a hall. Still, that hall had something of the character of the unifying Temple of Jerusalem under the reforming King Josiah. Although the Puritans were theologically barred from reference to any priesthood, save that of Jesus Christ, and even referred to their local meetinghouses as "synagogues," and were hence uncomfortable with a central priestly temple, for more than just economic reasons they could have thought of their College as being the spiritual and intellectual center of the Colony and eventually of the United Colonies. They easily thought of there having been "colleges in Israel" with "overseers."

A further clue as to how the Board was conceived is given by William Hubbard (1621–1704), pastor in Ipswich, an Overseer, who was appointed

---

[26]*Massachusetts Bay Colony Records*, II, 30, described by Morison, *The Founding of Harvard College*, 325ff.

[27]The Board of Overseers, however, was put in abeyance from 1686–1708 (except for one meeting on June 12, 1690) due to the loss of the Charter of the Colony itself and its replacement by a new charter for the royal Province. Morison, *Seventeenth Century*, 1: 327, n. 4.

[28]Morison, *The Founding of Harvard College*, 328.

[29]Act of Elizabeth 43 (1601), c. 281.

[30]*A General History of New England: From the Discovery to 1680*, 2d ed. (checked against the MS) (Boston, 1848), 237.

temporary president or rector of the College in 1688. Looking back to 1638 he said: "[I]t was a matter of great encouragement . . . to see one of the Schools of the Prophets set up; that from thence they might be supplied with persons fit to manage the affairs both of church and state at such a time when a supply was likely to fail elsewhere . . . . [U]nder whom [Dunster] that which was before but, at best, *Schola Illustris*, grew to the status or perfection of a College, and flourished in the profession of all liberal sciences."[31] Looking back in his *General History* and commenting on the Board as reorganized by the act of 1642, Hubbard said further that it was "a needful provision for the taking care of the sons of the prophets, over whom we know of old they were set that were able, both as prophets to teach, and judges to rule and govern."[32]

Schools of the prophets or "colleges" in Israel were readily inferred from such references to "sons of the prophets"[33] and were associated principally with Bethel, Hebron and, near Hebron, a city of three names: Kirjath-Sepher (City of books), Kirjath-Sannah and Debir.[34] In the Septuagint each city was rendered "*polis grammaton*," city of scribes. The judge-seer Samuel was reared in a priestly house in Bethel and later dwelt in Ramah. Samuel, the anointer of Saul and then of David, was regarded by the Reformed and hence by the New England Puritans as the head of the first school of the prophets—in the language of William Hubbard, at once a prophet and ruler in succession to the judges.[35] On this view Elijah and Elisha were seen, in their turn, as contributors to the academic tradition of scholarship in Israel. One repository of this kind of thinking, later referred to by Increase Mather on the same topic, was the work of Jacob Alting, professor of Groningen.[36] Dunster's successor, Hebraist President Charles Chauncy (1654–72), in his sermon after commencement in 1655, "Gods mercy shewed to His people in giving them a faithful ministry and schooles

---

[31]Ibid., 247.

[32]Ibid., 372ff. Emmanuel College could be thought back upon as such a school of the prophets (see below nn. 55–58), and the scriptural *loci* of Israelite prophetic schools, long since introduced into medieval university lore and collaterally strengthened by medieval and current rabbinical literature, were accessible to the Puritan divines and much used by them in their efforts to understand the needs of a biblical commonwealth in the wilderness and biblical sanctions for education beyond grammar schools. Morison has a substantial note on the school of the prophets in *The Founding of Harvard College*, 5, n. 1, but he does not take note of the strong scriptural and post-biblical Hebraisms in the sources adduced by the Reformed writers. I developed this further in my "*Translatio Studii*," 163–171.

[33]II Kings 2:3, 5.

[34]There are four biblical verses referring to the once Canaanite Kirjath-Sepher taken over in the period of Joshua and the judges, Joshua 15:15, 49; Judges 1:11, 12.

[35]See I Samuel 1–12, within which, the older and simpler account is preserved, 9:1–10, 16.

[36]J. Alting, *Hebraeorum respublica scholastica: sive historia academiarum* (Amsterdam, 1652), esp. 61–86.

of learning for the continual supplyes thereof,"[37] defended a trilingual education in Latin, Hebrew and Greek (alongside Aramaic and Syriac) and a broad curriculum. He also referred to "the College near Jerusalem" to which Hilkiah the priest at the behest of reforming King Josiah repaired to consult Huldah the Prophetess (2 Kings 22:14). And a third President, Increase Mather (1685–1701) referred to "the College of Elisha" in Jerusalem, evidently ascribing the founding of the "academy of Solomon" to the anointed prophet (1 Kings 4:34). There is more to say about the College as a school of the prophets, but with respect to the Overseers it is of interest that, at a later point (c. 1663), Jonathan Mitchell, minister in Cambridge, could write "of sundry Schools or colleges in Israel wherein scholars (or sons of ye prophets) were trained up, some of which Elijah (as their visitor) did visit."[38] "Visitor" here would be the older English term for "Overseer." Cambridge was referred to by Cotton Mather as New England's Kirjath-Sepher and Ramah.[39]

When, in 1701, Connecticut was considering a second New England Puritan college, there came from in and around Boston several advisory letters that throw further light on Harvard's Board of Overseers. Among them was a letter from Increase Mather, enclosing a much longer substantive letter from a "well-wisher to the Welfare of that Religious Colony," presumably from his son Cotton Mather. In this longer letter it was proposed that a synod of teaching elders and messengers from the churches of Connecticut be called "[t]o resolve upon an University, that shall be, The School of the Churches." The first president thereof was to be chosen by the same synod, and to see to it that "the pastors of such Twelve Churches, as the Synod shall pitch upon, be . . . the State Inspectors of the University."[40] In his proposal, Cotton Mather acknowledged that without concurrence of the local civil government and the Crown, this wholly synodal college might, indeed, not be able to grant the usual degrees of an English University; but Cotton Mather proposed that the graduate therefrom "intending the service of the Churches . . . be styled 'Instructus Ecclesiae', and that a graduate with any other intention be styled 'Ornatus Patriae'."[41] Although Cotton Mather's plan was not accepted in Connecticut as such, it throws light on how both the

[37](Cambridge, 1655). A copy of this sermon is available in New York Public Library and a photostat copy in Harvard University Archives; an excerpt from it is printed in P. Miller and T. Johnson, eds., *The Puritans: An Anthology* (New York, 1938), 705–08.

[38]*A Modell for the Maintaining of Students . . . at the College in Cambridge*, reprinted in *Harvard College Records, III*, Publications of the Colonial Society of Masssachusetts, 309.

[39]C. Mather, *Magnalia Christi Americana* (Boston, 1702), Book 4.12.6.

[40]F. Dexter, *Documentary History of Yale University . . . 1701–1745* (New Haven, CT, 1916), 1–34, esp. 2 and 4. As noted (above n. 25), "*Inspectores*" had become, through Henry Dunster's choice, the Latin term for Overseers, while Cotton Mather attached renewed importance to the replication of the covenantal apostolic Twelve, as in the provision in the Bay Colony for Twelve in 1636.

[41]Ibid.

Mathers understood their own College and its Board of Overseers. Surely, the recurrent number of 12 overseers cannot but suggest the judge-seers of the 12 tribes of the Old Covenant before the kings and also the 12 apostles of the first generation of the nascent Church of the New Covenant. The Mathers, in any case, must have looked back upon the original committee of Twelve of 1636 as indeed six ruling and six teaching elders constitutive of the emergent Board of the Reverend the Honorable the Board of Overseers.

Harvard College was always conceived to be a *school*, never a gathered *church*, even though prayers and sermons were part of the severely scheduled weekly regimen. On the Sabbath they all joined with the town in the services in the meetinghouse of the church in Cambridge. (So strong was this feeling that it was not until 1814 that a church was duly gathered "within the walls," of which the President and several professorial families became members.[42]) The sense of the College as, indeed, a school of the prophets and, in some new way, the central high place of New England as the New Israel, survived as late as 1722, when the convert from Judaism, rabbinically trained Judah Monis, tutor in Hebrew (1688–1734), was baptized in College Hall by the pastor of the First Church rather than in the local meetinghouse, with a great concourse.[43] So singular an event seemed to be best transacted at the symbolic center of New England, where a teacher of the Old Covenant was already serving as a teacher for the New.

C. The Corporation and Organic Metaphors for the College

It was the second board, the Corporation of 1650, that largely took over the more traditional collegiate character of Reformation Tudor colleges and thereby continued, in part, the medieval universitarian tradition. Other corporate and organic traits of the *Academia* of old Christendom, however, were also transmitted and developed in symbiosis with the Corporation. In other words, the corporate sense of the College, and of the University that grew out of it, is not monopolized by the interior history of only the Board that bears the corporate name, the oldest continuous corporation in the United States.[44]

If the New England Puritans were nominalists, as it were, in their ecclesiology, they were at least moderate nominalists in their conception of their College. In the history of corporations and partnerships from the time of Roman law right into the age of Sir Edward Coke a number of Latin terms were available to denote fictional persons at law, aggregates that collectively had a responsibility and a privilege different from that of a chance assemblage of persons, for example, *"corpus," "collegium," "societas"* and

[42]Meeting in University Hall designed for the purposes of a chapel, it was constituted a church in the presence of the pastor of the First Church and had provisions for baptism and communion.

[43]B. Colman, et al., *Discourse on the Baptism of Judah Monis* (Boston, 1722).

[44]J. Davis, *Essays in the Earlier History of American Corporations* (Cambridge, MA, 1917), 20ff.

"*universitas.*"[45] Much legal learning goes into distinguishing between a body that is an institutional creature of the state (*Anstalt*) in the tradition of Roman law and a body that is a fellowship or partnership that rises up and assumes collective responsibility (perhaps regulated by the state) in the tradition of German law (*Genossenschaftsrecht*). Within these legal collectivities there is attention as to whether the head of the body can function only with the consent of the fellow members (for example, the chapter) or whatever the collectivity be convened and consulted.[46]

Public and private corporations were not clearly distinguished in England in the seventeenth century and hence not in the eastern seaboard colonial charters for cities, corporate towns, and in corporate societies for business, military, philanthropic and educational purposes. Among these corporations, the corporation sole, for example, of a parson, persisted in colonial/provincial law, even if not always by name, alongside the much more common corporate aggregate.[47] Corporations in England were normally created by letters patent or by charter from the Crown,[48] although it was admitted that corporations could be created by Act of Parliament. Moreover, many bodies that exercised corporate powers by immemorial custom, by prescription or at common law without a specific grant were deemed to have obtained the implicit consent of the king.

That there is a distinctively Christian, as opposed to Graeco-Roman,

---

[45]Berman, *Law and Revolution*, 606, n. 40, citing P. Gillet, *La personalité juridique* (Malmes, 1927). Berman, dealing primarily with the Papal Revolution under Gregory VII Hildebrand, which he assesses as creative in its universalizing thrusts beyond the canon law, mentions the English or Puritan Revolution in ibid., 15, 21, 24. Earlier, Frederic William Maitland (d. 1906), legal scholar of England and the Church of England, translator also of the Berlin authority on natural law and corporations, Otto von Gierke (d. 1921), recognized the significance of corporations or *corpora mystica* and found in them Roman law and German antecedents. Maitland was also disposed to see the Christian component by way of canon law. See Maitland's chapters "The Corporation Sole," "The Crown as Corporation," "The Body Politic," "Trust and Corporation," in F. Maitland, *The Collected Papers*, ed. H. Fisher, 3 vols. (Cambridge, 1911), 3: 210–270, 285–303, 321–404.

[46]Berman devotes a whole section to "Corporation Law as the Constitutional Law of the Church," in *Law and Revolution*, 215–21. Berman does not cite Ernst Kantorowicz, who covers some of the same ground from antiquity into the Tudor period in his *The King's Two Bodies: A Study in Medieval Political Theology* (Princeton, 1957).

[47]Davis, *Essays in the Earlier History*, 20ff., 49, 75.

[48]Hence the dictum of Edward Lord Coke (d. 1634) of 1612 that "none but the King alone can create or make a corporation." *Case of Sutton's Hospital*, 10 Coke 33b.

It has been shown, however, in the High Erastian Anglican-Puritan controversy over competing conceptions of the corporation that, despite his dictum, Coke in general sought to articulate the inherent substance in the corporation of prescription and to safeguard its implied sphere of unencumbered competence and inviolability, and the same for even a royally-chartered corporation. The Puritans and common lawyers sought to safeguard the plenary competence of a corporation or society without undue interference from the royal prerogative. D. Little, "Coke and the Law of Corporations," *Religion, Order, and Law: A Study in Pre-Revolutionary England*, 3d ed. (Chicago, 1984), 189–217.

strand in all corporate theory in the Tudor period from the Middle Ages has been argued and therewith also even the distinctiveness of the English development in the Tudor and early Stuart periods.

All over Europe in the Reformation era the medieval conception of a clerical university had been transformed into a national or princely territorial, that is, civil institution, comprehensively serving the objectives of both sword and crozier. The Tudor colleges in England further dissolved the old line between chivalric and clerical education and made the college responsible for both political and ecclesiastical careers. While not clear-cut, the Tudor and Stuart lawyers, behind the envisioners of Harvard College, were original in largely replacing the notion of the legal corporation as a metaphor of an organological *corpus* of head and varying members with the notion of a body politic replicating itself by the legal fiction of a self-perpetuation of functions.[49] Therewith the concept of the *universitas* eventually superseded the more organological unity of head and limbs as the corporational succession in perpetuity in time into eternity.[50] Yet both these successional and

[49]In corporational theory and speculation, thought moved from the organological imagery of members of a body politic to succession in function in perpetuity. This point is illuminated by Kantorowicz, *The King's Two Bodies*, 409–31. Kantorowicz gives considerable attention to Tudor theory and practices into the reign of James I, but without special attention to university corporations. However, out of his resistance to the academic oath imposed by the Board of Regents at Berkeley, where he was professor of medieval history, Kantorowicz wrote a tract for the time, in which he drew contemporary implications of his conviction as to the relative autonomy of church, state and university, symbolized by the three gowns of the clergy, the judges and the professors. *The Fundamental Issue: Documents and Marginal Notes in the University of California Loyalty Oath* (n.p., 1950), which has been placed in a larger setting in tribute to the scholar by R. Giesey, "Ernst H. Kantorowicz Scholarly Triumphs and Academic Travails in Weimar Germany and the United States," *Publications of the Leo Baeck Institute, Yearbook* (1985): 191–202.

[50]Medieval law among canonists, legists and common lawyers alike had come to know indeed at least five kinds of "bodies politiques" or *corpora mystica* or corporations. The term *corpus mysticum* itself was derived from Scripture in a combination of Jesus' words at the Last Supper: "This is my body . . . " and from Pauline references to the eucharistic body of Christ and to the Church as the body of Christ, "Now you are the body of Christ and individually members of it" (I Cor. 6:15, 12:12, 27; Col. 2:19; etc.). In quoting Genesis 2:24, "For this reason man shall leave his father and mother and be joined to his wife and the two shall become one 'flesh'," the author of the epistle to the Ephesians declares: "This is a great *mystery*, and I take it to mean Christ and the Church" (5:33). In the course of the eucharistic controversies in the Carolingian period the eucharistic bread transmuted was for the first time called in quasi-Pauline language the *corpus mysticum*. By the thirteenth century this seemed to the Latin scholastics as insufficiently precise for what was henceforth to be called directly the sacramental transubstantiated *corpus Christi*. And as this usage spread, the older term *"corpus mysticum"* was freed first in extension to the whole Church, again in time and space (in the original Pauline sense but with *mysticum* now reinforcing it), then to the Christian kingdom, eventually to the village, the city and also to the whole world as all mystical collectivities, mystical bodies. The modern scholastic Latin for medieval Christendom interpenetrating society, the *corpus Christianum*, belongs to this line of usage (though of nineteenth century scholarly invention). See, generally, H. de Lubac, *Corpus Mysticum*, 2d ed. (Paris, 1949); Kantorowicz, *The King's Two Bodies*, 409-31. Berman cites the

organic concepts or metaphors of the corporation were, in the terms of the presentation here, "organic" as distinguished from "covenantal" or "voluntarist," the motif prevailing in New England Puritan society.

English jurists failed to make a clear distinction between the body politic and the supra-individual personage of the royal or abbatial or episcopal dignity. Tudor jurists, in effect, fused two different currents in corporate thought, the organic and the successional. From this fusion a number of interrelated concepts of the corporation emerged.

Richard Hooker, that major Elizabethan theorist of the *Ecclesia Anglicana*, said of Parliament as representing the whole English Body, politic and ecclesiastical, and, by implication, of other *corpora mystica* within the realm: "Wherefore as any man's deed past is good as long as him selfe continueth: so the act of a publique *societie* of men done five hundreth yeares sithence standeth as theirs, who presently are of the same societies, because corporations are immortall: we were then alive in our predecessors, and they in their successors do live still."[51] Tudor England had been, in a word, altogether replete with corporational imagery, even to the point of some confusion. Francis Bacon had written, reflecting impatiently on the common confusion of the day about the king as corporation or as corporation sole, the king in two bodies, corporate and natural: "Some say [such and such pertains] . . . to the Law, some to the crown, some to the kingdom, some to the body politic of the king: so there is confusion of tongue amongst them. . . ."[52]

A comparable confusion is evident in the rise of Harvard. The corporate unity which had once been called "*corpus mysticum*," "*dignitas*" or "*universitas*"—in reference to several organic unities besides the *studium generale* from medieval into early modern times—had once been distinguished from the collective unity of a *societas* or partnership. But now the fellows (*socii*) of the College were granted by the General Court the status of a corporation or a "body politique" in perpetuity.[53] In trying to descry the organic, as distinguished from the covenantal or voluntarist, thrusts in New England's first College, the late medieval and early modern terms can indeed be illuminating but also misleading.

In any event, the "organic" character of the College (and the later University) that issued from the act of foundation in 1636 and the charter of incorporation in 1650 does not adhere to, or subsist wholly in, that part of the institution that came exclusively at Harvard to bear the name of The Corporation. For easily explained historical circumstances, the dignity of the

---

same scriptural passages as decisive for the evolution of the concept of the corporation in the law of Western Christendom in his *Law and Revolution*, 216ff.

[51]R. Hooker, *The Laws of Ecclesiastical Polity*, ed. W. Hill, Folger Library Edition (Cambridge, MA, 1977) 1: 103.

[52]*Post-nati*, 651, quoted by Kantorowicz, *The King's Two Bodies*, 448, n. 427.

[53]See above n. 37.

Corporation came to be attached to the President and Fellows, although the nomenclature long remained fluid, and there came to be tutors and resident fellows who were not members of the Corporation.

It is quite plausible that when President Dunster petitioned for incorporation, and when the General Court granted the charter, the model of an integral English college was generally in the mind of all. Foremost as model was Emmanuel College, a Tudor Puritan college.[54] In the incorporation of Emmanuel in 1584, there had been a Master (Laurence Chaderton), eight fellows (who taught and studied on stipends provided by the endowment) and several social-economic classes of students, namely, four scholars, a number of fellow-commoners (students who dined with the fellows) and pensioners and sizars (undergraduates who received a certain quotient of aid, the size). The reason that the Harvard Corporation became discrepant from this earlier Puritan collegiate model lay: (1) in the difficulty of maintaining a comparable corps of resident teaching/studying fellows on the stipends that could be raised in New England; (2) in the relative youth of the students of all ranks; and (3) in the greater disposition of the New England fellows and tutors to leave Cambridge in response to a pastoral call. Consequently, the Harvard Corporation of President, Treasurer and five other Fellows became by the end of the seventeenth century, non-residential, non-salaried, deriving their living from other sources than the endowment, except for the resident President.[55] Nevertheless, the Emmanuel College model remained potent. In the statute of its foundation, Sir Walter had in 1584, reinforced by supplement in 1587, expressly indicated the purpose of Emmanuel as a "seed-ground" for fellows and scholars devoted to sacred theology, a seminary, "a seed-plot of learned men for the supply of the Church."[56] Harvard College similarly called itself and was called a seminary.[57]

[54]The founder of Emmanuel College, Sir Walter Mildmay, however, disavowed directly to Queen Elizabeth the adjective she had used in querying him about his "Puritan Foundation," as this adjective was construed by her to imply disloyalty to the Established Church and hence to her State, as it had been used exhortingly by Calvin. For the royal exchange with Elizabeth, see T. Fuller, *History of the University of Cambridge* (London, 1655), 2: 147, quoted by Morison, *The Founding of Harvard College*, 93. For Calvin's usage in 1556, see S. Neal, *The History of the Puritans, or Protestant Non-Conformists*, 4 vols. (London, 1732–38), 1: 72, quoted by Quincy, *History*, 1: 351. Neal, whose *History of New England* incited Thomas Hollis to his philanthropies of Harvard in 1721 and 1728, received an honorary M.S. from Harvard on January, 1721. His *History* was, in part, based on the *Magnalia* and yet aroused some local criticism because of the occasional critical treatment of local worthies and their institutions. See C. Shipton, ed., "Sibley's Harvard Graduates," *Massachusetts Historical Society* 6 (1942): 594–97.

[55]President Increase Mather was himself non-resident and resisted attempts to dislodge him from his parsonage of the Second Church of Boston.

[56]E. Schuckbergh, *Emmanuel College* (London, 1904), 23; ibid., 24, quoted by W. Hudson, "The Morison Myth Concerning the Founding of Harvard College," *Church History* 8 (1939): 151, 153.

[57]The term seems to have been English Counterreformational in origin. There are two related metaphors in the adaptation of the horticultural *seminarium* for a priestly (then a ministerial)

Emmanuel College in 1588 (thus, near its inception) had adopted the order to meet as a whole body for a periodic postprandial "mutual conference and communication of giftes" (sanctioned by I Cor. 14:23ff.), which meeting was to be opened by the Master with prayer for all "Prophets and Sonnes of the Prophets." Daily services were also held in the College chapel without surplice or the use of the Book of Common Prayer (at communion the elements were received while the members were seated around a table).[58]

For all the scriptural imagery and covenantal sanctions prevailing in the Bay Colony at large, Harvard College was, as of 1650, incorporated by the General Court as a "body politic" with several immunities reminiscent of medieval papal and imperial charters for a *studium generale*. While ideas of corporate thinking were inchoate,[59] and the distinction between a partnership or society of fellows (*socii*) and a corporation was even less clear in the Colony than in England, the Court could not but have been aware that the making of a corporation had been, up to then, the prerogative of the Crown.[60] Yet, on May 30, 1650, in the aftermath of the Second Civil War, the High and General Court of the Bay Colony—considering themselves the colonial counterpart of the Rump Parliament of some 50 Independent members surviving from the Long Parliament—granted a corporation to the College fully cognizant of their quasi-sovereign gesture.

The charter is notable in several other respects. Modeled on English college charters (evidently from the drafter's memory), the charter did not expressly accord the right to grant degrees, even though, or perhaps because, the College, under the Overseers, had already granted its first degrees in 1642. (As already suggested, the Board of Overseers may have been serving in this capacity as an academic *universitas*.) Instead of degrees and academic matters, the phrasing of the charter of the Corporation stressed the economic, financial and disciplinary aspects of college life and exemptions from the burden of temporal order:

[F]or the advancement of all good literature, arts, and sciences in Harvard College . . . and all . . . necessary provisions, that may conduce to the education of the English and Indian youth of this country, in knowledge and godliness, it is therefore ordered . . . that the said Col-

---

school, that of priestly progeny and that of divine seedlings. John Fisher, martyred bishop of Rochester, seems to have been the source of the first and Reginald Cardinal Pole, the mediator if not the originator of the second.

[58]William Hubbard, class of 1642, looking back on Harvard beginnings, called the whole of life and discipline in new Cambridge "one of the Schools of the Prophets . . . that from thence they [the Colonists] might be supplied with persons fit to manage the affairs both of church and state." W. Hubbard, *General History* (Cambridge, MA, 1848), 247; cf. above, n. 24; Morison, *The Founding of Harvard College*, 228.

[59]Morison, *Seventeenth Century*, 9ff.

[60]CF above n. 48.

lege . . . shall be a Corporation, consisting of seven persons . . . and that the said seven persons or the greater number of them, procuring the presence of the Overseers . . . and by their counsel and consent, shall have power . . . to elect a new President, Fellows (*socii*), or Treasurer . . . , which said President and Fellows shall forever hereafter . . . be *one body politic and corporate* in law . . . , and shall have perpetual succession . . . and also may sue and plead, or be sued and impleaded . . . in all Courts and places of judicature. . . . And shall have power . . . to make a common seal for the use of the said Corporation [evidently different from the Overseers' *Veritas* seal of 1642]. . . . choose such officers and servants . . . and make such orders and by-laws . . . [as necessary], provided the said orders be allowed by the Overseers. . . . And further be it ordered . . . that [all properties] to the President or College appertaining . . . shall from henceforth be *freed from all civil impositions, taxes, and rates*; all goods to the said Corporation, or to any scholars [students] thereof appertaining, shall be exempted from all personal civil offices, military exercises or services, watchings, and wardings. . . . [61]

Socius was first used of the Corporation fellow in 1650.[62] The College was the first of only two corporations chartered by the Bay Colony.[63] The mystery of "the body politique" created by the Court of the Bay Colony—itself the expansion of a royally chartered commercial planters' corporation become a commonwealth—was probably mostly subliminal with most of the magistrates and deputies who granted the College charter of 1650. It is, nevertheless, plausible that the petitioner, President Dunster himself, was for his part quite aware of what he sought for the College under its Overseers, namely, an organic college with teaching fellows incorporated, to enjoy the semi-autonomy of an English College of resident teaching and governing fellows, fellow-commoners and all the rest.

Even though the College, as Corporation, because of the youthfulness and transience of most of the co-opted tutors among the fellows, soon evolved into something more likè a non-residential board of trustees of a charitable trust, the corporational, as distinguished from a covenantal, sense of the College was duly transmitted in the genetic code. For, in the course of time, other organic traits would develop, some of them distinctive to the American college, to perpetuate the organic metaphors and the tissues of loyalty in academic institutional life.

[61]Morison surmises that the charter was drawn up by Richard Billington, magistrate and Overseer, the only qualified trained lawyer at the time, drafter of the *Laws and Liberties*, 1648. See Morison, *Seventeenth Century*, 1: 9ff. The parchment charter is preserved in the Harvard University Archives. It is printed in full as accurately as can be rendered in print by Morison, *The Seventeenth Century*, 5–8; by Quincy in modernized spelling and punctuation in *History*, 1: 589–91. The long quotation presented here represents a selection of about one third of the whole.

[62]Quincy, *History*, 2:269.

[63]The other of 1652 was for water delivery in Boston.

The academic oath, for example, the analogue to the ever renewable church covenant and to the solemnly repeated town covenant, did not develop at Harvard.[64] The oath and the covenant were alike solemn pledges. The covenant represented a scriptural revival for the formation and sustenance of the town and church. The oath could have been, by analogy and precedent, incorporated into the usage of the Board of Overseers of the Corporation and required of the other tutors and the young "scholars" of the College. The academic oath, indeed, had strong precedent in the medieval university. It was originally made to the (elected) rector by teachers in the various faculties. There were also oaths taken by the degree recipients at commencement. The solidarity and independence of any university, achieved through this academic oath to the rector, was partly undercut by making of it an oath of allegiance to the king, first in the reign of Louis XI of France (d. 1483). A consequence of the Reformation was that the oath was generally sworn in many parts of Christendom by transfer from the rector to the prince or king in the nationalization of the university in an age of confessional conflict.[65] There were three kinds of oaths in English society at the time: the oath of office, the oath of allegiance to the state or university or college and the test oath.

The founding fathers of Harvard, through the Board and the Corporation, had much experience with Stuart oaths in and out of the university. They were not disposed to replicate this system, the consequences of which they had themselves in part evaded when required on oath to uphold the formularies of the Church of England. Moreover, there was a scriptural injunction against oaths (Matt. 1 5:36ff.). However it came about, the members of the Board, the Corporation and the teaching staff did not take any oath in the seventeenth century at Harvard.

It has been argued, on the basis of a very careful sifting of the Harvard archival material, that the degree-granting privilege exercised by the College as of its first commencement of 1642 were the immunities of 1650 not

[64]Samuel Eliot Morison first wrote about academic oaths at Harvard when he took the lead in resisting the enactment of the Teachers' Oath by the Legislature in 1935. See Morison, "Harvard and Academic Oaths," *Harvard Alumni Bulletin* 37 (1934): 682–86. He carried the historical argument further in "Three Oathless Centuries in Massachusetts," Remarks at the Hearing to Repeal the Teachers' Oath Act (of 1935) at the State House Boston: Massachusetts Society for Freedom in Teaching, 3 Joy Street, 1936. These were spirited communications, although in the second Morison records but dismisses as precedent the oaths of the Hollis professors. The substance of each communication appears, alongside the testimony of Gaetano Salvemini, exile from Fascism, in *Massachusetts Law Quarterly* 21 (1936). Morison said it was certain that no oath was required of Charles Chauncy when, on renouncing further discussion in public on pedobaptism, he succeeded Baptist Dunster, whose doubts about the scriptural basis of the practice he initially and diffidently shared. For Kantorowicz on the academic oath, see above n. 49.

[65]P. Kibre, "Academic Oaths at the University of Paris in the Middle Ages," *Essays in Medieval Thought, Presented in Honor of Austin Patterson Evans* (New York, 1955), 123–37.

instances of colonial collegiate Puritan polemical parallelism with the two Anglican universities about to be overwhelmed in the turmoil of civil war, but rather a natural development overseas of more ordinary forces, even though Englishmen subsequently and elsewhere were not given to establishing colleges and universities, unlike, for example, the Spaniards.[66] The boldness of the College in granting degrees and any high theory of the quasi-sovereign colonial collegiate corporation are on this view explained as a consequence of simple confusion as between a corporation as charitable trust and a corporation as a body politic. Harvard degrees may have, indeed, gained acceptance primarily because, henceforth, they were honored in Oxford and Cambridge as equivalent to their own, and usage consolidated precedent.[67] According to the less dramatic view of what the revolutionary Puritan society of semi-Erastian non-Separating Congregationalists had accomplished, the College evolved quite simply in a quite natural growth from an advanced "high school" through college to embryonic academy/university without much distinctively theological and constitutional reflection on what was taking shape. But the thrust of the present study is that this development was at once revolutionary and conservative.

The College as a whole and not only its largely non-residential Corporation surely became a kind of *corpus Christi mysticum*, without, of course, resort to the full terminology. In a society where communicant membership in the local church depended upon the eternal decrees of the Almighty and on the congregationally verified private experience in each believer of the confirmatory covenant of grace, and where in the church of predestined saints each believer clove individually to Christ as a Husband,[68] the venerable image of the church as Bride and Mother came to attach gradually and distinctively to the common College of New England as a mystical body, a fostering mother. The College of President, tutors and young "scholars" in their early teens was a kind of domestic church, a *mater ecclesia academica*, that was bound through the storied generations back through the English university-colleges to the University of Paris and then much further back to the reputed colleges of biblical Palestine. This unique mystical body stood in contrast to the voluntaristic, covenantal, gathered Cambridge church, which alone administered communion to the President, probably to most of the tutors, but to only those few young scholars who could qualify experientially (as with their fellow youths of village and town).

---

[66]Hoffmann, *Commonwealth College*. For the observation on the English reserve about founding colleges elsewhere in the empire, see F. Rudolph, *The American College and University* (New York, 1962), 4; and earlier observers noted by O. and N. Handlin, *The American College and American Culture: Socialization as a Function of Higher Education* (New York, 1970), 6.

[67]Cf. Bailyn, et al., *Glimpses of the Harvard Past.*

[68]See T. Shephard, *The Autobiography of Thomas Shepard* (Boston, 1832).

The College was a uniquely central academic body, where selected and intellectually qualified youths were still under discipline for the acquisition of saving truth in the three languages of the cross, preparatory to their becoming ministers for the local churches and magistrates and merchants in the theocracy.

In 1652 Dunster lengthened the B.A. course from three to four years in accordance with usage in Old Cambridge and accordingly reduced the term for the M.A. from three to two years (in a temporarily controversial transition), confirmed by the Overseers. Thereupon Harvard degrees, indeed, gained readier acceptance in Oxford and Cambridge as equivalent to their own, since the mother universities were themselves under the Puritan Protectorate of Oliver Cromwell.

In the era of the founding of Harvard the term "university" was not often used of the College, although it did appear as early as 1647 in a law providing for schools "to instruct youth sofar as they may be fitted for the Universitie."[69] The Latin *"Universitas,"* with its corporate resonance, is not documented in the founding century in New England. The more common Latin universitarian term was, in fact, *"Academia,"* used commonly in the seventeenth century on the Continent but also used of the English universities. In the (only provisionally operative) Charter of 1692 with its perduring seal, *Christo et Ecclesiae,* Harvard College is denoted in Latin as the *Academia.*

During the period of uncertainty, between the end of the Congregational Puritan government of the Bay Colony and that of the Province, with its royally appointed Governor, there were altogether five attempts to secure a new College Charter.[70] The view generally prevailed that "with the cow dead, the calf in her belly is dead." The first of these five trial charters was the most significant because it was proposed by Increase Mather, who had himself negotiated the new provincial charter and who had immersed himself during his four years under three sovereigns in England (James II, William II and Mary) in the history of universities and their governance and degree-granting authority. In fact, the College operated under the provision of Mather's proposed College charter from 1692 to 1696.

Although the magisterial historians of Harvard have been harsh on President Increase Mather (1685–1701), in his self-aggrandizing pomposity, his conception of the University and the Corporation shed much light on the New England Puritan mind in the late seventeenth century with respect to its academic center.

Increase Mather, who had a pretty clear idea of what would be acceptable to the Crown, sought and obtained from the new provincial legislature

---

[69]*Massachusetts Bay Colony Records,* I, 213, 203, quoted by Morison, *Seventeenth Century,* 1: n. 72.

[70]They are all printed by Quincy, *History,* 1: 594–600.

the provisional grant of the new charter of incorporation,[71] which named ten Fellows as constitutive of the Corporation, with Mather continuing on as President or Rector. The provisional grant described the Corporation as "a body politic and corporative at law" with "perpetual succession," and lodged with the Corporation the right to confer degrees, including the higher degrees in theology, law and medicine. Mather also called the Corporation "a society." Missing from his charter of 1692 was any provision for the Board of Overseers or for any other visitorial committee. It was, indeed, for want of such a provision that his proposed College charter was finally rejected by the Crown. Another notable feature of the Corporation, as reconceived by Mather, was that it was still non-residential. Even he resisted residency, as he considered his post in the Second Church of Boston to require him to maintain his parsonage there. (He was also obsessed with the desire to return to England as agent of the Province and intended to make his removal thither his major change.) Thus his Corporation consolidated authorities and responsibilities that had been previously lodged in the two Boards, the Corporation now becoming briefly like the Overseers both non-residential and visitorial. At the same time, his enlarged Corporation was not representative of the government through authorities *ex officiis*. Indeed, the Corporation and hence the Academy in Cambridge, as it was now styled, was for four years understood as separated from the provincial government, all with the approval of Mather's friend and protege, Sir William Phips, the royal Governor.

The Corporation of 1650 was, nevertheless, in 1708 found, after five attempts at a new charter, "not to have been void or nulled." The Corporation, reduced from ten back to the original seven Fellows, nevertheless carried over some gathered strength, not only of law and prescription, but also from the brief episode under Mather's consolidative charter for the Academy. For Mather's Corporation had proceeded to award, besides the earned doctorate in theology to its esteemed drafter, also two earned bachelor degrees in theology, one of them to John Leverett, the President of Harvard from 1708–24; these higher degrees were never subsequently challenged.

Besides the Corporation and the Board, other corporational motifs are detectible from near the beginning of Harvard history in its constitutional, statutory and customary law, as the College as a whole with her *alumni* gradually assumed the prerogatives of a university community. The College as a whole became part legal *ficta persona*, part *corpus mysticum*, by convention, custom and accumulated emotional heritage and devotion. It remained distinct from the churches of the Standing Order and partly independent from the government, whether that of the town, Colony, Province or Commonwealth. It evolved as third eminence, alongside the

---

[71]Quincy deals with the Mather Charter, *History*, I, ch. 4; Morison, *Seventeenth Century*, I.

churches and the state, even in the period of the largely undisturbed Congregational Puritan theocracy.

D. The Alumni of Alma Mater, *Academia Harvardiensis*

Neither the documents constitutive of the Board of Overseers nor those constitutive of the Corporation include any phrase like *"mater universitatae"* or *"matrix"* of a university in anticipation of the rise of several colleges about the original college as there had been, for example, in the Elizabethan charter of Trinity College Dublin, 1591, likewise a single-college university.[72] Harvard College, however, was in organic development (if not in conceptualization) the mother of the later full-fledged University, and its degrees were and still are given corporately by the President and Fellows of Harvard *College* on recommendation to the Board of Overseers. The maternal and organic metaphors were frequently used to describe the fecund central institution of the whole of New England until 1701 (when Yale was founded) as *Alma Mater* with her loyal and supportive *alumni*.

It is striking that, while in their intensely spiritual, almost mystical, communicant church life, the Puritans became brides to Christ their Husband,[73] in their College life, their College became for them a nurturing collective mother figure, *Alma Mater*, and they her *lifelong* "sons." Among our few surviving American collegiate Latin terms felt to be pulsatingly classical, the terms *"alumni"* and *"alumnae,"* with Latin masculine and feminine plurals variously pronounced, and *"Alma Mater,"* too, are alike essentially American Latinisms and specifically Harvard contributions in their specialized American collegiate usage.

"Alumni" is almost unintelligible to Europeans, who consider themselves *"anciens éléves,"* doctors, licentiates or simply graduates of such and such a university in any of their tongues, but not lifelong *alumni* in the extended American sense. They will generally have for their university no generic endearing name.[74]

The oldest recognized usage in English of *"alumnus"* in the collegiate sense is in a passage not from some London imprint but from the *Diary* of a New Englander, Samuel Sewall, dated October 3, 1696: "Lt. Govr/ William Stoughton/complemented [sic] the President [Increase Mather] &c,

---

[72]Here the fellows of the college convened as a university senate to grant degrees. Morison, *The Founding of Harvard College*, 121–125, esp. n. 2.

[73]Cf. above text at nn. 4–6. Charles du Fresne Du Cange (d. 1688), *[Novum] Glossarium mediae et infimae Latinitatis*, incomplete A–O (Paris, 1934), 1: 210.

[74]*"Alma Mater"* in a classical dictionary designates the Great Mother Goddess Cybele or Ceyres. The multivolume *Du Cange*, ibid., has no leads. Under the entry *"alumni,"* one finds either nurslings of a pedagogue or of a day school under a governess for the children of prosperous families in the late Middle Ages and the Renaissance, or men fed at some lord's manorial table.

for all the respect to him, acknowlg'd [sic] his obligation and promis'd his Interposition for them as become such an Alumnus to such an Alma Mater."[75] Here is perhaps the earliest usage in English context of "*alumnus*" in the sense of a graduate loyally supporting his university in need, the nursling, as it were, taking care of his Fostering Mother in her old age or hour of trial.[76]

Sewall, the later Chief Justice and Diarist, had been a member of the Harvard class of 1671. He was resident fellow in the sense of tutor in 1674, recipient of the Master's degree in 1674.[77] He certainly would have been present at the commencement in 1677 and heard President Urian Oakes (acting or full President, 1675–84) in a witty Latin address twice refer to the College in a startling Latin trope, as a feminine rather than a masculine *corpus mysticum*:

> The fecundity of *Mater Academia* seems a happy omen, since this year she has brought forth six sons, whom she offers to be adored [with degrees] by your testimonials and suffrages. *Alma Mater* does not grow barren while she grows old; every year she grows big with a new *foetus*. Behold your sons, not unworthy of such a mother, whom she has brought forth in this turbulent year, who since she is poor, shows neither heaped-up wealth, nor Attalian garments . . . ; but useful sons, children trained up to honest disciplines, gentlemen educated like gentlemen (*liberi liberaliter educati*) . . . .[78]

When, then, a score of years later in a precarious moment in the career of the College, Sewall used the term "*alumnus*" in the sense of a supportive graduate—if he did not himself coin the term—he was then drawing on Harvard usage (perhaps strengthened by his own observations of old England college life in Cambridge and Oxford) that had begun to establish itself between 1645 and 1696, as all New England looked to its academic

---

[75]*The Diary of Samuel Sewall, 1674–1729*, ed. M. Thomas, 2 vols. (New York, 1973), 1: 357.

[76]As late as 1653, the academically creative Henry Dunster, appealing in his final distress for the testimony of loyal graduates of the College, wrote of them as "Accademical persons," not yet as *alumni*. See his Memorandum in self-defense when he espoused believers' baptism, printed by Morison, *The Seventeenth Century*, Appendix E, 451. President John Leverett (1708–24) would show a preference for "*Harvardinates*" in place of "sons of the Prophets," "sons of Harvard," ibid., 567. However, in Latin as in the deed of John Bulkley to Harvard in 1645, "*alumnus*" is used of himself in gratitude to President Dunster and the College. The Deed is printed by Quincy, *History*, 1: 505ff.

[77]Sewall defended in the affirmative the thesis question in Latin. "Whether original sin be both a sin and a punishment."

[78]"Oratio Cantabrigiae Nov-Anglorum in Comitys Academicis habita," August 14, 1677, Harvard University Archives, quoted and translated by Morison, *Seventeenth Century*, 2: 434 (emphasis added). Morison used the reference to *Liberi liberaliter educati* in general support of his view that Harvard College offered more than ministerial training.

center in Cambridge as the central shrine of the Reformed New Israel under a royally appointed Governor.[79]

In time, the sons of the prophets of Harvard would become sons of Fair Harvard, symbolized as feminine *Alma Mater*, to whom the *alumni* would remain loyal after success in the ministry, magistracy and business affairs, and to whom they would return annually at commencement, eventually to file past, in review, the current incumbents of the governing boards under whose tutelage they had once studied. In no such way are the graduates of European universities so linked together in supportive involvement as among Americans. Such sentiment likely developed because the boys who entered, sometimes younger even than those who enter a modern junior high school, were required by strict statute to reside at the College, and, as they ate, slept and worshiped much as in their natal homes, they developed an attachment as to a governess to whom a child will remain lifelong connected. No accounts of obstreperous behavior, violent conduct between the classes dining in the commons or the records of penalties imposed on them can obscure the growth of an unusual attachment to the College that has almost no counterpart among graduates of European university faculties. What was to become a distinctively American four year communal residential stage in the life of young people between their secondary and their professional education was shaped for posterity in Cambridge, a cultural artifact of New England civilization.[80]

III. THE *TRIPLEX MUNUS CHRISTI*

A. Church, Commonwealth and College

In the seventeenth century there was a common acceptance of the Reformed concept of the biblical theocracy, reflecting in its institutions the threefold office of Christ in *Academe*, in the local church and in the local and colonial government.

As did many Calvinists, New England societies took as scriptural a concept of Jesus Christ as Mediator between God and man (I Tim. 2:5) in three offices as Prophet, Priest and King (*propheta/doctor, sacerdos, rex*). This threefold office of Christ (*triplex munus Christi*) sanctioned in the New England theocracies the partial separation of authorities, the temporal, the ecclesiastical and the academic, in the town: the town hall, the church and

---

[79]Early usage for the Latin term in "the American sense" was in John Eliot's dedication in Latin of a copy of his *Indian Bible* (Cambridge, MA, 1663) for the library of his alma mater: "For Jesus College. Accept, mother, I pray, what a most humble *alumnus* offers, a son ever having thy prayers." S. Morison, *Builders of the Bay Colony* (Boston/New York, 1930), 291; cf. Morison, *The Founding of Harvard College*, 116.

[80]This usage and the feeling toward the college so developed over the generations that educated American men and women still think of themselves as belonging to the academic class of such and such a year wherever they are.

the academy occasionally to this day are seen painted white around a New England common.[81]

The *triplex munus Christi*, though not in any clear triadic formulation found in Scripture, had ample scriptural support. The Old Testament anticipated Jesus as the Christ in three offices. Kings and prophets were regularly anointed. Of the prophetic office, however, only Elisha among the Old Testament prophets is recorded as having been anointed to it (I Kings 19:16).

The *triplex munus Christi* was first formulated by the Church Fathers, notably Eusebius of Caesarea, the father of church history, and was liturgically and otherwise prominent in the ancient Church. Use of the *triplex munus Christi* largely lapsed or collapsed into the royal and priestly offices in the Middle Ages.

The *triplex munus Christi* became suddenly widespread at the outset of the Reformation Era, evidently having been reformulated for the first time by Erasmus in 1522.[82] (The role of Jesus Christ as mediator in his humanity and divinity became prominent in the lands of the Reformation to the extent that the role of Mary as Mediatrix receded or was indeed cut off.) Andreas Osiander of Nuremberg in 1530 wrote of Christ as annointed Prophet, King and High Priest. Martin Bucer of Straussburg in 1536 called Jesus "King of kings, high priest, and chief of the prophets."[83] In 1550 the Polish reformer, John Laski, superintendent of the Strangers' Church in London until the accession of Mary, gave prominence to Jesus Christ the Mediator in his *triplex munus* in several variants, but usually as King, Teacher/Prophet/Doctor and Pontifex.[84] Although Laski's writings were known to the founding fathers of New England, it was John Calvin's *Institutes* as of 1559 that promoted the term to universal status in New England.

The *triplex munus Christi* was thus well known to prospective New Englanders. It was clearly formulated in William Ames's *Marrow of Divinity*, the basic text in theology in Harvard for 150 years.[85] It appears, for example, in the church covenant of Dedham in 1638, which reads in part: "We doe . . . in ye name and presence of God, and of our Lord Jesus Christ . . . solemnly enter into covenant with ye the Lord our God professing . . . ye

[81]In the town of Sanbornton, New Hampshire, the three edifices are placed symmetrically on the hill and can be viewed from some distance as the architectural embodiment of the New England local sense of the threefold office of Christ.

[82]I have dealt with Erasmus in "Erasmianism in Poland, . . . , 1518–1605," *The Polish Review* 22 (1977): 3–50, esp. 31, 36–38.

[83]In his *Commentary on Psalms* (1536).

[84]The order of the three offices was not immediately stabilized. I have dealt with this in my "*Translatio Studii*." Since the term was substantially used in the documents of Vatican II, it was freshly studied by L. Schick, *Das Dreifache Amt Christi in der Kirche*. (Europäische Hochschulschriften, Reihe XXIII Theologie 171) (Frankfurt/Bern, 1982).

[85]W. Ames, *Marrow of Divinity*, trans. J. Eusden (Boston, 1968; original Latin ed., London, 1629), 132, 148.

Lord Jesus Christ our blessed Redeemer, to be ye only priest, prophet, and king of his church. . . . "[86] It appears in the covenant of the church in Woburn in 1642. The Confession of Faith of the church in Windsor, Connecticut (which had left Dorchester to become part of Thomas Hooker's colony) incorporated the *triplex munus Christi* in its covenant of 1647, which reads in part: "We . . . do here bind ourselves, in the presence of men and angels . . . to chose the Lord to serve him, and to walk in all his ways, and to keep all his commandments and ordinances, and his Christ to be our king, priest, and prophet . . . ."[87]

The *triplex munus Christi* also finds a prominent place in the Westminster Confession of Faith of 1647, adopted for substance of doctrine in every respect in the Cambridge Platform of the synod of 1648, save for the eschewing of presbyterian polity. When this Confession was substantially recast as a fully Congregationalist Declaration of Faith, in which New England divines had a hand, and adopted at the Savoy Palace in London right after the death of Oliver Cromwell in 1658, it was significantly amplified to read: "It pleased God in *a covenant made between them both*, to be the mediator between God and Man: the prophet, priest and king, the head and saviour of his Church, the heir of all things, and judge of the world."[88]

Calvin's appropriation of the *triplex munus Christi* in 1559 had long been influential. Yet, in his systematization of the fourfold ministry out of the disparate testimony of the New Testament, Calvin regarded the prophets along with the apostles as exercising extraordinary ministries that had lapsed with the close of the apostolic age. Nevertheless, some of his Puritan followers in England[89] interpreted I Corinthians 14:23ff. as legitimating lay prophecying or the right to discuss the meaning of Scripture under the inspiration of the same Holy Spirit that originally inspired the written Word. The Puritan William Perkins, however, already in his influential *The Art of Prophecying* (1592), insisted on the exclusively clerical privilege of prophecy, and he limited its scope: "There are two parts of Prophecie: Preaching the Word, and Conceiving of Prayer . . . And every prophet is partly the

---

[86]*The Record of Baptisms and Admissions to the Church and Dismissions Therefrom, Transcribed from the Church Records of the Town of Dedham, Massachusetts (1638–1845)*, ed. D. Hill (Dedham, MA, 1888), 12ff.; A. Lamson, *A History of the First Church in Dedham* (Dedham, MA, 1939), Note C, 82, of the town covenant of 1636, 32ff., see also above n. 20.

[87]W. Walker, ed., *The Creeds and Platforms of Congregationalism*, introd. D. Horton (Boston, 1960), 156.

[88]Walker, ed., *Creeds and Platforms*, 340–402, esp. 375ff.

[89]This understanding is evident, for example, in the prophecyings of Emmanuel College (above n. 54) which were evidently influenced by Jacob Acontius or Jacopo Aconcio (c. 1566). Aconcio gave wide circulation, from Transylvania to England, to the interpretation of I Corinthians 14:23ff. as the *lex sedentium*, the scriptural sanction for lay participation in reconstruing the sense of Scripture under the guidance of the Spirit that inspired it. This interpretation seems to have been taken over from the Anabaptists.

voyce of God, to wit, in preaching and partly the voyce of the people in the act of praying."[90] Accordingly, freedom of prophecy was largely clericalized also in New England and eventually institutionalized as the Thursday lecture. But the principle remained that the minister in the church, whether called pastor or teacher, was typologically the living counterpart of the ancient prophet. Calvin himself, while disallowing lay or even ministerial prophecy in the ancient Hebraic critical sense, did derive the office of teacher in the church, the second of his four ministries, from the sanction of Christ's prophetic office. Both he in Geneva, and Theodore Beza in Lausanne, understood the Reformed academies in their towns as the institutional extension of Christ's prophetic office among them.

At Harvard from near the beginning, the President of the College was a living *propheta*. We have already noted the practice of mutual conferences for prophecying in Emmanuel College[91] and how several New England divines envisaged their own College as modeled on the ancient schools of the prophets.[92] President Chauncy, already cited, distinguished in the Israelite School of Prophets or the "college of anointed Elisha" between "the sons of prophets" who were taught and disciplined and such other prophets as Elisha himself who had their calling *immediately* from God. He was emphatic on this point since the "calling of the Prophet is such an honour as the title was given to the Lord Jesus himself."[93]

Here we see the generic idea of prophecy as biblical study and discussion moving toward the elevation of the President of Harvard College as the Prophet for his school, society and church, with Christ himself understood as the preeminent *Propheta/Doctor* to whom the university was dedicated, and from whose sanction it could be construed as one of the three higher instances of the (by now hampered) bibliocracy within a royal province.

It is quite plausible, therefore, that the new seal of the Harvard *Academia*, undoubtedly conceived by Increase Mather, dedicated *Christo et Ecclesiae*, 1692[94] reflects his view in a parlous moment for the Harvard of the

---

[90]R. Henderson, *The Teaching Office in the Reformed Tradition: A History of the Doctoral Ministry* (Philadelphia, 1962). For the passage from Perkins, *Ars* (1592), see the English version of 1607 in W. Perkins, *Works*, 3 vols. (London, 1606–16), 3: 646.

[91]See above text at n. 54.

[92]See above text at nn. 33–39.

[93]H. Dunster, *Gods Mercy* (Cambridge, MA, 1655).

[94]Published as *Disceptatio scholastica* (Leiden, 1633). The first university of the Netherlands, Leiden (1574), had, amid Renaissance festivity, been dedicated to Minerva and the Muses. When the stockholders of the Estates of Friesland proclaimed the institution of the second university of the Netherlands in Franeker, they declared that in the divine Name it was dedicated "non Pallidi aut Musis, sed Christo et Ecclesiae."

Franciszek Lyra has traced the motto to the Polish theologian Jan Makowski of Franeker. See F. Lyra, *Grounds for Connections: The Pattern of Polish-American Literary Relations* (Warsaw, 1976), 91; restated in another context in "The Polish Bookshelf in Colonial America: A

original vision of Congregationalist errand in the wilderness. With the loss of a directly elected Governor under the new Provincial Charter that he himself had negotiated, it is likely that Increase Mather, who had studied extensively in the history and lore of universities, was thinking now of the international Reformed Church when he dedicated the New England *Academia* to the *Ecclesia*. For, although a Congregationalist, Mather had become more positive about synodal or presbyterial polities of the international Reformed Church (stretching from Scotland to Poland) of which he could see William of Orange from the Netherlands as the leading force as William III.

The Mathers, presidential father and historian son, could not readily have thought of their own congeries of Massachusetts congregations, now under a royal Governor, *in the singular* as *the* Church. In the singular, even in Latin, the word would have denoted for them either (1) the eternal and invisible Church of the elect; or (2) the international Reformed alliance, a community extending from Derry to Debrecen, joined in looking back to Calvin as their common master.

"*Academia*" in the new seal of 1692 represented the formal claim to universal status of a plenary university. Indeed, Mather himself, having in his provisional charter for the College called for the right of the Corporation to grant higher degrees, accepted from his Corporation the rank of *doctor* in theology as an earned degree. Moreover, in dedicating the *Academia Harvardiensis* as a "body politic and corporate in law," to Christ (the supreme *Doctor/Propheta*), as in a way its invisible Head, Mather must have, indeed, considered the "*Ecclesia*" of his seal to be equally universal in scope in the Reformed sense. His seal of the Harvard Academy could be construed also as a gesture of defiance of any attempt gradually to anglicanize (in the sense of episcopalianize) the College under a royal Governor.[95]

President Increase Mather, with his son Cotton, fondly identified new Cambridge with Kirjath-Sepher, Bethel, Ramah (where Samuel had been born, then dwelt) and Hebron, and the College as a replication in New England of "the universities of Palestine" at the time of Joshua, who himself was the type of Jesus Christ. To his glory their university was established (*In Christi gloriam*) and to him with the Church it was rededicated. This idea was also evoked in a sermon on the death of Increase Mather (1723) by the Reverend Benjamin Colman.[96] Giving expression to the common view that "Elijah and Elisha, after Samuel, seem to have been the Heads and

Preliminary Survey," *American Studies* 1 (Warsaw, 1986): 93–105, where he shows that Maccovius was read in America. For the older account, see C. Clapp, "Motto of Harvard College: Christo et Ecclesiae," The Colonial Society of Massachusetts, *Transactions* (1922–24), 59–83; and most recently, M. Hammond, "Latin Inscriptions in Harvard Buildings," ibid., 306, 334ff.

[95]Morison held that *Ecclesia* in the new seal "meant simply the Church of Christ in New England." *Seventeenth Century*, 493.

[96]Of the Brattle Street Church in Boston.

Presidents of Israel's Colleges," Colman mourned and lauded Mather as "Patriarch and *Prophet*," "Minister, Scholar, and *Doctor*."[97] Colman observed further that prophets, indeed, belonged to "a Supreme Order, and, though called Gods on earth yet must die like men."[98] In the funeral sermon for President John Leverett (1708–24), who had suddenly died in office, the same Colman the next year declared: "Prophets were their masters and presidents, and the Spirit of prophecy rested upon many of them,"[99] implying that the mourning students had sat at the feet of a latter-day prophet, like "the Sons of the Prophets [who] were the Scholars that dwelt and studied and worship'd in the Colleges of Israel."[100]

In his eulogies Colman had no reason to recall how one Harvard President had been prophetic in the Old Testament sense of an institutional and social critic. This was President Dunster.

B. President Dunster as *Propheta* in the Socially Critical Sense

Harvard's first President, Henry Dunster (1640–54), was a prophet in the socially, covenantally critical sense of the Hebrew prophet and suffered exile for his stand. Dunster, as ranking Hebraist of New England, came diffidently to the conclusion that pedobaptism, the sacramental connective tissue of the Colony, was not scriptural and assimilable to Old Testament circumcision. The Cambridge Synod of 1648, which had largely adopted the Westminster Confession of Faith,[101] persevered in pedobaptism and its restriction as a right only of experiential full (communicant) parents within the covenant. The conscientious younger generations of born New Englanders, in many cases, unable to testify to a saving experience, looked forlornly on the unbaptizable babies and fretted when they were themselves locally denied communion and were, *ipso facto*, denied the privilege of electing church officers and also the political franchise as freemen of the commonweal and town.[102]

No society in the history of all Christendom ever faced such a religiopolitical crisis, or such a strange one for upright conscientious married people of large families, men of marital prowess, still bearing the marks among their leaders of university education. A great monastic congregation of local abbeys, like that of Cluny, could recruit itself over the generations by taking in oblates who, on coming of age, would take the monastic vow of

---

[97]*Funeral Discourse upon the Death of the Very Reverent and Aged Dr. Increase Mather* (Boston, 1723), 26.

[98]Ibid., 13ff.

[99]B. Colman, *The Master Taken up from the Sons of the Prophets: /A Sermon Preached at Cambridge/Upon the Sudden Death/of the Reverend and Learned John Leverett,/President of Harvard College* (Boston, 1724), 2.

[100]Ibid., 3.

[101]R. Pope, *The Half-Way Covenant: Church Membership in Puritan New England* (Princeton, 1969).

[102]Walker, ed., *Creeds and Platforms*, 301–39.

stability, chastity, poverty and obedience and, as Cluniac Benedictines, rule vast domains and influence even the course of papal history. But the Bay Colony—a kind of conjugal and marital coenobitism based upon fecundity and disciplined faith, tutelage, pedobaptism, domestic and ecclesiastical discipline and, in young adulthood, the probationary owning of the church covenant (the counterpart of the monastic vow)—found itself near an impasse by the middle of the century.

Eventually resort was taken to the so-called "Half-way Covenant" of the synod of 1662. This covenant permitted members who had been baptized through the faith of their own parents, who lived respectable lives, who owned the church covenant and who promised thereby to support and obey the local church, to have their progeny baptized even though they could not recount a saving conversion experience and, therefore, could not partake of communion and participate otherwise in church offices.[103]

It is before this taut and precarious compromise, widely opposed (initially by Increase Mather), that is placed the forced resignation of the first President of Harvard, who had in his way discharged the prophetic office of social critique in scriptural and reasoned argument. In a society where pedobaptism was the religion in that it provided the ligaments between the generations, President Dunster came to the point where he considered it a major truth that only experiential believers, hence only adults, should be baptized.[104] He in whose presidential home the *Bay Psalm Book* had been printed, who had composed the Rules of the College, including the plenary purpose therein of godliness, now said: "All instituted Gospel Worship hath some express word of Scripture, but Pedobaptism hath none."[105]

Dunster had come to this politically and theologically explosive view by much biblical study and reflection. Some of his own infants, indeed, had been baptized by established usage under the ministry of young Jonathan Mitchell in First Church, Cambridge. But then three fully Calvinist Baptists from Newport, who had penetrated the Bay Colony as far as Lynn, ended up at the whipping-post in Boston. Obadiah Holmes, their steadfast leader, received thirty stripes in 1651.[106]

[103]See above text at n. 4.

[104]For further information on Dunster, see above at nn. 19–25.

[105]Dunster MS., 289, quoted by N. Wood, *History of the First Baptist Church of Boston (1665–1899)* (New York, 1980; reprint of Philadelphia, 1899 ed.), 26.

[106]Released in pain, having made their way back to Rhode Island, another of their number, John Clarke, a physician, arranged to have published in London *Ill News from New England: or A Narrative of New England's Persecution wherein is declared That while Old England is becoming new, New-England is becoming Old* (London, 1652). The minister in Lynn, Thomas Cobbes, where the three Rhode Islanders had foregathered with a brother in faith, retorted with *The Civil Magistrates Power* (London, 1653), citing Romans 13:3 and Canticles 2:15: "Take us the foxes, the little foxes which spoil the vines," the three Baptist foxes pleading, as it were, to be trapped! See E. Gaustad, *Baptist Piety: The Last Testament of Obadiah Holmes* (Washington, DC, 1978).

Dunster, as the leading biblical scholar of the Bay Colony, and his wife withheld their next infant from baptism. Dunster scripturally remonstrated with his pastor, Mitchell, who later reported: "It was a dismal thing to me, that I should live to see *truth* or peace dying or decaying in poor Cambridge."[107] Afterwards "in the defence of the comfortable truth [the baptism of infants]" it is reported by Cotton Mather that Mitchell "preached more than half a score of ungainsayable sermons, while his own church [in Cambridge] was in some danger by the hydrophobie of anabaptism."[108] And the son of the first minister of the Cambridge Church, Thomas Shepherd, Jr., would presently pun in an election sermon: "Anabaptism is an Engine framed to cut the throat of the Infanttry of the Church."[109]

Truth, here linked not merely to a rite but more particularly to the age at which it might be administered, in prevailing modern perspective, seems marginal, even to some trivial. Yet it was by infant baptism that the leadership of the Colony felt bound to old Christendom and behind that to ancient Israel in covenant. By it, too, ministers, magistrates and midwives all understood themselves to be bonded to each other in a regenerate society. It took intellectual courage in Dunster, as the ranking *Propheta* of the Colony, to allow his scholarly religious conviction to jeopardize all that he had built up almost single-handedly. He had even contributed a hundred acres to the College. He it was who undoubtedly designed the Overseers' seal of *Veritas* of 1642.[110]

Because of his eminence, Dunster was summoned to defend his newly won position as President in a two-day disputation in Latin with nine other ministers and two ruling elders of Boston and vicinity on the thesis: "Believers visibly only are to be baptized." (We have already adduced his Memorandum in connection with the institution of Overseers.[111]) Adversely judged by his peers, in October, 1654 the President was forced to resign. After two petitions he was allowed to remain until March, 1655 in the house that he himself had built and where the Colony's press was located. In April he was indicted by the grand jury. Writing to the county court thereafter, he said simply: "I conceived then [at the Boston disputation] and so do still, that I spake the truth in the feare of God, and dare not deny the same or go from it untill the Lord otherwise teach me."[112]

---

[107]C. Mather, *Magnalia Christi Americana*, quoted by J. Chaplin, *Life of Henry Dunster, First President of Harvard College* (Boston, 1872), 105.

[108]Ibid., 107.

[109]Sermon (1672), quoted in Wood, *History*, 35.

[110]See above text at n. 28. For a recent study of the hermeneutical richness of the seal, see J. Rosenmeier, "*Veritas*—the Sealing of the Promise," *Harvard Library Bulletin* 16 (1968): 26–37. The seal did not prevail until its rediscovery by President Quincy and it was flown on a banner at the bicentennial of the University in 1836.

[111]Dunster Memorandum, 1654 in Wood, *History*, 26, adduced in another connection above, n. 19.

[112]Chaplin, *Life of Henry Dunster*, 118.

The expelled President was settled over a church in Scituate outside the bounds of the Bay Colony. The principal teacher of the College and its virtual architect went into exile in the Separatist Congregational Plymouth Colony, whose magistrates for their part did not feel it proper on their Separatist principles to interfere with his now Baptist ministry.

In his scholarly quest for truth respecting the sacramental connective tissue of society, indirectly groping also for the proper scriptural limits of the temporal and the ecclesiastical authority over informed conscience in religion, Dunster in his testimony in reasoned formulation and in self-sacrificial deed confirmed the intermittent tradition of the teacher as prophetic in the exercise of critical judgment on even the religion that upholds both church and state, sustains the cohesiveness of the commonwealth and validates the social compact. The founding educator President, the ministerial scholar, Henry Dunster, left the memorable precedent of a reasoning nonconforming nonconformist in academia.

Although the presidential scholar-critic was brought down, Dunster testified valiantly to the way in which membership in "the supreme order" of truth (Colman's phrase) could be understood in relation to the two other orders of this tripartite theocracy, the church and the commonweal.

Of the institutions reflecting the threefold office of Christ, the College was the most organic of all the three of the Colonial theocracy and its Provincial successor. The magistracy, the ministry and collegiate school-mastery were symbolized from near the close of the seventeenth century by the judicial gown, the ministerial gown and the distinctive quasi-clerical "prophetic" academic gown of the President of the College (and eventually of all of its professors and of the graduates on the occasion of their receiving degrees).

IV. INTO THE NINETEENTH CENTURY

It was no doubt in the interest of the emerging model of all American higher education that both its governing boards were for the most part non-residential except for the President and several tutors, among the latter of whom there were also Fellows for shorter or longer terms. The Province-wide character of the oversight and financial support from the non-resident Fellows, along with their occasional intramural disciplinary decisions, protected the College from becoming ingrown.

By the first constitutional convention of the new Commonwealth, Harvard College/Academia, having suffered some loss of immunities during the Revolution, was incorporated in the Constitution of Massachusetts in 1780. Under the new republican government, it was itself referred to with a flourish by its drafter, John Adams, as "the Republic of Letters" in Cambridge and was for the first time officially called a University. Of this state University, certain ministers of the still Standing Order and the Governor, the Lieutenant Governor, the Council and the Senate, with the President of the Corporation, were deemed constitutive *ex officiis* of the Reverend the Honorable the Board of Overseers, which retained the right of visitation, of co-participation with the Corporation of Seven Fellows in the granting of degrees and in the approval of recommendations from the Corporation on faculty appointments.[113] A much more religiously pluralistic electorate could henceforth exercise considerable influence on the College through the largely elective senior board.

Although called a University in the Constitution of 1780, Harvard established its first graduate school, Medicine, in 1782, and the Law School in 1817.

The emergence of the Divinity School at Harvard in 1819, as a graduate department, took place during a major thrust forward in the reconstitution of Harvard, punctuated by a student rebellion that enormously strained the College as it sustained a transition from college to something like true university status.

In 1819, the *New England Patriot* sought to undermine Harvard by agitating for the withdrawal of state support on the charges that it supported both snobbish aristocracy and atheism, the last charge in part directed at the Unitarian patronage of the Divinity School. And the rural Calvinist and urban Catholic electorate behind the two charges could have become decisive in the second Constitutional Convention of 1820, concurrent with the establishment of the new State of Maine. In defense of the chapter on "the Republic of Letters in Cambridge," Daniel Webster wrote the report of the committee. (He had already won national renown for his successful defense before the Supreme Court, in 1819, of the colonial charter of his own *Alma Mater*, Dartmouth College, against comparable political pressure from the New Hampshire legislature.) His report exonerated the College of the charges of sectarianism and atheism and recommended that all her privileges be upheld but that, henceforth, the ministers of all denominations, and not those only of the Standing Order, become eligible for election to the 16 clerical places on the Board of Overseers. The Standing Order of Congregational churches and ministers—Trinitarian and Unitarian—would gradually have come to the end of all its privileges by 1833. Webster's conciliatory amendment was, strangely, rejected on referendum; and it was not until a legislative act of 1843 that the clerical places on the Board of Overseers were opened to ministers of any denomination.[114]

In 1821, George Ticknor, professor of Romance languages, communicated to the Board of Overseers his sense of the inadequacy of his *Alma Mater* to the new assignments of the age: "We are neither an University— which we call ourselves—nor a respectable high school—which we ought to

---

[113]Printed by Quincy, *History*, 2:507–09, Document XX.
[114]Morison, *Three Centuries*, 218, 257ff.

be—and with *Christo et Ecclesiae* for our motto, the morals of the young men who come to us are corrupted."[115]

Ticknor, for his part, was pressing for less rote learning and recitation and for departments to guide students in graded instruction for four demarcated classes divided by merit and progression. Concurrently, on a different tack, several instructors revived the Sever claim of 1720. In a Memorial to the Corporation they sought to gain seats on the Corporation as resident Fellows, holding that resident tutors should be Fellows as "a matter of chartered right" in reference to the Charter of 1650.

Leadership in this constitutional demarche was in the hands of German-trained Edward Everett, the first Eliot Professor of Greek literature, and Andrews Norton, Dexter Lecturer on Biblical Literature, a major figure in the emerging Divinity School. As the Corporation regarded itself as unqualified to respond to the Memorial by the very terms thereof, it left it to the Board of Overseers to delve into the constitutional history.

In the *Report* of their Committee on the Memorial of the Resident Instructors, of January 6, 1825, it was reaffirmed that the Corporation had in fact the immemorial charter right to co-opt whomsoever it chose, that residency, teaching and other qualifications pressed by the Memorialists had never been required of Fellows of the Corporation in the past. As a result of this intensive examination of the College records and the agitation for reform, *The Statutes and Laws of the University in Cambridge, Massachusetts* was issued in June, 1825, with 153 laws arranged in 13 chapters. In this the immediate government of the College, namely the President and instructors, were for the first time called "the Faculty." Some of Ticknor's reforms were therein embodied. In the same year Ticknor published his own research in university constitutional history, largely in defense of non-residential Fellows in the Corporation which was above intramural machinations and which offset the endemic tendency of any coterie of established scholars to seek its own self-interest.[116]

Once the Faculty had been established as the term for "the immediate government of the College," the distinctive institutions and terminology of American university government with reference to professors, tutors, lecturers and instructors had evolved into now familiar form and nomenclature. Distinctive American usage goes back to the first third of the nineteenth century when faculty meetings presided over by the president became regularized and when the teaching staff, in varying ranks and different titles, became, collectively, the faculty.[117] Students came to refer to their teachers

[115]Ibid., 230; Bailyn, et al., eds., *Glimpses of Harvard Past*, "Why [President] Kirkland Failed," 19–44.

[116]G. Ticknor, *Remarks on Changes Lately Proposed or Adopted in Harvard University* (Boston, 1825). Cf. Bailyn, et al., *Glimpses of the Harvard Past*, 29ff., 39.

[117]W. Craigue and J. Hulburt, *A Dictionary of American English on Historical Principles*, 4 vols. (Chicago, 1938–44), 2: 919.

not always in their individuality as professors but in their participatory collectivity as "faculty members,"[118] or unindividualized, as "the faculty."

The fully rounded University became organically "complete" in 1865 when it was fully separated from the state, and the Board of Overseers was elected by the national and eventually international alumni body. By then, of course, it had long since slipped even the collective memory of the institution that they had once been modeled on the *episkopoi* of Ephesus in Acts 20:28, that the legal notion of a body politic (ecclesiastical or academic) combined Roman and scriptural ideas of a perpetual body, that the transcendent Head of the Harvard Corporation, specifically, had been vaguely felt to be Christ, not the king, and that the alumni, as its nurslings transplanted to the various fields of endeavor, had become on American soil much more integral to the completeness and complexity of the American university than ever their counterparts in old Christendom.[119]

[118]I have not ascertained when or where this common usage started.

[119]The alumnus with whom I sat at the table on the eve of Prince Charles' Address to the first Convocation of Harvard's 350th Celebration, said with extraordinary emotion and resolve, "If this University should ever be destroyed by some cataclysm, God forbid, it would be rebuilt exactly as it is by its world-wide alumni!"

LAW AND PEACE IN PREREVOLUTIONARY RUSSIA: THE CASE OF V. F. MALINOVSKII

William E. Butler

The organized peace movements since the First World War have been confounded in ways that they were not in the post-Napoleonic period by the combination of ideological conflict and national security self-righteousness. The fragile system for international security constructed in the aftermath of the First World War collapsed institutionally when confronted by another national leader bent on reducing Europe and the world; in its place a stronger institutional framework was fashioned wherein bitter ideological and political rivalry led to both sides professing a policy of peace through strength and each mobilizing peace movements on their behalf. So accustomed have we become to "peace as an instrument of foreign policy" that we have lost sight of the intellectual currents that gave rise to important innovations and developments in the law of warfare at sea and on land, the peaceful settlement of international disputes and the conclusion of a host of international conventions that functionally made the notion of an international community more of a reality. Least of all are we aware that Russian thinkers have had some part in this process. Leo Tolstoy, to be sure, was a powerful voice universally renowned and respected as an expression of conscience making its point through an unforgettable portrayal of the Napoleonic wars. But Tolstoy's *War and Peace* was not the first work in the Russian language to bear that title nor to address that theme. One of the most original and interesting, published as Napoleon was beginning to consolidate his authority, was V. F. Malinovskii's Discourse on war and peace.

I. Diplomat, Pacifist, Publicist and Educator

Vasilii Fedorovich Malinovskii, born at Moscow in 1765, graduated from the Faculty of Philosophy at Moscow University in 1781. His pre-university life and education has not been recorded, but the Malinovskiis were among the most venerable of Moscow families, tracing their ancestry back to 1041. Malinovskii's father served Moscow University in his capacity as an Archpriest of the Russian Orthodox Church and was well known to "old Moscow society."[1] After completing his studies at the university, Malinovskii entered

---

[1]"Vasilii Fedorovich Malinovskii," *Pamiatnaia knizhka imperatorskogo Aleksandrovskogo litseia na 1856–1857 god* (St. Petersburg, 1856), 130. This account corrects a number of errors in

State service as an archivist in the Moscow Archive of the College of Foreign Affairs under G. F. Müller. He was involved in literary activities of the day and close to N. M. Karamzin, among others. While in archival service he evidently mastered the English language sufficiently to qualify for appointment to the Russian diplomatic establishment abroad.

In the autumn of 1789, he received his first assignment, as translator/interpreter to the Russian Mission in London. There he spent two years, resident at least part of the time in nearby Richmond, preparing in spare hours his treatise on war and peace[2] and a translation of Alexander Hamilton's report on the use of manufactures.[3] England evidently made an enduring positive impression on Malinovskii. His anonymous biographer reported:

> A close acquaintance with this enlightened and industrial country made a profound impression on V. F.; he retained his memories of this period to the end of his days; he loved to chat about England and knew how to give the great figures and true dignitaries of that country their just due.[4]

Probably in late 1791, Malinovskii returned to Russia, anxious, apparently, to become involved in that part of the world where Russian energies were concentrated: the Black Sea and Balkan regions in the war against Turkey. He was attached to the Russian Army to assist at the peace negotiations in Jassy. On the basis of his services at the Peace Congress, he petitioned to become an assessor of the College of Foreign Affairs but ended up being attached to the College without a special assignment or post because of his unwillingness to use his numerous contacts to advantage. In 1798, however, he was made a *nadvornyi sovetnik,* and two years later he was elevated to the next rank and appointed Consul General in Moldavia, where he served until May, 1803.

Recalled to Moscow in connection with Alexander I's reorganization of state service, Malinovskii continued to devote much of his time to writing and translating. He petitioned to become *stats-sovetnik* in 1805 and was awarded the Order of St. Vladimir in 1806. The return to St. Petersburg brought a period of economic privation for Malinovskii. He took part in the founding of the Russian Bible Society[5] and likewise was a founder and

---

[N. Koshanskii], "Izvestie o zhizni Malinovskago," *Syn Otechestva,* part 13 (St. Petersburg, 1814), no. 18, 220–223.

[2]Ibid. The end of Part One is designated as "Richmond. 1790."

[3]The translation was published much later as [A. Hamilton], *Otchet general-kaznacheia Aleksandra Gamil'tona, uchinennyi Amerikanskim shtatam 1791 g. o pol'ze manufaktur i otnoshenii onykh k torgovle i zemledeliiu* (St. Petersburg, 1807).

[4]"V.F. Malinovskii," 131.

[5]I. Seleznev, *Istoricheskii ocherk imperatorskogo byvshaga tsarskosel'skago nyne Aleksandrovskago litseia* (St. Petersburg, 1861), 45.

fervent supporter of the Philanthropic Committee. Yet, in June 1810, he appealed to Count N. P. Rumianstev for "rent money" to augment his inadequate salary.

His writings and translations were prodigious. The Malinovskii archive in Pushkinskii dom contains dozens of translations from English, Turkish, Hebrew, ancient Greek, German, French and other tongues. Philosophical works were favoured, but Shakespeare was included, as were several books of the Bible, presumably as part of his interest in the Bible Society.[6] The religious works were unknown to the public and kept within the family. In connection with Alexander I's ministerial reforms, Malinovskii drew up a Memorandum on the Emancipation of Slaves[7] in 1802. The following year he published a weekly journal, *Osennie vechera*,[8] all of the articles of which were apparently his own. That same year he completed reflections begun at Belozerka (1799) in his diary on transforming the State structure of Russia,[9] an essay on the "asian peoples"[10] and an epic tale intended for his journal about a hermit who returns to a provincial Russian city after years of absence and deplores the "French morality" which he sees as subverting the moral fibre of society.[11]

Malinovskii's most notable publication, however, was his *Razsuzhdenie o mire i voine* (1803), begun at Richmond in 1790. The second part was completed in 1798 at Belozerka, near Pavlovsk, and eventually Malinovskii saw it through to publication. We shall examine the contents below. From a letter of Kochubei, *circa* late 1802 or early 1803, it is evident that Malinovskii left London for Jassy partly to witness the evils of war against Turkey in person and gather additional data for his Discourse.[12] The peace negotiations, at which he served as secretary, frustrated that object of his journey because the battles had ended.

Malinovskii's translation of Alexander Hamilton's report on the use of manufactures appeared in 1807. He also left in manuscript form several political articles on the Jews and land ownership, on the history of Russia as

---

[6]E. Arab-Olgy, "Vydaiuschiisia russkii prosvetitel," in V. Malinovskii, *Izbrannye obshchestvenno-politicheskie sochineniia* (Moscow, 1958), 45.

[7]Printed for the first time in Malinovskii, *Izbrannye*, 111–114. The Memorandum was drafted by Malinovskii in Jassy and sent to the Minister of Internal Affairs, V. P. Kochubei (1768–1834). A friend of Malinovskii's from London and the Peace Congress at Jassy, Kochubei was one of the young liberals who took part in the Emperor's secret committee to prepare a program of social and governmental reform.

[8]Publication began on September 26, 1803. Evidently Malinovskii proposed to publish 12 weekly issues a year during the three months of autumn.

[9]First published, interestingly, during the First World War by V. Semevskii in *Golos minuvshego* 10 (1915): 247–264 and reprinted in Malinovskii, *Izbrannye*, 115–132, with annotations.

[10]Printed for the first time in ibid., 133–135.

[11]"Pustynnik," published in ibid., 136–145.

[12]The letter to Kochubei was first published in *Chteniia v imperatorskom Obshchestve istorii i drevnostei rossiiskikh pri Moskovskom universitete* (Moscow, 1863), no. 1, chap. 5, 172–175.

well as an article published during the Napoleonic wars concerning a general peace.[13]

Malinovskii achieved greatest renown during 1811 when he was appointed the first director of the Tsarskoe Selo (later Aleksandrovskii) Lycee and, *inter alia*, encouraged the development of international legal studies in Russia. The appointment occasioned much speculation among the *cognoscenti* of the day. Baron M. A. Korff attributed the directorship to Malinovskii's marriage in London to Sofia Andreevna Samborskaia (1772–1812), daughter of Andrei Afanas'evich Samborskii (1732–1815), clergyman, agronomist and author of books on English agronomy.[14] The "English connection" surfaced time and again in Malinovskii's career. Samborskii had served with the Russian Mission in London, became spiritual tutor to the future Emperor Alexander I and his brother Konstantin in 1784 and was close to Alexander's law reformer, adviser and confidant, M. M. Speranskii. Moreover, Malinovskii's interest in the Bible Society was believed to have originated in England.

D. F. Kobeko attributed Malinovskii's appointment to the latter facet of his activities. A letter dated June 16, 1811 from Malinovskii to his brother P. F. Malinovskii praises the efforts of Senator M. I. Donaurov, A. K. Razumovskii (1748–1822) and R. A. Koshelev on his behalf.[15] All three were elected vice-presidents of the Bible Society in 1813. Like-minded individuals in their attitude toward the propagation of the faith, Kobeko suggested, they were interested in placing their people in high positions and conversely in attracting important individuals to their ranks.[16]

Malinovskii's tenure as Director of what was to become the most distinguished Russian Lycee was auspicious but all too brief. He died at the age of 49 in 1814 and was buried in the Bol'sheokhtenskii Cemetery.[17]

II. AUTHORSHIP OF THE DISCOURSE

Although it is beyond doubt that V. F. Malinovskii is the author of the Discourse, the title page does not bear an author's name. The designation "Richmond. 1790" appears at the end of Part One and "Belozerka near Petersburg in 1798" at the end of Part Two, followed by the initials "V. M."

[13]"Obshchii mir," *Syn Otechestva* (1813): 1 (10), 235–244. The article appeared anonymously but is confirmed as Malinovskii's by contemporary sources. It is either a conspectus or a continuation of the 1803 Discourse.

[14]One of these, *Opisanie prakticheskogo anglinskogo zemledeliia* (Moscow, 1781) was published under the supervision of the first Russian law professor at Moscow University, S. Desnitskii.

[15]Printed in *Zhurnal Ministerstva narodnogo prosveshcheniia* 7 (1915): 30–32 and Malinovskii, *Izbrannye*, 153–155.

[16]D. Kobeko, *Pervyi direktor tsarskosel'skogo litseia* (Petrograd, 1915), 15. Also see Kobeko, *Imperatorskii tsarskosel'skii litsei; nastavniki i pitomtsy, 1811–1843* (St. Petersburg, 1911).

[17]Seleznev, *Istoricheskii*, 45.

in Russian. These data correspond with Malinovskii's career and places of residence, and Malinovskii himself confirms his authorship in letters to Count A. R. Vorontsov and G. R. Derzhavin. On August 16, 1803, Malinovskii wrote to Vorontsov that he had the "honor to present my work to the public, a book on war and peace."[18] In a letter addressed to Derzhavin dated August, 1812, Malinovskii reminds him of the "book on peace and war written by myself in England and the nearby vicinity; there is a continuation."[19]

One of the copies of the Discourse held by the Lenin Library bears a presentation inscription in the hand of Malinovskii's son, I. V. Malinovskii: "To the Honorable Vladimir Dmitrievich Serdiukov, in memory of worthy and beneficial activities in the Iziumskii uezd during his service based on justice, from an acquaintance of his late father—a work by my father. Ivan Malinovskii. 27 December 1862. Village of Kolpina."[20] Apparently, the original manuscript of the book remained in the Malinovskii family for many years, but its present whereabouts are unknown.

Malinovskii's authorship likewise has been unquestioned by scholars who have alerted an international readership to the significance of his contribution in the literature of international law. One of Russia's most distinguished international lawyers, D. I. Kachenovskii, addressing the London Peace Society during his visit to England in 1858–59, recited extracts from the Discourse to his audience.[21] These extracts were published in the *Herald of Peace* (July, 1859)[22] and reprinted in the organ of the American Peace Society in the same year.

III. A Scheme for International Peace and Security

Although Malinovskii's Discourse can properly be relegated to the literature proposing schemes for perpetual peace in Europe, it is, as Grabar suggests, "a comprehensive and independently conceived work."[23] The first part written in England concerns the reasons adduced on behalf of war, the misfortunes of war, the advantages of peace and the true causes of war. War, said Malinovskii, is a "spontaneous evil and a combination of all the evils in the world."[24] It combines "all the savageness of beasts with the art of human

---

[18]*Arkhiv kniazia Vorontsova* 30 (Moscow, 1884): 394.

[19]*Sochineniia Derzhavina* 6 (St. Petersburg, 1871): 239.

[20]That volume bears the rubber-stamp *ex libris* of V. E. Grabar (1865–1956). Grabar reports the existence of a "second edition" of the Discourse published in 1803, but neither his own copy, nor others examined, nor any other bibliographic reference source indicates the existence of such an edition. See. V. Grabar, *Materialy k istorii literatury mezhdunarodnogo prava v Rossii 1647–1917 gg.* (Moscow, 1958); 167. The reference is deleted in the English edition.

[21]See *Russkii invalid*, 131 (1861).

[22]*Herald of Peace* (July, 1859), 71.

[23]Grabar, *Materitly k istorii*, 167.

[24]V. Malinovskii, *Rassuzhdenie o mire i voine* (St. Petersburg, 1803).

reason directed toward the destruction of people."[25] Enlightened Europe should show an example of how to eradicate this evil "through the restoration and confirmation of a universal and indissoluble peace."[26] Love of man and moderation manifested in war "mitigate the cruelties of war no more than do the humanity and softheartedness of the hangman."[27] We consider ourselves "more enlightened than the ancient nations"; our Christian faith truly gives us an advantage over them. Their law approved of their going to war, whereas our God is a God of peace and love. Europeans "still have made no attempt to eradicate war. Peace, as they so often declare it among themselves, just like war, does not deserve the name: it is merely a respite from war and could be more properly termed an armistice concluded for an indefinite period."[28] After an attack on the Danish astronomer Tycho Brahe and Nicolaus Copernicus and the notions of their day, which "sheltered behind constellations and animals" and engaged in discourses about "useless metaphysical subtleties," the author turned on the monks: "The idle crowd of monks, whose prosperity is dependent upon the ignorance of nations, have maintained themselves, and the greater part of the people have given an absurd respect to those extravagant and wealthy monks, who have converted the God of Peace into a God of War."[29] All "those who differ in their opinions about the predominant faith are damned, deluded, and unfortunate, and are to be killed in order to please God."[30]

Although the domestic order of States has been strengthened, "the general administration of Europeans among themselves has remained in a barbaric state," disputes continuing to be resolved by fire and sword,[31] whereas the "prosperity of our State is inseparable from the general prosperity of Europe."[32] The wars of Europe have "become as unacceptable and harmful to all in general as were the internecine wars of barons in former times."[33]

As for arguments adduced in favour of war, Malinovskii examines several and refutes them. Some view war and pestilence as nature's corrective against overpopulation. Leave future prosperity to our descendants, he says, "for they, of course, will find enough places to live and the means to maintain themselves."[34] Against the view that Europe at peace in the long term will forget how to wage war and fall prey to other nations, Malinovskii contends that Europe united can be overcome by no one. Indeed, the

---

[25]Ibid., 2.
[26]Ibid., 2–3.
[27]Ibid., 3.
[28]Ibid., 7.
[29]Ibid., 8.
[30]Ibid., 9.
[31]Ibid., 10.
[32]Ibid., 11.
[33]Ibid.
[34]Ibid., 14.

present situation is the worse because "Asians, Americans, and Africans are entwined in our wars and, little by little learning the art of warfare, may use this against their teachers by taking advantage of their divisions and disunity."[35]

The power and might of states is not dependent upon territorial possessions or increased population to be acquired by wars; indeed, these may lead to a state's decline. States will acquire more pride, more enemies and more reasons for others to reduce this power, he said, documenting his case by reference to the respective positions of Sweden and Denmark. "Conquests are now different and virtually impossible."[36]

Malinovskii eloquently decried the prejudices of nations. The various traits of peoples, their shortcomings and virtues so diverse, should actually bind them closer together that they "might through their mutual virtues help one another with regard to their mutual shortcomings."[37] In his chapter on "Respect for War, Heroism, and Magnanimity of Spirit", he reserved his highest accolade for the "lawmaker" or legislator, for through his exercise of wisdom the lawmaker reaches millions of people over many races and centuries.[38]

The misfortunes of war are assessed on behalf of society as a whole. "War destroys the primary bases of society, the safety of life and property. Laws punish by death certain unfortunate murderers and thieves, but the keepers of those laws, the rulers of nations, in not knowing how to avert war, subject the entire State to murder and plundering."[39] Peace, on the other hand, would bring "prosperity and justice" to Europe. The appearance of nations and lands would be altered beyond recognition.[40]

Malinovskii concluded his analysis of the causes of war before he departed England. The European powers, he wrote, "habitually consider their neighbors to be implacable and natural enemies ... always ready to attack the enemy or to repulse his attack, just like people living in the world."[41] The only rules which "European powers observe among themselves are the rules of politics."[42] "Like the ancient rites of Egyptians, they are concealed from the common people—the priests send them away from the inward parts of the Temple, and with reason."[43] The Italians "introduced their politics into European cabinets where they have been presented to this day. The monks hurried to confirm them, rose to State office, and sowed

[35]Ibid., 15.
[36]Ibid., 23.
[37]Ibid., 29.
[38]Ibid., 39.
[39]Ibid., 45.
[40]Ibid., 65.
[41]Ibid., 69.
[42]Ibid., 69–70.
[43]Ibid., 70.

there the principles of pretence, injustice, and secrecy which bear sufficient witness against politics,"[44] since it is "useful and decorous in the behavior of dishonorable people to endeavor to deceive one another, but not in the conduct of nations."[45] The "management of politics by individuals at court could not make it more perfected, more accustomed to injustice and guile." Cardinals Richelieu and Mazarin are considered the most outstanding ministers, yet "coercion, deceit, arrogance, baseness, and perfidy marked their behavior."[46]

Malinovskii condemned political writers who "within the political composition of Europe are maggots born in the wounds of the human body."[47] They "defend the sophistry of politics, confirm its most ridiculous rules, and justify it in matters which it would itself be ashamed to admit to."[48] He divided the political writers into three categories: (1) "those writers who apologize for the fact that there are those who are blinded by love for their fatherland";[49] (2) the "most dangerous of all political writers are those write *ex officio* or in the interest of the court" (in their works "truth and the law of nations yield their place to injustice and lies"); [50] and (3) "the most common political writers, the newspaper writers; they write in order to write ... [O]ften the newspaper writers are suborned to think in a particular way."[51]

At Belozerka, where the family dacha was situated in beautiful surroundings, Malinovskii directed his attention to the antidote, to ways in which the international system could rid itself of the habit of war. He began with the "law of nations" [*obshchenarodnye zakony*], or what we call international law. States, like individuals, he reasoned, "need to base their behavior on absolute rules which, without prejudicing their independence, restrain them within the bounds of common advantage ... Every sovereign power administers its internal affairs according to its own discretion, and any interference, direct or indirect, is a violation of its independence."[52] The "establishment of rules or laws of nations and the observance thereof is not interference in internal affairs since they may be confirmed only by consent; but having this by common discourse it is impossible to return to particularity."[53]

"Nations," he adds, "conclude peace treaties, treaties of alliance, and defensive treaties, and these serve as the rule and law of conduct *inter se* which are changed as frequently as do the chief inducements of interest of

[44]Ibid.
[45]Ibid. 70–71.
[46]Ibid., 71.
[47]Ibid., 75.
[48]Ibid., 76.
[49]Ibid.
[50]Ibid., 77.
[51]Ibid., 78.
[52]Ibid., 81.
[53]Ibid., 82.

those who are concerned in them. Those who are bound are both the judges and the judged, both the aggrieved and those who aggrieve."[54] Under these conditions "there is neither security of a court, nor justice, nor equality."[55] The "vanquished has recourse to the mediation of other nations, but when the victor spurns this . . . then they seek place by force and armed mediation commences," but the mediators often have their own advantage in view. And "from this the political and cabinet correspondence and negotiations continue increasingly and, like clouds, gather and portend the threat of war from new alliances."[56]

Malinovskii distinguished among levels of alliance. A general alliance might subsume all the advantages of special alliances. "In this sense, instead of treaties there should be laws to confirm the independence and ownership of territory and of nations and to establish the conduct of all nations."[57] For the observance of such laws a general council "should be established, composed of plenipotentiaries of the allied nations. This council should preserve general security and ownership, prevent any disturbance of the peace, and decide disputes between nations submitted according to an established procedure, and its decisions must be unanimously implemented by all the allies (nations)."[58] If the decision of the general council were not implemented, "the recalcitrant power shall be excluded from all general privileges and intercourse, and in the event of obduracy, a common force shall be used to enforce the law."[59] The country housing the headquarters of the council shall be deemed "sacred and independent for the perpetual and safe sojourn of council plenipotentiaries. . . . Its personnel shall be inviolate in all territories."[60]

All negotiations, said Malinovskii, would take place through mutual plenipotentiaries in the council: "the custom of maintaining envoys will be superfluous. And in fact that custom serves only a hostile policy. What advantages does it have?" Consider "how much harm has been caused by its false, exaggerated, biased reports, its interference in internal affairs, and its illegal means of finding out secrets. One may regard wars as arising from envoys as much as from the maintenance of standing armies."[61] The movement of armies usually is preceded by the stirring of passions through the emotional words and reports of envoys. "With the elimination of this practice politics will return to its own stable simplicity."[62]

[54]Ibid., 83–84.
[55]Ibid., 84.
[56]Ibid., 85–86.
[57]Ibid., 86–87.
[58]Ibid., 87.
[59]Ibid., 88.
[60]Ibid., 87.
[61]Ibid., 89.
[62]Ibid., 90.

The "first laws should concern frontiers." Then "trade will unite the most remote nations and will appertain to the law of nations and must have precise provisions , . . . and in order to avoid disagreements, foreign merchants must be subject to identical laws."[63] Third, it is necessary, as is done in treaties of alliance, to define the *casus foederis* "even more precisely in the general alliance." This *casus* shall be an attack, and, therefore, the "*casus* of an attack must be determined precisely." An attack, he said, is self-defining: it is the entry of a foreign army within one's frontiers. Politicians "today vainly justify themselves in such instances by manifestos and disguise their intentions under various pacific or generally useful pretexts. The incursion of a foreign army is always a violation of independence and an appropriation of another's power."[64] Except when parrying an attack, the author doubted whether there could be another instance of a just or lawful war. An "insult to national honor" ought to be punished by a reprimand, since powers are obliged to respect one another. Finally, to remove any incentive for war, Malinovskii said it was essential to deprive an aggressor "of the expectation of acquisitions and advantages, and therefore all European powers, often having precisely demarcated their frontiers," must "acknowledge them to be mutually absolute and guarantee their integrity so that they may not be disturbed by war or conquest; equally, the advantages of trade should be absolute and might be changed only by mutual and voluntary consent."[65]

The tribulations of war could be confined, Malinovskii proposed, by limiting the spatial sphere in which European powers might engage in war. If Europeans quarrel, why should America, Africa and Asia become embroiled? European settlements in those parts of the globe should be neutral territory, with European powers stationing only enough troops there to ensure protection against the local inhabitants. To this policy he proposed to add stipulations against European powers seeking further possessions, punishment of those responsible for committing an attack, compensation for losses sustained and compulsory negotiations or proceedings between nations.[66] Malinovskii did not favor disarmament *per se* but noted that war is always preceded by movements of troops and arms. Such movements should be confined to imminent expectation of an attack, and the council should be notified of any such movements beforehand.[67]

The author then turned to "objections against despotism and independence" that would preclude the establishment of the "general alliance." An "independent power, like a private individual, has no right to begin a quarrel

---

[63]Ibid., 90–91.
[64]Ibid., 91–92.
[65]Ibid., 94.
[66]Ibid., 94–95.
[67]Ibid., 95–97.

without mediation and trial."[68] Any power "endeavors to prove the justness of its war, but who can decide justness without laws?"[69] The principal merit of politics is "to know how to give the appearance of justness and honor to all affairs and expectations. Manifestos concerning wars show that there is no certain way to decide their justness: since both belligerent powers are right or both are guilty, or sometimes one might imagine that the politicians recognize two justnesses, one true and the other false."[70]

The author then contraposes the natural state of society to a state, or civil society. Legal order should exist not merely between private individuals united in a civil society, but, likewise, between nations. But "treaties among powers are merely an expression of will and continue so long as they are not changed: their sole rationale is advantage, and therefore they are violated or respected as imminent ... and they are mistakenly called an obligation when their violation holds out nothing. Frederick the Great," he adds, "having written that a Sovereign is not obliged to keep his word to the detriment of his nation," said that "all powers think and do this."[71] Power, "while observing justice only among others but itself not submitting to this, stands on the outside of the power of untruth, asserting itself to be within justice. And these two grounds, as opposite as light and darkness, destroy one another."[72] European powers "constitute a single society, by reason of Christianity and of their mutual relations. In place of the fact that each power concedes its absolute right to spontaneously govern itself in its disagreements, it receives the major advantage of mutually, with others, preserving itself from spontaneous misfortune. The Christian regions ... are bound in every possible way to endeavor to settle their disputes peacefully and may not consider their rival an enemy, until he is recognized as such by all society."[73]

In the chapter entitled "Unification by Consent," Malinovskii argues that the "slightest violation of universal laws is equally dangerous and harmful to all . . . . The rulers of a nation who have violated an oath to society subject their nation to the danger of vengeance and are guilty before it."[74] In an unusual reference to his London stay, he adds: "In England representations are made by the people to the King concerning war and peace. In this fortunate land the people are allowed to judge their government in quarrels with other powers."[75]

The final chapter undertakes to draw the "consequences" of the Dis-

[68]Ibid., 99.
[69]Ibid., 101.
[70]Ibid.
[71]Ibid., 104–105.
[72]Ibid., 109.
[73]Ibid., 111.
[74]Ibid., 114–115.
[75]Ibid., 115–116.

course. "Since no nation can exist without laws of justice, so too entire nations cannot live without observing them, and not by destroying one another."[76] The "observance of justice between nations is as essential as it is between private individuals . . . ." Nonobservance of justice between nations also "violates it for each of them separately, subjecting the innocent to destruction and death."[77] "War," continues Malinovskii, "cannot be lawful when there are no laws between nations. These laws of nations are duties and obligations based on their own well-being . . . . When all governments are agreed on the unity of their intentions, they will be agreed on everything . . . Politics must be the science of rights and laws among nations, just as jurisprudence is among private individuals."[78]

A "just war is a punishment of a nation; if war is begun spontaneously without a trial and the decision of impartial persons, it is murder." The use of force gives a "right to defense, but even the most just vengeance may become force if it is left to the will of the aggrieved."[79] "Peoples and their governments may be united under the protection of laws, having no single leader except the Rulers of the Universe."[80]

IV. THE NAPOLEONIC WARS: A VINDICATION

By all accounts, and by the date on the book itself, Malinovskii had completed the Discourse before events in France brought Napoleon to power. While there are occasional acerbic references to French diplomacy, there is no reason to believe that Malinovskii pretended to see the pan-European conflagration in the offing, pertinent as many features of his diagnosis were to those happenings. And though the clouds of war were beginning to gather by the time the book appeared in 1803, the same holds true, though by then Malinovskii was beginning to apply propositions in the Discourse to continental foreign policy in his journal *Osennie vechera*.

By 1812–13 the scene had changed completely. Malinovskii's letter to Derzhavin[81] appears to confirm that his essay[82] on a "general peace" was envisaged as a continuation of the Discourse. Whatever the case, Malinovskii believed the time had truly arrived for his diagnosis to take effect. "A general peace," he wrote, "is no longer a chimera . . . Germany and virtually all of Europe desire it . . . ."[83] Having restored "freedom by their common efforts, all are aware that this cannot be preserved without their common

---

[76]Ibid., 117.
[77]Ibid., 118–119.
[78]Ibid., 123.
[79]Ibid., 124.
[80]Ibid., 125.
[81]*Sachineniia Derzhavina*, 6: 394
[82]*Syn Otechestva*, 10:234
[83]Quoted from the text reprinted in Malinovskii, *Izbrannye*, 94.

consent and already they do not rush, as before, to seek any private advantage or conclude a separate peace . . . . Entire States and peoples, as one man, endeavor collectively to overcome the common enemy and are as one joyously and solemnly celebrating their mutual triumphs."[84]

The previous treaties of alliance against Napoleon should now be transformed into one common or general new alliance which "would serve as a kind of *ulozhenie* (codex) and confirm reliable and stable rules for the security and integrity of possessions."[85] Further, he urged that the "general spirit of heroism, love for the fatherland, and disposition of nations to defend and assert their rights, together with intolerance of force and suppression," would lead the present generation to preserve the fruits of their common achievement for posterity.

The "confluence of present circumstances," he rightly foresaw, "constitute an epoch; we will be accountable to posterity, and will ourselves bitterly regret it, if we do not take advantage of them."[86] In printing Malinovskii's last article, the editor of the journal noted that shortly after receiving the manuscript for press the allied monarchs had proclaimed their grand alliance.

Malinovskii died in 1814, before the Congress of Vienna brought into being the framework for the structure of Europe in which he had placed such hopes. The Napoleonic wars also led to the formation in England, the United States and other countries of the organized peace movement—in England, the London Peace Society and in the United States, the American Peace Society. Unbeknownst to them (but perhaps inspired by English literature of that genre in the 1790s) until Kachenovskii's address in England, a Russian writer had made a substantial and original independent contribution to proposals for restructuring the international system. His untimely death perhaps deprived Russia and the international peace movement of an influential voice in post-Napoleonic Europe.

[84]Ibid.
[85]Ibid., 97.
[86]Ibid., 97–98.

II. Religious Perspectives on Law

CONCEPTIONS OF NATURAL LAW, FROM TROELTSCH TO BERMAN

James Luther Adams

The Spanish Cardinal Merry del Val once said that for the Protestant the Bible is a wax nose to be twisted any way one pleases. Something similar could be said of the concept of natural law. Indeed, at one time the Roman Catholic solution with respect to natural law as well as to the Bible was to provide ecclesiastical guidance. In the *Syllabus of Errors* (1864) appears under the rubric, "Concerning Errors Regarding Natural Ethics and Christian Ethics" the papal declaration, "Let him be anathema who asserts that the knowledge of philosophical and ethical things, as well as the civil laws, can and should be exempt from divine and ecclesiatical authority." It is difficult to conceive of anything more bewildering, indeed nonsensical, than this demand, for natural law by definition is the expression of human reason. Canonists have told me that the encyclical is not in all respects of permanent validity but was intended for the immediate situation.

The idea of natural law may be traced back to ancient Greece and Rome and has been a centerpiece of discussion for over 1,500 years. Indeed, Julius Stone in a conversation has suggested that the idea has been a "basket" for value theory for a millennium and a half.

Natural law has generally made the claim to provide a rational ethical standard that is discoverable through human powers of apprehension and thus does not depend upon special divine revelation. It is not surprising, therefore, for its meaning to have been subjected to diverse and even to contradictory interpretations. Because of this and because of the ways in which the idea has been made the weapon of special interests it has been abandoned in wide circles. Besides all of this the conception of even positive law has undergone radical change.

The legal realists assert that law is what the judges decide it is. In this view the positing of natural law is only a sign of human vanity. As a protest against this vanity Justice Oliver Wendell Holmes, Jr. reminded his students that man is in the belly of the universe; the universe is not in the belly of man. By law he meant no metaphysical truths or grand moral principles but rather the incidence of the public force through the instrumentality of the courts. Nevertheless, a version of natural law, in one form or another, has been adopted in recent years (for example, by Jerome Frank, Lon Fuller and Harold Berman). Of special significance is the fact that in Nazi Germany a conception of natural law was appealed to by judges who were opposed to racist views of "justice." In certain quarters this conflict gave rise to new interest in and respect for the crucial function of natural law as the ground for the criticism of positive law.

The history of the idea of natural law has filled libraries for centuries, as is readily evident in the massive work of Otto Gierke, *Natural Law and the Theory of Society*.[1] The development of and the contradictory views of natural law are recurrent themes in Harold Berman's *Law and Revolution: The Formation of the Western Legal Tradition*.[2] Here we see that in face of great social and legal change canon law was created as the first European legal system. In all of this the church was the principal carrier of natural law theory. Berman, therefore, gives considerable attention to the scholastic dialectic.

I. TROELTSCH ON NATURAL LAW

Probably no scholar has provided a more comprehensive account of the development of natural law from the beginning of Christianity through modern secularization and then to its decline than Ernst Troeltsch (1865–1923).[3] For an understanding of the ways in which Troeltsch spells out the emergence of a natural law doctrine in early Christianity one must first take into account his interpretation of the character and dynamic of primitive Christianity. His whole outlook in these matters was something he had to struggle for in the context of theological and philosophical conflicts of the latter part of the nineteenth century in Germany.

Troeltsch was one of the most original and penetrating cultural analysts of his time. Along with Max Weber, his colleague at Heidelberg, he was a pioneer in the burgeoning discipline of sociology of religion. He was especially aware of the ethical and philosophical problems characteristic of a pluralistic society with its tensions between church and state. But not only tension was evident. That could be present at any time. More significant was "the anarchy of values" following upon the decline of the traditional faith community with its obsolete supernatural sanctions inherited from the Middle Ages. This "anarchy of values"—a phrase coming from Wilhelm Dilthey—was evident on all sides, particularly as a consequence of positiv-

---

[1] *Natural Law and the Theory of Society*, trans. E. Barker (original German ed., Berlin, 1881; original trans., Cambridge, 1931, 2 vols.; paperback ed., Boston, 1957).

[2] (Cambridge, MA, 1983).

[3] *The Social Teaching of the Christian Churches*, 2 vols., trans. O. Wyon (New York, 1931; paperback ed., 1960); "Das christliche Naturrecht," *Aufsätze zur Geistegeschichte und Religionssoziologie*, ed. H. Baron (Tübingen, 1925), 156–65; "Das stoisch-christliche Naturrecht und das moderne profane Naturrecht," in ibid., 166–90. The ensuing discussion draws upon manuscript translations to be published in 1988 by T. & T. Clark (Edinburgh) and Fortress Press (Philadelphia), eds. J. Adams and W. Bense.

ism and relativism. One could not expect guidance from theologians who were terribly at ease in Zion, partly because in Germany they were coercively supported by the state and partly because they hugged the shore of their orthodoxy and their bibliolatry. The new, relatively liberal theology of Albrecht Ritschl (1822–1889) attracted Troeltsch, but eventually he became convinced that its social gospel of building here and now the Kingdom of God was not supported by historical studies. The liberal message was something subjectively read into the Gospels. In this view Troeltsch was speaking as a member of the Religious-Historical School; indeed, he was recognized as the dogmatic theologian of this School. He found in the Gospels no social philosophy of the kind promoted by Ritschl (or later by the Social Gospel in the United States). On the contrary, Jesus proclaimed an apocalyptic gospel affirming the coming of a new age. He offered no plan for overcoming oppression or for instituting social reform. The conflict he waged was against false religious leaders. There was here also a profound mystical element (though Jesus "was himself not a mystic"), relating the individual immediately to God and at the same time combining this individualism with a universalism. Since the churches were waiting for the Second Coming, primitive Christianity possessed no social philosophy for ongoing history. It, therefore, appropriated from Stoicism elements analogous to its own ethos; it adopted a conception of moral natural law, the source of legal rules and institutions. In Stoicism this was viewed as a law that rules the whole world, the divine reason. For the Stoics as well as for the Christians this moral natural law was rooted in the divine will.

Amos Wilder goes further than Troeltsch in seeing in the teaching of Jesus elements or equivalents of natural law.[4] He finds natural law to be "implicit in the world view of Israel and of Jesus." Through a careful analysis of texts in the Gospels he delineates equivalents of natural law in the teaching of Jesus.

In the history of the idea of natural law one finds considerable variety of content. The Stoic view excluded coercion, the differentiation of power or social class and private property which gives rise to such differentiation. This included the idea of humanity construed as a community of totally free people—all of this issuing from the divine reason. But none or little of this was practicable in the world's present state.

Consequently, a distinction was made between an absolute and a relative natural law. The former was realized in the Golden Age at the beginning of human history, with the proton, but its realization was thwarted by the rise of human passions, greed, the lust for power, egoism and violence. The Christians could readily discern the analogy with the biblical

---

[4] A. Wilder, "Equivalents of Natural Law in the Teaching of Jesus," *The Journal of Religion* 26 (1946): 125–35. This article came out of a two year study of natural law by Protestant theologians in the Middle West. It was published along with an article by the present writer, "The Law of Nature in Graeco-Roman Thought," *The Journal of Religion* 25 (1945): 97–118.

conception of the Creation and Fall. But they had a more exalted conception of the *eschaton*. Moreover, they did not renounce the absolute natural law so completely as did the Stoics. On the other hand, they knew from the biblical tradition that a standard was required for the present harsh order of state and law, the protection of property by law, war and brute force, slavery and domination. This Troeltsch called relative natural law. It presupposes the Fall, and it restrains and heals sin by means of rationally ordered organizations of coercion. For inventing the term "relative natural law" Troeltsch was criticized by Emil Brunner.[5] But Ernest Barker follows Troeltsch by adopting the term.[6] It is worth noting that Gierke in discussing Ulpian's (c. 220 A.D.) twofold conception of natural law speaks of the distinction "between the 'absolute' and the 'conditioned' dictates of reason. The latter is the only form of natural law in which it could be applied to the real world."[7] For the Christians the relative natural law was identified with the Decalogue, the expression of divine reason manifesting itself under the present conditions of the state of sin.

There have been numerous attempts to classify conceptions or interpretations of natural law. Troeltsch, the sociologist, devised a comprehensive scheme in terms of his typology of religious associations, the church type, the sect type and the mystical. This typology appears and reappears in his writings with a richness of formulation, notably in *The Social Teaching of the Christian Churches*, in the essay on "The Stoic-Christian Natural Law and Modern Secular Natural Law" and in the essay on "The Social Philosophy of Christianity."[8] These ideal types are for Troeltsch not merely abstract, transhistorical concepts. They serve as the basis for periodization in Christian history and for identifying the dynamics of the Christian movement in history. They also indicate different types of organization and membership in terms of which the Christian movement related itself to the surrounding world, the larger society. We can give here only abbreviated formulations of these widely familiar concepts.

The most important and central sociological form is the church-type, best illustrated by the medieval church. Here salvation is something given with the divine decree of salvation, as something in principle already realized, independent of personal achievement and perfection. One is born into the church. It is for the masses and for all classes. This type can compromise with existing structures of society which persist in the state of sin and in which the members have to live. Relative natural law is characteristic here.

---

[5]*Justice and the Social Order*, trans. M. Hottinger (New York, 1945), 270, 273.

[6]Gierke, *Natural Law and the Theory of Society*, xxxvii.

[7]Ibid., 233.

[8]Troeltsch, *The Social Teachings*; also id., *Die Sozialphilosophie des Christentums* (Zurich, 1922); "The Ideas of Natural Law and Humanity in World Politics," trans. E. Barker, in Gierke, *Natural Law and the Theory of Society*, Appendix I, 201–22.

The sect revolts against the church. The point of departure for the medieval sects was the Gregorian reform and revolution within the church. The sects are rigorous in their application of the evangelical ethic. They do not base their arguments upon learned patristic or Aristotelian researches into the Law of God but upon the plain Law of Christ or the Sermon on the Mount, the absolute law of nature. This conception permits a good deal of variety of interpretation, forms of inequality as well as of equality. By the appeal to an absolute natural law the sects give to their biblicism "an illuminating reason and a passionate sentiment." The sect does not build upon an objectively and institutionally available grace. The members belong mainly to the lower classes. The "note" of the typical sect is the piety of the members. The sect refuses to surrender to the general state of sinfulness. Compromise is rejected, and, therefore, relative natural law is rejected. One is a member of the sect by choice. Therefore, the sect substitutes the voluntary association for the institutional church. In general one may say that orientation to absolute natural law is characteristic.

The sects may be divided into two main groups: the withdrawing sect avoids state and law, often forming small groups separated from the world; the aggressive sect attempts to transform the world (even by force). By far the most important here are the Anabaptists and their progeny who form independent, democratic congregations such as among the English Independents and the American Pilgrims. Gradually, however, the radical natural law feature is pushed into the background. Yet some of these groups become forerunners of modern socialism with an egalitarian natural law, which, in certain quarters, gradually loses the religious foundation.

Mysticism constitutes a third type. Here the aim is immediacy of experience in the relationship to God. The historical and institutional elements are, at best, merely a stimulus and a means to the inner or suprahistorical communion with the divine. This mystical type can appeal to the doctrine of the Spirit in the New Testament, especially to John and Paul. It tends to remain aloof from the world and society, entailing a disjunction between the inner and the outer worlds. Consequently, it is not concerned with institutional organizations. Ultimately, then, mysticism is a radical, noncommunal form of individualism. Natural law scarcely plays a role. This sort of mysticism may be found in all periods, interwoven with church and sect.

These three types appear in successive periods of Western history, finally coming to fruition in the Free Church. Here we see the advent of the denomination as a type. This concept is not explicitly delineated by Troeltsch, though it is always just under the surface. So much for the theory of periodization. It will be noted that a difference between the church-type and the sect-type appears in the attitude toward compromise. Whereas compromise is characteristic of the church-type, it is rejected by the sect-type. We have already observed that in the third century Ulpian held that the only way to affect "the real world" is through relative natural law. Troeltsch speaks of this as compromise. For him the concept refers to the characteristic, indeed the indispensable, way for Christianity to affect the surrounding "real world." The concept appears from the very earliest to the latest of his writings.[9] The history of Christianity, Troeltsch says, is "a tremendous, continuous compromise between the Utopian demands of the Kingdom of God and the permanent conditions of our actual human life."[10] Compromise is inevitable in the ethical involvement of Christianity in the world, where the attempt is made to realize ethical purposes so far as possible. Compromise in this sense is related to the tension between spirit and nature, life and thought, ideal and reality, moral norm and economic interests, church and state, the individual and the state, science and religion, church and religion, asceticism and the worldly ethic—in short, it is the catalytic link between Christianity and the world. Yet, life itself, of course, remains sinful—a mixture, that is to say, of nature and the divine life.

In spelling out the ramifications of this schema, Troeltsch sets forth a metaphysical interpretation. One might momentarily call it a form of animism (the view that all things possess a natural life or vitality). Each of the polar entities represents an intrinsic, dynamic reality—all together unfolding "the vitality, multiplicity and freedom of the world in God, and indeed the creative freedom of God Himself."[11]

I have referred to this view as a form of animism. It would be nearer to a Troeltschean conception if we spoke of it as "the primacy of the will."[12] Absolute and relative natural law must be seen in the context of the idea of compromise and its metaphysical presuppositions.

We must now turn to a consideration of Lutheranism and Calvinism. Troeltsch writes at length on Martin Luther's doctrine of natural law. Under the influence of the rediscovery of Aristotle, the Thomistic doctrine of natural law is formulated, furnishing a precondition for theocracy or the universal rule of the church. Liberty, equality and common property are regarded as the true Christian ideals, but these ideals belonged to the original state in Paradise. Since the Fall, relative natural law prevails as a punishment and as a restraint of sin. In relative natural law sanction is found for the monogamous family with patriarchal power of the man, for the state with the rule of force, of war and of law, also for the regulation of the just

[9]The term appears frequently in *The Social Teachings*, beginning with the treatment of Paul (ch. 1, sec. 2) and then repeatedly in *Christian Thought: Its History and Application*, published posthumously (Westport, CT, 1923), *passim*. See index of the volume.

[10]Ibid., 165.

[11]"Contingency," *Hastings Dictionary of Religion and Ethics*, ed. J. Hastings (New York, 1931), 2: 139.

[12]Here one may see a similarity between Troeltsch and Tillich. (Tillich spoke of Troeltsch as his "mentor.") See J. Adams, et al., eds., *The Thought of Paul Tillich* (San Francisco, CA, 1986), esp. Introduction by the present writer.

price and for the condemnation of wholesale trade and usury. One can see here that at one time the church conservatively protects the power structure and at another time progressively protects the rights of the individual. The church claims the service of the entire society. The state, the product of sin, becomes the bulwark of order and liberty.

Luther rejects Roman theology and canon law. He does not accept the dual morality of Catholicism, the distinction between a lukewarm mass-Christianity and a monastically inclined elite. For the same reason he does not recognize the hierarchical structure of society with its steps leading from nature to grace, from the forms of life ruled by natural law to the realm of grace in the church. He cannot, therefore, set the natural and the Christian law side by side, but must draw the one into the other. He has to realize the Christian law immediately within and by means of the forms of life ruled by natural law. He accomplishes this by means of the doctrine of vocation. In accordance with natural law, society is divided into a system of vocations and classes. But something more is needed. The vocational division of labor based on natural law must be inspired by the spirit of Christian love through the preaching of the Word.

In accordance with natural law, big business, speculation and a credit economy are excluded as well as any revolutionary spirit. The relative natural law is, therefore, extremely conservative. All order and welfare depend upon obedience to the authorities—whatever they may be at a particular time. Even when the authorities abuse their power they must be obeyed. Resistence destroys the social order based on natural law. The authority is based upon reason and the divine will—the relative natural law. Therefore, Luther could oppose the peasants when they made their de-mands for reform. In this way he did away with the Stoic and rationalist elements of natural law, even though he did view the Decalogue as equivalent to natural law.

This whole view of Luther has been vigorously disputed, for example, by Karl Holl who asserts that Luther presented a new conception of community in both the secular and the religious realm, an organic view of the community analogous to the Pauline view of the body of Christ. Yet because of sin there is a need for law and coercion. But the nature of community—like God's own nature—is to love and to evoke love.[13]

John Calvin takes over the Lutheran-Catholic natural law but with an important difference. He does not adopt the Lutheran transmutation of natural law into a law of divinely sanctioned authority. He, therefore, retains the ancient Catholic natural law with its mixture of rationalistic-individual-istic and irrational-authoritarian elements. Calvin forbids resistance to duly

---

[13]We have given here only a suggestion of Holl's critique of Troeltsch. For an extensive account of this critique, see the Introduction by W. Bense to K. Holl, *The Reconstruction of Morality*, eds. J. Adams and W. Bense (Minneapolis, 1979).

constituted authority by the private individual. It is reserved for a subordinate authority. If the highest authority fails, the subordinate authority may step into its place and carry out the natural and the divine law. We may call this the institutionalization of dissent, but it is a dissent belonging to a constituted group authority. The control of power is a corporate control. In short, we have here a corporate constitutionalism. Clearly, we see in Calvin not only a theologian but also a trained lawyer.

In later Neo-Calvinism, constitutional dissent could spread within the society in a democratic direction. Here natural law becomes popular sovereignty. Authority rests with the people, not with private individuals but through duly constituted corporate representatives. Another deviation from Luther and from Catholic natural law is to be seen in Calvin's declaration that usury and commerce are permitted by natural law. As a consequence of this (urban) ethos Calvinism was able in good conscience to form alliances with the countries and the social classes representing the rise of the capitalist economy.

An even more far-reaching transformation of Calvinist natural law occurs in the English Revolution of the seventeenth century and in America under the influence of the Independents whose orientation was Anabaptist and sectarian. To be sure, Oliver Cromwell resorts to force. But, in the democratic direction, relative natural law of the sinful state is replaced by a conception of democratic equality and self-government, an approach to absolute natural law.

Viewing the variety and taking into account the separation of church and state, Troeltsch asserts that the general distinction between the church and the sect has been wiped out. Looking back over the whole period to the Middle Ages he finds only two fully elaborated social philosophies, Roman Catholicism and Calvinism.

But more must be said here. We can discern a great difference between Calvin's position as a whole and that of Luther and Lutheranism. Calvin speaks about the identity of natural law with the Decalogue, but the whole Old Testament law and the history of Israel are viewed as illustrations of natural law. The state is never regarded as a mere antidote to the fallen condition and a penalty for evil. It is chiefly regarded as a good and holy institution appointed by God. Moreover, private property likewise seems to be a directly divine institution. Indeed, political and economic institutions are regarded as divine institutions for the purpose of preserving social peace and harmony. For Calvin, then, the relative natural law is a divine institution. (We leave aside here a discussion of Calvin's use of the Ten Commandments, apart from noting that the moral law which has permanent validity is chiefly associated with the Commandments that inculcate the worship of God and the mutual love of men.)

Another possibility (a surprising one indeed) is realized—the decline of universal natural law. This takes place under the rubric of Romanticism. But there were several kinds of Romanticism. A. O. Lovejoy used to speak of "three Romanticisms."[14] In the lecture delivered only a few months before his death,[15] Troeltsch sees Romanticism as bringing about the demise of natural law in nineteenth century Germany. This essay gives a remarkable synoptic view not only of natural law with its history but also of the Romantic turn in the direction of historical jurisprudence in the *Volksgeist*, the spirit of the people. This Romanticism centers attention not on the universal, the idea of humanity, but on the positive, the particular, the individual, the unique, the spiritually organic, superpersonal creative forces belonging to a *Volk*. As Ortega y Gasset today describes this view, human being has no nature but only a history.[16] This whole movement separates Germany from Western Europe. With its appeal to the old Teutonic poetry of the Volsungs (which inspired Wagner) it leads finally to a curious mixture of mysticism and brutality. One could say here that Romanticism was dehumanized to go on all fours, "brutalizing romance and romanticizing cynicism." It makes law something that lies outside the moral boundaries, a demoralized law. This entails a total and fundamental destruction of any idea of a universal natural law. With a basic philosophy of pantheism this German view adopts what has been called "the principle of identity": it discerns a spiritual and divine essence inherent in a new kind of community supported by a stern realism. In this new community, the state in following its "legitimate political interest" is elevated to the position of a sort of deity. The consequence is a contempt for the idea of a universal humanity. Here we encounter a blind worship of power and success. Uniqueness has become what we might call "uniquity." Bismarck, the "Iron Chancellor," is its symbol and incarnation. These pages are a severe indictment of an ingredient of German culture by a German. In reading these pages of the essay one can see an anticipation of the Third Reich of the Nazis.

Despite these demonic perversions of individuality, this toad, ugly and venemous, wears yet a jewel in his head. Troeltsch asserts that by virtue of the very idea of individuality the German theories have contributed to historical investigation and to the understanding of history. They have created the historical sense as a "specific and definite thing." What is needed, however, is not merely the historical but the universal historical. This is to be found not in Germany but in the great representatives of Western Europe. This does not mean, however, that we turn in this direction with an uncritical eye. The ideas of Western Europe, and especially of capitalism with its lopsided individualism, are today under a new scrutiny at the hands of socialism (which has its own limitations). The needed return to the West is a return to natural law. In the context of his philosophy of history,

---

[14]A. Lovejoy, *Essays in the History of Ideas* (Baltimore, 1948, 1970), 228–53.

[15]*Die Sozialphilosophie.*

[16]Cited by G. Iggers, "German Historical Thought and the Idea of Natural Law," unpublished paper presented to the College of Social Studies, Wesleyan University, March 9, 1964.

Troeltsch looks for a new dynamic synthesis to be created not by an individual but by a generation of cooperation.

II. BERMAN ON NATURAL LAW AND HISTORY

We turn now to a discussion of Harold Berman's treatment of natural law. Like Troeltsch, he laments that law has become increasingly secular, pragmatic and political. But, partly due to his centering attention on jurisprudence, he takes a path somewhat different from that of Troeltsch. In his 1980 address at the Chicago Divinity School, entitled "The Moral Crisis of the Western Legal Tradition and the Weightier Matters of the Law," he says that law "no longer seems to be rooted in an ongoing tradition and guided by a universal vision."[17] What has been lost is a sense of the rootedness of law in the moral order of the universe and a sense of its transcendent qualities, the sense that it points to something beyond itself, to something dealt with by theology. In place of this rootedness, law is viewed as something "wholly instrumental, wholly invented, wholly pragmatic." Along with this attitude has come finally also a deep skepticism about law as a manifestation of justice. Equally mistaken is the antinomian view that confuses law with legalism. Here Berman would probably approve of T. S. Eliot's phrase that "the spirit killeth, the word giveth life."

These views are far distant from the "medieval marriage of jurisprudence and theology."[18] In the generations after Gregory VII, the symbol of a revolution in the history of the church, a distinction was made between divine law and human law, and within human law a distinction between ecclesiastical and secular law. The link between divine law and human law was natural law which helped to determine the priorities between enacted law and customary law. The subordination of positive law to natural law was re-enforced by the dualism of secular and ecclesiastical law. According to Gratian, the laws of the church itself were to be tested by their conformity to natural law.

But how did the breakdown of the marriage come about, the divorce between jurisprudence and theology? Berman sets forth the singular view that the divorce began with Anselm (1033–1109) who thought it is possible to prove "by reason alone" what faith knows through divine revelation. Although Anselm held that faith enlightens reason, the latter has its own principles of operation. This strategy was calculated to persuade the unbeliever; it also purported to harmonize articles of faith. In jurisprudence of the period one sees the same reliance on reason alone. When, later on, the

---

[17]*Criterion* 19 (1980): 15–23.

[18]H. Berman, an unpublished essay "The Marriage of Jurisprudence and Theology in Western Christendom" (c. 1969).

principal law-making and law-enforcing functions were transferred to the sole jurisdiction of the national state, the foundation was laid for the separation of jurisprudence from theology and ultimately for the complete secularization of legal thought. This process did not take place all at once. It reached its fruition in the crisis of the twentieth century.

In Berman's view, adherence was lacking, not only to natural law theory but also to the historical school. At the same time, the regnant school is the positivist school that treats law as essentially a particular type of political instrument, a body of rules "posited" by the state. Berman probably would consider Troeltsch's presentation of the Romantic historical outlook as a perversion of the historical school. In any event, his presentation gives major attention to jurisprudence.

Berman laments the fact, however, that the historical orientation has almost been lost. He, therefore, spells out the historical jurisprudence stemming from Savigny, "the most important German legal figure of the nineteenth century." His theory of law was directed against ideas prevailing in France after the Revolution. Legislation was viewed as the primary source of law. In this view the legislator is obliged to protect "the rights of man" or "the greatest good for the greatest number." But these views leave out of account traditions of the past with their "prerogatives and prejudices," words that reflect Burke's conception of the nation as a community of generations. Law is, therefore, considered to be an integral part of the common conscious-ness of the nation, "internal, silently operating powers." It must never become merely a body of ideal propositions [natural law] or a mere system of rules promulgated by the state [positivism]. It must always be an expression of the *Volksgeist*, a particular expression of the social and historical consciousness of a people at a given time and place. Berman compares this conception to that of the American "unwritten constitution," the national ideals, "the community values." Savigny's historical school held that the ultimate source of law is the older Germanic tradition of popular participation in law-making and adjudication as well as the more modern German tradition of scholarly interpretation and systematization of the common law, the *ius commune*. This common law, like the English common law, the traditional unenacted law, had been the common consciousness of the nation as it had developed through the generations by virtue of the *Volksgeist*.

We should note here that, as with positivism and natural law, signifi-cant criticisms have been made of the historical theory. I assume that the questions press upon us. How does one determine the *Volksgeist*? Does it include the Romanticism that, in Troeltsch's view, separated Germany from Western Europe and which suppressed natural law? Are we to assume that a judge in deciding a technical point in contract law is reflecting the

Volksgeist? In any event, one must recognize, as Berman emphasizes, that the common memory is highly selective, as in post-Nazi Germany.[19]

Now we come to the *pièce de resistance*: Berman's address in January, 1987 before the American Society of Christian Ethics, entitled "Toward an Integrative Jurisprudence: Politics, Morality, and History."[20] The term "integrative jurisprudence," as Berman points out, was used previously by Jerome Hall. In this scenario Berman proposes something similar to Troeltsch's demand for a dynamic synthesis. We should recall here that in his *The Interaction of Law and Religion* (1974) Berman suggested that we may be entering a new period to replace the period of particularism and fragmentation. In this new period one may encounter a new synthesis, interaction between and within all spheres, between the immanent and the transcendent, between the individual and the community, between and within the academic disciplines.

The 1987 lecture proposes to bring together three main schools of jurisprudence—positivist, historical and natural law. They became separated in the eighteenth and nineteenth centuries when legal philosophy was divorced from theology. Since that time each of these schools has developed in various directions. Berman agrees with Hall that the three can be brought together only by giving a broader definition to law than that which is usually adopted. He, therefore, defines the *actualization* of law as its essential feature. It is a type of social action, a process in which rules and values and traditions—all three—coalesce and are actualized. Pre-Enlightenment Christian writers from Aquinas to Blackstone, though characterized as natural law theorists, were also positivists and historicists. The common source of these three they found in the triune God.

In proposing integrative jurisprudence, then, Berman asserts that it is not a new thing. It has already appeared in Western legal theory. But, as we have seen, he holds that an authentic integration will require a recovery of the historical dimension. Germany in the 1920s and 1930s forsook historical jurisprudence and adopted an extreme positivism, thus also abandoning natural law theory. The rule of the state was glorified and made supreme over both history and the moral law of justice.

On the other hand, the historical school has found an echo in such figures as Maine and Maitland in England and in certain ways in Pound and Llewellyn in the United States. But a major trend turned attention to instruments and processes of legal development. More and more this trend issued in a sociology of law.

Yet, in England and America, judges have applied a historical jurisprudence combined with principles of reasonableness and fairness. Here again

---

[19]See E. Fraenkel, *The Dual State* (New York, 1941) for an account of the conflict in the courts of Nazi Germany between Nazi racist law and rational natural law.

[20]H. Berman, "Toward an Integrative Jurisprudence: Politics, Morality, and History." (Unpublished article.)

we encounter an integrative jurisprudence. In the United States, outstanding examples are Joseph Story and Benjamin Cardozo.

In recent decades the integration of the principal schools has been sidetracked by the decline of the historical approach. A spurious, a blind historicism centers attention on what has been said by lawmakers of an earlier time, on the belief that law expresses what has been said in past formulations of the spirit of freedom and equality. These views turn out to be futile attempts to repeat the past. Berman speaks of them as historical positivism and historical moralism. The essence of historical jurisprudence is not historicism but historicity. Law is an ongoing historical process developing from the past into the future. A genuine historical jurisprudence helps to determine the scope of freedom of legal action, the standards according to which law should be enacted and interpreted and the goals toward which the legal system strives. Therefore, hope is the nerve of this move into the future.

Looking toward the future, Berman sees the possible development of world law. The West is no longer the center; the West is in the larger world. He spells out in considerable detail the possibility of a broader law than the national law. Again, the need for an integrative jurisprudence is stressed. Accordingly, he asserts that history alone—and especially national history alone—is as futile and as demonic as politics alone or morality alone. What is needed is the sense of history, the sense of destiny, the sense of mission in America and throughout the West. As against current nationalism the idea must be emphasized that the body of law is binding on the state.

In all of this one must recognize that a revolutionary as well as an evolutionary element has appeared in the development of the Western legal tradition. Every nation looks to its revolutionary past. This means that historical jurisprudence must be alert not only to the living past but also to the times in which we live. To know the times is essential to any healthy jurisprudence. And a healthy jurisprudence will call for an integrative jurisprudence that seeks what both Troeltsch and Berman have defined as a new synthesis. Berman would agree with Troeltsch in holding that the human obligation is a response to a more-than-human truth and justice.

For a theological interpretation of the needed interaction between the philosophies of law we turn to Paul of Tarsus. In the *First Epistle to the Corinthians* we read, "The body does not consist of one member but of many. If the foot should say, 'Because I am not a hand, I do not belong to the body', that would not make it any less a part of the body." This is true also of the ear and the eye. "If the whole body were an ear, where would be the sense of smell?"[21] In short, any philosophy of law that is isolated from the others brings about distortion, for "if one member suffers, all suffer together."

[21]I Cor. 12:17.

This twelfth chapter of the *Epistle* is followed by the encomium of love. Accordingly, Harold Berman in an address given in 1963 at the Episcopal Theological School in Cambridge concludes that "law is a process creating conditions in which sacrificial love personified by Jesus Christ, can take root in society and grow."[22]

[22]"Law and Love," *Episcopal Theological School Bulletin* 56 (May, 1964): 12.

RELIGION AND THE CRIMINAL LAW:
TYPES AND CONTEXTS OF INTERACTION

W. Cole Durham, Jr.

It would be difficult to name any one individual who has done more in recent years to rekindle American interest in the interaction of law and religion than Professor Harold Berman. His scholarship has explored this interface on many fronts and has often paid particular attention to criminal law.[1] This emphasis is not surprising, since the reciprocal influence of law and religion is often most visible with respect to criminal norms and institutions.

In this essay, my aim is to further the work that Professor Berman has helped to reinvigorate, not by providing an in-depth study of some particular area in which the interaction of criminal law and religion is evident, but instead by attempting to sketch and categorize in a provisional way the incredibly broad range of types and contexts in which that interaction can be and has been experienced. Only when one begins to appreciate the multiplicity of the possible types and contexts of interaction and their constantly shifting, overlapping and interpenetrating influence on each other does one become conscious of the full complexity and richness of the interconnection between law and religion. My hope is that, while cataloguing these types and contexts may seem at first to yield little that is not obvious or commonplace, this essay will contribute to the process of thinking concretely about the range of ways in which religious and legal dimensions of human culture influence each other.

I. POSITIVE AND NEGATIVE DIMENSIONS OF INTERACTION

In the spirit of such concreteness, let me begin with two situations that might, at first, seem to have little to do with the relationship of law and religion. The first has to do with an incident that filled the national press a

---

[1]See generally H. Berman, "Love For Justice: The Influence of Christianity upon the Development of Law," *Oklahoma Law Review* 12 (1959): 86; id., *The Interaction of Law and Religion* (Nashville, 1974); id., "The Religious Foundations of Western Law," *Catholic University Review* 24 (1975): 490–508; id., "The Background of the Western Legal Tradition in the Folklaw of the Peoples of Europe," *University of Chicago Law Review* 45 (1978): 553–97; id., "The Interaction of Law and Religion," *Capital University Law Review* 8 (1979): 345–56; id., *Law and Revolution: The Formation of the Western Legal Tradition* (Cambridge, MA, 1983); id., "Religious Foundations of Law in the West: An Historical Perspective," *Journal of Law and Religion* 1 (1983): 3–43; id., "Law and Belief in Three Revolutions," *Valparaiso Law Review* 18 (1984): 569–629.

couple of years ago when a young woman sought to recant testimony that had led six years earlier to a rape conviction.[2] What drew particular fire from the press was the trial judge's decision to let the original conviction stand, despite the new testimony.

The case had all the earmarks of classic injustice: an innocent man was being returned to prison to serve the balance of a 25- to 50-year sentence for a crime he did not commit. To be sure, there were inconsistencies between the new testimony and the original proof at trial that could have led a reasonable fact finder to question the new testimony. The convicted party himself told a reporter after the hearing that he was not surprised by the decision, since he had researched Illinois law and found that no one had ever been freed on recanted testimony.[3] What no one mentioned amid all the uproar is that the tradition of discrediting recanted testimony is centuries old, tracing back at least to medieval canon law, if not before. Whether the oaths of witnesses were regarded as "a summoning of Divine vengeance upon false swearing, whereby, when the spectators see the witness standing unharmed, they know that the Divine judgment has pronounced him to be a truth teller,"[4] as in medieval law, or whether the oath is merely "a method of reminding the witness strongly of the Divine punishment somewhere in store for false swearing,"[5] as it became later, it is clear that "the solemnity of the religious sanction imports a reference to religion and morals. . . ."[6] At least in early periods, the rule prevailed that "[i]f evidence given on oath must be believed because it is so given, the witness who has sworn to it cannot be allowed to retract it."[7]

The second situation is one noted by Professor Berman in connection with the insanity defense:

> If a sane man is convicted of murder and sentenced to death, and thereafter, before the sentence is carried out, he becomes insane, his execution will be postponed until he recovers his sanity. Generally speaking, this is the law in Western countries and in many non-Western countries as well. Why? The historical answer, in the West, is that if a man is executed while he is insane he will not have had the opportunity freely to confess his sins and to take the sacrament of holy communion. He must be allowed to recover his sanity before he dies so that his soul will not be condemned to eternal hellfire but will instead have the opportunity to expiate his sins in purgatory and ultimately, at the Last Judgment, to enter the kingdom of heaven.[8]

[2]"More Than a Case of Rape," *Newsweek* (April 22, 1985), 21.
[3]Ibid.
[4]J. Wigmore, *Evidence in Trials at Common Law* (Boston, 1970), 3: 2349 (§1816); W. Holdsworth, *A History of English Law* (London, 1944), 9:189.
[5]Ibid.
[6]Ibid.
[7]Ibid., 206.
[8]Berman, *Law and Revolution*, 166.

What these two legal curiosities have in common is that they both evidence the vanishing religious background that was once the substance and the matrix of criminal law. They remind us of both the continuities and discontinuities between past and present. Consciousness of the religious content of these legal relics evokes an ambivalent response. On the one hand, they remind us of the profoundly religious roots of many of our deepest convictions about criminal law. The discounting of recanted testimony reminds us of religiously grounded ideals of due process and evidentiary caution. The quirk in insanity procedure reflects the principle of culpability, with its insistence on *mens rea* and moral accountability, and the principle that excessively harsh or disproportionate punishments should be avoided. On the other hand, the dissonance between the implicated religious ideals and the seemingly bizarre practical results reminds us of the darker side of the criminal law's religious heritage—of religion's legacy of superstition and abuse. Religion's refining influence on criminal law has too often been matched by episodes of witchburning and the prosecution of heresy—both literally, as in medieval times, and figuratively, whenever overzealous prosecution has been justified by reference to religious values.

To understand the relationship between contemporary criminal law and religion, both the affirmative grounding of criminal law in religion and the negative reaction of secularized criminal law against religion must be taken into account. Scholars too often ignore one or the other of these contrasting approaches to the issue of interaction. The religiously oriented literature is replete with works that seek to establish the moral and religious grounding of the criminal law by tracing the religious genealogy of particular crimes,[9] or that note the passing of a pre-secular age when a stronger bond between religious and legal values still prevailed.[10] At the same time, the more

[9]See, e.g., S. Feigin, "Homicide in Ancient Oriental Law and in Babylonian-Assyrian Contracts," *Hatekufa* 32–33 (1947): 740–65 (Hebrew); J. Ostrow, "Tannaitic and Roman Procedure in Homicide," *Jewish Quarterly Review* 48 (1958): 352; id., "Tannaitic and Roman Procedure in Homicide," *Jewish Quarterly Review* 53 (1961): 160; B. Jackson, *Theft in Early Jewish Law* (Oxford, 1972); H. Jacobs, "Theft in Early Jewish Law," *Journal of Jewish Studies* 24 (1983): 91; H. McKeating, "The Development of the Law on Homicide in Ancient Israel," *Vetus Testamentum* 25 (1975): 46; M. Sulzberger, *The Ancient Hebrew Law of Homicide* (Philadelphia, 1915); B. Cohen, *The Talmudic Law Concerning the Alteration of Objects Obtained by Robbery* (New York, 1927).

[10]See, e.g., Berman, *Interaction*, 21–30; id., "Religious Foundations," 3–5; K. Bünger and H. Trimborn, eds., *Religiöse Bedingungen in frühen und in orientalischen Rechten* (Wiesbaden, 1952); I. Cornelison, *The Relation of Religion to Civil Government in the United States of America* (New York/London, 1895; reprint, New York, 1970); see generally Lord Denning, "The Influence of Religion on Law," *Christian Legal Society Quarterly* 2 (1981): 12–18; G. Dilcher and I. Staff, eds., *Christentum und modernes Recht: Beiträge zum Problem der Säkularisation* (Frankfurt, 1984); Z. Falk, *Law and Religion: The Jewish Experience* (Jerusalem, 1981); S. Guterman, "The Interaction of Religion, Law and Politics in Western Society: Its Historical Character and Influence," *University of Miami Law Review* 17 (1963): 439–68; J. Morden, "An Essay on the Connections Between Law and Religion," *Journal of Law and Religion* 2 (1984):

secular sources are all too prone to assume that the path of progress lies in stripping away residual religious vestiges from an enlightened criminal system.[11]

The point is straightforward but, nonetheless, important. One cannot hope to obtain a comprehensive picture of the interaction of law and religion without considering both the positive influences and the negative reactions. Only by paying attention to both poles of this interaction can we expect to develop a realistic sense of the ways in which reciprocal influences are structured. The types and contexts of interaction on the positive side, where law and religion strengthen, mold and reinforce each other, are often quite different from those on the negative side, where the aim is to disentangle a tainted and tattering alliance.

II. REFLECTIONS ON THE NATURE OF INTERACTION: TOWARD A MORE FLUID MODEL

Any effort to explore the relationship between criminal law and religion is plagued from the outset by the need to confront the myriad ways in which the two may interact. This problem is further compounded by the vagueness of the term "religion." In a more extensive study, the breadth of the definition of religion could conceivably be important for determining the ultimate scope of work—that is, for expanding or narrowing the range of human actions, beliefs and institutions that might count as religious and whose bearing on criminal law needs to be considered. For present purposes, however, an expansive definition will suffice: religion is any institutional arrangement or set of doctrines and beliefs that offers some means of relating individuals or groups to what is taken to be the ultimate nature of reality.[12] The effort here, after all, is to mark out a broad set of types and contexts of interaction, and any premature definitional limitation on the scope of inquiry would be unfortunate.

Within the expansive domain contemplated by this definition, the fact

---

17–19; W. Naucke, "Christliche, aufklärerische and wissenschaftstheoretische Begründung des Strafrechts (Luther-Beccaria-Kant)," in Dilcher and Staff, eds., *Christentum*, 213–221; D. Van Ness, *Crime and Its Victims* (Downers Grove, IL, 1986); R. Wilson, "Nomos: The Biblical Significance of Law," *Scottish Journal of Theology* 5 (1952): 17–19.

[11]See H. Achenbach, *Historische und dogmatische Grundlagen der strafrechtssystematischen Schuldlehre* (Berlin, 1974), 19–26 (modern "scientific" conceptions of culpability are essentially post-Enlightenment developments, despite links to earlier tradition); J. Hall, "Biblical Atonement and Modern Criminal Law," *Journal of Law and Religion* 1 (1983): 279 (notes that modern ethics and penal theory tend to supplant biblical notions of atonement with the idea of being responsible for one's own crimes); L. Radzinowicz, *Ideology and Crime: A Study of Crime in its Social and Historical Context* (London, 1966), 1–28; G. Stratenwerth, *Die Zukunft des strafrechtlichen Schuldprinzips* (Heidelberg, 1977), 5–8.

[12]Cf. "Religion," in W. Reese, *Dictionary of Philosophy and Religion: Eastern and Western Thought* (New York, 1980), 488.

that criminal law and religion constitute fundamental, interconnected dimensions of culture escapes no one, but the methodological questions concerning the nature of the interconnections are elusive and pose some of the deepest questions in social theory.[13] Naive causal models suggesting, for example, that a particular religious idea causes a particular type of statute or practice to be adopted fail to capture the full richness of the interaction, and are as likely to mislead as to prove useful.[14] More sophisticated theories can often be equally problematic.

Sir Henry Maine described the relationship between criminal law and religion as an evolving one, starting with fusion of religion and law and moving toward separation. In his words, "there is no system of recorded law, literally from China to Peru, which, when it first emerges into notice, is not seen to be entangled with religious ritual and observance."[15] This fusion of law and religion is as evident in criminal law as in other fields.[16] The path of progress moves, according to Maine, from this primitive blurring of law and religion toward more sophisticated systems in which the realms of law and religion are more clearly delineated.

Maine's view corresponds to a typical way of thinking about the relationship between law (including criminal law) and religion.[17] This way of thinking recognizes religion as an important co-founder of the criminal law, but one whose contribution can be dispensed with once a more advanced stage of civilization is attained. This type of view is important not only as a historical curio, but because of its residual (if sometimes merely

---

[13]The methodological questions about how criminal law and religion interact are merely sub-issues of much broader questions about how religion interacts with culture in general. See, e.g., C. Geertz, *The Interpretation of Cultures* (New York, 1973), 87–141; R. Merton, *Social Theory and Social Structure*, rev. ed. (New York, 1968), 96–100; T. Parsons, *Essays in Sociological Theory, Pure and Applied* (Glencoe, IL, 1949), 61–63; R. Unger, *Knowledge and Politics* (New York, 1975), 12–16; id., *Law in Modern Society: Toward a Criticism of Social Theory* (New York, 1975), 57, 76–86, 127–33, 238–44.

[14]Consider, e.g., the *Caroli constitutio criminalis*, a German criminal code enacted by the Catholic Emperor Charles V in 1532. The *Carolina* remained an important source of German criminal law for the next three and a half centuries and has been characterized as "an achievement of the spirit of the Reformation." See, e.g., C. von Bar, et al., *A History of Continental Criminal Law*, trans. T. Bell (Boston, 1916), 211. The *Carolina* was based largely on the *Bambergensis Halsgerichtsordnung*, drafted by Freiherr Johann von Schwarzenberg and enacted in 1507. E. Schmidt, *Einführung in die Geschichte der deutschen Strafrechtspflege*, 3d ed. (Göttingen, 1965), 109. Since Luther's denunciation of papal indulgences did not occur until 1517, a strict causal theory would make it difficult to say that the law reforms involved were caused by the Lutheran Reformation. On the other hand, Schwarzenberg did become Lutheran, and his reforms are not totally independent of the religious reformation. Berman, "Law and Belief," 582–89. Deeper connections between the legal and religious reforms are obscured by a narrow causal reading of the events.

[15]H. Maine, *Dissertations on Early Law and Custom* (London, 1891), 5.

[16]Ibid., 40–45.

[17]See, e.g., C. Lobingier, "Common Roots of Law and Religion," *Temple Law Quarterly* 19 (1946): 390, 392; E. Revillout, *Cours de droit egyptian* (Paris, 1884), 1: 48.

subliminal) force in a wide range of contexts in which the influence of religion on law is subtly (or not so subtly) disparaged. Part of the tacit rhetorical appeal of deterrence over retributivist theories, for example, is that the latter are tainted by their association with a literal version of the *lex talionis* and other features of "primitive" religion. The very use of the term "retributivism" to describe deontological or culpability-oriented theories of punishment conjures up images of primitive society, thereby shading argumentation in favor of instrumentalist and consequentialist theories. We have lost our naiveté about the march of progress, and, for that matter, about the nature of what is "modern" and what is "primitive," but arguments from modernity are still made, and, when they are, they tend to downgrade the role of religion in criminal law.[18]

Maine's arguments that law and religion were fused in ancient legal systems rested in large part on analysis of ancient codes and on noting the recurrent tendency for such codes to intermingle religious and secular matters. Maine treated the codes as collections of existing customs, subsequently altered by fictions, equity and legislation.[19] He interpreted the seemingly random interspersing of religious and secular norms as a sign that no sharp conceptual distinctions were made between religious and secular dimensions of social activity.

In 1935, A. S. Diamond subjected Maine's account to a withering attack.[20] Countering Maine's picture of a fusion of law and religion in early cultures, Diamond argued that core criminal offenses were secular *ab initio*. The mere juxtaposition of religious and secular provisions in ancient codes was not sufficient warrant to conclude that the secular offenses were infused with a religious aura. Diamond acknowledged that the frontiers of law and religion touch at two points: in the area of sacral crimes and in the administration of oaths or ordeals in litigation.[21] For the most part, however, he contended that the separation of law and religion was quite evident from early periods and at virtually all stages of social development.[22] In fact, he argued, given that scribes tended to be clerics in virtually all early cultures, it is actually remarkable how little of the extant codes are religious.[23]

---

[18]I am conscious that notions of increasing differentiation of concepts and social structures can be invoked in ways that do not imply acceptance of naive unilinear conceptions of evolution and progress. See, e.g., B. Jackson, "Reflections on Biblical Criminal Law," *Journal of Jewish Studies* 24 (1973): 8, 13. Too often, however, arguments that implicitly assume that what is "modern" is better than what is "primitive" in the context of criminal law do not display this sophistication.

[19]H. Maine, *Ancient Law: Its Connection with the Early History of Society and Its Relevance to Modern Ideas* (London, 1861).

[20]Most notably A. S. Diamond, *Primitive Law Past and Present* (London, 1971; first published in 1935). (Citations in this article are to the 1971 edition.)

[21]Ibid., 47.

[22]Ibid., 48. Ethelbehrt's Code, e.g., which emerged in a society exhibiting primitive characteristics, was entirely secular and contained no religious rules or sanctions. Ibid., 58–59.

[23]Ibid., 47.

There are a number of problems with Diamond's position,[24] but my principal point in raising the Maine/Diamond debate here is to highlight a deeper methodological point. While Maine and Diamond are at odds on many points, they are at one in taking an essentially "either-or" attitude toward the relation of criminal law and religion. Either the criminal law is infused with religiosity, or it is secular, or it is at some transition point in between. The reality is that the criminal law may be both religious and secular at the same time, or that individuals within a particular culture may see it, at alternating moments, as one and then the other and then the other again.

The methodological rigidity implicit in the positions of Maine and Diamond is parallel in many ways to that discernible in a debate between Lévy-Bruhl and Malinowski concerning the nature of "native thought." Lévy-Bruhl interpreted native thought primarily in mystic terms, whereas Malinowski interpreted it in a more secular common sense manner.[25] Clifford Geertz's commentary on this debate is worth quoting at length:

The movement back and forth between the religious perspective and the common-sense perspective is actually one of the more obvious empirical occurrences on the social scene, though, again, one of the most neglected by social anthropologists, virtually all of whom have seen it happen countless times. Religious belief has usually been presented as a homogeneous characteristic of an individual, like his place of resi-

---

[24]His grouping of codes by stages of economic development rather than by chronological time, ibid. [Introduction], may allow him to manipulate his data to some extent. For example, "Early Codes" that Diamond views as secular are all drawn from Europe in the early Middle Ages. The fact that economic development in Europe at the time may have been comparable to development levels in the Near East at extremely early periods does not preclude the possibility that early Europeans could have been sensitized to the secular/religious distinction as a result of awareness of cultures that were chronologically earlier but developmentally "later." Diamond is also unduly wedded to an Austinian conception of law as sanction. Thus he sometimes seems to imply that unless rules have religious, as opposed to secular, sanctions, they are not religious rules. Describing Christian areas in early Europe, e.g., he states, "[t]here are no religious rules of conduct—that is to say, rules with religious and not secular sanctions, in the continental codes of Europe, but several contain a separate section on ecclesiastical law." Most significantly, Diamond is so intent on showing that a secular outlook is discernible from very early times that he fails to pay sufficient attention to significant interaction between secular and religious outlooks. At one point, while arguing that the law had only minimal contacts with religion (i.e., certain crimes that are so abhorrent to the community that they become both crimes and breaches of religious norms, and use of religion in procedure to ascertain truth by ordeal), he states essentially as an aside, "Otherwise religion serves chiefly to reinforce the devotion of the people to its traditional code of conduct, and it must be rarely, if ever, that it leads to new law or amendments of the law." Ibid., 326. But, obviously, the larger issue is not merely whether religious consciousness was a source of values but whether it had an impact on their vitality. Maine did not necessarily claim that religion was a source of secular law. See Lobingier, "Common Roots of Law and Religion," 392, n. 14.

[25]L. Lévy-Bruhl, *How Natives Think*, trans. W. Clare (New York, 1926); B. Malinowski, *Magic, Science, and Religion, and Other Essays* (Garden City, NY, 1948).

dence, his occupational role, his kinship position, and so on. But religious belief in the midst of ritual, where it engulfs the total person, transporting him, so far as he is concerned, into another mode of existence, and religious belief as the pale, remembered reflection of that experience in the midst of everyday life are not precisely the same thing, and the failure to realize this has led to some confusion, most especially in connection with the so-called primitive-mentality problem. Much of the difficulty between Lévy-Bruhl and Malinowski on the nature of native thought, for example, arises from a lack of full recognition of this distinction; for where the French philosopher was concerned with the view of reality savages adopted when taking a specifically religious perspective, the Polish-English ethnographer was concerned with that which they adopted when taking a strictly common-sense one. Both perhaps vaguely sensed that they were not talking about exactly the same thing, but where they went astray was in failing to give a specific accounting of the way in which these two forms of "thought"—or, as I would rather say, these two modes of symbolic formulations—interacted, so that where Lévy-Bruhl's savages tended to live, despite his postludial disclaimers, in a world composed entirely of mystical encounters, Malinowski's tended to live, despite his stress on the functional importance of religion, in a world composed entirely of practical actions. They became reductionists (an idealist is as much a reductionist as a materialist) in spite of themselves because they failed to see man as moving more or less easily, and very frequently, between radically contrasting ways of looking at the world, ways which are not continuous with one another but separated by cultural gaps across which Kierkegaardian leaps must be made in both directions .... [26]

What this passage stresses is the need, in analyzing the interaction of law and religion, to examine the innumerable contexts in which the interaction occurs with full awareness of the *Gestalt*-type switches back and forth between religious and nonreligious orientations. As Ze'ev Falk has stated, "a philosophy of law or religion must speak of consciousness as the forum where legal as well as religious concepts are formulated."[27] Ultimately, it is within the consciousness of an individual, or in the interacting consciousnesses of the members of society, that the interaction of law and religion occurs. The fact that religion and law exist side-by-side in consciousness, as both Maine and Diamond, in effect, recognized, is not nearly so interesting as understanding the more fluid ways in which they reciprocally influence each other as consciousness moves back and forth (or fails to move back and forth) between religiously charged and secular outlooks.

[26]Geertz, *Interpretation*, 119–20.
[27]Falk, *Law and Religion*, 25.

III. TYPES OF INTERACTION BETWEEN
CRIMINAL LAW AND RELIGION

The range of interactional contexts and the types of interaction worthy of exploration in the field of criminal law and religion are virtually limitless. In what follows, I make only a few initial forays into this vast domain. My aim here is merely to provide an overview of some of the types and contexts of interaction I have in mind. My list makes no claims for completeness. Even the categorization of "types" and "contexts" is crude and haphazard, and the various categories are not to be thought of as being mutually exclusive.

By using the word "type," I do not mean to suggest anything as sophisticated as Weber's notion of ideal types. I have in mind merely a number of different ways or modes in which religion interacts with criminal law. My list of types of interaction includes the following: (1) reception or transplantation of religious norms into criminal law; (2) religious reinforcement of secular norms; (3) shared conduits of cultural meaning; (4) shaping the external structures of normative systems; (5) providing the narrative context for legal materials; (6) molding the deep structures of criminal law; (7) shaping fundamental concepts; and (8) grounding the moral striving that drives the institutions of criminal justice. I shall comment on each of these in turn.

A. Reception or Transplantation of Religious Norms into Criminal Law

Law grows as much by reception and transplantation[28] as by revolution. Legal systems, by nature of their subject matter and their complexity, are too cumbersome to be created *ex nihilo*. Revolutionary belief structures and ideology invariably play a filtering role in determining what is received or transplanted and what is rejected. They also provide the energy necessary to overcome legal inertia. But the bulk of legal growth in criminal law as elsewhere occurs through a continuing process of borrowing, tinkering, comparing, patching up and rethinking. Thus, one thinks of the reception of Roman law in what is now civilian Europe, the reception and transplantation of European law in the Americas and the Third World, and the ongoing borrowing of legal ideas among nations.

Reception can entail renewal as well as mere borrowing; renewal and borrowing can involve underlying values and norms as well as statutes and legal procedures. Legal systems are often imbued with religious values as a result of reception at this level. The spread of Islam suggests one obvious set

---

[28]The focus on reception and transplantation is suggested by the work of Professor Alan Watson, who has studied these processes from a comparative law perspective with great acuity and depth. See, generally, A. Watson, *The Making of the Civil Law* (Philadelphia, 1981); id., *Legal Transplants: An Approach to Comparative Law* (Edinburgh, 1974).

of examples. More significant for the West has been the "reception" of biblical values, mediated, to be sure, through different religious traditions in different places and at different times, but exerting an ongoing influence nonetheless. Examples of European laws with biblical antecedents are numerous.[29] When the reception process is religiously motivated, or religiously dictated, interactions may be particularly obvious or significant.

B. Religious Reinforcement of Secular Norms

Religious values tend to shore up legal values by inducing law-abiding behavior among citizens. Despite the inroads of secularization, much of the population in most countries is motivated to obey secular laws (for example, laws against murder or theft) because doing so comports with religious norms. Where clashing religious values or conscientious belief of dissenters are involved, opposite results may ensue. In such situations, religious belief may prompt civil disobedience or even civil war. Witness contemporary Lebanon and Northern Ireland, or, to take a more historical example, the English Civil War. In general, however, religious values tend to be a stabilizing force.

Until the French and American Revolutions, European political thinkers tended to assume that religious beliefs (and homogeneous religious beliefs at that) constituted a vital bonding influence in society.[30] It was assumed that religion played a vital role in inculcating acceptable patterns of human behavior. Read in context, Matthew Hale's oft-quoted statement that Christianity is a part of the common law[31] reflects this concern. The passage occurs in *Taylor's Case*,[32] in which the defendant was charged with "uttering of divers blasphemous expressions, horrible to hear, [viz.] that Jesus Christ was a bastard, a whoremaster, religion was a cheat; and that he neither feared God, the devil, or man."[33] In support of the conviction, Hale stated that

> such kind of wicked blasphemous words were not only an offence to God and religion, but a crime against the laws, State and Government, and therefore punishable in this Court. For to say, religion is a cheat, is to dissolve all those obligations whereby the civil societies are preserved, and that Christianity is parcel of the laws of England; and therefore to reproach the Christian religion is to speak in subversion of the law.[34]

[29]See, e.g., J. Goebel, "King's Law and Local Custom in Seventeenth Century New England," *Columbia Law Review* 31 (1931): 423ff.

[30]The early reformation notion articulated in the Peace of Augsburg (1555) that the prince should determine the religion of his people (*cuius regio eius religio*) is linked to this idea.

[31]The history of this notion is traced in J. Spiegel, "Christianity as Part of the Common Law," *North Carolina Law Journal* 14 (1984): 494.

[32]R. Taylor, 1 Vent. 293, 3 Keb. 607, 86 Eng. Rep. 189 (1676).

[33]Ibid.

[34]Ibid.

Locke's reluctance to tolerate Catholics and atheists is attributable to the same concern to protect the religious bonds of society (in particular, the validity of oaths).[35] The framers of the United States Constitution pressed forward with the "noble experiment" of religious liberty, despite anxieties about the ultimate consequences of religious pluralism for the stability of society.

In the interim, we have substantial historical experience validating the proposition that religious liberty can be squared with social stability. But theorists continue to point to the significance of religion as a social force reinforcing secular norms. Thus, Alexis de Tocqueville contended that religion was vital to the preservation of democratic institutions, because it alone could temper the materialistic pursuits which would otherwise be the undoing of a democratic society.[36] While the law in a free society allows people to do as they wish, he maintained, "there are things which religion prevents them from imagining and forbids them to dare."[37] Taking another tack, Emile Durkheim noted the reciprocally reinforcing influences of law and religion. In a sense, that is the point of his notion that punishment serves to reinforce the collective conscience.[38] In any event, the notion that, on balance, religious belief tends to reinforce obedience to secular norms is a solid bit of practical wisdom.

C. Shared Conduits of Cultural Meaning

Criminal law and religion may interact in a variety of ways in contexts where they act in tandem or in parallel in transmitting or embodying cultural values. Both law and religion, for example, react to shifting images of man.[39] A criminal code designed for the hardy pioneers of nineteenth century individualism differs markedly from one designed for the hapless victims of twentieth century industrialization and urbanization.

Professor Berman has suggested that the principal ways in which law channels and communicates transactional values are through ritual, tradition, authority and express or implicit claims of universal validity.[40] Both law and religion operate through these channels, often at the same time. Oath-taking, for example, is a ritual that has simultaneous legal and religious significance. Core substantive crimes such as murder and theft reflect overlapping secular and religious affirmations of the sanctity of life and property. The scope of criminalization (for example, of "victimless crimes")

---

[35]See J. Locke, *A Letter Concerning Toleration*, ed. P. Romanell (New York, 1955), 52.

[36]A. de Tocqueville, *Democracy in America*, ed. J. Mayer trans. G. Lawrence (Garden City, NY, 1969), 444–45.

[37]Ibid., 292.

[38]E. Durkheim, *The Division of Labor in Society*, trans. G. Simpson (New York, 1933), 108–09.

[39]See, e.g., H. Jescheck, *Das Menschenbild unserer Zeit und die Strafrechtsreform* (Tübingen, 1957).

[40]Berman, *Interaction*, 31.

reflects both religious and secular tradition. The close association of criminal law and religion in such areas leads to reciprocal modeling of ideas and institutions, and both come to reflect deeper societal values and sources of cultural meaning.

D. Shaping the External Structures of Normative Systems

At least in the West, religion has had a profound impact on the way the criminal law is organized. The most obvious example of this is the traditional division of the elements of crime into internal and external elements—what the common law knew as *mens rea* and *actus reus*, or what the Model Penal Code refers to as culpability elements, on the one hand, and conduct, result or circumstance elements on the other.[41] The origins of this structure can be traced back at least to New Testament models of sin and action.[42] It mirrors Christian doctrines about the relationship of internal and external behavior.[43] The structure received significant elaboration by medieval scholars,[44] and, while it is now largely secularized, it is an obvious and pervasive residuum of religious thought. The impact of the canon law on structuring the general part of criminal law and in systematizing criminal law as a whole cannot be overestimated.[45]

E. Providing the Narrative Context for Legal Materials

"No set of legal institutions or prescriptions," writes Robert Cover,

> exists apart from the narratives that locate it and give it meaning. For every constitution there is an epic, for each decalogue a scripture. Once understood in the context of the narratives that give it meaning, law becomes not merely a system of rules to be observed, but a world in which we live.[46]

David Daube taught us how to discern law in the interstices of biblical narrative,[47] and, increasingly, hermeneuticists and semioticists are persuading us that all law is embedded in deeper normative landscapes.[48]

[41]Model Penal Code §§ 13 and 2.02 (Proposed Official Draft, 1962).

[42]See notes 123–136 and accompanying text, below.

[43]J. Sklar, *Legalism: Law, Morals and Political Trials* (Cambridge, MA, 1964), 45.

[44]See notes 152–172 and accompanying text, below.

[45]Berman, *Law and Revolution*, 185–204, 253–54; S. Kuttner, *Kanonistische Schuldlehre von Gratian bis auf die Dekretalen Gregors IX, systematisch auf Grund der handschriftlichen Quellen dargestellt* (Citta del Vaticano, 1935), 65; T. Plucknett, *A Concise History of the Common Law*, 5th ed. (Boston, 1956), 305–06.

[46]R. Cover, "The Supreme Court, 1982 Term—Foreword: Nomos and Narrative," *Harvard Law Review* 97 (1983): 4–5.

[47]D. Daube, *Studies in Biblical Law* (Cambridge, 1947).

[48]With regard to legal semiotics, see B. Jackson, *Semiotics and Legal Theory* (London, 1985), 130–36. For discussions of hermeneutics and law, see D. Hermann, "Phenomenology, Structur-

Differing religious traditions place similar criminal laws in differing narrative contexts. Catholics, Lutherans and Calvinists have different accounts of the role of the civil magistrate and concomitant differences in their understanding of the role of criminal law in society. Differing attitudes toward the Fall yield differing attitudes toward the prospects of reforming criminal offenders. The idea of the Last Judgment provides the background for earthly judgments—both as an ideal of perfect judgment and as a threat of ultimate punishment. Penance (*poenitentia*) is identified with punishment (*poena*), and both are linked with an account of progress toward salvation.[49]

F. Molding the Deep Structures of Criminal Law

By "deep structures" I mean something different from the narratives in which norms are imbedded. Deep structures are paradigmatic features of criminal norms, or perhaps more accurately, paradigmatic ways of seeing or understanding criminal norms. The best examples of what I have in mind are George Fletcher's "patterns of liability": the patterns of manifest criminality, subjective criminality and harmful consequences.[50]

This is not the place to describe these patterns in any detail. Brief examples from the law of attempts and the law of homicide will have to suffice to give some notion of what is at stake.[51] The law of attempts deals with the general problem of determining where the state should intervene in the continuum ranging from mere "bad thoughts" at one extreme to the actual consummation of crime at the other. Within a legal culture or legal consciousness aligned with the pattern of manifest criminality, the impulse is to allow intervention only at a very late stage, when the criminality represented by the consummated crime is nearly manifest. This orientation

---

alism, Hermeneutics and Legal Study: Applications of Contemporary Continental Thought to Legal Phenomena," *University of Miami Law Review* 36 (1982): 398–409; S. McIntosh, "Legal Hermeneutics: A Philosophical Critique," *Oklahoma Law Review* (1982): 1–72. This area has been explored much more extensively in German legal literature. See, e.g., J. Esser, *Vorverständnis und Methodenwahl in der Rechtsfindung: Rationalitätsgarantien der richterlichen Entscheidungspraxis* (Frankfurt, 1972); W. Hassemer, *Einführung in die Grundlagen des Strafrechts* (München, 1981), 77–80, 113–59; id., *Tatbestand und Typus: Untersuchungen zur strafrechtlichen Hermeneutik* (Köln, 1968); J. Hruschka, *Die Konstitution des Rechtsfalles: Studien zum Verhältnis von Tatschenfeststellung und Rechtsanwendung* (Berlin, 1965); A. Kaufmann, *Analogie und "Natur der Sache": Zugleich ein Beitrag zur Lehre von Typus* (Karlsruhe, 1965); M. Kriele, *Theorie der Rechtsgewinnung, entwickelt am Problem der Verfassungsinterpretation* (Berlin, 1967); F. Müller, *Juristische Methodik*, 2d rev. ed. (Berlin, 1976).

[49]See Berman, *Law and Revolution*, 168–78.

[50]The three patterns are discussed at length in the first half of G. Fletcher, *Rethinking Criminal Law* (Boston, 1978). There they provide the framework for Professor Fletcher's analysis of the "special part" of criminal law. The patterns are recapitulated briefly in ibid., 388–90 (§5.3.3).

[51]These examples are discussed at much greater length in ibid., 131–97, 235–42, 341–88.

in the law of attempts has yielded tests for attempt liability which insist that conduct does not amount to an attempt unless it is the "last proximate step"[52] prior to consummation or unless the act in question "unequivocally" shows criminal intent on the face of it.[53] Within a system dominated by the pattern of subjective criminality, in contrast, one is likely to encounter a much lower threshold of attempt liability. Thus, in Model Penal Code jurisdictions, attempt liability requires only that there be "an act or omission constituting a substantial step in a course of conduct planned to culminate in . . . [a] crime."[54]

According to George Fletcher, the pattern of harmful consequences derives fundamentally from the law of homicide, and involves crimes where there is (1) a concrete harm to a personal interest (death, bodily injury, destruction of property); (2) there is a need to distinguish harmful consequences resulting from natural processes from those that result from human action; and (3) there liability for negligence or omissions makes sense.[55] Although attempted crimes obviously aim at harmful consequences, they do not fit within this pattern in his view, since attempt liability is conceived as deriving from either the threat an attempt poses to the peace and order of the community (manifest criminality) or from the actor's intent to violate a protected interest (subjective criminality), and not from the actual occurrence of harm itself (which is obviously absent where all that has happened is an attempt).[56] The situation is quite different with respect to the law of homicide. Many ancient or primitive legal systems apparently assumed that a person (or animal) that caused the death of another was tainted by the event, and, therefore, subject to punishment aimed at purging the taint.[57] The taking of life was thought of as a desecration, regardless of whether the death was the result of intentional, negligent or accidental conduct. Under biblical law, propitiation was required even in the case of a murder by a person unknown.[58]

The importance of such deep structures or patterns within legal culture is that they are strongly influenced by religious ideas. Primitive homicide rules requiring expiation of accidental deaths or of the acts of unknown murderers appear as bizarre affronts to our deepest moral intuitions about the importance of personal culpability as a prerequisite for punishment. If such rules ever made sense, it seems to us, they did so only in the context of

---

[52]*Regina v. Eagleton*, 6 Cox C.C. 559 (Crim. App. 1855).

[53]*King v. Barker*, [1924] N.Z.L.R. 865 (N.Z. Court of Appeal); J. Salmond, *Jurisprudence*, 7th ed. (London, 1924), 404.

[54]Model Penal Code § 5.01 (1) (c) (Proposed Official Draft, 1962).

[55]Fletcher, *Rethinking*, 385.

[56]Ibid., 341, 387.

[57]Ibid., 343–49.

[58]Deuteronomy 21:1ff.; A. Phillips, *Ancient Israel's Criminal Law: A New Approach to the Decalogue* (Oxford, 1970), 93–95.

pervasive (but now alien) religious world-views—that is, the deep structures of criminal liability then dominant were religiously molded.

Further, the older patterns of thought exert a residual hold by continuing to shape modern contours of liability and our intuitions about them. For example, the fact that consent is not a defense to homicide reflects at least in part the view that life is not merely a secular interest, disposable at the will of its possessor.[59] The religious view that life has transcendent value lies close to the surface beneath the secular veneer of this rule. Pressures for a subjectivist law of attempts stem not only from concerns with deterring dangerous conduct emanating from the criminal mind, but also from the religious notion that a person who has sinned in his heart is just as culpable as a person who commits a crime. Riddles about whether consummated crimes should be punished more severely than attempts[60] thus reflect a tension between religiously grounded intuitions about culpability (that is, that moral culpability depends on inner intent rather than on the fortuity of whether that intention is successfully actualized in the external world) and another set of originally religious intuitions about the taint (liability) that derives from causing harmful consequences. The rhetoric of such discussions is now thoroughly secularized, but the underlying patterns of liability track structures with religious roots.

I do not regard George Fletcher's patterns as an exhaustive list, nor, so far as I know, does he. Moreover, patterns of criminality are not necessarily mutually exclusive. At any given time, one or another may be dominant, and several may be at work in shaping the contours and the categories, the intuitions and the arguments of the law. At other times, certain patterns may virtually disappear from view. This point deserves emphasis because many of the interactions of religion and deep structure that have been most significant for Western criminal law may have occurred during the ascendency of a fourth pattern: the pattern of betrayal. A great deal more work needs to be done to document such a pattern, but its broad contours can be sketched briefly. From this perspective, the locus of criminality lies not in manifest action, the subjective state of the actor or the harm caused, but rather in an act of betrayal. Such acts would naturally be perceived as bearing the critical hallmark of criminality in heroic, feudal, family or clan based societies, or in any other social setting where individuals are highly dependent on each other personally (as opposed to anonymously) for defense or survival. In such societies, the notion of betrayal becomes paradigmatic for crime in general. It serves as a filter through which all or a large portion of the criminal activity in a society is perceived, interpreted

---

[59]Fletcher, *Rethinking*, 236.

[60]B. Burkhardt, "Is There a Rational Justification for Punishing an Accomplished Crime More Severely Than an Attempted Crime?" *Brigham Young University Law Review* (1986): 553; S. Schulhofer, "Harm and Punishment: A Critique of Emphasis on the Results of Conduct in the Criminal Law," *University of Pennsylvania Law Review* 122 (1974): 1497.

and ordered. Viewed through this lens, the topography of crime appears rather different than when seen from the perspective of the other patterns. Just as homicide is the archetypal crime in the pattern of harmful consequences, so treason becomes the archetype in the pattern of betrayal. Where the jarring of collective expectations or a base motive or the harm caused are the common denominators of crimes in other patterns, breach of faith (for example, breach of the king's peace) becomes central to criminality within the pattern of betrayal. Honor is likely to become a crucial value in a society in which betrayal is the central wrong, because it is honor that withstands betrayal. In medieval Switzerland, for example, all crimes came to be classified in terms of relative affronts to honor.[61] A different ordering of crimes is to be expected within the pattern of betrayal. Dante's perception of fraud and embezzlement as crimes more heinous than manifest theft,[62] for example, makes sense in the setting of what might be called a betrayal (or, more positively, a loyalty) culture. Blood feuds appear nothing less than barbaric to us, but, from a betrayal perspective, any lesser response might appear to be an inadequate display of respect toward those to whom loyalty is owed. Ritual oath-taking, aimed at renewing and reaffirming interpersonal bonds, seems a little stilted to us, but it is critical in a society where loyalty relationships are central.

There can be little doubt that the trappings of this pattern of criminality are foreign to us. But my sense is that this is precisely the pattern that was predominant during the medieval period that Professor Berman rightly identifies as crucial to the formation of Western criminal law. If correct, this suggests that the pattern of betrayal was the starting matrix mediating the interaction of law and religion during the formative period of Western criminal law. It may well be that one of the strongest impacts of religion on criminal law in the West was to provide alternative models of law and moral responsibility that ultimately supplanted the pattern of betrayal. This hypothesis needs much fuller exploration and testing than can be provided here. However, even cursory review of Professor Berman's work on the medieval foundations of criminal law provides interesting evidence for the theory.

At the outset it is worth remembering that in many ways, the early Judaic-Christian tradition was pervaded by signs of loyalty culture. Whether or not one accepts the notion that Israel's covenant relationship with Yahweh was modeled on Hittite suzerainty treaties,[63] with the commands of the

---

[61]von Bar, *History of Continental Criminal Law*, 142–45.

[62]Dante, *Divina Commedia*, Canto XI, lines 52–60, in Dante, *Opere*, ed. M. Porena and M. Pazzaglia (Bologna, 1966).

[63]G. Mendenhall, "Ancient Oriental and Biblical Law," *Biblical Archaeologist* 17 (1954): 26–46; id., "Covenant Forms in Israelite Tradition," *Biblical Archaeologist* 17 (1954): 50–76; cf. Phillips, *Ancient Israel's Criminal Law*, 3.

Decalogue constituting stipulations imposed on Israel by Yahweh,[64] there is no question that the basic models of religious and social life were based on loyalty. The fundamental wrong was breach of faith. During the Middle Ages, this notion became linked with feudalism and ideals of honor. As Professor Berman put it in his study on the roots of the Western legal tradition in European folklaw, "[t]he bonds of kinship, of lordship units, and of territorial communities *were* the law."[65] Religious and social models reinforced each other; each could be interpreted in terms of the other. The Christian penitentials (guidelines for penances for various sins) that prolif-erated throughout Europe helped to reinforce folklaw and to maintain the sanctity oaths on which it rested.[66] In the Christian setting, the betrayal by Judas was the archetypal crime, and betrayal in general was a fundamental form of wrongdoing. The crime of *lèse majesté* (high treason) and its derivatives, applying not only to betrayal of the sovereign but to injuries to a wide range of feudal relations, were very important for the practical administration of criminal law.[67] More generally, the notion of "felony" appears to have been linked at early stages with betrayal. The term "felon," which originally suggested being full of bitterness or venom, attached itself soon after its initial emergence to the class of crimes which "consist of a breach of that trust and faith which should exist between man and lord."[68]

Many of the key legal metaphors reflected loyalty structures. Professor Berman notes that such metaphors "were chiefly feudal, though they had religious overtones—metaphors of honor, of satisfaction for violation of honor, of pledge of faith, of reciprocal bonds of service and protection."[69] Some ideas, such as the notions of purgatory, penance and the Last Judgment, began to generate some of the abstract notions of law, justice and punishment that lie at the core of modern legalism,[70] but many of the key conceptions continued to be framed in terms consonant with a betrayal culture. Anselm's conception of the atonement, for example, turns on curing the breach caused by sin by satisfying God's honor. In *Cur Deus Homo*,[71] Anselm reasoned that in order to rectify disobedience, man must either be punished for his sin or make satisfaction for dishonoring God.[72] Since only God can provide such satisfac-tion (man does not have enough to offer), but only man ought to provide it (God has done nothing wrong), the atonement can only be made by the

---

[64]Ibid., 3–9.

[65]Berman, "The Background of the Western Legal Tradition," 587 (emphasis in original).

[66]Ibid., 577–79, 583.

[67]von Bar, *History of Continental Criminal Law*, 41–45, 163–64.

[68]F. Pollock and F. Maitland, *The History of English Law*, 2d ed. (Cambridge, 1968), 2: 465.

[69]Berman, *Law and Revolution*, 165.

[70]Ibid., 166–73.

[71]Anselm, *Cur Deus Homo*, J. Migne, *Patrologia Latina* (Paris, 1844–55), 158: 359–431. See J. McIntyre, *St. Anselm and His Critics: A Reinterpretation of the Cur Deus Homo* (Edinburgh, 1954).

[72]Berman, *Law and Revolution*, 177.

God-Man, Jesus Christ.[73] In the process of conceptualizing the atonement in terms of restoring honor—a sensible move within a betrayal culture—Anselm began to distinguish the demands for the protection of honor from the demands of punishment. In the context of the atonement and original sin, punishment was an unacceptable option because the punishment deserved was total destruction, which God did not want man to suffer.[74] But the actual sins of baptized, penitent Christians could be expiated by temporal punishments in this world or in purgatory.[75] In Professor Berman's view, the distinction between satisfaction of honor and punishment may have opened up the way to supplant Germanic notions of "reconciliation as an alternative to vengence,"[76] with more general conceptions of justice. By the time of St. Thomas Aquinas, this development led to the notion that "since crime, in contrast to tort, is a defiance of the law itself, punishment, and not merely reparation, must be imposed *as the price of the violation of the law.*"[77] Thus a Christian concept, first interpreted against the background of the pattern of betrayal, ultimately paves the way toward more general conceptions of law and punishment. Punishment comes to be seen not as vengeance for betrayal but as abstract and equal administration of justice for all.

G. Shaping Fundamental Concepts

Closely related to interactions at the level of patterns of criminality are interactions relating to shifts in fundamental conceptions such as harm and culpability. The latter will be discussed in more detail in the next section. But a few words can be said here about some of the ways in which religion has shaped our concepts of harm. One of the most significant interactions of religion and law in this area has to do with the notion of harm as evil. Evil in its primary sense is a religious notion with Judaic-Christian roots. The notion is in many ways alien to Greek culture. For Aristotle, badness of character is a defect of virtue, and it is difficult to distinguish between failure to be good and evil itself.[78] Evil plays a role in the universe of Shakespearian tragedy that is not matched in Greek tragedy. More to the point here is that sin has an association with evil that goes beyond mere moral default, and sin was for generations a key notion behind the criminal law.[79] Harm defined in terms of evil is necessarily infused with religious overtones.

---

[73]Ibid.

[74]Anselm, *Cur Deus Homo*, 158: 379, 381.

[75]Berman, *Law and Revolution*, 182–83.

[76]Ibid., 183.

[77]Ibid., citing T. Aquinas, *Summa theologiae*, II-II, Q. 62, Arts. 3–6.

[78]A. MacIntyre, *After Virtue: A Study in Moral Theory* (Notre Dame, 1984), 175.

[79]See generally A. Louch, "Sins and Crimes," *Morality and the Law*, ed., R. Wasserstrom (Belmont, CA, 1971), 73–85; W. Katz, "Christian Morality and the Criminal Law," *Religion, Morality and Law*, ed. A. Harding (Dallas, 1956), 54–71.

In recent years, the significance of the concept of harm and its breadth has had primary relevance to the debate about the enforcement of morals. Ever since John Stuart Mill asserted his "one very simple principle" for ascertaining the appropriate scope of societal coercion, namely that "the only purpose for which power can be rightfully exercised over any member of a civilised community, against his will, is to prevent harm to others,"[80] harm has been viewed as a critical factor in assessing the appropriate scope of criminal law.[81] The seductive allure of Mill's harm principle derives from its apparent neutrality. Regardless of the value differences that may divide us in a secular, pluralistic society, we can at least agree, it would seem, that palpable harm to ascertainable individuals constitutes appropriate grounds for state intervention. The difficulty, of course, is that harm is anything but a neutral concept. From a purely secular standpoint, a battery is clearly a harm, whereas homosexual conduct between consenting adults in private may appear victimless. But, from a religious perspective, the homosexual conduct may appear to be far more harmful. Adultery statutes tend to lose their operative grip in an increasingly secular culture. On another front, how does one compare the harm involved in losing an arm to an industrial accident (obviously palpable enough) with the harm of entrusting a child to a secular age? Wrestling with a harm of the second type, the Supreme Court in *Wisconsin v. Yoder* [82] held on free exercise grounds that a state's interest in compulsory education did not outweigh the religiously-based right of Amish parents to shield their children from perceived harms of secularization. There are, of course, questions about the extent to which religiously grounded assessments of harm may be introduced into political discourse in a society adhering to principles of separation of church and state.[83] My point here is merely that prevailing religious or secular world-views, by pouring content into critical terms such as "harm," exert great influence on the operative scope of criminal law.

[80]J. Mill, *On Liberty* (1859), reprinted in *The Philosophy of John Stuart Mill: Ethical, Political and Religious*, ed. M. Cohen (New York, 1961), 196–7.

[81]The literature of the enforcement-of-morals debate is, of course, extensive. Among the major disputants in this fray are the following: P. Devlin, *The Enforcement of Morals* (London, 1965); R. Dworkin, "Lord Devlin and the Enforcement of Morals," *Yale Law Journal* 75 (1966): 986ff.; J. Feinberg, *The Moral Limits of the Criminal Law*, 4 vols. (New York, 1984), H. Hart, "Immorality and Treason," *The Listener* (July 30, 1959): 162–63; id., *Law, Liberty and Morality* (Stanford, CA, 1963); id., "Social Solidarity and the Enforcement of Morality," *University of Chicago Law Review* 35 (1967): 1ff.; G. Hughes, "Morals and the Criminal Law," *Yale Law Journal* 71 (1962): 662ff.; S. Kadish, "The Crisis of Overcriminalization," *Annals* 374 (1967): 157ff.; B. Mitchell, *Law, Morality and Religion in a Secular Society* (London, 1967); R. Wasserstrom, ed., *Morality and the Law* (Belmont, CA, 1971).

[82]406 U.S. 205 (1972).

[83]See, e.g., K. Greenawalt, "Religiously Based Premises and Laws Restrictive of Liberty," *Brigham Young University Law Review* (1986): 245–97; L. Tribe, *American Constitutional Law* (Mineola, NY, 1978), 928.

H. Grounding the Moral Striving that Drives the Institutions of Criminal-Justice

A significant if largely forgotten issue of moral theory has to do with answering the question why one should obey moral rules, including the moral rule that one ought to obey the law. Assuming a particular rule is applicable, why ought one to obey it? This, it should be remembered, is the original context of Hume's formulation of the is/ought dichotomy,[84] and, in this setting at least, it seems fairly clear that identifying the logical divide between descriptive and prescriptive statements does not get one very far in finding an answer to the question about the grounds of moral motivation. Kant tried to find an answer by grounding moral obligation in a categorical imperative that is, in turn, grounded in reason,[85] but this grounding can be challenged by those not compulsive about being reasonable[86] or by those who have grown skeptical, as many have in the twentieth century, about the depth of man's rational veneer.[87] The full range of religious participation in the shaping of moral vision and moral striving is obviously a topic that goes beyond the scope of this paper. Mention of one perhaps non-obvious role will have to suffice. John Stuart Mill premised his argument for a free market of ideas on the need to prevent inadvertent crushing of the thought of moral pilgrims whose truths would (otherwise) ultimately prevail. Lord Devlin responded that Mill "did not really grapple with the fact that along the paths that depart from traditional morals, pimps leading the weak astray far outnumber spiritual explorers at the head of the strong"[88]—that is, the very legitimate concerns for protecting the openness of the marketplace of ideas must be tempered with the recognition that some idea generators are more likely to yield higher moral vision than others. While Mill was, no doubt, correct that extreme care must be exercised to avoid inadvertent trampling of incipient truth, there is wisdom in Devlin's recognition that a totally unfettered *laissez faire* approach in this domain may allow the prime seedbeds of moral vision to become overgrown weed patches. What is needed is some type of filtering mechanism that maximizes the likelihood that moral pimps do not prevail over pilgrims. The priority accorded to

---

[84]D. Hume, *A Treatise of Human Nature*, ed. L. Selby-Bigge (Oxford, 1888), 464–69.

[85]I. Kant, *Groundwork of the Metaphysic of Morals* (1785), trans. H. Paton (New York, 1964); id., *Critique of Practical Reason* (1787), trans. L. Beck (Indianapolis, 1956).

[86]R. Nozick, *Philosophical Explanations* (Cambridge, MA, 1981), 4.

[87]See, e.g., W. Barrett, *Irrational Man: A Study in Existential Philosophy* (Garden City, NY, 1958); C. Lasch, *The Culture of Narcissism: American Life in an Age of Diminishing Expectations* (New York, 1978); H. Marcuse, *Eros and Civilization: A Philosophical Inquiry into Freud* (New York, 1955); id., *One-Dimensional Man: Studies in the Ideology of Advanced Industrial Society* (Boston, 1964); P. Ricoeur, *Freud and Philosophy: An Essay on Interpretation* (New Haven, CT, 1970).

[88]P. Devlin, "Mill on Liberty in Morals," *University of Chicago Law Review* 32 (1965): 215–35, reprinted in Devlin, *The Enforcement of Morals*, 102–33.

religious liberty in most Western nations can be interpreted as just such a filtering device. Significantly, the right to religious liberty does not obviate the need for more secular protections such as freedom of the press and other media or freedom of association. Instead, it recognizes that religious individuals and communities have been particularly fruitful sources of moral vision, and they are in need of special protection. It provides, in effect, a non-preemptive filtering device that helps to foster patterns of individual and communal life that have been among the most fruitful through time in generating human conceptions of the good. Note that it is not merely the internal meditation and dialogue within religious groups but also the competition among them that has promoted moral striving. Historically, there have obviously been times when religious movements have gone too far in attempting to throttle rival world-views, but, in general, one of the critical roles they play in grounding and fostering moral vision is a filtering function that helps to sort out and clarify the highest human values and the human propensities that interfere with their achievement.

IV. Contexts of Interaction

In the last analysis, the contexts of interaction between criminal law and religion are as numerous as individual lives and settings of individual and collective action. But a number of salient contexts deserve mention.

A. Biography

In dealing with a topic as vast as criminal law and religion, there is a tendency to focus so intensively on historical and cultural perspectives that the role of individual biography is overlooked. Yet, in the last analysis, it is clear that this interaction occurs within individual consciousness. More than that, historical and cultural changes are obviously prompted by individuals acting on their beliefs. Depending on the focus of the particular biographer, much can be learned from biographies of leading legal figures.[89] For example, Newmyer's[90] and McClellan's[91] biographies of Story explore in

[89]See, e.g., L. Baker, *John Marshall: A Life in Law* (New York, 1974), 751–53; Berman, "Law and Belief," 609–613; E. Heward, *Matthew Hale* (London, 1972); W. Holdsworth, *History of English Law*, 6: 574–95; D. Yale, *Hale as a Legal Historian* (London, 1976); C. Swisher, *Stephen J. Field: Craftsman of the Law* (Washington, 1930), 79–80.

[90]R. Newmyer, *Supreme Court Justice Joseph Story: Statesman of the Old Republic* (Chapel Hill, NC, 1985), 183–84, 244. Other references to this debate include: J. Story, "Value and Importance of Legal Studies," *The Miscellaneous Writings of Joseph Story*, ed. W. Story (Boston, 1852), 517; id., "Art. V—Christianity a Part of the Common Law," *American Jurist* 9 (April, 1833): 346–48; M. Peterson, *The Jefferson Image in the American Mind* (New York, 1960), 96–98.

[91]J. McClellan, *Joseph Story and the American Constitution: A Study in Political and Legal Thought* (Norman, OK, 1971), 118–59.

some detail Story's dispute with Jefferson about the relationship of Christianity and the common law. Biographies of Brandeis often touch on his religious concerns.[92] Similarly, biographical accounts of the attitudes of major religious leaders toward criminal law and other law-related issues can yield significant insights.[93]

B. Judging

Closely related to the context of biography is the more concrete setting of judging. A judge's religious (or non-religious) outlook cannot help but color the way he or she perceives a broad range of value questions. It has long been obvious that Oliver Wendell Holmes's bad-man view of the law is not helpful in the hour of judgment. The interaction here tends to be much more complex than one might think.[94] While one can easily imagine judges with fixed religious views who decide cases according to those views and then try to drum up post hoc "neutral" rationalia, the situation is generally much more complex. A judge might feel religiously bound to respect the oath he or she took on assuming judicial office, and this might dictate upholding the Constitution and constitutional rights that run counter to his or her personal beliefs (for example, in the domain of abortion or school prayer). Conscious of personal religious beliefs and biases, a judge may bend over backwards to respect and protect the rights of litigants with contrary views.

At another level, the moment of judgment itself becomes a type of religious experience or at least a crisis of conscience. I remember talking one afternoon with a trial judge who had just come from a sentencing hearing in a capital case. Because of certain mitigating circumstances in the case, she was able to reach a decision of life rather than death. But her comment on the intensity of the experience was revealing: "I earned my entire salary for the year this afternoon." Just as there are few atheists in foxholes, there are probably many outwardly secular judges who resort to higher sources when searing decisions must be made.

[92]P. Strum, *Louis D. Brandeis: Justice for the People* (Cambridge, MA, 1984), 261, 291.

[93]See, e.g., H. Bornkamm, *Luther in Mid-Career 1521–1530*, trans. E. Bachmann (Philadelphia, 1983), 109–42 (dealing with Luther's entry into matters of jurisprudence, beginning with his work on marriage and continuing through his work on temporal authority); W. von Loewenich, *Martin Luther: The Man and His Work* (Minneapolis, 1986), ch. 21; R. Kingdon, "Calvin and the Government of Geneva," *Calvinus Ecclesiae Genevensis Custos*, ed. W. Neuser (Frankfurt, 1984), 49–67; J. Baur, "Gott, Recht und weltliches Regiment im Werke Calvins," *Schriften zur Rechtslehre und Politik* 44 (Bonn, 1965); J. Bohatec, *Calvin und das Recht* (1934; reprint, Aalen, 1971); B. Hall, "John Calvin, the Jurisconsults and the 'Ius civile'," *Studies in Church History*, ed. G. Cumming (Leiden, 1966), 3:202–16.

[94]Cf. R. Dworkin, "Hard Cases," *Harvard Law Review* 88 (1975): 1057–1109; reprinted in R. Dworkin, *Taking Rights Seriously* (Cambridge, MA, 1977), 81–130.

C. Popular Consciousness

The conceptions of criminal law and justice operative at the level of popular consciousness are never so sophisticated or refined as those that evolve among legal professionals and theorists. They are often strongly molded by a crude sense of justice that is, in turn, shaped by prevailing religious outlooks. Whatever the technical operation of the *lex talionis* may have been in biblical law,[95] the idea exerts a powerful modeling influence in shaping notions of proportionality in punishment.[96] Popular attitudes toward capital punishment are the most obvious example. Another example, noted by Professor Berman, would be the role that notions of purgatory and penance played in catalyzing the development of elaborate rules and standards of moral and, ultimately, criminal liability in the early Middle Ages.[97]

Paying attention to popular consciousness may be particularly significant from the standpoint of gaining a full understanding of the way religious and criminal norms interact, since the interactions at that level may be quite different from those being experienced by the professional elites likely to write about such things. One must also bear in mind that popular consciousness is filled with its own profusion of eddies and currents. Fringe groups may see religious and legal realities in ways quite different from dominant groups.

The phenomenon of witchcraft—an obvious sore spot in the history of the interaction of religion and criminal law[98]—provides an interesting case in point. A major flaw in conventional accounts of witchcraft is a failure to take popular consciousness seriously. Professor Trevor-Roper, one of the leading historians of the subject, emphasized the views of the educated and indicated his lack of concern with what he called "those elementary village credulities which anthropologists discover in all times and at all places."[99] Recent scholarship has made it clear just how much can be learned by

---

[95] W. Albright and C. Mann, *The Anchor Bible: Matthew* (Garden City, NY, 1971), 68 (the law of retaliation operated as a humanizing check on blood feud); A. Alt, "Zur Talionsformel," *Kleine Schriften zur Geschichte des Volkes Israel* 1 (1953): 341–44; D. Daube, "Lex talionis," *Studies in Biblical Law* (Cambridge, 1947); id., *The New Testament and Rabbinic Judaism* (London, 1956), 255–59; E. Fisher, "Lex Talionis in the Bible and Rabbinic Tradition (Reply to Encyclical of Pope John Paul II, Dives in Misericordia)," *Journal of Ecclesiastical Studies* 19 (1982): 582–87; J. Harris, *Lex Talionis and the Jewish Law of Mercy* (London, n.d.).

[96] The idea of the *lex talionis* was foreign to early Germanic law, but, by the time of the later Middle Ages, it found its way in its well-known Mosaic form into various south German statutes. von Bar, *A History of Continental Criminal Law*, 109. It was also clearly significant in Swedish and Finnish law. Ibid., 296.

[97] Berman, *Law and Revolution*, 166–73.

[98] For a description of witchcraft laws and abuses, see von Bar, *A History of Continental Criminal Law*, 45, 226–27, 243, 299.

[99] H. Trevor-Roper, "The European Witch Craze of the Sixteenth and Seventeenth Centuries," *Religion, the Reformation and Social Change* (New York, 1967).

focussing on such "village credulities." Carlo Ginzburg's *Benandanti*[100] contends that at the level of village culture witchcraft issues were connected with widespread fertility rites and that the questions as perceived by involved locals were often quite at odds with the expectations of clerics and their witch-hunting manuals.[101] Much of the recent scholarship on witchcraft has gone toward expanding and refining our understanding of the phenomenon at the level of popular consciousness.[102] These studies obviously do nothing to alter post-Enlightenment abhorrence of the penalization of witchcraft, but they do underscore the significance of popular consciousness as a context in which religion and criminal law interact.

D. Theories of Punishment

Traditional theories of punishment—retributivism, general and special deterrence, isolation and reform—are typically framed as theories describing the (true) grounds for justifying and legitimating punishment as an institution.[103] While, undoubtedly, there is earnestness in the assertions of the advocates of rival theories, awareness of millennia of such wrangling[104] ultimately leads one to suspect that one may be dealing more with time-tested rhetorical postures or sophisticated stock arguments. Classical rheto-

[100]C. Ginzburg, *The Night Battles: Witchcraft and Agrarian Cults in the Sixteenth and Seventeenth Centuries*, trans. J. and A. Tedeschi (Baltimore, MD, 1984).

[101]A version of this thesis was advanced earlier in M. Murray, *The Witch-Cult in Western Europe* (Oxford, 1921).

[102]See, e.g., Burke, "Good Witches," *New York Review of Books*, (February 28, 1985), 32; Eliade, "Some Observations on European Witchcraft," *History of Religions* 14 (1974): 149; P. Klaniczay, "Benandanti—kresnik—zduhac—taltos," *Ethnographie* 94 (1983): 14; E. Le Roy LaDurie, *La sorcire de jasmin* (Paris, 1984); M. Wilson, "Witch Beliefs and Social Structure," *American Journal of Sociology* 56 (1951): 307.

[103]H. Acton, *The Philosophy of Punishment* (London, 1969); J. Andenaes, *Punishment and Deterrence* (Ann Arbor, MI, 1974); G. Ezorsky, ed., *Philosophical Perspectives on Punishment* (Albany, NY, 1972); A. Ewing, *The Morality of Punishment* (London, 1929); J. Feinberg and H. Gross, eds., *Punishment* (Encino, CA, 1975); R. Gerber and P. McAnany, eds., *Contemporary Punishment: Views, Explanations and Justifications* (Notre Dame, 1972); A. Goldman, "Toward a New Theory of Punishment," *Law and Philosophy* 1 (1982): 57–76; S. Grupp, ed., *Theories of Punishment* (Bloomington, IN, 1971); H. Hart, *Punishment and Responsibility: Essays in the Philosophy of Law* (New York, 1968); W. Hassemer, K. Lüderssen and W. Naucke, *Hauptprobleme der Generalprävention* (Frankfurt am Main, 1979); J. Mabbot, "Punishment," *Mind* 48 (1939): 162–67; M. Mackenzie, *Plato on Punishment* (Berkeley, CA, 1981); J. Murphy, *Punishment and Rehabilitation* (Belmont, CA, 1973); id., *Retribution, Justice and Therapy: Essays in the Philosophy of Law* (Dordrecht/Boston, 1979); id., "Marxism and Retribution," *Philosophy and Public Affairs* 2 (1973): 217–43; A. Norrie, "Thomas Hobbes and the Philosophy of Punishment," *Law and Philosophy* 3 (1984): 299–320; E. Pincoffs, *The Rationale of Legal Punishment* (New York, 1966); A. von Hirsch, *Doing Justice* (New York, 1976); N. Walker, "The Efficacy and Morality of Deterrents," *Criminal Law Review* (1979): 129–44; F. Zimring and G. Hawkins, *Deterrence: The Legal Threat in Crime Control* (Chicago, 1973).

[104]The antecedents of such argumentation can be traced back to the Greeks and beyond. See, e.g., M. Mackenzie, *Plato on Punishment* (Berkeley, CA, 1981).

ric referred to such devices as *topoi*—as devices which could define the topography of argumentation.[105] *Topoi* provide argumentative orientations for surrounding problems, seeing them from all sides, and generating insightful solutions through the dialectic interplay of theories dealing with the problems they address. Differing *topoi* may be wielded with differing levels of effectiveness in different contexts. Religious and secular belief systems of those engaged in a *topoi*-generated dialogue will obviously influence the effectiveness and persuasiveness of rival *topoi*. Without going into great detail, my point is that theories of punishment function as *topoi*, and religion interacts with criminal law in the context of theories of punishment by affecting the relative force of rival argumentative postures. In general, retributive arguments win stronger acceptance with religious audiences (unless they can be recast in ways that enhance their appeal in secular settings); deterrence theories are more prone to find acceptance in secularist circles. Part of the reason for the difference has to do with the relationship between *topoi* and background narrative: retributive arguments mesh better with religious narratives than with secularist accounts of the nature of existence and justice.

E. Institutional Contexts

Institutional interaction provides the grist of traditional institutional histories. One thinks, for example, of the major role the church played in substituting imprisonment for harsher sanctions with the aim of bringing the offender to repentance through contemplation.[106] Similarly, religious influence played a mixed role with respect to the institution of torture: sometimes aiding and abetting and other times ameliorating the practice.[107] Reform movements in criminal law since the Enlightenment have often involved coalitions of religious and secularist groups.[108]

During much of the history of the West, church institutions had substantial control over criminal law. Ecclesiastical courts heard not only cases involving canon law crimes but also cases involving criminal offenses of clerics. Recent research indicates that, in addition, ecclesiastical courts

[105]Aristotle, *Topica*, trans. E. Foster, Loeb Classical Library (Cambridge, MA, 1960); Cicero, *Topica*, trans. H. Hubbell, Loeb Classical Library (Cambrige, MA, 1949). The leading modern work describing the relationship between *topoi* and law is T. Viehweg, *Topik und Jurisprudenz: Ein Beitrag zur rechtswissenschaftlichen Grundlagen-forschung*, 5th rev. ed. (München, 1974).

[106]Plucknett, *A Concise History*, 305.

[107]On the history of torture, see J. Langbein, "Torture and Plea Bargaining," *University of Chicago Law Review* 46 (1978): 3; id., *Torture and the Law of Proof: Europe and the Ancien Regime* (Chicago, 1976).

[108]*American Friends Service Committee, Struggle for Justice—A Report on Crime and Justice in America* (1971); G. McHugh, *Christian Faith and Criminal Justice: Toward a Christian Response to Crime and Punishment* (New York, 1978); D. Van Ness, *Crime and Its Victims*, 193–207.

heard a large number of cases of secular offenses committed by lay individuals.[109] Sometimes, the ecclesiastical courts would act as legal gap fillers. Secular courts seldom prosecuted infanticide, but ecclesiastical courts often did.[110]

In addition to the direct control of the ecclesiastical courts over large areas of criminal behavior, ecclesiastics also had substantial direct control over secular criminal courts. During the Middle Ages, the Church came to control a great number of the existing civic tribunals.[111] Furthermore, even the tribunals that remained in control of secular magistrates tended to be staffed by clerics trained in the canon law. Close ties between the study of canon law and Roman law in the universities tended to reinforce the influence of the former. Cooperation and compromise between church and state officials further extended the influence of religious institutions.[112]

Institutional interactions are particularly visible in the context of jurisdictional disputes. Here one thinks first of such early confrontations as the dispute between Becket and Henry II over the immunity of "criminous clerks."[113] Later, there is the steady shrinking of the jurisdiction of ecclesiastical tribunals—particularly over criminal matters. Lockean arguments that ecclesiastical entities should not be allowed to assert jurisdiction over civil and, particularly, criminal matters are an important landmark in this development.[114] Finally, in our own time, waning enthusiasm of secular tribunals to prosecute consensual sex offenses can be viewed as a refusal to take jurisdiction over the "arguably religious."

While such jurisdictional disputes (except for their secularized versions in the domain of debates about overcriminalization and the enforcement of morals) are now of mainly historical character, they have clearly left their mark on the law. The original force of the distinction between murder and manslaughter—still the basic divide running through the law of homicide—was to delineate homicides eligible for the benefit of clergy from those that were not clergyable.[115]

---

[109]R. Helmholz, "Crime, Compurgation and the Courts of the Medieval Church," *Law and History Review* 1 (1983): 11.

[110]Ibid.

[111]von Bar, *History of Continental Criminal Law*, 89.

[112]See, e.g., W. Jones, "The Two Laws in England: The Later Middle Ages," *Journal of Church and State* 11 (1969): 111 (suggesting that medieval historiography tends to overplay confrontations between church and state, thereby underestimating the significance of cooperation).

[113]See, e.g., C. Duggan, *Canon Law in Medieval England: The Becket Dispute and Decretal Collections* (London, 1982).

[114]Locke, *Letter Concerning Toleration*, 22–23.

[115]See Plucknett, *A Concise History*, 445–46. See also L. Gabel, *Benefit of Clergy in England in the Later Middle Ages* (New York, 1969); Holdsworth, *A History of English Law*, 3: 293. ("Benefit of Clergy and the institution of Sanctuary and Abjuration are the two most important instances in which ecclesiastical law influenced the medieval criminal law.")

On another front, Professor Berman has suggested that an array of procedural reforms connected with the Puritan Revolution can be viewed as examples of the interaction between law and religion. These included the termination of the inquisitorial system in the Court of Star Chamber, the Court of High Commission and in criminal cases in Admirality, Chancery and other courts and the expansion of the jurisdiction of the common law courts; the transformation of the role of the jury; the abolition of the *ex officio* oath; the abolition of prerogative courts; recognition (and reinforcement) of rights of *habeas corpus* and rights against self-incrimination, ex post facto laws, excessive bail, cruel and unusual punishment and other such rights that have become the core of procedural due process.[116] Many of these developments can be explained on purely secular grounds, but this would overlook the very real interplay of religious and secular forces in the minds of those who brought these changes about.

The foregoing list, while hardly exhaustive, will suffice to give some impression of the variety of institutional contexts in which further study is needed. In general, a more detailed sense for the multitude of types and contexts of interaction should help to deepen and focus research in this area. To round out the discussion of contexts, I turn in the final section to one area in which the interaction of criminal law and religion has been extraordinarily important: the evolution of conceptions of criminal culpability. Even in this limited area, I cannot hope to provide a comprehensive account of legal and religious interaction, but I hope to be able to convey a somewhat richer sense of its complexity than has been possible in other sections of this article. Here, as elsewhere, my debt to Professor Berman will be apparent.

V. Religious Foundations of the Culpability Principle

The culpability principle—that is, the notion that it is unjust to punish someone unless the person may fairly be held accountable for the criminal conduct in question[117]—is obviously a core principle in our criminal jurisprudence. It lies behind the *mens rea* requirement,[118] a large number of legal defenses,[119] the culpability provisions of the Model Penal

---

[116]Berman, "Law and Belief," 598–601.

[117]With the culpability principle, I have in mind what German criminal theorists refer to as the *Schuldprinzip*. The German literature on this notion is extensive. See, e.g., H. Achenbach, *Historische and dogmatische Grundlagen*; W. Englemann, *Irrtum und Schuld nach der italienischen Lehre und Praxis des Mittelalters* (Berlin, 1922); A. Kaufmann, *Das Schuldprinzip*, 2d rev. ed. (Heidelberg, 1976); M. Liepmann, *Die Entstehung des Schuldbegriffs* (Danzig, 1891); E. Wolf, *Strafrechtliche Schuldlehre: Erster Teil: Die gegenwartige Lage, die theoretischen Voraussetzungen and die methodologische Struktur der strafrechtlichen Schuldlehre* (Mannheim/Berlin/Leipzig, 1928).

[118]G. Fletcher, "The Theory of Criminal Negligence," *University of Pennsylvania Law Review* 119 (1971): 401ff.

[119]P. Robinson, *Criminal Law Defenses* (St. Paul, MN, 1984), 1: 91–101.

Code[120] and our general aversion to strict liability crimes.[121] As a key value in our criminal jurisprudence, it is also one with clear religious roots. Christian theology in general and canon law in particular have exerted a major formative influence on theory and practice in this area.

Ideally, a study of the interaction of law and religion in the development of the culpability principle would trace this conception to its roots in Greece and the ancient Near East and then trace its development down to the present.[122] All that can be done here is to describe a few high points in this lengthy history.

A. Judaic-Christian Roots of Culpability

The starting point is the emergence of the Judaic-Christian notion that righteousness is ultimately a matter of internal disposition, a matter of the heart. A vast literature could be cited here,[123] but reference to a few biblical passages is perhaps a better way to introduce this theme. One thinks of Samuel's admonition to Israel, "prepare your hearts unto the Lord,"[124] or the later statement in Isaiah, "Hearken unto me, ye that know righteousness, the people in whose heart is my law . . ."[125] The theme sounds again in Jeremiah: "I will put my law in their inward parts, and write it in their hearts."[126] By the time of the New Testament, the notion has been universalized: "For when the Gentiles, which have not the law, do by nature the things contained in the law, these, having not the law, are a law unto themselves: [w]hich shew the work of the law written in their hearts. . . ."[127]

The sensitivity to inward morality carries with it a sense for inward evil.

[120]Model Penal Code § 2.01 (Proposed Official Draft 1962).

[121]This is manifest, among other things, in the effort of the drafters of the Model Penal Code to reduce strict liability offenses to violations. See Model Penal Code § 104(5) (Proposed Official Draft 1962). For discussions of the issue of strict liability in criminal law, see M. Budd and A. Lynch, "Voluntariness, Causation and Strict Liability," *Criminal Law Review* (1978): 74–81; R. Wasserstrom, "Strict Liability in the Criminal Law," *Stanford Law Review* 12 (1960): 731ff.

[122]A few general, though now somewhat dated, accounts of the history of notions of culpability and *mens rea* are available. See, e.g., A. Levitt, "The Origin of the Doctrine of Mens Rea," *Illinois Law Review* 17 (1922): 117–37; A. Löffler, *Schuldformen des Strafrechts in vergleichend-historischer and dogmatischer Darstellung* (Leipzig, 1895); F. Sayre, "Mens Rea," *Harvard Law Review* 45 (1932): 974–1026. For a more recent discussion, see G. Fletcher, "The Theory of Criminal Negligence: A Comparative Analysis," *University of Pennsylvania Law Review* 119 (1971): 408–26.

[123]See, e.g., Bahya ibn Pakuda, "The Duties of the Heart," *The Judaic Tradition*, ed. N. Glatzer, rev. ed. (Boston, 1969), 305–308; G. von Rad, *The Message of the Prophets*, trans. D. Stalker (London, 1968); G. Robinson, *The Twelve Minor Prophets* (New York, 1930); H. Robinson, *Inspiration and Revelation in the Old Testament* (Oxford, 1946), 69–91; G. Vermes, *Jesus and the World of Judaism* (London, 1983), 44–49.

[124]I Sam. 7:3.

[125]Isaiah 51:7.

[126]Jer. 31:33.

[127]Rom. 2:14–15.

Thus, the Psalmist laments, "For their heart was not right with him, neither were they steadfast in his covenant."[128] Proverbs counseled, "Lust not after her beauty in thine heart,"[129] a theme that was echoed with greater force by Jesus: ". . . whosoever looketh on a woman to lust after her hath committed adultery with her already in his heart."[130] The sensitivity to inner corruption recurs: "But those things which proceed out of the mouth come forth from the heart; and they defile the man. For out of the heart proceed evil thoughts, murders, adulteries, fornications, thefts, false witness, blasphemies: These are the things which defile a man: but to eat with unwashen hands defileth not a man."[131]

The discrepancy between divine and human insight into the inner seat of morality became particularly significant for the evolution of legal analysis of culpability. Consciousness of this difference is evident in Samuel's statement in the process of choosing David: "for the Lord seeth not as man seeth; for man looketh on the outward appearance, but the Lord looketh on the heart."[132] The idea is discernible in the Psalms: ". . . for [God] knoweth the secrets of the heart."[133] And again in Luke: "Ye are they which justify yourselves before men; but God knoweth your hearts."[134]

Biblical references such as those just cited provided the theological backdrop for the evolution of legal conceptions of culpability. Greek thought, particularly that of the Stoics, also contributed to the interiorization of moral life.[135] But, in contrast with Greek conceptions of virtue and vice, which saw vice primarily as a defect in character, the Judaic-Christian conception placed a greater emphasis on the notion of breach of divine law— on acts of disloyalty to God.[136] And it is with respect to this type of breach or sin that later theologians, philosophers and legal thinkers began to transmute background religious values into functional legal concepts.

B. Religious Foundations of *Mens Rea*

The insistence on *mens rea* as an element of serious crime is one of the most deeply held principles in Anglo-American criminal law. The phrase "*mens rea*" is first encountered in the writings of Augustine in a sermon dealing with perjury. There Augustine reasoned that a man who testifies that it rained at a certain spot, believing that it did not and ignorant of the fact that

---

[128]Ps. 78:37.
[129]Prov. 6:25.
[130]Matt. 5:28.
[131]Matt. 15:18–20.
[132]1 Sam. 16:7.
[133]Ps. 44:21.
[134]Luke 16:15.
[135]MacIntyre, *After Virtue*, 168.
[136]Ibid.

it actually did, is guilty of perjury. For Augustine, the issue of culpability turned on the extent to which the arguably perjured word comes from the mind. His conclusion was, *"Ream linguam non facit nisi mens rea"*[137] ("it does not make the tongue guilty unless the mind is guilty").[138]

A brief overview of the subsequent history of the notion of *mens rea* may be helpful. As Pollock and Maitland noted,[139] the phrase passed from Augustine via some intermediate source that dropped the reference to "tongue" (*linguam*) into the *Leges Henrici Primi*[140] (a compilation dating from about 1118 that sought to state "a body of true English law that was neither Roman nor canon law"[141]). Pollock and Maitland speak of receiving a "shock of surprise"[142] at finding the shortened maxim (*Reum non facit nisi mens rea*) in that context, apparently because Henry I's compilation was pervaded by the notion of absolute liability regardless of evil intent.[143] At about the same time the Augustinian phrase was wending its way into the *Leges Henrici Primi*, it was absorbed into canon law as well.[144]

During the centuries that followed, as a result of the institutional influence of the Church, the dissemination of the notion that guilt was a necessary condition for punishment in the widely circulated penitential books,[145] and the refinement of culpability theory in the more sophisticated doctrines of canonists and moral theologians, the criminal law moved in the direction of insisting on a generalized requirement of blameworthiness.[146] This development was part of a much broader shift in dominant patterns of liability. Harm-oriented conceptions of law, which structured *prima facie* liability in terms of harmful results regardless of fault, were gradually being supplanted by act-oriented patterns, for which culpability concerns were central.[147] The legitimacy of betrayal culture, with its patterns of blood feud and kinship-group revenge (and the concomitant lack of concern for individual fault) was being undermined by Christian conceptions of forgiveness and by the emergence of centralized state power anxious to minimize breaches of civil peace and security. The *mens rea* formula found in the *Leges Henrici Primi* was appropriated as a convenient label for articulating the newer

---

[137]Augustinus, *Sermones*, no. 180, c.2, Migne, *Patrologia Latina*, 38: 974.

[138]The translation here is derived from Levitt's explanation of the history of the passage. "The Origin," 117, n.1.

[139]Pollock and Maitland, *History of English Law*, 2: 476 n.5.

[140]*Leges Henrici Primi* c.5, §28. See Sayre "Mens Rea," 983.

[141]Ibid., 978.

[142]Pollock and Maitland, *History of English Law*, 2: 476.

[143]See Sayre, "Mens Rea," 983. To use the German terminology, the *Leges Henrici Primi* was pervaded by *Erfolgshaftung*—i.e., liability keyed to harmful consequences or results.

[144]*Decretum*, c.3, C.22, Q. 2 (ca. 1140).

[145]Berman, "Background of Western Legal Tradition," 577–86.

[146]Sayre, "Mens Rea," 988–94.

[147]Cf. Fletcher, *Rethinking*, 238–40.

ideas.[148] Ultimately, it emerged in Coke's *Third Institute* in the form in which it has come down to common lawyers ever since: "*actus non facit reum nisi mens sit rea.*"[149]

Within the common law tradition, there has been a tendency to convert the generalized normative requirement of blameworthiness associated with the early *mens rea* notion into precise descriptions of mental states for individual crimes.[150] In recent years, excessive rigidity in thinking of *mens rea* as particularized positive mental states has led to disputes in borderline areas, such as whether negligence (which by definition involves the absence of a mental state) is a form of *mens rea* and whether it may justifiably be punished.[151]

The foregoing glimpse of the road *mens rea* has traveled from Augustine to the present suggests at the most general level the nature of interaction of law and religion in the domain of culpability: ideas of religious origin find their way into the law and help mold its fundamental categories.

C. The Separation of Crime and Sin

In modern secular culture, we are accustomed to thinking about the separation of crime and sin as part of a larger separation of religion and politics. In a pluralistic society, we assume that behavior which is to be criminalized must be announced in advance and that criminal sanctions should be justifiable in terms of secular interests. In the medieval world, a parallel separation of crime and sin emerged, but its basis was much different.

The starting point of analysis in medieval culture was with the religiously grounded notion of sin. Sin could lie in any form of deviation from divine law, whether inward or outward, and any form of sin manifested disobedience to God. Yet, early on, the need emerged to distinguish between sin and canonical crime. One of the motivating considerations was the canon law of ordination.[152] According to the New Testament, "a bishop must be blameless."[153] The Latin version of this verse provided "*oportet episcopum esse sine crimine*" ("a bishop must be without crime").

Augustine had stressed that the passage did not require that "a bishop must be without sin."[154] The question, then, was what differented crime from conduct that did not preclude ordination as a bishop?

[148]Ibid., 988.

[149]Sir Edward Coke, *Third Institute* [1644], ed. E. Brooke (London, 1797), 54, 107.

[150]Sayre, "Mens Rea," 994–1016; J. Hall, *General Principles of Criminal Law*, 2d ed. (Indianapolis, 1960), 70–104.

[151]Fletcher, "Theory of Criminal Negligence," 408–26; J. Hall, "Negligent Behavior Should Be Excluded from Penal Liability," *Columbia Law Review* 63 (1963): 632ff.

[152]There was also a need to differentiate offenses warranting excommunication. Kuttner, *Kanonistische Schuldlehre*, 4.

[153]Titus 1:7.

[154]Kuttner, *Kanonistische Schuldlehre*, n. 1.

For Peter Abelard the issue was essentially jurisdictional. In harmony with some of the biblical passages noted above,[155] Abelard took the position that God judges the heart, where only inner intent matters, but human fora, including canon law courts, need to be able to identify external characteristics of crime.[156] Abelard assumed that all human punishment can attach only to outer conduct, involving active engagement of the will in bringing about actions and results. In addition, he believed that crime must have three characteristics.[157] First, it must involve grave sin. Not even all mortal sins are grave enough to constitute crime. Simple greed, for example, was not sufficient. The act must be sufficiently opprobrious that it brings infamy to the individual. Second, a crime must be manifested in an outer act, in order that it can come to judicial cognizance.[158] Third, the act must be vexatious to the Church (*ecclesiam scandalizant*). That is, even morally offensive acts should not be punished unless harmful in some way to the Church.

As Stephan Kuttner has noted, Abelard could, theoretically, have developed a concept of crime from his analysis that was not dependent on the concept of sin.[159] Leaving aside the element of sin, one still has in the residue the insistence on outer acts, vexation for the church and infamy for the offender.[160] But freeing crime from theological considerations was foreign to Abelard's enterprise. Ecclesiastical crime and punishment remained connected with divine punishment for sin; they constituted part of divine justice. The limits on crime were derivative not from the substance of the religious category of sin but from the evidentiary limits implicit in human judging. Taking these limits seriously, Abelard drew the radical conclusion that retributive punishment of inner guilt lay beyond human competence and that church punishment must be restricted to the more limited task of preventing or deterring crime and thereby protecting the social order from harms.[161] In this he was not followed by later canonists, who strove to reconcile the inscrutability of inner culpability with retributive punishment. In their view, the Church possesses sufficient outer indicia

[155]See notes 124–34 above.

[156]Kuttner, *Kanonistische Schuldlehre*, 4–5.

[157]Ibid., 5; Berman, *Law and Revolution*, 187–89.

[158]This insistence is linked to a persistent strain in Western legal systems that Fletcher characterizes as the pattern of manifest criminality. Fletcher, *Rethinking*, 81, 115–18, 232–33. It is particularly evident in the law of attempts, which has always required more than mere preparation for liability. Ibid., 141–46. This pattern has deep linkages with the notion of the rule of law, with its insistence on sharp legal categories that can help avoid excessive discretion in the administration of justice.

[159]Kuttner, *Kanonistische Schuldlehre*, 5.

[160]Ibid.

[161]Ibid., 25. Professor Berman indicates that Abelard relied on a conclusive presumption to bridge the gap between crime and sin. Berman, *Law and Revolution*, 189. This appears to flow from a misreading of Kuttner, who indicates that it was subsequent canonists who attempted to rescue the notion of punishment for guilt (*Schuldstrafe*). Ibid., 25–27.

of guilt to reach an assessment of inner guilt that approximates the result of divine judgment.[162]

The effort to work out an ecclesiastical conception of crime can be followed through Gratian[163] and the Decretists who commented directly on his work.[164] But the essential picture has already emerged. Like Abelard, they viewed gravity of the sin, externality of the conduct and vexation for the Church as necessary conditions for making conduct legally cognizable as a crime. Unlike Abelard, they tried to reconcile punishment for culpability with the true content of guilt. They viewed human limitations in discerning inner motivation as a human weakness, but not as a jurisdictional bar.[165]

What is significant for my purposes is to see how the borderline between internal motivation and externally cognizable conduct is drawn against the background of Christian theology. The precise contours of the canonical conception of crime are not nearly so significant as the dichotomy between inner motivation and external action that they presuppose. The resulting categories, despite disputes about their precise boundaries, have shaped criminal thought for centuries. Crimes have subjective and objective dimensions.[166] Offenses are conceptualized in terms of *mens rea* and *actus reus* elements, or they are analyzed in terms of culpability elements, on the one hand, and result, conduct or circumstance elements, on the other.[167] Mere thoughts are not to be punished.[168] More generally, the realm of practical reason is divided into the internal domain of ethics and the external domain of law. One of the more salient examples of this is the structure of Kantian moral and legal philosophy, where moral life is subdivided into two parts, one ruled by a doctrine of justice (*Rechtslehre*)[169] which deals with laws that refer only to "freedom in its external exercise,"[170] and another governed by a doctrine of virtue (*Tugendlehre*),[171] with laws that refer to freedom "in both the internal and external exercise of will."[172] But the division is certainly not restricted to Kant and runs through many of our

[162]Kuttner, *Kanonistische Schuldlehre*, 25–27.

[163]Ibid., 6–8.

[164]Ibid., 8–22.

[165]Ibid., 25–27.

[166]Fletcher, *Rethinking*, 504–14.

[167]P. Robinson, *Criminal Defenses*, 1: 62–69; Model Penal Code 1.13 (9), 2.02 (Proposed Official Draft, 1962).

[168]G. Dworkin and D. Blumenfeld, "Punishment for Intention," *Mind* 75 (1966): 396–404; H. Morris, "Punishment for Thoughts," *Monist* 49 (1965): 342–76.

[169]I. Kant, "The Metaphysical Elements of Justice," Part I of the *Metaphysic of Morals*, trans. J. Ladd, (Indianapolis, 1965).

[170]Ibid., 13.

[171]I. Kant, "The Doctrine of Virtue," Part II of the *Metaphysic of Morals*, trans., M. Gregor, (Philadelphia, 1964).

[172]Kant, "Metaphysical Elements of Justice," 13.

deepest assumptions about the relation of law and morals. In short, the distinction of crime and sin worked out in medieval theory molded the framework within which most of the fundamental debates about culpability and legal accountability have been carried on ever since.

VI. Conclusion

The shaping of the doctrine of culpability is, of course, only one of innumerable areas in which more intensive study of the interaction of law and religion in criminal law is needed. Even in that limited area, what has been said here has not even begun to scratch the surface of what can and should be done. But my aim has not been to provide a comprehensive treatment of relationships between law and religion in criminal law. It has been to identify with greater specificity the plethora of types and contexts of interactions one needs to think about as one explores this complex interface. The significance to virtually all of the types and contexts of interaction that have been discussed in this article becomes apparent as one reflects on the isolated strands in the history of the doctrine of culpability that have been described above. This is worth summarizing briefly, as a way of reflecting back over what has been said. The fact that there is both a positive and negative dimension to the interaction is apparent from the sifting that has gone on in the course of development. The religious insistence on fair accountability as a precondition for punishment has been accentuated, but, over time, it has also been secularized. Older notions of grounding crime in religious notions of sin have been left behind in modern pluralistic societies. Thought over the centuries about notions of culpability has been profoundly molded by the endless *Gestalt*-type back-and-forth in individual conscious-ness between religious and secular interpretation, analysis and experience of issues of criminal responsibility. It is not as though there are two fixed and hermetically sealed options—religious and secular—that one alternates between. Having perceived an issue of culpability in a context charged with religiosity changes the way one sees the situation when the charge fades and the situation is examined through secular lenses. Penetration by the numi-nous changes the secular landscape, and vice-versa, and this happens in many ways. Sometimes religious norms are transplanted into secular law. This is clearly what happened with *mens rea*, which commenced its journey as a phrase in a sermon by Augustine and now is the fundamental axiom of criminal culpability. At the same time, religious notions of culpability serve to reinforce secularized legal notions. Religiously grounded ideas about when it is fair to hold someone accountable help to mitigate pressures for excessive zeal in prosecution. This is one of the many ways in which notions of culpability have constituted a shared (religious and secular) conduit of cultural meaning. Assessment of culpability has been a key issue in both religious and secular contexts, and analyses from the two domains have inevitably exerted reciprocal modeling influences on each other. The fact that notions of culpability have been critical in shaping the structure of the criminal system—its divisions into internal and external dimensions of liability, among other things—has already been noted. The narratives of final judgment and individual penance have provided crucial backgrounds for the emergence of key notions of criminal culpability. The emergence of Christian notions of culpability had a tremendous impact in supplanting the patterns of betrayal and result-oriented liability (*Erfolgshaftung*) and pressing criminal systems toward the pattern of subjective criminality with its tendency to put issues of culpability at the center of criminal analysis. Finally, with respect to types of interaction, there can be no doubt that religious notions of culpability have helped to ground and motivate modern notions of culpability. Even in our post-Enlightenment world, where the culpability principle tends to be justified in terms of arguments with utilitarian or Kantian ancestries, religious perceptions continue to play a role in reinforcing moral intuitions.

Turning to contexts of interaction, the detailed development of culpability concepts—of more particularized *mens rea* requirements with respect to particular crimes and defenses—has clearly occurred in the contexts of individualized judging and biography. It is to the thought of individuals such as Augustine, Abelard, Coke and others that we have turned to trace the history of culpability. The influence of the penitentials in shaping culpability rules attests to the significance of popular consciousness as a context of interaction. Religious views on punishment and culpability are intimately tied to abstract philosophical theories of punishment. Finally, the institutional contexts in which law and religion have interacted with respect to culpability are extensive. It was in the institutional setting of clarifying for ordination, for example, that it became necessary to distinguish the ecclesiastical concept of crime from sin. Issues of perjury and false oath-taking first gave Augustine's statements on *mens rea* their currency. Here in particular, the range of interactions has been slighted, but again, that has been unavoidable here.

What I have tried to describe is a point of departure for further work on the relationship between criminal law and religion. From my perspective, this article still represents work in process, and suffers from all the defects that are associated with that stage of research. I have no doubt that my incomplete and tentative list of types and contexts of interaction could be usefully expanded, and I am convinced of the need for deeper research into the areas suggested by those I have identified. My hope at this point is that the framework of analysis I have suggested here will contribute to the efforts that Professor Berman has done so much to motivate, the revitalization of research in the domain of criminal law and religion.

CASTING THE PRIESTS OUT OF THE TEMPLE: JOHN AUSTIN AND THE RELATION BETWEEN LAW AND RELIGION

John V. Orth

On Sunday, July 14, 1833, John Keble preached the Assize Sermon at Oxford, the Church of England's contribution to the medieval pageantry that still surrounded the periodic visits of the royal judges. Devoted to "National Apostasy,"[1] the sermon was the anguished response of an earnest churchman to contemporary political developments. During the preceding year the Reform Act[2] had enfranchised thousands of Englishmen hitherto excluded from politics, including many Protestant nonconformists. Even as he spoke, a parliament elected along new lines was legislating for the state-supported church in Ireland, suppressing in the process ten ancient Irish bishoprics.[3] In his alarm at secular interference in church affairs Keble imagined the worst:

> The case is at least possible, of a nation, having for centuries acknowledged, as an essential part of its theory of government, that, as a Christian nation, she is also a part of Christ's Church, and bound, in all her legislation and policy, by the fundamental rules of that Church—the case is, I say, conceivable, of a government and people, so constituted, deliberately throwing off the restraint, which in many respects such a principle would impose on them, nay, disavowing the principle itself. . . .[4]

"Is APOSTASY too hard a word," asked the preacher, "to describe the temper of that nation?"[5] For the benefit of the assembled judges, Keble expressed the hope that

---

[1] "National Apostasy," reprinted in J. Keble, *Sermons Academic and Occasional* (Oxford, 1848), 127–48. For his text the preacher chose I Samuel 12:23 (AV): "As for me, God forbid that I should sin against the Lord in ceasing to pray for you: but I will teach you the good and the right way." The text expresses the prophet's reaction to the Israelites' demand that they become like other people with a king to rule them, despite the kingship of God.

Keble (1792–1866), author of *The Christian Year* (London, 1827), a best-selling collection of sacred verse, was Professor of Poetry at Oxford. Keble College is named in his memory.

[2] 2 & 3 Will. 4, c. 45 (1832).

[3] 3 & 4 Will. 4, c. 37 (1833).

[4] Keble, *Sermons*, 134.

[5] Ibid., 138 (emphasis in original).

[t]he very solemnity of this day may remind them, even more than others, of the close amity which must ever subsist between equal justice and pure religion; Apostolical religion, more especially, in proportion to her superior truth and exactness. It is an amity, made still more sacred, if possible, in the case of the Church and Law of England, by historical recollections, associations and precedents, of the most engaging and ennobling cast.[6]

For all Church of England men, Keble thought the need to draw down God's blessing during the time of peril contributed

one motive more to exact punctuality in those duties, personal and official, which the return of an Assize week offers to our practice; one reason more for veracity in witnesses, fairness in pleaders, strict impartiality, self-command, and patience, in those on whom decisions depend; and for an awful sense of God's presence in all.[7]

"National Apostasy" was more than an isolated cleric's *cri de coeur*; it was also the trumpet call to a new movement within the Established Church. Before the year was out, the first of the momentous *Tracts for the Times* had appeared, and the Oxford Movement had begun. Keble's own contributions to the famous *Tracts* emphasized the "Apostolical Succession," taking a high line on "submission to authority," the rights of clergy and the dangers of free thinking.[8] Thirty years later John Henry Newman, by then a Roman Catholic priest, recalled the effect of Keble's Assize Sermon and confessed that he had ever "kept the day" as the start of a great religious revival.[9]

The years surrounding the Reform Act of 1832 offered other instances of legislation concerning religion, in addition to the Irish Church Act. In the complicated politics that preceded franchise extension, nonconformists gained greater legal security; the outright repeal of the repressive Corporation Act in 1828[10] rendered annual indemnity acts unnecessary. Roman Catholics, too, benefited from legislative tolerance; in 1829 they were relieved—emancipated, as it was called—from Tudor-Stuart penal laws.[11] After the Reform Act, legislation altered the perquisites of the Establishment. Biblical-sounding tithe was commuted to a money payment based on

[6]Ibid., 145.

[7]Ibid., 146.

[8]*Tracts for the Times* (London, 1833–41), nos. 4, 40, 52, 54, 57, 60. Attribution of the anonymous tracts to Keble is in W. Lock, *John Keble* (London, 1895), 83–85, 98–102. Keble is also described as the author of *Tracts* nos. 13 and 89.

[9]J. Newman, *Apologia pro Vita Sua*, Modern Library (1950; 1st ed. 1864), 63.

[10]9 Geo. 4, c. 17 (1828) (repealing in part 13 Car. 2, st. 2, c. 1 1661).

[11]10 Geo. 4, c. 7 (1829). On the penal laws see Charles Butler's note in the edition of *Coke on Littleton* that he prepared with Francis Hargrave in 1794 (vol. 3, n. 346). The note was subsequently issued as a pamphlet, *Historical Account of the Laws Respecting Roman Catholics* (London, 1795).

the market price of grain.[12] The Church's monopoly on marriage was finally broken.[13] The function of recording baptisms, marriages and funerals was transferred to a registrar of vital statistics.[14]

Since England was, as Keble claimed, a "Christian nation," seemingly secular issues became charged with religious significance. After a prolonged evangelical campaign, slavery was finally abolished in 1833.[15] No sooner had the labor system based on the ownership of "human souls" been ended by act of parliament than a new series of statutes dealing with the conditions of factory work was inaugurated[16] amid applause from socially conscious clergy. Simultaneously, the middle class movement for free trade in grain that culminated in the celebrated repeal of the Corn Laws in 1846[17] was conducted with religious fervor. For symbolic purposes, however, nothing can equal the National Fast solemnly proclaimed for March 21, 1832 to invoke the Deity to end an epidemic of cholera.[18] Not all Englishmen, however, shared the religious outlook of Keble. In some cases the preacher had grounds for using the hard word "Apostasy." When Spencer Perceval, pious son of the former Prime Minister, first moved in parliament for a general fast, many members were uncomprehending. "General *what?*" they cried.[19] Henry Hunt, the radical orator, sarcastically observed during a later debate that one-third of the people of Britain already fasted involuntarily,[20] and the National Union of the Working Classes parodied the National Fast Day as National Farce Day.[21] Throughout the century undoubtedly more Englishmen observed July 14 as Bastille Day than as the day of Keble's Assize Sermon.

During the agitation that led up to the passage of the great Reform Act, a series of lectures on jurisprudence was delivered[22] to a small class at the

[12]6 & 7 Will. 4, c. 71 (1836).

[13]6 & 7 Will. 4, c. 85 (1836).

[14]6 & 7 Will. 4, c. 86 (1836).

[15]3 & 4 Will. 4, c. 73 (1833).

[16]3 & 4 Will. 4, c. 103 (1833). For an overview of the whole series of statutes see B. Hutchins and A. Harrison, *A History of Factory Legislation*, 3d ed. (London, 1926).

[17]8 & 9 Vict., c. 22 (1846) (reducing duty to nominal level).

[18]Proclamation by Privy Council (Feb. 6, 1832) ("For a general fast in England and Ireland (21st March) to beseech God to remove the grievous disease.") *Handlist of Proclamations Issued by Royal and Other Constitutional Authorities, 1714–1910*, in *Bibliotheca Lindesiana* (Wigan, Lancs., 1913), 8: 308.

For a novelistic account of the official service of intercession see M. Edelman, *Disraeli in Love* (New York, 1972), ch. 2.

[19]*Hansard Parliamentary Debates*, 3d ser. (1830–31): col. 81 (Dec. 23, 1830).

[20]Ibid., cols. 204–05 (Feb. 7, 1831).

[21]*Poor Man's Guardian*, March 24, 1832, cited in A. Briggs, *The Age of Improvement, 1783–1867* (New York, 1959), 254, n. 1.

[22]Based on a misleading statement years later, the misapprehension has arisen that the lectures began in 1828. In fact, the first series seems to have been delivered from November 16, 1829, to July, 1830. See W. Morison, *John Austin* (Stanford, CA, 1982), 21.

newly established University of London.[23] The lecturer, born in 1790 and therefore two years Keble's senior, was John Austin.[24] Though Austin's class was small,[25] it was select, including John Stuart Mill,[26] Edwin Chadwick,[27] J.A. Roebuck,[28] Edward Strutt,[29] John Romilly,[30] Charles Villiers,[31] Charles Buller[32] and George Cornewall Lewis.[33] Like many other

[23]In 1836 the University was incorporated and became University College. With King's College, founded in 1829 by adherents of the Church of England, it formed the University of London, which (with many additional components) continues to exist. On legal education at University College see G. Keeton, "University College, London, and the Law," *Juridical Review* 51 (1939): 118–33 and J. Baker, "University College and Legal Education, 1826–1976," *Current Legal Problems* 30 (1977): 1–13.

[24]Thomas Carlyle described John Austin in a letter to his wife as a "lean grey-headed painful-looking man, with large earnest timid eyes and a clanging metallic voice . . . ; a very worthy sort of limited man and professor of law." Carlyle to Mrs. Carlyle, September 4, 1831, reprinted in J. Froude, *Thomas Carlyle: A History of the First Forty Years of His Life, 1795–1835* (New York, 1882), 2: 153.

[25]Names of students, taken from the University register, are in H. Bellot, *University College, London. 1826–1926* (London, 1929), 187–88.

[26]John Stuart Mill (1806–73). Son of Bentham's principal collaborator, Mill was already acquainted with John Austin's pedagogy, having studied Roman law with him during the winter of 1821–22. See *The Autobiography of John Stuart Mill* (New York, 1924; 1st ed. 1873), 45. Mill later made major contributions to economics, notably in his *Principles of Political Economy*, 2 vols. (London, 1848). He also propounded a world famous philosophy of individual freedom in his essays *On Liberty* (London, 1859) and *The Subjection of Women* (London, 1861). In *Utilitarianism* (London, 1863) he restated Benthamism for his generation. He also served briefly in parliament, 1865–68.

[27]Edwin Chadwick (1800–90). As secretary to the Poor Law Commission, Chadwick drafted a famous report on sanitation that led to passage of the Public Health Act (1848), creating a Board of Health on which he subsequently served.

[28]J. A. Roebuck (1801–79). An independent middle-class radical, Roebuck sat in parliament almost continually from 1832 until his death. As a member of the Royal Commission on Trade Unions in 1867–69, he opposed improvement in the legal status of labor organizations.

[29]Edward Strutt (1801–80). After serving from 1830–47 and 1851–56 in parliament, Strutt was created Lord Belper. From 1871–79 he was president of the council of University College, London.

[30]John Romilly (1802–74). Son of the celebrated law reformer, Romilly sat in parliament from 1832–36 and 1847–52. He was successively Solicitor-General, Attorney General and Master of the Rolls. Romilly was created a baron in 1865.

[31]Charles Villiers (1802–98). Younger brother of the Earl of Clarendon, Villiers served in parliament, 1835–98, where he was an outspoken opponent of protectionism and, in his early years, of the Corn Laws. He was later Judge Advocate-General and President of the Poor Law Board.

[32]Charles Buller (1806–48). Elected to parliament in 1830, Buller voted for the Reform Act that eliminated his own constituency. In 1838 he accompanied Lord Durham to Canada on a mission that led to the reform of colonial administration. He later served as secretary to the Board of Control, Judge Advocate-General and head of the Poor Law Commission.

[33]George Cornewall Lewis (1806–63). In 1836 Lewis served with his former teacher Austin on a mission to investigate the colonial government of Malta. For an analysis of the Austin-Lewis Report, which appears in *Parliamentary Papers* (1837–38), vol. 29 and (1839), vol. 17, see W. Rumble, *The Thought of John Austin: Jurisprudence, Colonial Reform, and the British Constitution* (London, 1985), ch. 5. [This analysis should be read in conjunction with the background

students at the new university, Austin's were later prominent in public life as exponents of utilitarianism, the philosophy of social reform propounded by Jeremy Bentham. Indeed, the University of London had been founded by Benthamites to offer higher education to those, especially dissenters in religion, to whom the two existing universities did not cater. Both Oxford and Cambridge conditioned the awarding of degrees on subscription of the Thirty-Nine Articles, the official creed of the Church of England,[34] and Oxford—Keble's university—imposed the religious test at matriculation as well.

Unlike Keble's Assize Sermon, Austin's lectures on jurisprudence were seeds that fell on stony ground. The illustrious class that attended the first series of lectures was not equalled the following year. In fact, at the commencement of the next academic year Austin had no class at all, and only three students appeared the following week.[35] The course limped along with a few students for several years. (It would be interesting to know whether Austin canceled class on the National Fast Day.) Finally, in 1835, the lecturer gave up and resigned. The principal fruit of Austin's effort was a little-noticed volume of lectures, *The Province of Jurisprudence Determined*,[36] published in mid-1832, at almost the exact moment of the adoption of the Reform Act. Perhaps due to the political furor at the time, the "Scotch reviewers" for the influential *Edinburgh Review* did not comment on the lectures, although John Stuart Mill gave his former teacher high marks in *Tait's Edinburgh Magazine*.[37]

As staked out by Austin, the province of jurisprudence is "positive law," that is, "law set by political superiors to political inferiors."[38] Law, as defined by Austin,[39] includes divine as well as human law, both proceeding

---

information supplied by L. Hamburger and J. Hamburger, *Troubled Lives: John and Sarah Austin* (Toronto, 1985), ch. 5.] Lewis went on to a distinguished career as a man of letters and cabinet minister. After editing the *Edinburgh Review*, he was successively Chancellor of the Exchequer, Home Secretary and Secretary for War.

[34]The Thirty-Nine Articles, printed in most editions of the Book of Common Prayer, were adopted by Church convocation in 1563 and published by royal ordinance. In 1571 they were sanctioned by parliament in the Subscription Act. 13 Eliz., c. 12 (1571); see also 5 Anne, c. 5 (1707) [incorporated in Act of Union of England and Scotland, 5 Anne, c. 8, § 7 (1707)].

[35]Morison, *Austin*, 22.

[36]J. Austin, *The Province of Jurisprudence Determined* (London, 1832) [hereafter cited as Austin, *Province* (1832)]. Despite misleading indications, the 1954 edition of the *Province* published by H. Hart does not reprint the 1832 text; instead, it is based on one of the posthumous editions prepared by S. Austin and R. Campbell. See notes 45 and 46 below.

[37]*Tait's Edinburgh Magazine* 2 (1832): 343–48.

[38]Austin, *Province* (1832), 1.

[39]"A law, in the most general and comprehensive acceptation in which the term, in its literal meaning, is employed, may be said to be a rule laid down for the guidance of an intelligent being by an intelligent being having power over him." J. Austin, *The Province of Jurisprudence Determined*, ed. H. Hart (New York, 1954), 10 [hereafter cited as Austin, *Province* (ed. Hart)]. This definition does not appear in the 1832 edition.

de haut en bas. What determines the difference, according to the lecturer, is politics. God is in the right place, so to speak, but he is not there politically. Moral law is marked off from God's law because it is made by men and is, therefore, "positive morality."[40] Backed by sanctions, laws are, in Austin's words, "a *species* of commands."[41] This emphasis on hierarchy, force and command reminded many, not least his wife, that Austin had served for many years in the army during the Napoleonic wars. Military life left "permanent traces ... in his character and sentiments," reminisced his widow.[42] (For one scholar "[h]is jurisprudence always smacked of the drill-sergeant."[43])

While allegedly more concerned with positive law than morality, the lecturer, nonetheless, paid considerable attention to the "commands of the Deity." Indeed, three of his six lectures (Lectures II – IV) were devoted to the Supreme Commander and divine law. To no one's surprise, perhaps, Austin's God is a figure more at home with Benthamite utilitarians than Anglican priests.

While the law professor's work did not flourish like the preacher's—*The Province of Jurisprudence Determined* sold slowly and then went out of print—Austin's day was to dawn, although he did not live to see it. After his death in 1859, his remarkable widow Sarah[44] prepared a new edition of *The Province* and added two volumes of previously unpublished *Lectures on Jurisprudence.*[45] After Sarah's death, the editorship passed to Robert Campbell who produced new and more complete editions.[46] Mid-Victorian England was receptive to Austin's views. This time around, a long and

[40]Austin, *Province* (1832), 4.

[41]Ibid., 6 (emphasis in original).

[42]S. Austin, "Preface [to 2d ed.]," reprinted in J. Austin, *Lectures on Jurisprudence, or the Philosophy of Positive Law*, 3d ed., ed. R. Campbell (London, 1869), 1: 3 [hereafter cited as Austin, *Lectures* (3d ed.)].

[43]F. Hearnshaw, "John Austin and the Analytical Jurists," *The Social and Political Ideas of Some Representative Thinkers of the Age of Reaction and Reconstruction, 1815–65*, ed. F. Hearnshaw (New York, 1932), 163.

[44]Sarah Taylor Austin (1785–1867). Married in 1819, she carried on a lively intellectual program of her own. Her translations, including works by Ranke and Guizot, provided financial support. For materials on her life assembled by her granddaughter, see J. Ross, *Three Generations of English Women: Memoirs and Correspondence of Mrs. John Taylor, Mrs. Sarah Austin, and Lady Duff Gordon* (London, 1888), 1:30–296; 2:1–173. On Sarah Austin's work as a translator see Hamburger and Hamburger, *Troubled Lives*, 66–75, 130–31, 135, 140.

[45]J. Austin, *The Province of Jurisprudence Determined*, 2d ed., ed. S. Austin, 3 vols. (London, 1861–63) (vols. 2 and 3 are entitled "Lectures on Jurisprudence, or the Philosophy of Positive Law"). When Sarah Austin said in her preface, "I have altered nothing, except the position of the Outline. . . . ," reprinted in Austin, *Lectures* (3d ed.), 24, she did not mean that the second edition merely reprinted the first. She meant that she had made only those changes contemplated by her husband sometime between 1832 and his death in 1859: "I have inserted all the scattered memoranda I have been able to find, relating to alterations and additions which he meditated." Ibid.

[46]Austin, *Lectures* (3d ed.). The definitive edition is the 5th (1885).

appreciative notice by John Stuart Mill appeared promptly in the *Edinburgh Review*.[47] Despite continuing expressions of public religion, a secular spirit was, as Keble had feared, ever more evident. When a renewed outbreak of cholera in 1853 had brought a call for another national fast, Lord Palmerston summarily dismissed it. Overcrowding and unsanitary conditions caused the infection. Said the Prime Minister: "When man had done his utmost for his own safety, then is the time to invoke the blessing of heaven to give effect to his exertions."[48] By mid-century the Puseyites, intellectual descendants of Keble and the Oxford Movement, ironically opposed national fasts as unwarranted governmental interferences in religion.[49]

Increasing professionalism was, meanwhile, altering English legal education. The intellectually inane practice of supposedly learning law while "keeping terms" at the Inns of Court was yielding to new university training. The promise of Blackstone's Vinerian lectures a century earlier was finally fulfilled by new schools of jurisprudence at the historic universities. Austin's lectures were much needed grist for the academic mills. At Oxford—Keble's university—they promptly became required reading.[50] In 1875 Campbell produced a one volume abridged edition for student use,[51] and, 30 years later, while Campbell's abridgment was still in print,[52] W. Jethro Brown published an edition of the key lectures complete with notes and questions.[53] The legal professoriate became disciples almost to a man.[54] Qualifying or refining one thing or another in Austin's work, they created the Austinian tradition. Markby,[55] Amos,[56]

[47]*Edinburgh Review* 118 (1863): 439–82, reprinted in J. Mill, *Dissertations and Discussions: Political, Philosophical, and Historical* (London, 1867), 3:206–74.

[48]Quoted by O. Chadwick, *The Victorian Church, An Ecclesiastical History of England* (New York, 1966), 5:490.

[49]Ibid.

[50]F. Lawson, *The Oxford Law School, 1850–1865* (Oxford, 1968), 39.

[51]J. Austin, *Lectures on Jurisprudence, or the Philosophy of Positive Law*, The Student's Edition, abridged by R. Campbell (London, 1875).

[52]J. Austin, *Lectures on Jurisprudence, or the Philosophy of Positive Law*, The Student's Edition, abridged by R. Campbell, 12th impression (1913; reprint ed., St. Clair Shores, MI, 1977).

[53]W. Brown, *The Austinian Theory of Law* (London, 1906) (reprinting Lectures I, V, and VI).

[54]James Bryce may have been the exception: he held that John Austin's "contributions to juristic science are really so scanty, and so much entangled with error, that his book ought no longer to find a place among those prescribed for students." J. Bryce, "The Methods of Legal Science," *Studies in History and Jurisprudence* (New York, 1901), 616.

[55]William Markby (1829–1914). Justice of the High Court of Calcutta, 1866–78, Reader in Indian Law at Oxford, 1878–1900, Markby published the once widely read *Elements of Law Considered with Reference to the Principles of General Jurisprudence* in 1871. In 1876 he wrote on "Analytical Jurisprudence" in the *Law Magazine and Review*, 4th Ser. 1: 617–30. He contributed the article on John Austin in the famous 11th ed. of the *Encyclopaedia Britannica* (1910–11). (His wife Lucy was Sarah Austin's niece. Markby had assisted Sarah in preparing her husband's manuscripts for publication.)

[56]Sheldon Amos (1836–86). Professor of Jurisprudence at University College, London, 1869–78—that is, a successor of Austin's—Amos published a *Systematic View of the Science of Jurisprudence* in 1872. (His father, Andrew Amos, had been Professor of English Law at the University of London, 1829–37—that is, a colleague of Austin's.)

Clark,[57] Hearn,[58] Holland,[59] Salmond,[60] Hart[61]—a succession of "philosophers of positive law" span the century from the "reception" of Austin to the
present day. Analytical jurisprudence or, as it is now more often called, legal
positivism has become characteristic of the English legal establishment.
Only in recent years has an anti-positivist challenge been issued, ironically
from within the stronghold of Oxford.[62] In America, notwithstanding all the
differences engendered by federalism and judicial review, Austinian influences are also found. Academic jurisprudence, in the person of Harvard law
professor John Chipman Gray, accepted Austin *mutatis mutandis*.[63] Justice
Oliver Wendell Holmes knew his Austin, reading the *Lectures* again and
again during his "shaping years."[64] Through Holmes, Austin reached the
legal realists who dominated American academic law between the two world
wars.[65]

But the triumphant Austinianism of the last 100 years is not necessarily
to be identified with the Austin of the empty lecture halls of the early 1830s
whose unnoticed book seemed destined for the dustbin of history. Three of
Austin's six lectures in the *Province of Jurisprudence Determined*—the three
treating of God and divine law—remained to all intents and purposes
interred even after the posthumous editions of his work achieved success.

[57]E. C. Clark (1835–1917). Regius Professor of Civil Law at Cambridge, 1873–1914, Clark
published *Practical Jurisprudence, A Comment on Austin* in 1883.

[58]W. E. Hearn (1826–88). Dean of the Faculty of Law at the University of Melbourne, Australia,
1873–88, he published *The Theory of Legal Rights and Duties: An Introduction to Analytical
Jurisprudence* in 1883.

[59]Thomas Erskine Holland (1835–1926). Chichele Professor of International Law and Diplomacy at Oxford, 1874–1910, he published *Elements of Jurisprudence* in 1880, which remained
the standard textbook for more than half a century.

[60]John W. Salmond (1862–1924). Professor of Law at the University of Adelaide, New Zealand,
1897–1906, he published *Jurisprudence* in 1902. The 12th edition of *Salmond on Jurisprudence*
by P. Fitzgerald was published in 1966.

[61]H. L. A. Hart (1907–   ). Professor of Jurisprudence at Oxford, 1952–68, he published *The
Concept of Law* in 1961. With J. H. Burns he has edited the legal works of Jeremy Bentham. In
1954 he republished John Austin's *The Province of Jurisprudence Determined*. See note 36
above. He has written on "Postivism and the Separation of Law and Morals," *Harvard Law
Review* 71 (1958): 593–629. Hart contributed the article on John Austin in the 15th ed. of the
Encyclopaedia Britannica (1974).

[62]R. Dworkin, *Taking Rights Seriously* (London, 1977) and *Law's Empire* (Cambridge, MA,
1986). Dworkin (1931–   ) succeeded H.L.A. Hart as Professor of Jurisprudence at Oxford in
1969. Since 1977 he has also been Professor of Law at New York University.

[63]J. Gray, *The Nature and Sources of Law* (New York, 1909).

[64]E. Little, "The Early Reading of Justice Oliver Wendell Holmes," *Harvard Library Bulletin*
8 (1954): 169, 177, 181, 183, cited in *Justice Oliver Wendell Holmes: The Shaping Years,
1841–1870* (Cambridge, MA, 1957), 194, note d.

For an elaborate argument that Holmes's legal philosophy was largely derived from Bentham
and Austin see H. Pohlman, *Justice Oliver Wendell Holmes and Utilitarian Jurisprudence*
(Cambridge, MA, 1984).

[65]W. Rumble, "The Legal Positivism of John Austin and the Realist Movement in American
Jurisprudence," *Cornell Law Review* 66 (1981): 989, n.13.

Brown's reprinting of the key lectures in 1906 omitted precisely those lectures, passing directly from Lecture I to Lecture V.[66] What appealed to legal professionals in the second half of the Victorian era was not Austin's preference for divine utilitarianism over Keble's version of "Apostolical religion" but rather the loose connection in Austin's philosophy between law and any brand of religion. The first question on "general jurisprudence" set for the law examination at Oxford at Michaelmas Term, 1872 was: "Is it necessary to lay down any theory or system of Morals as a foundation for a system of Jurisprudence?"[67] Sir Henry Maine answered the question in print a few years later: "the truth is that Austin's system is consistent with *any* ethical theory."[68] Echoing Maine, Markby added: "Not only is Austin's conception of law independent of ethics; it is equally independent of politics and religion, and this very independence is one of its greatest merits."[69] A contrary answer, one linking law and religion, might have proved embarrassing. It was only the previous year that academic posts at Oxford and Cambridge had finally been opened on equal terms to all men regardless of creed.[70]

Not only was Austin's revived philosophy timely in its separation of law and religion; it also satisfied the late-Victorian taste for scientific method and terminology. Drawing on European systems of Roman law,[71] which he had studied in Germany during 1827–28 while preparing his lectures, Austin provided a closely-reasoned "analysis of pervading notions,"[72] such as legal right, duty, person, thing, fact and forbearance. Although intended by Austin as a necessary first step toward the Benthamite goal of codification, his analytic notions proved of most enduring use in common law pedagogy. Not only was English law being fitted for university study, but in America a whole new system of graduate legal education was being established. In

[66]See note 53 above. Modern casebook editors have followed Brown's example. See, e.g., G. Christie, *Jurisprudence: Text and Readings on the Philosophy of Law* (St. Paul, MN, 1973), 471–594 (reprinting substantially all of Lectures I, V, and VI, but only parts of Lectures II and III and none of Lecture IV).

[67]Lawson, *Oxford Law School*, 192.

[68]H. Maine, *Lectures on the Early History of Institutions*, 4th ed. (London, 1885; 1st ed., 1874), 368 (emphasis in original). A modern scholar has done all that is humanly possible to hold Austin's system together with utilitarianism. See Rumble, *Thought of Austin*, ch. 3 (previously published in the *American Journal of Jurisprudence* 24 (1979): 139–80).

[69]W. Markby, "Analytical Jurisprudence," *Law Magazine and Review*, 4th ser., 1 (1876): 617, 624.

[70]34 & 35 Vict., c. 26 (1871). Earlier acts had freed from religious tests matriculation at Oxford and admission to degrees at either university (except in the faculty of theology). 17 & 18 Vict., c. 81 (Oxford, 1954); 19 & 20 Vict., c. 88 (Cambridge, 1856).

[71]See M. Hoeflich, "John Austin and Joseph Story: Two Nineteenth Century Perspectives on the Utility of the Civil Law for the Common Lawyer," *American Journal of Legal History* 29 (1985): 38–56.

[72]Austin, *Lectures* (3d ed.), 34, 353–524. In keeping with Austin's "Outline of the Course of Lectures," Lectures XII–XXVII are labeled "Analysis of Pervading Notions."

1871, Dean Christopher Columbus Langdell of the Harvard Law School compiled the first casebook and taught the first class using the Socratic method. Both innovations were premised on the Austinian assumptions that law is a science and that it consists of a limited number of fundamental principles.[73] "Teaching law as a science"[74] became the hallmark of legal education at Harvard and, ultimately, at all American law schools. Analysis of "fundamental legal conceptions" was carried to near perfection in the next generation by Wesley Newcomb Hohfeld.[75] Recently, Professor Berman has observed that "in the late nineteenth and early twentieth centuries . . . there was an excessive concern with logical consistency in the law, which still exists in some quarters. . . ."[76]

The fate of his doctrine would not perhaps have been wholly welcome to Austin. He would certainly have regretted the failure of codification, and it is not at all clear how he would have answered the examination question on law and religion—or what grade he would have received.[77] In 1832 he had maintained that "divine law is the measure or test of positive law and morality: or (changing the phrase) law and morality, in so far as they *are* what they *ought* to be, conform, or are not repugnant, to the law of God."[78] Nonetheless, even the author admitted that his extended discussion of God and divine law "may seem somewhat impertinent,"[79] since what lay within the province of jurisprudence was descriptive, not normative. The principal reason that Austin gave for his seeming impertinence was the need to refute jurists who drew from Roman law a distinction between "positive law and morality fashioned on the law of God" (*jus gentium*) and "positive law and morality of purely human original" (*jus civile*).[80] The purpose of this distinction was to locate a source for natural law in the laws common to all nations. This concept of natural law, along with all others not his own, Austin furiously rejected: "[T]he only *natural law*, of which it is possible to speak without a metaphor, or without a blending of objects which ought to be distinguished broadly" is "[t]he whole or a portion of the laws set by God to men."[81] Although Austin maintained that divine laws are "laws properly so

---

[73]C. Langdell, *Cases on Contracts* (Boston, 1871), viii.

[74]C. Langdell, "Teaching Law as a Science," *American Law Review* 21 (1887): 123–25.

[75]W. Hohfeld, *Fundamental Legal Conceptions As Applied in Judicial Reasoning and Other Legal Essays*, ed. W. Cook (New Haven, CT, 1923) (reprinting essays published 1909–17).

[76]H. Berman, *Law and Revolution: The Formation of the Western Legal Tradition* (Cambridge, MA, 1983), 41.

[77]Although one of the examiners for Michaelmas Term, 1872 was J. Bryce, who gave Austin low marks in general, see n. 54 above, there is no reason to think that Bryce was not "Austinian" in regard to the relations between morals and jurisprudence. See J. Bryce, "The Relations of Law and Religion," *Studies*, 638–68 (contrasting Christianity and Islam).

[78]Austin, *Province* (1832), xiii (emphasis in original).

[79]Ibid., xi.

[80]Ibid., xii.

[81]Ibid., 2 (emphasis added).

called,"[82] he insisted that only positive laws, "laws which are simply and strictly so called,"[83] and which are all made by men, are the proper subject of jurisprudence.

Unlike more orthodox utilitarians, Austin was not radically irreligious. His wife came from a family with strong dissenting traditions,[84] and both husband and wife remained religious, although unchurched.[85] John Stuart Mill recalled that Austin professed "a kind of German religion, a religion of poetry and feeling with little, if anything, of positive dogma."[86] Austin's early lectures are peppered with references, of which Keble would have approved, to God's perfect wisdom and goodness.[87] Even more would Keble have approved of Austin's flattering digression on the "great and excellent writers, who, by the strength of their philosophical genius, or by their large and tolerant spirit, have given imperishable lustre to the Church of England, and extinguished or softened the hostility of many who reject her creed," although the lecturer's purpose was to rank Dr. Paley with "the Berkeleys and Butlers, with the Burnets, Tillotsons and Hoadlys."[88] William Paley, the eighteenth century Cambridge philosopher and divine, was useful to Austin because of his incipient utilitarianism as well as for his admission that revelation did not disclose the whole duty of man. Concerning revelation, Austin spoke sparingly, but with respect. For him, it was the source of truth and light.[89] The lawyer, indeed, conceded more than would, perhaps, be demanded by those who spent their lives studying Scripture. Within its own dispensation, he said, it stated men's duties "distinctly and precisely."[90]

But, in the undefined area beyond the pale of revelation, an area which Austin implied was very extensive, religion gave way to utilitarianism—or, to put it in other words, utilitarianism and true religion became one and the same. God himself was a Benthamite: "Inasmuch as the goodness of God is boundless and impartial, he designs the greatest happiness of all his sentient creatures."[91] While the Anglican Mr. Keble might have shared such a theological assumption, the same could not be said of all Christians. Believers in predestination would have had to concede with Martin Luther that "it is difficult to believe in God's mercy and goodness when he damns those

[82]Ibid., vii.
[83]Ibid.
[84]Hamburger and Hamburger, *Troubled Lives*, 8, 16–18.
[85]Ibid., 92 (Sarah); 170–71 (John).
[86]Mill, *Autobiography*, 125.
[87]Austin, *Province* (1832), 35–36, 40, 48, 60, 70, 86, 90, 92–93, 134, n. 353.
[88]Ibid., 81.
[89]Ibid., 32.
[90]Ibid., 33. In a note that seems to have been composed early in life but that was not published until after his death, Austin retracted this generous concession: "All divines, at least all reasonable divines, admit that no scheme of duties perfectly complete and unambiguous was ever imparted to us by revelation." Austin, *Province* (ed. Hart), 186.
[91]Austin, *Province* (1832), 36.

who do not deserve it."[92] For this part of the Christian tradition God is "utterly incomprehensible and inaccessible to human reason."[93] The ineluctable conclusion is that "His justice also must be incomprehensible."[94] Notwithstanding this long-running theological debate, Austin confidently proclaimed utility the best index to God's will: "From the probable effects of our actions on the greatest happiness of all, or from the tendencies of human actions to increase or diminish that aggregate, we may infer the laws which he has given, but has not expressed or revealed."[95] Calculations of utility were not, however, to be left to each individual; Austin denied, in other words, "the priesthood of all [utilitarian] believers." Utilitarian experts took over from the apostolic priesthood for whom Keble made such high claims.

Austin, himself of course an expert, exemplified the dictates of utility without compromise: "For example, if a poor man steals a handful from the heap of his rich neighbour. . . . "[96] The necessitous thief has long troubled lawyers and theologians. Blackstone, with his unscientific notion of the nature of laws in general, explicitly recognized that the poor may "demand a supply sufficient for all the necessities of life, from the more opulent part of the community," although in keeping with his general complacency about the state of English law and society, the Commentator limited the demand to proper channels: "by means of the several statutes enacted for the relief of the poor"—specifically, in other words, by the old Poor Law.[97] Austin who was (unlike Blackstone) describing a "general jurisprudence" not rooted in time or place considered the matter only from the point of view of God or utility *sub specie aeternitatis*. From that vantage point, property appeared to Austin to be most utilitarian:

> Without security for property, there were no inducement to save. Without habitual saving on the part of proprietors, there were no accumulation of capital. Without accumulation of capital, there were no fund for the payment of wages, no division of labour, no elaborate and costly machines: there were none of those helps to labour which augment its productive power, and, therefore, multiply the enjoyments of every individual in the community. Frequent invasions of property would bring the rich to poverty; and, what were a greater evil, would aggravate the poverty of the poor.[98]

[92]Quoted in R. Bainton, *Erasmus of Christendom* (New York, 1969), 189. (Because Bainton recast Luther's tracts into direct discourse, ibid., 198 n. 36, the quoted words may not be a direct citation.)

[93]Ibid.

[94]Ibid.

[95]Austin, *Province* (1832), 36.

[96]Ibid., 37.

[97]W. Blackstone, *Commentaries on the Laws of England* (Oxford, 1765–69), 1: 127. [The statutes, especially the Elizabethan Poor Law, 43 Eliz., c. 2 (1601), are described in ibid., 1:347–53.]

[98]Austin, *Province* (1832), 37–38.

In literal terms the final beneficiaries of the inviolability of property were the poor, but their "happiness" was maximized only at the cost of individual deprivation. If Austin's God was benevolent, it was with the stern benevolence of the new Poor Law which authorized workhouses for able-bodied paupers where conditions would always be "less eligible" than those enjoyed by the worst-off workingman.[99] As administered by Austin's pupil Edwin Chadwick, this harsh regime earned the undying hatred of the poor whose sufferings in these "Poor Law Bastilles"[100] were vididly described by Charles Dickens.[101]

Austin's God acts not on particulars but on universals: "For example, certain acts are pernicious, considered as a class. . . . Further: Such are the motives or inducements to the commission of acts of the class, that, unless we were determined to forbearance by the fear of punishment, they *would* be frequently committed. Now," concluded Austin, "if we combine these *data* with the wisdom and goodness of God, we must infer that he forbids such acts, and forbids them *without exception*."[102] Thus does utilitarian reasoning reinforce the Sinaitic Commandment: "Thou shalt not steal." What impresses about Austin's chain of thought is his insistence on the harshness of divine law. Human legislation is, to be sure, often described as referring properly only to classes, not to particulars. The judicial function, by contrast, is typically described as the application of universals to particular cases. Aristotle had long ago recognized that "where it is necessary to speak universally, but impossible to do so correctly, the law takes the most general case, though it is well aware of the incorrectness of it."[103] The philosopher had introduced equity as "the correction of the law where it is defective by reason of its universality."[104] But then Austin dismissed the "notions of the ancients" for being "perfectly vague as to the bounds which separate laws from morality."[105]

In a later lecture on divine law Austin returned to his earlier example and elaborated upon it. A "solitary savage"—man in the state of nature—kills a hunter and steals food to satisfy his "gnawing hunger." He is, in turn, attacked but kills his assailant. "Tried by the test of utility," said the lecturer, the difference between the two actions is immense:

> The general happiness or good demands the institution of property. . . .
> Were want, however intense, an excuse for violations of property; could
> every man who hungers take from another with impunity, and slay the

[99]4 & 5 Will. 4, c. 76 (1834). See A. Brundage, *The Making of the New Poor Law. . . . The Politics of Inquiry, Enactment and Implementation, 1832–39* (New Brunswick, NJ, 1978).

[100]F. Engels, *The Condition of the Working Class in England*, trans. and eds. W. Henderson and W. Chaloner (Stanford, CA, 1958), 324. (According to the translators, "Poor Law Bastilles" appeared in English in the first [German] edition, 1845.)

[101]See, e.g., C. Dickens, *Oliver Twist* (London, 1838).

[102]Austin, *Province* (1832), 39–40 (emphasis in original).

[103]Aristotle, *Nichomachean Ethics*, 5.10.1137b 11–28.

[104]Ibid.

[105]Austin, *Lectures* (3d ed.), 601.

owner with impunity if the owner stood on his possession; that benefi-cent institution would become nugatory, and the ends of government and law would be defeated.—And, on the other hand, the very principle of utility which demands the institution of property requires that an attack upon the body shall be repelled at the instant. . . .[106]

Much in the way of preciseness is left to be desired by this judgment. A justification of stealing to prevent death by starvation—a case of "intense" want, in other words—would not apply to "every man who hungers." Nor would such a justification necessarily include the use of deadly force against the owner. But the tendency is clear enough. The God of the utilitarians will admit killing in self-defense, but never stealing. "Thou shalt not steal" rather than "Thou shalt not kill" seems to be all the law and the prophets.

In dealing with Austin's hypothetical case, a traditionalist like Keble would doubtless have first consulted divine law, by which he would have meant revelation alone. Perhaps he would have turned to the Gospel story about the hungry disciples who picked ears of corn on the Sabbath and ate them. Defending his followers against the charge of Sabbath-breaking, Jesus cited with approval the Old Testament case of King David and his troops whose hunger drove them to enter the temple and eat the shewbread.[107] Then he would have turned to natural law, probably justifying himself with the Pauline text: "what the law requires is written on their hearts."[108] In Austin's system, of course, natural law is collapsed into divine law, and divine law is formally equated with revelation plus utility, although in practice the content of divine law is drawn only from utility. In effect *sola utilitata* displaces *sola scriptura*.

Yet, even in positive law, Austin's chosen province, it is doubtful whether he accurately analyzed the hypothetical situation. The case of the necessitous thief is, of course, only one example of a larger problem, that of a citizen who encounters a conflict between a positive law and an imperative moral claim. Austin's view, as paraphrased by one scholar, is that the citizen has three options:

> (1) he may use his political power and his social influence to get the law changed; (2) he may refuse to obey and pay the penalty; (3) he may, if he regards the situation as serious enough, organise a rebellion and endea-vour to destroy the State, in the hope of setting up a new one more in accordance with his conscience.[109]

The catalogue is incomplete. The citizen may, of course, obey the law and forego his moral claim, perhaps in the belief that obedience even to an unjust

---

[106]Austin, *Province* (1832), 100–01.
[107]Matthew 12:1–5 (citing I Samuel 21:4–7); see also Mark 2:23–28 and Luke 6:1–5.
[108]Romans 2:15 (RSV).
[109]Hearnshaw, "John Austin," 178.

law is itself a moral obligation. Yet, even as expanded, the list of choices is inadequate. Assume that the thief takes food to preserve his life. Subsequently arrested and tried, he pleads his necessity. Is it not likely that the thief will be acquitted? The jury may assert its ancient power to nullify a law by finding the accused not guilty, or the law may be construed not to apply to such a case. In the latter event, of course, the thief is not a thief at all, and— what is more interesting—the taking is not a violation of positive law.[110] In other words, the law against theft admits of an exception. This exception is created, of course, because of the moral sentiments of the human beings called upon to enforce it.

Events outside the lecture halls soon threatened to bring Austin's hypothetical case to life. A succession of bad harvests after 1836 (which, incidentally, made the debate about the repeal of the Corn Laws largely academic) along with a sharp downturn in the business cycle combined to produce the grimmest years of the nineteenth century in England. A financial pinch in 1841 sent the Austins seeking cheaper residences abroad, first in Carlsbad and Dresden, then in Paris. To thousands of Englishmen at home, however, the decade was to be simply the "Hungry Forties."[111]

The stringency in the Austin's family budget that sent them into voluntary exile was occasioned by the default of the American state of Mississippi on its public debt.[112] Mississippi bonds issued in the 1830s had sold well on the London market, being purchased by many middle-class English investors.[113] Few bond issues in history could have had such distinguished—and articulate—purchasers, among them the Reverend Sydney Smith, canon of St. Paul's, and William Wordsworth, the poet laureate. On the advice of George Grote, historian and banker, John Austin had invested a sizable amount of his savings.[114] When the financial Panic of 1837 struck the American economy, Mississippi suspended payment, never to this day resuming it.[115] Sydney Smith petitioned Congress,[116] while Wordsworth

[110]See, e.g., *Model Penal Code* § 3.02 (1980) (evil sought to be avoided must be greater than that sought to be prevented by the law defining the offense). In a leading English case, *R. v. Dudley and Stephens*, 14 Q. B. D. (1884), the court rejected necessity as a legal defense, preferring to leave it for consideration in the pardoning process. See A. Simpson, *Cannibalism and the Common Law: The Story of the Tragic Last Voyage of the Mignonette and the Strange Legal Proceedings to Which It Gave Rise* (Chicago, 1984) [reviewed by J. Orth, *Albion* 16 (1984): 440–41].

[111]J. Harrison, *The Early Victorians, 1832–1851* (New York, 1971), 12.

[112]Hamburger and Hamburger, *Troubled Lives*, 131–32.

[113]R. McGrane, *Foreign Bondholders and American State Debts* (New York, 1935), 51.

[114]Hamburger and Hamburger, *Troubled Lives*, 131.

[115]See B. Ratchford, *American State Debts* (Durham, NC, 1941), chap. 5. On the legal issues raised by Mississippi's repudiation, see J. Orth, *The Judicial Power of the United States: The Eleventh Amendment in American History* (New York, 1986), 44–46, 86–87, 140–41.

[116]*The Times* (London), (May 19, 1843), 5, col. 3.

composed a sonnet on the evils of default.[117] Charles Dickens even took a swipe at America in *A Christmas Carol*, calling something worthless "a mere United States' security."[118] John Austin, on the contrary, suffered in silence.

Silence was by then becoming a habit with Austin, perhaps in response to a succession of personal failures. After resigning as professor of jurisprudence, he failed to convince the Criminal Law Commission, to which he was appointed, of the merits of codification and so resigned.[119] He was appointed to lecture on jurisprudence at the Inner Temple but failed to keep an audience.[120] He was sent with a former student, George Cornewall Lewis, to report on the colonial administration of Malta but—despite some useful recommendations—he failed to complete his assignment.[121] While previous failures may have contributed to Austin's silence, he faced a special problem of his own creation in fashioning a complaint about Mississippi's default. In the *Province of Jurisprudence Determined*, the lecturer had defined law as the command of the sovereign. The distinguishing marks of Austinian sovereignty are: "(1) The *bulk* of the given society are in a *habit* of obedience or submission to a *determinate* and *common* superior . . . ; and (2) That certain individual, or that certain body of individuals, is *not* in a habit of obedience to a determinate human superior."[122] What this means in practice is that a sovereign is necessarily irresponsible, legally speaking. In other words, a sovereign cannot be compelled to answer in a court of law.[123]

In Great Britain Austin recognized sovereignty in that "body of individuals" composed of the monarch, the members of the House of Lords and the electorate of the House of Commons.[124] Assembled in person or by representatives in parliament, this sovereign is legally omnipotent. Indeed, the only legal limit to its power is derived from its omnipotence. What one parliament may do, the next may undo. Austin was very severe with Blackstone for asserting early in the Introduction to his *Commentaries* that

[117]W. Wordsworth, "To the Pennsylvanians," (1845), *Poetical Works of William Wordsworth*, ed. W. Knight (London, 1896), 8:179–80. See also Wordsworth's Additional Note (1850) on "Men of the Western World," (1842), ibid., 113. (The editor thinks these are the last lines for publication composed by the poet.)

[118]C. Dickens, *A Christmas Carol* (London, 1843), stave 2.

[119]S. Austin, "Preface [to 2d ed]," reprinted in Austin, *Lectures* (3d ed.), 11. On the work actually done by the Criminal Law Commission see R. Cross, "The Reports of the Criminal Law Commissioners (1833–1849) and the Abortive Bills of 1853," in *Reshaping the Criminal Law: Essays in Honor of Glanville Williams*, ed. P. Glazebrook (London, 1978), 5–20.

[120]S. Austin, "Preface [to 2d ed]," reprinted in Austin, *Lectures* (3d ed.), 11–12. Austin's posthumous *Lectures* consolidate his Inner Temple lectures with the earlier London University lectures, ibid., 27.

[121]On the Malta assignment see sources in n. 33 above.

[122]Austin, *Province* (1832), 199 (emphasis in original).

[123]Ibid., 268. See also R. Eastwood and G. Keeton, *The Austinian Theories of Law and Sovereignty* (London, 1929), 74–75.

[124]Austin, *Province* (1832), 241.

divine law is "superior in obligation to any other" and that "no human laws are of any validity, if contrary to this."[125] Austin called this "stark nonsense."[126] Whatever the ultimate value of Blackstone's passing observation, the Commentator himself receded from its implications later in the same Introduction. Taking up a hoary problem of English constitutional theory—whether a man can be a judge in his own case[127]—the Commentator recognized that the medieval verities were gone. Traditional thinking on the subject was summed up in the seventeenth century by Lord Coke:

> [I]f any Act of Parliament gives to any to hold, or to have conusans [sic] of all manner of pleas arising before him within his manor of D., yet he shall hold no plea, to which he himself is a part; for, as hath been said, *iniquum est aliquem suae rei esse judicem* [it is wrong for a man to be a judge in his own case].[128]

In the eighteenth century, Blackstone agreed that it was "unreasonable that any man should determine his own quarrel," and, therefore, advised contemporary judges to construe a general grant (such as the one supposed by Coke) to exclude that result, but he fully recognized the logic of parliamentary supremacy:

> [I]f we could conceive it possible for the parliament to enact, that he should try as well his own causes as those of other persons, there is no court that has power to defeat the intent of the legislature, when couched in such evident and express words, as leave no doubt whether it was the intent of the legislature or no.[129]

In the United States, as Austin readily admitted, the matter is not so simple. Austin accepted that the courts of the United States and of the several states are obliged to enforce only laws made in pursuance of the United States Constitution;[130] he took for granted, in other words, the doctrine of judicial review. In consequence, Austin located American sovereignty in the only body legally empowered to amend the Constitution, that is, the aggregate formed by the state electorates of three-fourths of the

[125]Blackstone, *Commentaries*, 1: 41.

[126]Austin, *Province* (ed. Hart), 185. This passage does not appear in the 1832 ed.

[127]The issue is—in jurisprudential terms—not whether a man can decide his own case, but whether such a decision-maker is, properly speaking, a judge.

I discussed this issue earlier in a review essay, "On the Relation Between the Rule of Law and Public Opinion," [review of R. Cosgrove, *The Rule of Law: Albert Venn Dicey, Victorian Jurist*] *Michigan Law Review* 80 (1982): 762, n. 49. The remainder of this paragraph is based on that discussion.

[128]*Dr. Bonham's Case*, 8 Co. Rep. 107a, 118b, 77 Eng. Rep. 638, 654 (K. B., 1610).

[129]Blackstone, *Commentaries*, 1: 91.

[130]Austin, *Province* (1832), 261–62. See U.S. Constitution, Art. VI, cl. 2 and *Marbury v. Madison*, 5 U.S. (1 Cranch) 137 (1803).

states.[131] As Henry Sidgwick long ago observed, there is something strange about attributing to the bulk of Americans a "habit of obedience" to a sovereign that had last acted in 1804, when the Twelfth Amendment was ratified, and that would not act again until 1865, when the Thirteenth Amendment was ratified.[132] In the concrete case of Mississippi's default, the bondholders sued the state and recovered a judgment,[133] but state officers refused to satisfy the judgment so the plaintiffs never got a cent. The sovereign remaining inert, the situation would seem to be one for applying Austin's legal fiction—that acts of inferior magistrates should be treated as if they were acts of the sovereign.[134]

In Austin's system there is no legal basis for criticizing this result. "No *positive* law is *legally* unjust"; this, according to Austin, is "indisputably true."[135] Aside from an appeal to positive morality—by definition, of no binding effect—the only appeal is to divine law, that is, revelation and utility. Since he said so little about revelation, there is no knowing how Austin would have constructed this argument. (Keble, with his wide knowledge of Scripture, would doubtless have known right where to begin.) As to utility, on the other hand, Austin would have been confident of his ground. Defaults are pernicious as a class. Inducements to defaults are such that, unless deterred by fear of punishment, they would be of frequent occurrence. The wise and good God, therefore, must forbid defaults *without exception*. The Mississipians were unlikely to be moved. Not having any present plans to borrow again, they took the punishment.

In 1848 the revolutionary *journees* in Paris whirled the Austins out of exile and back to England. First-hand experience of revolution accelerated John Austin's long-perceptible shift toward conservatism; as John Stuart Mill later recalled, his former teacher became "much more Tory" in his old age.[136] Breaking his long silence, Austin published a frankly reactionary pamphlet, "A Plea for the Constitution,"[137] opposing further franchise extension and even expressing retrospective doubt about the wisdom of the first Reform Act. Many of his arguments anticipated those later used by opponents of the second Reform Act,[138] opponents described in the biblical

---

[131]Austin, *Province* (1832), 264 and n.*. See U.S. Constitution, Art. V.

[132]H. Sidgwick, *The Elements of Politics*, 4th ed. (London, 1919), 27–28.

[133]*State v. Johnson*, 25 Miss. 625 (1853).

[134]Austin, *Lectures* (3d ed.), 548.

[135]Austin, *Province* (1832), 276, n.*.

[136]Mill, *Autobiography*, 126.

[137]J. Austin, *A Plea for the Constitution* (London, 1859). On Austin's few political pamphlets including "A Plea for the Constitution," see E. Ruben, "John Austin's Political Pamphlets, 1824–1859," *Perspectives in Jurisprudence*, ed. E. Attwooll (Glasgow, 1977), 20–41, and Rumble, *Thought of Austin*, chap. 6.

[138]30 & 31 Vict., c. 102.

language then current as sheltering in the "cave of Adullam."[139] Like the Adullamites, Austin failed to stop the spread of democracy. It was to be his last failure. "In December, 1859," as one historian cruelly remarked, "he failed to remain alive."[140]

For reasons wholly unconnected with the legal philosopher, the year of Austin's death proved to be an *annus mirabilis*. In 1859 Charles Darwin published his unsettling book *On the Origin of Species*.[141] Just as Austin did not deny God as lawgiver, so Darwin did not deny God as creator, but both shattered traditional images of the Deity. And both removed Him from the center of the process as previously understood. After his decorous references to revelation, Austin went on to depict a remote God whose benevolence worked the greatest happiness of the many at the expense of intense want for the few. Darwin necessarily dispensed altogether with revelation. While insisting in the famous last sentence of the *Origin* that "there is grandeur in this view of life," he limited God's part in it to breathing life "into a few forms or into one" and left the rest to the operation of the fixed laws of evolution.[142]

However much Austin and Darwin agreed on relegating God to the margin of their disciplines, they differed fundamentally in their intellectual approaches. As an analytical thinker, Austin concentrated on law as it is, while Darwin, as an evolutionist, stressed the process by which species came into being. It is, of course, possible to view law from an evolutionary as well as from an analytical perspective, since law also evolves through history. On the Continent, historical jurisprudence had flourished in Germany since the early nineteenth century and Austin had encountered it during his sojourn there in 1827–28. While welcoming its attack on natural law theories, he had objected to its rejection of codification. In contemporary England, too, an historical approach threatened to blur the distinction Austin drew between law and religion. In his Assize Sermon Keble had spoken warmly of the "Church and Law of England," joined by "historical recollections, associations and precedents,

---

[139]I Samuel 22: 1–2. The phase was first applied to the mid-Victorian opponents of franchise extension by John Bright. See A. Briggs, *Victorian People: A Reassessment of Persons and Themes, 1851–67* (Harmondsworth, Middlesex, 1955), 237, 245.

[140]Hearnshaw, "John Austin," 166.

[141]C. Darwin, *On the Origin of Species by Means of Natural Selection, or the Preservation of Favored Races in the Struggle for Life* (1859; facsimile ed., Cambridge, MA, 1966). See also J. Barzun, *Darwin, Marx, and Wagner: Critique of a Heritage*, 2d ed. (Garden City, NY, 1958). Describing his book as an essay on the "legacy of 1859," Barzun concentrates on—in addition to Darwin's *Origin of Species*—Marx's *Critique of Political Economy* (1859) and Wagner's *Tristan and Isolde* (1859). In the history of English literature, 1859 is notable as the date of publication of Charles Dickens's *A Tale of Two Cities*, George Eliot's *Adam Bede*, Edward Fitzgerald's translation of the *Rubaiyat of Omar Khayyam*, and the first edition of Alfred Tennyson's *Idylls of the King*.

[142]Darwin, *Origin*, 490.

of the most engaging and ennobling cast."[143] In fact, historical jurisprudence was postponed in England; it emerged only after Austin's death and was stimulated by Darwinism.[144]

Not only was 1859 the year of the *Origin of Species*, it was also the year of John Stuart Mill's essay *On Liberty*.[145] Mill had been a student of Austin's and had favorably reviewed his book, both the first and second editions.[146] While he applauded Austin's distinction between law and religion, he passed in silence over his former teacher's disquisition on divine law. Austin had defined the province of jurisprudence—positive law—by what it essentially is and does, although he acknowledged divine law (that is, utilitarianism) as a standard for criticism. Mill accepted Austin's definition of positive law but differed with him on the standard for evaluating a legal system. Theoretically, Mill could have disputed Austin's version of divine law; instead he concentrated on what Austin would have called "positive morality." Individualism, not utilitarianism, was the highest value in Mill's philosophy. Appropriating a scientific phrase, Mill defended "experiments in living"[147] and denounced any sanctions, whether legal (positive law) or social (positive morality).[148]

After 1859, other thinkers appeared, offering other ideologies ("isms") in place of Darwinism or individualism. Austin's utilitarianism faded further into the background, while Keble's "Apostolical religion" was reduced, as Professor Berman has observed, "to the level of a personal, private matter, without public influence on legal development."[149] Meanwhile Austin's "philosophy of positive law" became the basis of common law jurisprudence and of legal education, both English and American. His distinction between law and religion permitted lawyers to remain aloof from the ongoing dispute over religious (or "moral" or "ethical") values. Of course, values (however named) could not be permanently extirpated from law. So, soon after the triumph of Austinianism, "public opinion" achieved recognition as an essential datum for the under-

[143]Keble, *Sermons*, 145.

[144]W. Holdsworth, *The Historians of Anglo-American Law* (New York, 1928), 68–69, 71; id., *Some Makers of English Law* (Cambridge, 1938), 270; id., *A History of English Law*, eds. A. Goodhart and H. Hanbury (London, 1903–72), 15: 353–54.

[145]J. Mill, *On Liberty* [1859], ed. E. Rapaport (Indianapolis, 1978). Also in 1859 appeared Samuel Smiles's popular lectures on acquisitive individualism, *Self-Help*. On the conjuncture of Mill's essay and developments in labor law see J. Orth, "English Law and Striking Workmen: The Molestation of Workman Act, 1859," *Journal of Legal History* 2 (1981): 253.

[146]See nn. 37 and 47 above.

[147]Mill, *On Liberty*, 79.

[148]Mill was emphatic that liberty is not a legal concept only but a social one as well. He had experienced social sanctions because of his liaison with a married woman, Mrs. Harriet Taylor (to whom, incidentally, he dedicated *On Liberty*). See M. Packe, *The Life of John Stuart Mill* (London, 1954), 152–53. George Eliot (i.e., Mary Ann Evans) had been ostracized by society in 1854 because of her liaison with a married man, G. H. Lewes.

[149]Berman, *Law and Revolution*, 31.

standing of law.[150] But opinion is notoriously fickle and which of the many "publics" to attend to has proved difficult to decide. In consequence law has become—to quote Professor Berman again—"more fragmented, more subjective, geared more to expediency and less to morality, concerned more with immediate consequences and less with consistency or continuity."[151] Without the priests the temple is kept clean and functional, but the only sound is the clink of the moneychangers.

[150]R. Cosgrove, "The Reception of Analytic Jurisprudence: The Victorian Debate on the Separation of Law and Morality, 1860–1900," *Durham University Journal* 74 (1981): 47–56.
[151]Berman, *Law and Revolution*, 39.

BEYOND POSITIVISM: A THEOLOGICAL PERSPECTIVE*

Frank S. Alexander

Much that is written today seems to assume that our larger society is enabled to function by a combination of the individual's moral sense and social control through the threatened sanctions of state-made law. We need to remind ourselves that we constantly orient our actions toward one another by signposts that are set neither by morals, in any ordinary sense, nor by words in lawbooks.[1]

Lon L. Fuller

For over a century, legal positivists have set the basic terms for inquiry into the nature of law. They have treated law as a body of rules capable of objective analysis and the analysis of law as a scientific examination of those rules, to be conducted without reference to questions of what is "right" or "just." The strength of legal positivism lies in the simplicity of its concept of law as rules and the objectivity of its analysis of the meaning of the rules. Its strength, however, is also its weakness. For legal positivists have dwelt on the "words in lawbooks" to the exclusion not only of "morals" but also of the "signposts by which we constantly orient our actions toward one another."

Those who have opposed legal positivism have too often themselves been the victims of these basic terms of inquiry. For the most part they have taken as the starting point of discussion the positivists' assertion that law is separate from morals and have then sought to overcome that assertion by showing connections between the two. They have inquired into the nature of morals primarily in order to demonstrate the narrowness of legal positivism. In attempting to relate the "words in lawbooks" to "morals," they have, like their positivist opponents, often ignored what Professor Fuller calls the "signposts" of our reciprocal relationships.

What are these "signposts"? Unfortunately, Fuller gave only a few clues, toward the end of his career, to what it is by which people orient their actions toward one another. I shall argue here that we cannot find these signposts unless we ground our theory of law in an understanding of what it means to

---

* An earlier version of this essay formed part of a symposium on "The Constitution and Human Values: An Unfinished Agenda," the proceedings of which were published in *Georgia Law Review* 20 (1985): 811–1157.

[1] L. Fuller, "Human Interaction and the Law," *The Principles of Social Order*, ed. K. Winston (Durham, NC, 1981), 211, 246.

be human, both as individuals and as members of communities. Such an understanding must itself be articulated in terms of at least three topics, or analytical elements: (1) the element of individuality, which, in turn, is subdivided into human reason, personal responsibility and autonomy; (2) the element of community, which partially identifies that which individuals have in common; and (3) the element of purpose that informs and shapes both the individual and the community. These three elements, taken together, constitute the subject matter of ontology: the study of what it means to be human. In effect, then, I am proposing that we cannot effectively go beyond positivism without first examining certain basic philosophical and theological assumptions concerning human nature.

Contemporary American legal scholars who oppose positivism have not generally attempted to set forth in any systematic way their own theories of human nature. They have sometimes discussed questions relating to individuality, to community or to the purposive nature of existence, but they have generally neglected at least one of these three topics. To illustrate this, and to explore the consequences of such analysis, I have chosen three examples. The first, Philip Soper, while offering a strong concept of individuality, develops only a weak concept of community and largely ignores the concept of purpose. The second, Michael Perry, offers a strong concept of community but a weak and undifferentiated concept of individuality, and an even weaker sense of purpose. The third, Lon Fuller, in contrast to the other two, develops each of these three concepts, but his concept of community is abstract, and he fails to give substantive content to his concept of purpose.

Because of the general weakness of their ontology, contemporary American legal writers—nonpositivist as well as positivist—would benefit greatly from theology. Theology undertakes, as one of its major pursuits, to understand the nature of individual and collective being. The theological concepts of creation, covenant and redemption as expressed in the Judaic-Christian tradition have helped to form our assumptions concerning the nature of the individual person and of the community.

I. THE CONTEXT: THE METHODOLOGY OF LEGAL POSITIVISM

For at least a century, no single school of thought has had more influence in Anglo-American jurisprudence than legal positivism. This is reflected in the fact that adherents of alternative schools of law are more often evaluated for their success in criticizing positivism than for the premises underlying their own theories. Thus, to appreciate the strengths and weaknesses of the recent work of nonpositivist scholars, one must set out the basic positivist agenda to which they are reacting.[2]

[2]This brief summary of legal positivism is drawn primarily from John Austin and H. L. A. Hart because their works have been the catalyst for the responses of Soper, Perry and Fuller. To be

In addressing the question "what is law?" legal positivists start with an effort to define what is unique about law and to distinguish legal rights and duties from other kinds of claims and obligations. The legal positivist intends such a description to be abstract and universal; he is not interested in specific legal systems, but in law in general. In seeking to separate law from all other forms of human activity, he must define it in terms not of its content but of the form it must take in order to be law.[3]

Thus the task of the legal philosopher is to identify by observation the social phenomena that comport with this form. He can then describe and explain law objectively and neutrally. John Austin, the founder of English legal positivism, defined law as general commands of a sovereign authority enforced by threat of a sanction.[4] Thus he distinguished law from other forms of politics by its generality, and from morality by its source and its sanctions.

Austin's definition of law has been modified by H. L. A. Hart, perhaps the foremost legal positivist of this century.[5] Nevertheless, following Austin,[6] Hart insists on the separation of questions of morality or justice from the question of what is law: "It is in no sense a necessary truth that laws reproduce or satisfy certain demands of morality, though in fact they have often done so."[7] There are three justifications for this "neutral" approach to defining law. First, it permits one to talk about law objectively, without casting judgment on its virtue or vice. It is designed to identify the subject matter of the inquiry (the law), and to postpone questions of its desirability. Second, the approach is designed to avoid the confusion of law and morals (or value judgments) that may result either in an idealization of the law (as it is) or in a utopian legalism in which that which ought to be is made into law.

---

sure, legal positivism as a "school" of legal theory is inclusive of scholars other than Austin and Hart, many of whom may not share particular views.

[3]In contrast, theories of natural law tend to begin the analysis of "what is law?" with an inquiry into the authority of law and into the relationship of different kinds of laws. The emphasis, for natural law theories, is on the essential or inherent authority of propositions of law as derived from claims of belief in God or transcendent norms. In the legal realist tradition, and perhaps the more recent work in Critical Legal Studies, the question of "what is law?" finds a response more in terms of the policies the law is seeking to achieve and the allocation of power among the lawmakers and those subject to the requirements of the law.

[4]"Now jurisprudence, if it is anything, is the science of law, or at most the science of law combined with the art of applying it." J. Austin, *Lectures on Jurisprudence*, 2 vols.; 5th ed. (London, 1885), 1: 208.

[5]Hart retains Austin's description of law as that which gives rise to a legal obligation, "[T]he laws of any country will be the general orders backed by threats which are issued either by the sovereign or subordinates in obedience to the sovereign." H. Hart, *The Concept of Law* (New York/London, 1961), 25. Hart's difference with Austin derives primarily from Hart's perception that Austin's "gunman theory of law" contains a weak conception of obligation. There is a major difference, Hart points out, between the sense of obligation one feels to comply with a gunman's commands and the sense of obligation to comply with the command of a political sovereign.

[6]Austin, *Lectures*, 214–19.

[7]Hart, *The Concept of Law*, 181–82

Third, it allows the inquiry to be based on those aspects of human behavior that are more quantifiable and verifiable than beliefs, values or priorities that are difficult to prove or even to evaluate. With this empirical foundation the approach can be applied to the laws of any culture.[8]

Well aware that morality influences law in a number of respects,[9] Hart insists on a distinction between law and morals not only to protect the core concepts of both, but also to permit a concept of morals to be utilized in interpreting and criticizing laws. He describes five "truisms"—human vulnerability, approximate equality, limited altruism, limited resources, limited understanding and strength of will—that confirm the role of "conventional morality" in shaping law.[10] Hart describes these characteristics as the "core of good sense" of "Natural Law".[11]

Hart does not, however, suggest that these truisms provide a necessary moral content to law. Rather, he points out that in any given society at any particular time a community's legal standards may be more or less rigorous than its moral standards. This potential tension between accepted morality and existing law, Hart argues, should be recognized and protected. Hart thus argues in favor of what he terms a "wider" concept of law that includes those laws that may be morally reprehensible, but are, nonetheless, law. A "narrow" approach would exclude laws inconsistent with accepted morality. The latter approach, he suggests, would be inconsistent with the "scientific study of law as a social phenomenon" because "it would lead us to exclude certain rules though they exhibit all the other complex characteristics of law."[12]

Legal positivism attracts those who seek a concept of law that is independent of morals, on the one hand, and of history or culture, on the other. By abstracting and objectifying law, positivism purports to provide a

[8]Hart has identified two dangers against which the separation of law and morals, the "is" and the "ought," are intended to protect: "the danger that law and its authority may be dissolved in man's conceptions of what law ought to be and the danger that the existing law may supplant morality as a final test of conduct and so escape criticism." H. Hart, "Positivism and the Separation of Law and Morals," *Harvard Law Review* 71 (1958): 593, 598. These are consistent with the second and third justifications I identify. The first argument in favor of the separation of law and morals, that of allowing a common descriptive language free from necessary dependencies on moral judgments, is the methodological premise of positivism that is central to the thesis of this essay. Elsewhere I have compared Hart's view of the two "dangers" of conjoining law and morals with debates in Reformation theology on the relationship of law and gospel, and with Luther's view of the three uses of the law. See F. Alexander, "Validity and Function of Law: The Reformation Doctrine of Usus Legis," *Mercer Law Review* 31 (1980): 509, 524–29.

[9]"The further ways in which law mirrors morality are myriad, and still insufficiently studied . . . . No 'positivist' could deny that these are facts, or that the stability of legal systems depends in part upon such types of correspondence with morals. If this is what is meant by the necessary connexion of law and morals, its existence should be conceded." Hart, *The Concept of Law*, 199–200.

[10]Ibid., 189–95.

[11]Ibid., 194.

[12]Ibid., 205–06.

scientific basis for raising the question of justice or injustice of particular laws. Such a question can only properly be raised, it is said, after the existence of the particular law has been established by morally neutral tests. Yet positivism accomplishes this with a sleight of hand: it permits us to criticize any particular law as unjust only after we have accepted it, on positivist terms, as legally binding.

Positivism has thus made consideration of normative legal questions extremely difficult. For example, many of the writers concerned with the inadequacies of positivist concepts argue that law must contain some essential correlation with morality, for a concept of law that can embrace the laws of the Third Reich, genocide and apartheid stretches the meaning of law beyond limits. The response of the positivist is that such laws may well be unjust but the positivist analysis permits, if not encourages, this moral criticism of law. The nonpositivist fails to challenge the descriptive agenda— the ground rules—of legal positivism.

Positivism fails to deal with the more slippery, more inchoate, question of how law is based upon human nature. This approach does not preclude consideration of such a question; the question simply is not necessary to the definition of what law "is."[13] By beginning with the question "what is law?" the positivists push into the background the questions, "why is law needed?" "what is its purpose?" and "what ought it to be?"[14] These questions are thought by positivists to be secondary, to *follow* the question of what is law. They are thus ultimately left to others—political scientists, sociologists and other non-lawyers—to answer.

II. Elements of a Normative Jurisprudence

The only viable nonpositivist alternative that attacks positivism at its foundations is one which identifies the *signposts* which are neither laws nor morals in the ordinary sense—the signposts (in Fuller's words) by which "we constantly orient our actions toward one another." This means that we

---

[13]This is not to say that the leading legal positivists fail to recognize certain minimum concepts about human existence; rather, such normative propositions are relatively insignificant in the overall methodology of legal positivism. Because of the desire to provide a concept of law that is not historically or culturally biased, the positivist is constrained from identifying any more than a bare minimum of characteristics of the human condition.

[14]As Philip Soper has observed:

The positivist's insistence on maintaining his theory's purity forces him to say nothing about either the grounds for or the nature of normative judgments. Yet at the same time the positivist insists that law is a normative system. Insistence on the first position results in a theory that provides neither insider nor outsider with criteria to explain or justify the normative attitude that the second position posits as a characteristic of any legal system. As a result, the second position itself—the insistence that law is normative—begins to appear arbitrary.

P. Soper, A *Theory of Law* (Cambridge, MA, 1984), 30.

must ask a new first question: not "what is law?" but "what is the nature of our reciprocal relationships, our existence together?" This is, to be sure, a far more difficult question. Nevertheless, unless and until jurisprudence poses this question, we shall be unable to move beyond the positivist analysis to the questions that the positivist recognizes as valid but fails to address.

An inquiry into the nature of our existence together inevitably involves a consideration of both (1) individuality, including the nature of human reason, personal responsibility and autonomy; and (2) community, what individuals have in common and what holds them together. In turn, such a consideration must include an examination of (3) the purposes that guide individual and communal thought and action. An analytical distinction between *individuality* and *community* is to some extent artificial, for a person's perspective on one element has significant ramifications for his perspective on the other. Similarly, to treat *purposes* as a distinct analytical element is to divide, temporarily, a single thing into two parts. It should be emphasized, therefore, that these topics or "elements" are intended to form the building blocks of a single complex theoretical structure.[15]

A. Individuality

The element of individuality includes three issues: (1) the capacity or incapacity of the individual person to reason effectively; (2) the capacity or incapacity of the individual person to exercise his or her will; and (3) the character of the individual person as either an autonomous entity or as dependent upon others.

Law itself, and, therefore, every serious discussion of law, makes certain assumptions concerning the efficacy of human reason. At a minimum, individuals are assumed to be capable of perceiving that there is such a thing as law and that it permits or prohibits certain types of conduct. Thus all concepts of legal responsibility presuppose the ability of an individual to reason about choices which the individual may confront. When, in a particular instance, an individual is found not to possess the requisite degree of rationality, such person is found (at least with respect to the acts in question) incompetent to meet the standards of the law. Examples range from the insanity defense in criminal matters to guardianship proceedings in civil matters and presumptions of incompetency with respect to minors.

---

[15]I am not suggesting that all normative jurisprudence must contain these three elements. Nor am I suggesting that these three elements are exhaustive of all normative analysis. Indeed, even the theological perspectives on human nature elaborated in Part IV of this essay cannot be set within the context of these three elements alone. Rather, I suggest that this taxonomy offers, first, an analytical method for interpreting and evaluating recent nonpositivist scholarship, and, second, a vehicle for helping structure future inquiries in normative jurisprudence. A recent example of a similar form of inquiry, though one that does not follow the method of inquiring into ontological issues, is R. Hiers, "Normative Analysis in Judicial Determination of Public Policy," *Journal of Law and Religion* 3 (1985): 77.

Although related to the capacity to reason, the question of the extent to which individual choices are perceived as volitional addresses not so much the ability *to know* as the ability *to do*. Even if one assumes a very high degree of individual rationality in comprehending alternative courses of action, there remains the question of the ability of the individual to implement the choices that are made. Psychological perspectives on this aspect of human nature range from the extremes of radical Skinnerian behaviorism, in which all choices and actions are simply responses to external stimuli, to extreme libertarian assertions of complete knowledge and capability to act as one chooses. From the behaviorist perspective, there is little basis for moral responsibility, and legal responsibility must be based on considerations of public policy. From the libertarian perspective, one is liable as a legal matter for a very wide range of consequences of one's actions.

Closely related to the level of rationality and self-control that is an essential part of human nature is the degree of autonomy that may be imputed to the individual person. At one extreme, the society which law regulates may be viewed as a collection of autonomous individuals, each of whom consciously interacts with others to the extent necessary to fulfill his own physical and spiritual wants. From this point of view, the principal task of law is to protect individual liberty: each person is free to act as he or she chooses so long as he or she does not interfere unduly with the freedom of the other individuals in the society. At the other extreme, it is the common life of the community that gives each of its members his or her character. From the latter perspective, the principal task of law is to protect society against excesses of self-aggrandizement. Thus, in family law, we may define marital or parental relationships in terms of the nature of the separate individuals involved, or, conversely, we may perceive the existence of such relationships as major determinants of the nature of each individual.

B. Community

A theory of law cannot properly disregard the question of the nature of human community if only because the existence of law in any form presupposes some degree of human interaction. The ontological question is whether law emerges and develops because a number of individuals happen to find themselves together and need protection against each other or whether law emerges and develops as an integral part of a community to foster and protect interpersonal bonds that define the community. This element of analysis is also subdivided into three aspects: (1) why law is an integral part of community; (2) how membership in a community is secured; and (3) whether there is a common good which the law must serve.

Positivist theories do not usually address the question "why is law needed?" in explicit terms, but simply assume that its function is to preserve order: law provides a structure that makes possible the peaceful coexistence of individuals in society. This "prevention of chaos," or "Hobbesian Minimum," approach sees community only as that form of association which is necessary for survival. A radically different perspective would stress that a community is comprised of individuals who share a high degree of common aims or common beliefs and that these things which are held in common are constitutive of human nature. Under this approach, the nature and function of law is not simply that of making it possible for individuals to coexist. When a community is defined by shared beliefs, traditions or destiny, the role of law becomes an expression of and is responsive to such common meaning. By contrast, in the Hobbesian Minimum the signpost for law is only the order necessary to preserve individual existence.[16]

Traditional positivist theory has also failed to address the question of how one becomes a full member of a community and thereby a full participant in the operation of the laws of that community. As a result of this neglect, positivism has offered no satisfactory explanations of the individual's obligation to obey the law or the community's obligation to protect individual rights (including the individual's right to participate in changing the law). Criteria for membership in a community include majoritarian decision, common historical narratives, geography and the individual's own decision. By relegating the study of such criteria to political science, history and sociology, adherents of positivist theories of law have failed to deal adequately with the problems that arise from the inclusion of radically different cultures within one legal system and the extent to which such cultures are a part of the larger community from which law is derived.

Whether a community can be defined in terms of the common good, and whether it is a fundamental purpose of law to serve that common good, are necessary questions not only for moral philosophy (as the positivists assert) but also for legal philosophy, since they provide the social context both for making and interpreting laws. It is relatively easy to identify or postulate a concept of the common good for a uniform and homogeneous community, but in a society such as the American culture, in which many diverse religious, ethnic and cultural traditions compete and cooperate, the task is far more difficult.

C. Purpose

Although individuality and community are to be defined partly in terms of their purposes, it is useful to analyze purpose as a separate element or topic of legal theory if one is concerned to show that not only the individual

---

[16]For a recent explication of the multiplicity of approaches to the concept of community, see F. Kirkpatrick, *Community: A Trinity of Models* (Washington, 1986). Kirkpatrick describes and evaluates three models of human association: (a) the atomistic/contractarian model; (b) the organic/functional model; and (c) the mutual/personal model.

as such, and not only the community as such, but also the law as such is purposive in nature. This has two aspects. First, particular laws must be interpreted partly in terms of the purposes which they are designed to achieve. Taken in this sense, purpose has a relatively restricted meaning. Second, insofar as human nature is purposive in its very essence, legality—the whole body of law—is purposive in its essence.

Law thus bears an essential relationship to purposes of individual life. Community also must be understood as purposive; the law of a given community will relate to the history of that community's movement toward its purposes. One classic statement of such purpose is "to love Lord your God with all your heart and soul and strength."[17] Another more recent statement is "to form a more perfect Union, establish Justice, insure domestic Tranquility, provide for the common defense, promote the general Welfare, and secure the Blessings of Liberty to ourselves and our Posterity . . . ."[18] Both expressions of purpose give meaning and direction to the actor (whether the individual in an autonomous sense or the community), and that meaning and direction can determine the substance of law.

A theory of law needs to confront (1) the purposive character of human nature; and (2) the ways in which the purposes of human nature are related to individual and communal purposes. It is not proposed here that a purposive theory of law would foreclose debate concerning content of such purposes. On the contrary, one might take the subjective or relativist position, for example, that each individual should be left free to pursue whatever purposes he or she finds compelling, with the function of law being to maximize the freedom to achieve such purposes. An alternative position might argue that human nature is characterized by its orientation toward transcendent purposes, which purposes clarify the nature and function of law.

It can be shown that implicit in every legal theory are certain assumptions concerning these three analytical elements—individuality, community and purpose. We must examine these elements explicitly and in depth if we are to find the "signposts by which we orient our actions toward one another."[19] To the extent that we fail to make these elements an integral part of our theories, our conceptions both of law and of morals remain locked in the definitional ground rules of positivism.

[17]Deuteronomy 6:5. See also Matthew 22:37.

[18]United States Constitution, Preamble.

[19]In giving this bare sketch of a few of the questions concerning human nature that lie beneath the surface of any theory of law, I touch on matters that are within the province not only of philosophy but also of psychology and sociology. As will appear later in this essay, they are also within the province of theology. It is not my purpose here to exhaust the list of such questions, let alone try to answer them. It is my purpose, rather, to show the poverty of those schools of legal theory that do not even raise the questions while at the same time they assume the answers.

III. THREE EXAMPLES OF NONPOSITIVIST ANALYSIS

Philip Soper, Michael Perry and Lon Fuller are among the leading contemporary critics of legal positivism. They have each offered a creative analysis designed to pose alternatives to legal positivism. Though each of these writers makes significant advances beyond legal positivism, their inquiries have failed to address adequately the signposts that underlie their perspectives. As a result, the alternatives they propose are incomplete.

A. Philip Soper and the Nature of Obligation

In *A Theory of Law*[20] Philip Soper seeks to develop an approach to legal theory that encompasses "both the concerns of natural law and the core of the positivists' program."[21] He poses as the pivotal question not "what is law?" but "what must law be if it is to obligate?" He is thus primarily concerned not with the nature or form of law but with the nature of legal obligation.[22] His concept of obligation is focused on the source of one's duty to obey law: "That is what I seek: a theory of law that gives a generally applicable moral reason to comply apart from the sanction."[23]

Soper sets forth two premises that he maintains are necessary and sufficient for such a concept of obligation.[24] He states (1) that there must be a widespread belief that the enterprise of law in general is better than no law at all; and (2) that there must be "a good faith effort by those in charge to govern in the interests of the entire community, including the dissenting individual."[25] On these two premises, particularly the second, rest his entire theory of law.

The second premise contains two criteria, the requirement of "good faith effort" and the concept of the "interests of the entire community."

---

[20](Cambridge, MA, 1984). Critical discussions of this include T. Raz, "The Morality of Obedience," *Michigan Law Review* 83 (1985): 732; J. Fischer, "Obligation and Mutual Respect," *Yale Law Journal* 95 (1985): 437; K. Greenawalt, "The Natural Duty to Obey the Law," *Michigan Law Review* 84 (1985): 1. Soper responds to Greenawalt and Raz in P. Soper, "The Moral Value of Law," *Michigan Law Review* 84 (1985): 63.

[21]Soper, *A Theory of Law*, 55.

[22]"The virtue of the moral approach to legal theory is that it accepts the persistent association of obligation and law as elements of a legal system that must be explained; to ignore this feature is to prejudice in advance one's conclusions concerning the nature of law and its relevance to moral duty." Ibid., 10.

[23]Ibid., 62.

[24]Soper develops his concept of obligation in the context of a theory of *political* obligation, and then ties his understanding of obligation to the concept of an obligation to obey the law. In this sense, he departs from traditional positivist analysis first, by locating the substance of duties in the social and political context in the first instance, and only then viewing law as an aspect of political obligation. In contrast, the positivist analysis as developed by Hart begins with rules of recognition which then provide "authoritative criteria for identifying primary rules of obligation." Hart, *The Concept of Law*, 97.

[25]Soper, *A Theory of Law*, 80.

Soper places particular emphasis on the former, carefully avoiding any suggestion that community interests necessarily contain any specific requirement of the common good. In his exposition, Soper often identifies a good faith *effort* on the part of governing officials with a good faith *belief*. By so doing, he makes the quality of sincerity the central normative concept in *A Theory of Law*: "the sincerity of a belief rather than its accuracy [is] the critical ingredient in generating respect and obligation."[26]

This requirement of sincerity on the part of governing officials as a precondition of obligation leads Soper to two conclusions. First, the "justice" of a legal or political system entails a high degree of mutual respect among persons holding differing views. Such mutual respect requires that the governing officials be prepared to explain and defend from "normative" perspectives the rules and policies which they promulgate. "The state's 'duty to speak' is in fact a duty to respond to normative challenge about the use of force and thus implies that something more than monologue is required."[27] Second, the only fundamental right that is a necessary condition for law is the right to discourse. This right protects the existence of radical differences among persons *and* makes possible constructive exchanges of ideas.

Soper's primary emphasis is on the complex of moral values that gives to law a quality of obligation distinct from the obligations produced by force alone. In establishing sincerity, mutual respect and discourse as the pivotal features of his theory of law, Soper shifts jurisprudential inquiry away from the course prescribed by legal positivism. He invites us to engage in discourse about the nature of these values.[28] The manner in which Soper has addressed, or failed to address, each of the three analytical elements which I have postulated to be essential to a comprehensive analysis of law reveals the strengths and limitations of his theory.

1. *Individuality.* Of the three elements of *individuality, community* and *purpose,* the first is the one that is most clearly developed in Soper's theory of law. He argues, in effect, that the individual person is by nature autonomous, but that included in this autonomy is a sense of mutuality among persons. This concept of human nature is at the basis of the two premises he identifies as necessary for a legal system.

Soper supports his first premise—that a system of law in general is preferable to no law at all—by noting that without a system of law there would be little protection of those things that the individual has determined to be in his or her own interest. A system of law affords a measure of security,

---

[26]Ibid., 119.

[27]Ibid., 142.

[28]Soper admits that "[a] full political or moral theory would undoubtedly add a great deal in the way of flesh to these bones." Ibid., 143. His invitation is to pursue such theories precisely because he "sees an essential difference between law and force . . . [which] implies that moral discourse is rational, however difficult it may be to substantiate value judgments." Ibid., 160.

of protection, to the autonomous individual. "Acknowledgement of the value of law," he writes, "arises out of a rational appraisal of self-interest in the maintenance of a coercive order."[29] Soper does not imply, however, that the authority of particular laws turns on the consent of the individual to be obligated by it. He emphasizes not *consent* to the creation of a particular law but *assent* to the prior existence of a legal system in general. Drawing an analogy to a child's recognition of the peculiar features of a parent's command, as opposed to that of a stranger, Soper asserts that a legal system is recognized as having value not because one chooses the system but because one recognizes that the legal enterprise is an inherent part of both one's existence and the relationships among persons. Though he speaks of law as a shared enterprise, in the end he bases his concept of obligation to legal authority on human rationality. "The assault on autonomy must be assuaged by the appeal to reason alone rather than by the fact of a shared commitment."[30]

Soper's view of individuality is also manifest in his description of the qualities of sincerity and mutual respect that inform his second premise—that governing officials make a good faith effort to govern in the interest of the entire community. Soper argues that in order for obligations to exist the assertion of autonomy necessarily requires a mutuality of respect.[31] This does not mean simply that one party to a contract cannot insist on performance by the other party absent his own performance. It also involves a much deeper sense of mutuality of respect among individuals and sincere acknowledgment of the views of other persons. A legal system loses its morally binding character when it fails to acknowledge the importance of the views of each individual. Thus Soper projects a view of the autonomy of individuals not as isolated persons but as persons in relationships of discourse. Such discourse, he writes, "is not required as a means of enhancing personality," but is necessary to maintain "the individual's recognition of and tolerance for value disagreement; if that recognition and tolerance is not mutual, obligation again does not result."[32]

2. *Community.* Although Soper strikes a balance between individual autonomy and interpersonal relationships, he attaches only a minimal value to community as such. No particular characteristic of community, in Soper's view, is necessary for the existence of a legal system. Indeed, he expressly disclaims that his theory of law, and of obedience to law, presupposes that there is such a thing as a "common good," much less any particular conception of what that might be.[33] "[I]f the collective good is as abstract as the notion of a just society, there seems little to be gained in worrying about

[29]Ibid., 84.
[30]Ibid., 82.
[31]Ibid., 137.
[32]Ibid., 141.
[33]Ibid., 118.

whether it is enlightened self-interest or a theory of justice that in the end provides the criterion of acceptability."[34]

Despite this strong denial there are two ways in which Soper's theory contains at least a weak sense of community. First, he contends that officials must maintain a good faith belief that they are acting in the interests of the entire community if the legal system is to be morally obligatory. Thus, although he is unwilling to give content to "the common good," Soper resorts to a concept of the *entire* community to provide minimum substantive limitations on official actions that discriminate against individuals or groups. Otherwise, such actions might destroy either the minimal security that law is intended to provide or the mutual respect necessary for obligation to exist. Second, the test of "good faith belief" presupposes a shared commitment to the legitimacy of the legal system. Soper speaks of individuals in society sharing a "normative value," a commitment, with officials that "provides a basis for respect in the individual's recognition that if he were in charge he too could do no other than seek the common good according to his own light."[35] Though only by way of analogy, he suggests that just as the family enterprise is united by love and contains value, so the legal enterprise rests on basic interpersonal commitments.[36]

3. *Purpose.* Even though Soper states that a concept of obligation underlying law requires that law be viewed in terms of purposes,[37] the meaning which he attaches to such purpose remains elusive. He rejects existing social conventions and practices as justifications for legal obligation arguing instead that obligation must be grounded in purposes. But as with the element of community, Soper shies away from giving any specific content to such purposes. He again relies on the contention that the justification for legal obligation is the good faith effort or belief on the part of the governing officials that they are acting in the interests of the entire community. Thus for Soper "purpose" is not a defining characteristic either of individual autonomy or of community. It is a defining characteristic of a legal system insofar as a legal system is a shared enterprise. In speaking of

---

[34]Ibid. This disclaimer by Soper is not to be read as an agnostic view of the content of morals. Soper is making the epistemological point of humility rather than arrogance in the assertion of values. "That one cannot prove who is right in the case of value disagreement is not proof that the concept of truth in ethics is meaningless." Ibid., 150. Compare John Finnis' reliance on Leo Strauss's judgment that "knowledge of the indefinitely large variety of notions of right and wrong is so far from being incompatible with the idea of natural right that it is the essential condition for the emergence of the idea: realization of the variety of notions of right is the incentive for the quest for natural rights." J. Finnis, *Natural Law and Natural Rights* (Oxford, 1980), 29, quoting L. Strauss, *Natural Right and History* (Chicago, 1953), 10.

[35]Ibid., 137.

[36]Ibid., 78–9.

[37]"[T]he only adequate account of obligation from the viewpoint of the insider corresponds to the purpose theory." Ibid., 44.

the "purpose theory," Soper is referring to the fact that law consists of rules, or norms, each of which is directed to some end.[38]

The limited role which Soper attaches to the purposes of law is also implied in his treatment of the role of commitment. A theory of obligation, he states, presupposes a commitment to the legitimacy of the legal system, that is, a belief that the legal system possesses value. "[T]he belief in value, not the ability to ground that belief or to persuade others, . . . is critical to law and obligation."[39] Thus, even for the extreme relativist who denies the existence of common values, "the normative status of law depends on a far reaching noncontractual commitment by him and his equivalent officials to the basic values of the system."[40] In this theory what is important is not any specific purposes or goals of a legal system but the existence of a belief in the purposive nature of law in general.

Soper presents a theory of law in which the element of individuality is effectively elaborated but in which the elements of community and purpose remain weak and elusive. His view of individuality identifies four ontological signposts: the importance of human rationality, the ability to comprehend the statements and actions of government officials, the test of sincerity or good faith belief as the criteria for obligation and the corollary of sincerity, which is mutual respect. The element of community remains weak in content in that Soper does not indicate why individuals deal with one another at all. He eschews the Hobbesian Minimum as the function of law, yet he does not show how any other function of law relates to his perception of community. In addition, Soper is unwilling to say that there is such a thing as the common good, much less that it possesses any given content. Notwithstanding his belief that law is purposive in nature, the content of the purposes of law and their relationship to the purposes of individuality and community remain unclear. The particular goals or directions of individuals and communities are left entirely subjective, and legal obligation is dependent largely upon whether the beliefs of officials are sincerely held beliefs.

B. Michael Perry's Proposals

Because he presents normative questions as threshold questions in legal analysis, Michael Perry's work is a radical departure from legal positivism. In particular, he postulates that the ways in which we understand ourselves as individuals and as a community provide the foundations for our understand-

[38]Ibid., 79.

[39]Ibid., 149. Soper recognizes that "[t]he problem of commitment in legal theory is that legal theory cannot itself ground the commitment even though it shows that the commitment is essential to law and obligation." Ibid., 156. In this vein he seeks in his present theory only to demonstrate that commitment creates a bond between moral obligation and the legal system. At the same time he encourages us to pursue an understanding of the substance of the visions of a just society to which we are, or might be, committed.

[40]Ibid., 150.

ing of the nature and function of law. Though Perry has not attempted to set forth a systematic theory of law, he has set forth a theory of the relation of basic beliefs, or values, to the interpretation of legal documents, specifically, the United States Constitution. He argues that while the Constitution incorporates the value judgments of its authors, constitutional interpretation cannot, in certain situations, be limited to the values of the Framers.[41] In particular, Perry argues that constitutional resolution of human rights issues[42] cannot be accurately analyzed either descriptively or prescriptively in terms of eighteenth century values. Given this claim, Perry is forced to confront the question of what values, or whose values, provide the bases for constitutional policymaking in such cases.

Perry rejects both "tradition" and "consensus" as sufficient sources of such values. American culture, he points out, is composed of numerous different traditions and cultures, and many traditions (racial intolerance, religious bigotry) are hardly acceptable contemporary norms.[43] Similarly, he finds in our pluralistic culture no consensus on fundamental values sufficiently clear to provide a useful basis for decisions in human rights cases.[44]

Perry does, however, identify one "particular conception of the American polity that seems to constitute a basic, irreducible feature of the American people's understanding of themselves. The conception can be described, for want of a better word, as religious."[45] This self-understanding is not religious in the sense of sectarian or particular theistic beliefs. It is religious, in Perry's view, in the sense that it includes beliefs in a transcendent source of *obligation*, of *prophecy* and of *commitment*. The *obligation* consists of responsibilities to a higher law, a universal sense of justice among individuals and nations. The *prophecy* is based upon the belief that there are ultimate criteria of right and wrong and that the conduct of a community at any particular point in time is to be judged by those criteria. The religious character of *commitment* is expressed in the willingness to seek the right answers.

Our religious self-understanding has generally involved a commitment—though not necessarily a fully conscious commitment—to the

---

[41]He advocates what he terms a "non-interpretivist" or "nonoriginalist" method of adjudicating certain types of constitutional claims. M. Perry, "The Authority of Text, Tradition, and Reason: A Theory of Constitutional Interpretation," *Southern California Law Review* 58 (1985): 551; id., *The Constitution, The Courts, and Human Rights* (New Haven, CT, 1982).

[42]"Human rights" issues are defined by Perry to include "issues concerning the nature and extent of the (fundamental) rights of individuals vis-à-vis government." Ibid., 61. Such issues are those which arise primarily in the context of freedom of expression, equal protection, and other issues which arise in the context of "substantive due process." Ibid., 5.

[43]Ibid., 93.

[44]Ibid., 94.

[45]Ibid., 97.

notion of moral evolution, because in the main we have avoided the pretense that our current understanding of the moral universe—of ourselves, others, and the world we inhabit, and most fundamentally of the proper relationship among ourselves, others and our world—was perfect and complete. Rather, we know that we are fallible and that we must struggle incessantly to achieve a better—a broader and deeper— understanding. We also know that we are frail and that our frailty necessitates an ongoing struggle to bring our collective (political) practice into ever closer harmony with our evolving, deepening moral understanding.[46]

The religious character of American culture serves, in Perry's view, as a source of decisional norms in human rights cases. With this as a starting point, Perry has begun to confront in his most recent works the inevitable questions of pluralism and moral skepticism.[47] Does a common "religious" self-understanding, in Perry's sense of the term, provide any clear vision of values in a culture that is comprised of radically differing "religious" (and other) perspectives? Is it possible for moral arguments to be anything other than simply the assertions of different individuals or groups based on widely divergent moral premises? Perry answers that the fact of radical disagreements does not itself preclude a concept of an American culture as a community of shared traditions and aspirations.[48] Additionally, that there are divergent views on moral questions does not preclude the existence of moral reality. The very search for moral reality is one of the things that individuals have in common.

1. *Individuality.* Despite his focus on human rights, Perry does not examine in depth the nature of individual responsibility and autonomy that underlie the very concept of rights. He does indicate three attributes of human nature which characterize individuality. First, one's individuality "is partly constituted by one's fundamental beliefs."[49] These beliefs are simultaneously part of a collective or communal experience. Second, each person's development is highly dependent on others. "A person's experiential and thus cognitive condition would be extremely impoverished if she should not rely on other's experience."[50] Third, individual human nature is fallible in its ability to know and to do that which it has identified as desirable. Thus each individual is constantly in the process of revising and developing his or her own self-understanding.[51]

2. *Community.* Perry's perspective on the element of community begins

[46]Ibid., 99.

[47]See M. Perry, "The Authority of Text"; "Moral Knowledge, Moral Reasoning, Moral Relativism: A 'Naturalist' Perspective," *Georgia Law Review* 20 (1986): 995.

[48]Perry, "The Authority of Text," 596.

[49]Perry, "Moral Knowledge," 1034.

[50]Ibid., 1028.

[51]Ibid., 1037.

with the qualities we have in common. "[T]he facts that human beings are members of a single species, that they have at least some basic interests in common as members of the same species, and that they inhabit the same planetary environment explain where there *are* beliefs common to all human beings."[52] Cautious in specifying the content of such common beliefs, Perry emphasizes that the experience of common beliefs makes moral discourse possible.[53] At a minimum, each person shares with every other person the pursuit of moral reality. Belief in this moral reality, and the answers that result from pursuit of this reality, are not individualistic or isolated. Beliefs are "located" to a far greater extent in the experience of the community.

> [B]asic moral beliefs are less the property of individuals than of communities. That is, they are less the property of human beings *qua* particular individuals than of human beings *qua* members of particular communities. And, relatedly, the true test or measure of such beliefs is not the experience of just one person. It is, rather, the experience of the community . . . *over time.*[54]

A community, and more particularly a moral community, is "a group of persons united principally by their identification of themselves as the present bearers of, and participants in, a tradition."[55] By "tradition," Perry means "a particular history or narrative, in which the central motif is an aspiration to a particular form of life."[56] A tradition that is viable is a living, open, challenging tradition. It is living in the sense that it is not a fixed or static quantum of events or beliefs. It is constantly in the process of renewal and revision, of "moral evolution,"[57] as new beliefs and convictions are incorporated and older beliefs are discarded.[58] A community's tradition is open in that it does not require unity or homogeneity of norms or values. A community is composed of a multitude of persons, and thus its tradition

---

[52]Ibid., 1066–69.

[53]"Whether there are *shared human interests*—and, if so, whether the satisfaction of those interests is a useful adjudicatory standard—is much less important, *for purposes of assessing the possibility, in a given situation, of productive moral discourse,* than whether there are *shared beliefs*—beliefs shared with those with whom we happen to be in conflict at any given point, and with whom, therefore, we must (or at any rate want to) try to reason." Ibid., 1066–67. (Emphasis in original.)

[54]Ibid., 1037.

[55]Perry, "The Authority of Text," 557. Given the normative significance of community, it is not surprising that Perry suggests that everyone is a member not only of some moral community but also of a morally pluralistic political community. Perry, "The Authority of Text," 595. To become a member of a moral community there must be self-identification with the community though there may be other conditions as well. Ibid., 594.

[56]Perry, "Moral Knowledge," 1031.

[57]Perry, *The Constitution*, 99.

[58]"A religious tradition has ceased to live when (*inter alia*) the community that presently bears it is no longer sensitive to the need to criticize and revise the community's form of life in the light of new experiences and exigencies." Perry, "The Authority of Text," 558.

embodies diversity.[59] A tradition is challenging in the sense that it embodies a prophetic element that points to the aspirations of the community as continuing unfulfilled ideals.[60]

3. *Purpose.* As one of the roles of tradition for a community is the challenging, prophetic role, Perry expresses throughout his writings a sense in which human life is purposive. The central moral question for an individual, as well as for a culture, is "how particular human beings must live if they are to live the most deeply satisfying lives of which they are capable (or at least lives as deeply satisfying as any of which they are capable)."[61] The purposive quality of a community provides a context by which to evaluate both particular laws and the political process of lawmaking in that community. Perry has identified three such central aspirations of the American political tradition: (1) governance that is both responsive and accountable; (2) representative government; and (3) "liberty and justice for all."[62]

This purposive view of reality has two ramifications for Perry's analysis. First, it makes possible productive moral discourse. When individuals and separate moral communities claim different sets of ideals and aspirations, the result does not have to be a paralyzing moral relativism. "The aim, rather, is to identify a range of equally acceptable (unacceptable?) ways of life, and, beyond that, to achieve an ever more sensitive understanding of the advantages and disadvantages of different ways of life."[63] At the same time, the orientation towards purposes does not mandate an exclusive moral truth or a single way of life. The second ramification is that the characterization of life in terms of a multiplicity of aspirations reinforces the dynamic, dialogic character of law as part of human existence.

With his rich perspective on community, Michael Perry has begun to identify the signposts by which we orient our actions toward one another. By focusing on communities in historical context, with living, open and prophetic traditions, he points both to a source for understanding why individuals are in community and to a context for evaluating the laws of the

---

[59]"A tradition, then, connotes not consensus, but dissensus and consensus. A tradition is constituted in part by an argument as to how that which is shared should be understood and socially embodied." Ibid., 594.

[60]"There is the all too familiar danger, of course, that any effort to evaluate ways of life other than one's own is or will become, unwittingly or not, self-serving and imperialistic. Therefore, it bears emphasis that if there are common human interests the satisfaction of which is the measure for evaluating forms of life, then no way of life, including one's own, is immune to such evaluation. Indeed, one's own way of life is the least immune: a person should be most concerned to discover, not whether, but how she (and her community/tradition) can do better—how she can live in a more deeply satisfying way. Virtually any person—and her tradition/community—can always do better. The question is not whether but how." Perry, "Moral Knowledge," 1065–66.

[61]Ibid., 1024.

[62]Perry, "The Authority of Text," 577–580.

[63]Perry, "Moral Knowledge," 1065.

community. Purpose, for Perry, helps to define both individuality and community. The element of individuality, however, remains opaque.

C. Lon Fuller's Responses

Writing over a period of 50 years, Lon Fuller never attempted to set forth a systematic theory of law. Instead, his writings consist primarily of essays which, taken together, offer a comprehensive and integrated vision of law without reducing that vision to an analytical system.[64] These essays reflect his outrage with prevailing legal theories and legal theorists.[65]

Both traditional legal positivists and American legal realists of the 1920s and 1930s defined law as a body of rules laid down by the legislator or judge, independent of all values and moral judgments. Fuller, by contrast, defines law not as "rules" but as "an enterprise for making rules" and insists on the intricate interconnection of law and morals, the "is" and the "ought."[66] He seeks to present "[a] view that seems to recognize as the characteristic mark of law a set of concerns shared with morality."[67]

While he is hesitant to identify his own work as a system of natural law,[68]

---

[64]Fuller's most comprehensive descriptions of law are found in *The Morality of Law* (New Haven, CT, 1964) and *Anatomy of Law* (New York, 1968). His earlier essay, "Freedom—A Suggested Analysis," *Harvard Law Review* 68 (1955): 1302 also sets forth a clear summary of his views on freedom and liberty. A complete bibliography of the published writings of Lon Fuller is contained in Fuller, *The Principles of Social Order*, 305–308.

Professor Teachout has argued that "[t]o get to the heart of his jurisprudence, we must regard his essays rather as ethical performances that collectively give expression to an integrated ethical vision." P. Teachout, "The Soul of the Fugue: An Essay on Reading Fuller," *Minnesota Law Review* 70 (1986): 1073, 1092. The most recent study of Fuller's jurisprudence is R. Summers, *Lon L. Fuller* (Stanford, CA, 1984). Though he considers Fuller "one of the four most important American legal theorists of the last hundred years," ibid., 1, Summers concludes that the lack of a comprehensive general theory is a serious deficiency in Fuller's jurisprudence. Ibid., 107. As Kenneth Winston has observed, "If his almost casual manner of argument left him especially vulnerable to attack, his critics nonetheless failed, in my view, to touch his fundamental insight of the central place of moral theory in developing an adequate conception of law." K. Winston, "Introduction," *The Principles of Social Order*, 11, 44. See also D. Sturm, "Lon Fuller's Multidimensional Natural Law Theory," *Stanford Law Review* 18 (1966): 612.

[65]His critiques of legal realist philosophy and positivism show the limitations of such approaches and offer an alternative view that law is an enterprise involving reciprocity that gives a context for interpreting legal rules. For his perspectives on legal realism, see L. Fuller, *The Law in Quest of Itself* (Chicago, 1940); L. Fuller, "American Legal Realism," *University of Pennsylvania Law Review* 82 (1934): 429. His most famous response to legal positivism is L. Fuller, "Positivism and Fidelity to Law—A Reply to Professor Hart," *Harvard Law Review* 71 (1958): 630.

[66]"Certainly it is clear that the obligation of fidelity to positive law cannot itself be derived from positive law." L. Fuller, "American Legal Philosophy at Mid-Century," *Journal of Legal Education* 6 (1954): 457, 468.

[67]Fuller, *Morality of Law*, 130.

[68]"What I was advocating in my book [*The Law in Quest of Itself*] was not a system of natural law but the natural-law method." Letter from Lon Fuller to Thomas Reed Powell (undated), reprinted in Fuller, *The Principles of Social Order*, 294. Fuller subsequently described his desire "to discern and articulate the natural laws of a particular human undertaking, which I have

Fuller enumerates eight essential requirements or "desiderata" for any legal system to exist: (1) a requirement of generality—that rules exist; (2) a requirement of promulgation—that rules be published; (3) a limitation on retroactive laws; (4) a requirement of clarity—that rules be comprehensible; (5) an avoidance of contradictory rules—that laws not require conflicting behavior; (6) a requirement of possibility—that rules be attainable; (7) a requirement of stability—that rules not change precipitiously; and (8) a requirement of congruence—that rules be applied in a manner consistent with their enactment.[69] Fuller argues that these requirements constitute the "internal morality of law."

For purposes of the present analysis, the analytic elements of individuality, community and purpose that inform Fuller's concept of law are of primary concern. Of these three, the emphasis is on the purposive nature of reality that informs both the elements of individuality and community and the concept of law itself.[70] "[L]aw is the enterprise of subjecting human conduct to the governance of rules. Unlike most modern theories of law, this view treats law as an activity and regards a legal system as the product of a sustained purposive effort."[71]

Fuller ultimately rests his perspective on the significance of communication among persons. Communication with others makes possible the discovery for an individual of the sense of one's self, and the sense in which individuals are at once similar and diverse.

> If I were asked . . . to discern one central indisputable principle of what may be called substantive natural law—Natural Law with capital letters—I would find it in the injunction: Open up, maintain, and preserve the integrity of the channels of communication by which men convey to one another what they perceive, feel, and desire.[72]

---

described as 'the enterprise of subjecting human conduct to the governance of rules.'" Fuller, *Morality of Law*, 96. "It should be confessed, however, that the term 'natural law' has been so misused on all sides that it is difficult to recapture a dispassionate attitude toward it." Ibid., 102. Despite Fuller's own disclaimers, Summers places Fuller in the context of the natural law tradition, Summers, *Lon L. Fuller*, 65–68; Teachout resists placing him within any single tradition in jurisprudence, Teachout, "The Soul of the Fugue," n. 54.

[69]Fuller, *Morality of Law*, 33–94, 104.

[70]Douglas Sturm has identified "three postulated and universal norms" as underlying all of Fuller's writings: "(1) preserve human life, (2) keep alive the purposive side of man's nature, and (3) maintain communication." Sturm, "Multidimensional Natural Law," 161. Kenneth Winston has similarly identified in Fuller's writings three criteria for a conception of law: (1) a conception of law should be generous in including the historical and cultural diversity of legal forms; (2) the nature of legal regulation is a purposive and problem-solving enterprise; and (3) the aim of legal regulation is to promote moral order among persons. Winston, "Introduction," *Principles of Social Order*, 17–18.

[71]Fuller, *Morality of Law*, 106.

[72]Ibid., 186.

1. *Individuality.* Fuller's view of individuality is encapsulated in his summary of the three conditions for a concept of reciprocity:

> *First,* the relationship of reciprocity out of which duty arises must result from a voluntary agreement between the parties immediately affected; they themselves "create" the duty. *Second,* the reciprocal performance of the parties must in some sense be equal in value .... The bond of reciprocity unites men, not simply in spite of their differences, but because of their differences.... *Third,* the relationships within the society must be sufficiently fluid so that the same duty you owe me today, I may owe you tomorrow.[73]

The first of these conditions stresses the nature of the individual as a responsible moral agent with freedom of will: the capacity of the individual to make choices is critical to self-determination. The second condition reflects Fuller's view that a premise of reciprocity is equality: individuals will only resolve their differences voluntarily if each benefits thereby. The third condition is social: the principle of reciprocity depends on the fluid, dynamic character of society.

Fuller's first condition of reciprocity, namely, the nature of the individual as a responsible moral agent, is a substantive assumption. Each of the eight "desiderata" of law presupposes the capability of the individual to comprehend clear and predictable rules, and thus to govern his or her actions accordingly.

> To embark on the enterprise of subjecting human conduct to the governance of rules involves of necessity a commitment to the view that man is, or can become, a responsible agent, capable of understanding and following rules, and answerable for his defaults. Every departure from the principles of the law's inner morality is an affront to man's dignity as a responsible agent.[74]

As the individual is held accountable to laws that comport with the inner morality that Fuller has identified, the individual necessarily possesses the ability both to know and to do that which is required by law. In the alternative view, "that man is incapable of responsible action, legal morality loses its reason for being."[75] The legal system thus is premised on a high degree of free will in individuals, a freedom of the will that is part of the dignity of each individual.

Fuller tempers his emphasis on freedom of will, however, with a recognition of the fallibility both of human nature and of the legal enterprise itself. "I have insisted that law be viewed as a purposeful enterprise, dependent for its success on the energy, insight, intelligence, and conscien-

[73]Ibid., 23.
[74]Ibid., 162.
[75]Ibid., 162–63.

tiousness of those who conduct it, and fated, because of this dependence, to fall always somewhat short of a full attainment of its goals."[76] For Fuller, this failure to meet its goals is precisely what enables the legal enterprise to be an ongoing creative process of discovery of the goals of the enterprise itself.[77]

Fuller also describes limitations of freedom that are inherent in choice itself. Freedom does not lie in pursuit of unlimited choices, for "[i]f the individual had in fact to choose everything for himself, the burden of choice would become so overwhelming that choice itself would lose its meaning."[78] Instead, freedom lies in making a commitment to that which one has chosen, with the commitment itself precluding other choices.

Fuller's second condition for reciprocity—an equality among individuals—is implicit in interaction itself.[79] In entering into voluntary agreements each individual is free to select what is consonant with his or her own purposes. The fulfillment of such choices, however, is dependent on fulfillment of the contract or agreement. In this manner, individuals are not atomistic but dependent on others. As Douglas Sturm has observed, "Fuller's understanding of man is not individualistic. Forms of human association are not in all or in most instances a limitation on individual freedom or purposiveness. Rather the possibility of human choice and action are actually vastly increased by means of various forms of association."[80]

The third condition that Fuller identifies for reciprocity, namely, that it must be possible that the duty that you owe to me today could be the same duty that I owe to you tomorrow, presupposes a dynamic view of the nature of interpersonal relationships. The freedom of individuals to pursue their own purposes inevitably leads to constant change as interactions beget new interactions.

> "[F]reedom to" does point to one general social objective without which all others lose their meaning, that is, the objective of keeping alive the creative, choosing, and purposive side of man's nature. It is possible to argue about the areas in which the human function of forming purposes and deciding upon courses of action is best exercised. But, unless we are bent on collective suicide, it seems clear that it must be kept alive somewhere.[81]

[76]Ibid., 145.

[77]"In a sense, then, the thing we call 'the story' is not something that is, but something that becomes; it is not a hard chunk of reality, but a fluid process, which is as much directed by men's creative impulses, by their conception of the story as it ought to be, as it is by the original event which unlocked those impulses. The ought here is just as real, as a part of human experience, as the is, and the line between the two melts away in the common stream of telling and retelling into which they both flow." Fuller, *The Law in Quest of Itself*, 9.

[78]Fuller, "Freedom," 1311.

[79]L. Fuller, "Law as an Instrument of Social Control and Law as a Facilitation of Human Interaction," *Brigham Young University Law Review* (1975): 89.

[80]Sturm, "Multidimensional Natural Law," 622.

[81]Fuller, "Freedom," 1314.

2. *Community*. Fuller views community primarily as one in which law is a collective enterprise that is necessary for the actualization of individual choices. "The choices a man can make without requiring collaborative social effort for their realization are trivial."[82] A community or society, then, does not provide the initial motivation or reason for the pursuit of purposes that define and shape the individual. Individuals form associations, therefore, in order that they may enhance their individual freedom of action. This is not to say that Fuller's view of community is a minimalist view. He expressly rejects the view that the only function of community is to prevent evil.[83] A community also provides a structure for human interaction, though Fuller does not define the extent to which a community determines the substance of such interaction. His chief example of the way in which a community undergirds law and gives it content is customary law (as opposed to enacted law), which, he states, "not simply . . . serves to facilitate interaction, but . . . derives tacitly *from* interaction."[84]

In the concluding passages of *The Morality of Law*, Fuller addresses briefly the question of the nature of community.[85] Paraphrasing the Talmud, he states that a commitment *with* others if not *to* others is the bond of a community. "If we are not for ourselves, who shall be for us? If we are for ourselves alone, what are we? Whatever answer we may give to this last question, it must be predicated on the assumption that we are above all else human beings."[86] He returns to this question in his last important work, *Two Principles of Human Association*.[87] Here he identifies as the source of bonds of human association a principle of shared commitment and a legal principle. The first principle is operative when individuals are brought together by common aspirations and interests;[88] the second principle governs when individuals or groups enter into relationships primarily for the purpose of gaining something for themselves. Fuller stresses that most forms of human association represent a blend of the two principles.[89] He argues that when

[82]Ibid., 1312.

[83]Fuller, "Social Control and Human Interaction," 89.

[84]Ibid., 94.

[85]Fuller, *Morality of Law*, 181.

[86]Ibid., 183.

[87]L. Fuller, "Two Principles of Human Association," *The Principles of Social Order*, 67–85.

[88]"Association by the principle of shared commitment is perhaps best illustrated in its purest form in an association between a composer and a librettist. . . . An equally relevant example would be the collaboration in scientific research of a theorist with an experimentalist." Ibid., 72.

[89]Ibid. The stylistic usage of polarities and spectrums to express his perspectives runs throughout Fuller's writings and is a theme that is extensively explored in Teachout, "The Soul of the Fugue." In "Human Association," Fuller is careful to note that what he is describing are principles rather than forms of human association. In an earlier essay he had identified two fundamental forms of social organization: organization by reciprocity and organization by common ends. Fuller, "Freedom," 1316. The parallel seems to be that the form of organization by common ends reflects the principle of shared commitment, while organization by reciprocity incorporates the legal principle.

any association comes into existence by virtue of shared commitments, the association will over time come to be dominated by the legal principle. Once this occurs, the bond of shared commitments dissipates. In its place legalism comes to control human associations.[90] Although he stresses the importance of the legal principle in radically diverse and pluralistic societies, Fuller, nevertheless, views with anguish the loss of the principle of shared commitment:

> May there not be in human nature a deep hunger to form a bond of union with one's fellow which runs deeper than that of legally defined duty and counterduty? May a man not feel an urge to enter such a bond even though he knows that it may later be ruptured, against his will, by those who consider him unsuited to it? And may not the possibility of this rupture lend a special value to the association by attesting its importance to both sides?[91]

3. *Purpose*. The element of purpose is central to Fuller's jurisprudential writings. An individual's capacity to make conscious choices in order to achieve his or her purposes is the characteristic that renders human existence unique. "The whole man, taken in the round, is an enormously complicated set of interrelated and interacting purposes. This system of purposes constitutes his nature."[92] The ability to make choices constitutes the purposive aspect of human existence, and the actual choices made provide the substance of an individual's dignity. To preserve the purposive character of the human condition is the "one general social objective without which all others lose their meaning."[93] The quality of purposiveness also infuses the nature and function of the legal system. "In one aspect our whole legal system represents a complex of rules designed to rescue man from the blind play of chance and to put him safely on the road to purposeful and creative activity."[94]

[90]Fuller identifies eight "laws" that describe the transformation of the principle of shared commitment to the legal principle: (1) In most associations both principles are present; (2) In any specific case, either principle may control; (3) Initially, the principle of shared commitment is dominant; (4) An association governed by shared commitment is initially hostile toward internal groups dominated by the same commitment; (5) As an association moves towards the legal principle it needs internal groups that are dominated by the shared commitment; (6) An association moves towards dominance by the legal principle; (7) Dominance by the legal principle feeds on itself and becomes accelerative (creeping legalism); and (8) the distinctions between the political state and internal associations break down and result in "galloping legalism." Fuller, "Human Association," 76–78.

[91]Ibid., 85.

[92]Fuller, "Mid-Century," 472.

[93]Fuller, "Freedom," 1314.

[94]Fuller, *Morality of Law*, 9.

In Fuller's view, the quality of purposiveness gives movement and direction to individuals and communities over time.[95] Most critically, it is the conceptual foundation by which he is able to reject the sharp philosophical distinction between the law that is "posited" by those in authority and the "moral" law, the law as it ought to be. Fuller insists on the "metaphysical inseparability" of the "is" and the "ought."[96] Every norm or rule embraces both descriptive and prescriptive qualities that define the goal and set guidelines for its realization. This conjunction of the "is" and the "ought" is the statement of law as a movement toward a goal which has not yet been reached.

D. Implications

Soper, Perry and Fuller articulate their assumptions concerning human nature, assumptions that are considered irrelevant in a positivist approach to law. Although they are very different from each other in the nature of their interests and in the quality of their scholarship, each develops, to varying degrees, his conceptions of individuality, of community and of the role of purpose in individual and communal existence. Each thus identifies in his jurisprudence some of the signposts which guide our understanding of law. By failing, however, to address adequately one or more of these three elements, each of them presents an incomplete view of law.

Though Soper's theory expresses his perspective on individuality, his failure to develop a substantive concept of community leads to two difficulties. First, he provides no basis for answering the question of who counts as a full member of the community. The critical second premise of Soper's theory—that the governing officials must serve the interests of the entire community, including the dissenting individual—gives insufficient guidance, for there is no analysis of what creates or defines the entire community. We are told, in effect, that "everyone" in the community is to be served, but whether this includes aliens, Native Americans, Salvadoran refugees or the unborn depends on what is meant by "community." Although, in Soper's theory, official actions that destroy mutual respect lose the quality of obligation, the question of whose respect counts as "mutual" is, again, left unanswered.

Second, Soper's reluctance to recognize that there is a common good, much less that it has any particular content, eliminates any context for evaluating the actions of government officials. So long as the beliefs of the

---

[95]As Douglas Sturm has observed, "[I]n Fuller's understanding, purposiveness or 'freedom to' is not merely a fact about human nature; it is not simply the capacity required to orient oneself towards purposes and goals; it is itself a value, a purpose, albeit a highly general and abstract one." Sturm, "Multidimensional Natural Law," 614. "Rather the 'supreme end' or 'ultimate destiny' of man is a quality of living, a mode of developing again and again in each new moment of living, and in each new stage of development, in each new instant of action." Ibid., 619.

[96]Fuller, "Letter to Powell," 295.

governing officials are sincerely held, obligation exists. Apart from sincerity, the only substantive limit that Soper recognizes is the right of discourse with the officials. If discourse is permitted, however, the decisions of the officials must be followed regardless of how onerous or unjust they may be.

Soper's failure to develop a concept of purpose presents similar obstacles. If purpose is not recognized as an integral part of the individual or the community, there are few limits on the purpose of law. It thus becomes virtually impossible to call into question the legitimacy of a legal system itself. As Soper does not propose a view of communities set in an historical context, his conception of the *interests* of the entire community lacks the possibility of movement of an historical community over time toward any given purposes. There is thus little relationship between that which a community affirms as what ought to be and that which is at any particular point in time.

By leaving the elements of community and purpose largely undeveloped, Soper's theory leaves individual autonomy as the only signpost to guide our actions. His premise that the enterprise of law in general is better than no law at all offers but a threshold, a door which when opened leads to an empty room.

In contrast to Soper, Perry's emphasis is primarily on the element of community, to the neglect of individuality. By failing to develop adequately a concept of individuality, Perry, too, gives no basis for answering the question of who counts as a full member of the community. His requirement of self-identification with the history and tradition of a community as the criterion for membership leaves open the question whether a given body of law is morally obligatory for individuals who reject one or more of such traditions. Perry does not insist on homogeneity, but his insistence on self-identification is a substantial barrier for an individual who identifies with some but not other of the many diverse traditions of a society such as the United States.

Of the three scholars who are the focus of this inquiry, Lon Fuller offers the most comprehensive concept of the interconnections between law and human nature. Without expressly adopting the tripartite classification proposed in this essay, Fuller has, nevertheless, emphasized that to understand law properly one must explore its relationships to concepts of individuality and community, and especially to the purposive character of individual and communal life. Thus, where Philip Soper refrains from describing an essential nature of community, Fuller offers his view that shared aspirations create bonds among persons that give direction to law. Where Michael Perry leaves unaddressed the attributes of human nature that comprise one's individuality, Fuller points to the role of responsible choice in shaping the dignity of each person. Where the element of purposiveness plays no role in Soper's theory, Fuller finds it to be the definitional characteristic of human nature. Fuller's conception of individual autonomy is one that affirms the dignity of the autonomous individual without leaving the individual isolated. His conception of community reaches for substance beyond mere coexistence. His conception of purpose describes a basic orientation of human nature.

Fuller's quest for the signposts by which we constantly orient our actions toward one another is left incomplete, however, because he fails to identify what provides content to shared commitments and the purposes that define individuals and community. Apart from common sense, the lessons of experience and general clarity of thought, Fuller does not tell us where to turn to find the essence of such commitment or the substance of purpose. Thus, despite his description of human nature, as containing "a deep hunger to form a bond of union with one's fellow which runs deeper than that of legally defined duty and counterduty,"[97] Fuller provides few clues as to how such hunger is satisfied.

In Fuller's writings there is no sense of what could hold together a society that embraces radically diverse concepts of the most desirable form of life. As an alternative to the legal principle of human association, he offers the possibility of shared aspirations voluntarily chosen. Yet, as Fuller recognizes, once individuals no longer possess common aspirations, their association become dominated by the legal principle; the only cohesion provided by the legal principle is legalism.

Fuller's view of community, therefore, ultimately fails to provide any significance for law other than law as order. An individual interacts with others only insofar as the interaction serves to further the individual's own goals—though the goals may happen to be the same goals held by others. Community is, therefore, a *necessary* aspect of human existence but only in the sense that it is self-serving. There is nothing in Fuller's writings to indicate that a community possesses moral content above and beyond being a collection of individuals; there is even less possibility that the moral convictions and purposes of a community are *essential* to the individual.

This weakness of Fuller's jurisprudence is further reflected in his virtual disregard for history. The fact that every community has deep historical roots and traditions seems of little consequence to him. Thus he ignores the fact that both individuals and communities are able to call upon their own heritage or the heritage of others as a prophetic guide to the future. Because of its unhistorical character, Fuller's view of community is curiously abstract.

IV. THEOLOGICAL PERSPECTIVES

The recent writings of nonpositivist legal philosophers develop only in part the analytical elements of individuality, community and purpose which form the ontological foundations for their jurisprudence. As a consequence,

[97]Fuller, "Human Association," 85.

students of their theories have difficulty finding their way out of the predicament inherent in positivism: a body of law whose ultimate source is the will of the ruler is not morally obligatory, and, conversely, a particular law that is morally offensive cannot be challenged on legal grounds. The ontological fallacy of positivism is thus insufficiently exposed; the signposts pointing to a genuine alternative are obscured.

In this situation, it is useful for legal theory to turn to the insights of theology. Concepts of individuality and community have been central to the Judaic-Christian tradition. In particular, the biblical doctrines of creation, covenant and redemption provide significant perspectives on the nature of individuality and community, and the purposes which are central to each.[98]

A. Creation, Covenant and Redemption

The biblical doctrine of creation is the story of relationships.[99] It is the narrative of creation not of isolated things but of things existing in intimate relationship one with another.[100] It is the relationship between God as creator and all that is created, between the land and the water and the animate creatures within the environment, between humans—Adam and Eve. All of these relationships are characterized by two features. First, each thing, each entity, stands in a multitude of relationships which when taken together define the single entity. Second, the existence of such relationships permits each entity to have a distinctive character.

Each part of creation stands in relationship to God. Each part of creation also stands in relationship with the rest of creation. Any one person can be described in numerous ways, such as spouse, parent, child, sibling, teacher, lawyer, homeowner, fisherman or taxpayer; no single label serves to define that person. This multiplicity of relationships is not accidental or coincidental. Each distinct entity is dependent on one or more other entities. If any part of creation is described or examined solely in terms of one relationship, the description is incomplete.

For this reason the metaphor of the "body," the organic whole, as descriptive of creation runs throughout theological literature. Each part of the body, each part of creation, contributes something essential both to the remaining parts of creation and creation as a whole. One of the clearest

[98]I concur with Milner Ball's statement that "the biblical tradition is the most fruitful medium for understanding, judging, and celebrating the secular world, including law." M. Ball, *The Promise of American Law: A Theological, Humanistic View of Legal Process* (Athens, GA, 1981), 2.

[99]Genesis 1–2.

[100]"The doctrine of creation is not the story of an event which took place 'once upon a time'. It is the basic description of the relation between God and the world . . . All three modes of time must be used in symbolizing it. God *has* created the world, he *is* creative in the present moment, and he *will* creatively fulfill his *telos*." P. Tillich, *Systematic Theology*, 3 vols. (Chicago, 1951, 1955), 1: 252–253.

examples of this interdependence is the biblical description of the marriage relationship as ordained by God—a natural relationship in which family members possess a bond of dependence on each other as well as on God.

The interdependence of all creatures, as represented in the creation narrative, does not, however, limit in any way the distinctive character of each. As the creation of light made possible the separation of light and darkness, so also the creation of land made possible the distinction of land and waters.[101] Distinctive names were given to each entity in creation, and each part of creation retains separate significance in its relationship to God.

The biblical narrative of creation also provides a concept of power, of authority, that is manifest in the concept of covenant. Both the Old Testament and the New Testament are the stories of covenant—a covenant between God and creation, between God and people. The existence of the covenant *from the beginning* provides a concept of authority which is not dependent on individual assent to contracts or political sovereigns.

> In contrast to the social contract, the covenant tradition does not rest on a surrender of a preexisting individual power to another entity. The people and their power are created by covenant. To consent is to accept the proposition that the people become a people in the election of God. The covenant is a matter of receiving, not preserving, the self or its property. The attendant duty involves no submission . to a higher power or greater authority, but is a response to the present reality that has called the people into being. The content of the law is the covenant that creates the people.[102]

The theological concept of covenant is addressed in the creation story to the freedom of humans to respond to the covenant. The covenant is a promise in which humans are charged with responsibility—responsibility to respond to this promise. The covenant stands as a call to action; together with creation it describes the purposive quality of human nature.

Precisely because it points to human responsibility, the biblical tradition is also the story of failure to fulfill the covenant, and of redemption notwithstanding that failure. The creation narrative contains the story of forbidden fruit, of breach of promise and disobedience, that is a metaphor for the inability of humanity to do that which it is called to do. The sin is the selfish pride of human nature by which the individual declares his ultimate independence both from God and from other persons. This false assertion of power and independence leads to inevitable failure to know or to do in any complete sense that which is required. The biblical tradition is thus the story

---

[101]Genesis 1:3–10.
[102]Ball, *The Promise of American Law*, 14.

of the brokenness of humanity, of injustice, isolation and suffering.[103] It is the story of lawless authority.

The concept of redemption is integral to the story of creation of covenant and this description of broken reality. Redemption is the paradoxical affirmation of the breach of the covenant by humanity and, simultaneously, the affirmation that God fulfills the covenant in unequivocally accepting humanity as it is.[104] It is the statement that, notwithstanding our failure to achieve that which ought to be done, there is an open acceptance by God of who we are. Theologically, the concept of redemption permits, therefore, the simultaneous recognition of the *is* and the *ought*. The covenant stands as a statement of the ought, while the metaphor of the fall and the history of the covenant stand as a statement of what is.

B. Implications

One of the issues of individuality is whether the essential nature of human existence lies in the individual as an autonomous being or is in some sense found in relationships. An individual's self-understanding and sense of fulfillment could be predicated on the individual "I" which is central to a strong concept of liberty. From this perspective other persons have significance to an individual only insofar as they serve the individual's own goals or preferences.

An alternative perspective is found in the creation narrative and the concept of covenant. Theologically, each person is autonomous in the sense that one is never completely the same as, and never wholly dependent on, another. Nevertheless, each is heavily dependent on, and is inseparable from, others. One's knowledge of the individuality of one's self requires recognition of the separateness of the self from the rest of creation; yet a deeper understanding of one's individuality involves an affirmation of the

---

[103]It is important that the "Fall" be considered not so much as an aspect of the creation narrative as an integral part of the redemption narrative. This is necessary in order to avoid the implication that the Fall into sin is a description of an event at a particular point in time. The "self-centeredness" of each individual is instead a description of every point in time. Hence, it is an ontological rather than a chronological description.

> The relation of man's essential nature to his sinful state cannot be solved within terms of the chronological version of the perfection before the Fall. It is, as it were, a vertical rather than a horizontal relation. When the Fall is made an event of history rather than a symbol of an aspect of every historical moment in the life of man, the relation of evil to goodness in that moment is obscured.

R. Niebuhr, *The Nature and Destiny of Man*, 2 vols. (New York, 1941, 1964), 1:269.

[104]Robert Cover describes redemption in a similar manner:

> Redemption takes place within an eschatological schema that postulates: (1) the unredeemed character of reality as we know it, (2) the fundamentally different reality that should take its place, and (3) the replacement of the one with the other. The term "redemptive" also has the connotation of saving or freeing *persons*, not only "worlds" or understandings.

R. Cover, "Nomos and Narrative," *Harvard Law Review* 97 (1983): 1, 34–5.

relatedness between the self and the other person. This point has been developed most cogently by twentieth century theologians Martin Buber[105] and Dietrich Bonhoeffer.[106] Bonhoeffer's understanding of individuality derives from relationships:

> The ontological structure of man is thus located in the self-other relationship, just as the ontological structure of Christ is located in Christ's being-for-man, nature and history. Man is only man in the Thou-I, I-Thou relationship, just as Christ is only Christ in his *pro nobis sein* . . . . Turned in upon itself, the self is bound; it must be a self in mutuality with others if it is to touch the transcendent ground of its own essence.[107]

One example of the role of this theological perspective is the application of law in the context of marital and familial rights and duties. A marital or parental relationship could be defined in terms of the nature of the separate individuals involved. Creation and covenant, however, point to the existence of such a relationship as determinative (at least in part) of the nature of the individuals. Instead of obligations to others being derived from interactions among autonomous individuals, an appreciation of such obligations is essential to being an individual in the first place.

Creation and covenant similarly focus on the issues within the element of individuality which concern human reason and responsibility. The covenant tradition points to the existence of responsibility for our actions and stands as a call for the greatest degree of human responsibility in all relationships. It indicates a role for human rationality in the experience of personal relationships and places emphasis upon the exercise of individual and collective reason.

Such a theological perspective also addresses the nature of community. Community is, in essence, the "mutuality" of relationships within the "body" of creation. Insofar as each part of creation stands in relationship with every other part of creation, each person is a member of the creation community simply by virtue of his or her birth. This community is not one which is voluntarily chosen—one is born into it. The creation narrative further affirms, however, the multiplicity of smaller communities in which persons exist, whether the family, the profession or the nation. There may be a greater role of volitional choice in joining such communities, or defining membership in such communities. Nonetheless, the basic point remains that theologically each person is in community with others, in

---

[105]M. Buber, *I and Thou*, 2d ed. (New York, 1958).

[106]D. Bonhoeffer, *Ethics* (New York, 1955) and *Christ the Center* (New York, 1960).

[107]L. Rasmussen, *Dietrich Bonhoeffer: Reality and Resistance* (New York, 1972), 19.

numerous communities, each of which serves to create the individuality of that person.[108]

The covenant tradition gives a meaning to the common good of a community different from the meaning attributed to it from positivist jurisprudence. In Judaic-Christian thought, the good which is *common* in and for a community is the response of the community to an antecedent covenant. The good is not measured in terms of maximizing individual happiness or the social, economic and political welfare of a particular community. It is experienced in the response of the community to the covenant which led to the community's creation. In this manner all of existence, both individual and collective, is imbued with a sense of purpose which is a response to the antecedent grace of God.[109] As the story of a covenant being worked out through history, the covenant tradition is a dynamic movement through time. It is never static or precisely quantifiable. It is always in the process of discovery and response, of confusion and new responses.[110]

The theological concepts of covenant and redemption combine to caution against dogmatic insistence on uniformity and homogeneity. As all of creation is composed of distinct entities which are inseparable in essential ways, human judgments about the appropriateness of certain forms of life must be made with caution. As Robert Cover points out, permitting the law to serve as a vehicle for structure and order which constrains diversity and imposes judgment is violence itself.[111]

As these theological concepts contain, simultaneously, demands on human behavior and descriptions of the fallibility of human nature, they address the efficacy of human reason. Ability to reason about choices, and make commitments to those choices, is part of the creation narrative. Such ability, however, whether viewed in terms of the individual or the community, is deeply flawed. Thus, although individuals and communities are and must be held responsible for the consequences of their actions, such responsibility must always be viewed in the context of fallen reality.

In the biblical tradition the experience of law by both individuals and communities contains this simultaneous presence of the "is" and the "ought." The concept of redemption permits this tension to be transformative.

[108]In a recent essay Milton Regan probes the implications of differing views of the human condition in community. M. Regan, "Community and Justice in Constitutional Theory," *Wisconsin Law Review* (1985): 1073.

[109]R. Lovin, "Equality and Covenant Theology," *Journal of Law and Religion* 2 (1984): 206 [reviewing H. Berman, *Law and Revolution: The Formation of the Western Legal Tradition* (Cambridge, MA, 1983)].

[110]See E. Gaffney, "Of Covenants Ancient and New: The Influence of Secular Law on Biblical Religion," *Journal of Law and Religion* 2 (1984): 117.

[111]R. Cover, "The Bonds of Constitutional Interpretation: Of the Word, the Deed and the Role," *Georgia Law Review* 20 (1986): 815.

If law reflects a tension between what is and what might be, law can be maintained only as long as the two are close enough to reveal a line of human endeavor that brings them into temporary or partial reconciliation. All utopian or eschatological movements that do not withdraw to insularity risk the failure of the conversion of vision into reality and, thus, the breaking of the tension. At that point, they may be movements but they are no longer movements of the law.[112]

The legal enterprise itself is as fallible and broken as every individual. Creation and covenant reveal this brokenness and stand as judgment on the failure to achieve the justice. Redemption simultaneously calls for a continuing commitment to the justice of the covenant.

These theological concepts provide content to the ontological elements of individuality and community, and the purposes which characterize each of them. These concepts thus reveal signposts by which we orient our actions toward one another that are found neither in lawbooks nor in morals. The signposts consist of (1) a commitment to diversity among individuals and communities while affirming that each person is dependent on others in an essential way; (2) an emphasis on human responsibility and free will while acknowledging that reason and choice are inherently fallible; and (3) a sense of movement toward fulfillment of purpose in responding to the antecedent covenant of God and the possibility of transformation notwithstanding the failure to respond completely.

V. CONCLUSION

Nonpositivist jurisprudence can most effectively present alternatives to positivist theories of law when the methodology of positivism is avoided in the first instance. To achieve this, we should begin not with a definitional analysis of law as such, but with a discussion of the purposive nature of individuality and community, in which law has its roots. To the extent that one or more of these elements remains unaddressed, the resulting theory of law will be incomplete.

The theological concepts of creation, covenant and redemption directly address these ontological concerns and offer rich historical and conceptual perspectives for a comprehensive theory of law. If we can engage one another on the level of our convictions about the nature of individuality, the essential character of community and expressions of purpose, our views of law will be enriched. These theological perspectives on the nature of our being together as individuals in community are valuable not because agreement concerning them will be reached; on the contrary, it is likely that most legal scholars will reject them entirely. Yet a conscious rejection of them will require an analysis of their relation to alternative perspectives.

[112]Cover, "Nomos and Narrative," 39.

Eventually, it may be recognized that modern legal theory itself is secular theology, and that without theology we shall see very little into the nature of law, even though with it we will only see through the glass darkly.

In so far as man has the simplest vanity of self,
There is no escape from the movement toward fulfillment.
   And since all kind but fulfills its own kind,
Fulfillment is only in the degree of recognition
Of the common lot of our kind. And that is the death of vanity,
And that is the beginning of virtue.
The recognition of complicity is the beginning of innocence.
The recognition of necessity is the beginning of freedom.
The recognition of the direction of fulfillment is the death of the self.
And the death of the self is the beginning of selfhood.
All else is surrogate of hope and destitution of spirit.[113]

[113]R. Warren, *Brother to Dragons* (New York, 1953), 214–15.

THE ROLE OF CONSCIENCE IN JUDICIAL DECISION-MAKING

Lois G. Forer

"—now, having passed seventy, I believe I have my own voice."

Jorge Luis Borges

To participate in a *Festschrift* honoring Professor Harold J. Berman is a great privilege and an equally great responsibility. What can a busy judge write that will be worthy to stand beside the monumental scholarly works of Professor Berman? I shall not attempt the impossible but, rather, take this opportunity to explore from my own perspective and experience an issue of concern to Professor Berman, the role of conscience in the judicial process.

In his perceptive little book *The Interaction of Law and Religion* Professor Berman points out the unsatisfactory nature of both natural law and particularly the legal realism that so bemused legal scholars and judges in the first half of the twentieth century. He writes:

> Judicial decisions or statutes that purport to be merely hunches or experiments lack the credibility upon which observance of law ulti- mately depends—observance not only by 'the masses' but by all of us, and especially by judges and lawmakers.
> Once in 1947 when the late Thurman Arnold, who as a teacher and writer carried the theory called 'legal realism' to the point of genuine cynicism, was urging upon a class at Yale Law School his view that judges decide solely according to their prejudices, a student interrupted to ask whether when Arnold himself was on the bench he did the same. Arnold paused before answering; one had the impression that he was transforming himself from Mr. Hyde to Dr. Jekyll as the professor in him yielded to the judge. He replied, 'Well, we can sit here in the classroom and dissect the conduct of judges, but when you put on those black robes and you sit on a raised platform, and you are addressed as "Your Honor", you *have* to believe that you are acting according to some objective standard'.[1]

This book was a comfort and source of inspiration to me in its honest search not for fine honed multi-pronged arguments but for an ethical basis for the many decisions that a judge must make for which there is no positive law or precedent. A trial judge is on the firing line of the legal profession. I regret

---

[1] *H. Berman, The Interaction of Law and Religion* (New York/Nashville, 1974), 30.

the military metaphor but, unfortunately, it is appropriate. A trial judge sits alone on a raised bench in full view of the litigants, the lawyers and the press. Inevitably, one side or the other will be dissatisfied with the result, often very vocally so. The press may be, and often is, scathing in commenting on decisions.

On occasion, as has happened to me, a judge is accosted by the family and friends of a defendant whom one has convicted and by the friends and family of the victim of a crime who believe the penalty did not sufficiently avenge the crime. In civil cases, passions are also provoked by rulings viewed as pro- or anti-business or consumer, pro- or anti-labor or management, pro- or anti-women's rights, minority rights or involving countless other divisive social issues in our society.[2]

Unlike appellate judges, who have the opportunity to discuss the issues and attempt to reach a consensus, a trial judge is a solitary figure. Blame cannot be shared or responsibility diffused. That, I believe, is salutary. In reaching a decision, a judge should not be permitted to evade the onus of his or her verdict and opinion by claiming the protection of colleagues who form the plurality.

The disadvantages of acting alone are many. One rarely has the opportunity for searching debate with one's peers. Law clerks fresh out of school lack experience and a long perspective. They rarely have backgrounds in philosophy, comparative law and anthropology, the disciplines sorely needed by one who must make sensitive decisions affecting the lives of individuals and addressing public concerns. Faced with a novel question, or one that has been accepted as a given with little critical analysis, a judge would like to know how other probing minds and other societies have dealt with analogous problems. One would like to make an educated prognostication as to the social and economic effects of a ruling and not act on speculation or a "hunch."[3] Unfortunately one's colleagues on the trial bench are busy with their own cases and fending off criticisms of themselves. There is little opportunity to discuss the underlying moral issues that greatly disturb a thoughtful judge.

One searches for a kindred soul with whom to discuss these problems and from whom one can obtain enlightenment. One scans the literature seeking guidance. Exhortations to act with "principled neutrality"[4] are rarely helpful.

[2]I do not wish to leave the impression that trial judges are constantly under siege. The vast majority of cases are unreported and provoke no comment. I frequently receive letters from prisoners whom I have convicted and sentenced, thanking me for a fair trial. Victims also write in appreciation for the treatment they have received. I am gratified by the poll of local lawyers who voted me the "most respected" woman in the law. But neither adverse criticism nor praise mitigates the concern as to whether one's decision was ethically right.

[3]See, e.g., *Williams v. Florida*, 399 U.S. 78 (1980) in which the Supreme Court operating on a "hunch" sustained the constitutionality of a statute reducing the size of a jury to six members.

[4]See H. Wechsler, "Toward Neutral Principles of Constitutional Law," *Harvard Law Review* 73 (1959): 1 and R. Bork, "Neutral Principles and Some First Amendment Problems," *Indiana Law Journal* 47 (1971): 1, 20.

When I write a book or an article I usually feel like a castaway on a desert island who puts a note in a bottle and tosses it out into the restless sea. Will the bottle smash on a reef, sink to the murky depths, be washed up on a distant shore where the inhabitants are illiterate aborigines or perhaps sophisticates who will consign the bottle to the trash can? If by miraculous fortune the note is read, will the reader care? One of my books, *The Death of the Law*,[5] washed up on the stony shores of Massachusetts and was read by Professor Berman. I had read and reread his book. We became epistolary acquaintances, then pen pals, and happily good friends. It is, therefore, appropriate that in this *Festschrift* I address an issue that he has so eloquently raised. Whether one is a believing deist or, like myself, a non-believer, the question of conscience in judicial decision-making should, I am convinced, loom large. Significantly, the lay public appears to believe that conscience and ethics, not economics, positive law or self-interest are the basis of the entire structure of that complex institution we denominate as "the law." Playwright Arthur Miller, for example, sees the law "as a metaphor for the moral order of man."[6]

I agree with the late Judge Arnold, as quoted by Professor Berman, that one entrusted with the duties of a judge, on any level of court, must believe that he or she is acting according to some objective standard. That standard must be authoritative. Must it also be ethical? In the United States we lawyers and judges have been taught to seek those standards in the Constitution of the United States, the Constitutions of the several states, innumerable statutes, codes, rules of procedure and prior decisions of the courts.[7] These sources of law rarely provide a definitive, ineluctable answer to cases that are litigated to verdict. When the law is clear, lawyers sensibly prevail upon their clients to settle civil cases. In criminal cases, most frequently it is the facts, not the law, that are in dispute.

After 15 years on the trial bench of a very busy state court in a large metropolitan city, I am still astonished at the number of novel issues on which I am required to rule. Despite comprehensive legislative codes—the Uniform Commercial Code, the Model Penal Code, class action procedural rules and similar carefully drafted statutes and rules—lacunae that call for

---

[5](New York, 1975).

[6]*New York Times* (February 1, 1986), 30-H. Cf. Hans Kelsen's view that law is a science "incompetent to answer either the question of whether a given law is just or not, or the more fundamental question of what constitutes justice." H. Kelsen, "The Pure Theory of Law and Analytic Jurisprudence," *Harvard Law Review* 55 (1951): 44. See also E. Morgan, *Introduction to the Study of Law* (Chicago, 1926), 32.

[7]Few judges read law as literature. Literature deals in metaphor and fantasy. It seeks to reveal the inner nature of human beings, to plumb their souls. It creates an intimate relationship between author and reader. Legal writings, whether Constitutions, statutes or judicial opinions, are public documents. They are designed to be clear, external statements that all readers will view in the same way, regardless of personal experiences or sensitivities. For a contrary view, see "Symposium: Law and Literature," *Texas Law Review* 60 (1982): 373ff.

interstitial legislation and interpretation are inevitable. Even the wisest drafters cannot anticipate all problems. Human behavior is not wholly predictable. Unlike machines that function by rote, replicating the same motions (or malfunctioning in predictable fashion), human beings vary in their responses to the same stimulus. Someone is bound to engage in unanticipated conduct. Moreover, technology and science are changing the physical environment, the work place and even the family with such extraordinary and unprecedented rapidity that legislatures are unable to promulgate laws governing new conditions before conflicts ripen into litigation. Although it is common in contemporary jurisprudence to excoriate the "activist" judge, it should be remembered that trial judges do not have discretionary jurisdiction. They must decide the cases brought before them. They cannot decline to decide or defer consideration until the legislature has the opportunity to act.

It is not my purpose to defend the judiciary from any of the countless charges hurled against it, but, rather, to consider the role that conscience should play in judicial decisions. The claims of conscience arise primarily in two broad categories: (1) cases in which there is no clear, binding positive law either by statute or judicial precedent; and (2) cases in which the application of statutory law or binding precedent will lead to an unconscionable result.

The enormous body of literature by academics, jurists, philosophers, legal historians and politicians would constitute an insurmountable obstacle to anyone attempting to present a critique of natural law, positive law, critical legal studies and all the other schools of jurisprudence. I am emboldened to discuss the role of conscience in decision-making from the viewpoint of the judge by the example of Mr. Justice Brennan. In his 1986 Oliver Wendell Holmes, Jr. Lecture at the Harvard Law School, entitled "Constitutional Adjudication and the Death Penalty: A View from the Court," he declared:

> What I want to talk about is the process of constitutional adjudication. But let me be clear. I am not going to attempt a revised historical account of the eighth amendment; I will leave that task to the professional historians. Nor will I offer a new theoretical approach to the jurisprudence of the cruel and unusual clause—I leave that undertaking to the academics. Nor will I provide an overview of the current constitutional status of the death penalty—that is probably for the law reviews. And of course I shall not predict what the Court will do in the future—that is only for the soothsayers among us. What I will do is discuss how I, a sitting judge who must decide cases, have engaged in the process of answering the lawyers' contention that the Constitution prohibits the government from killing men and women for the crimes they commit. You will hear the story as I see it, from the Court.[8]

[8]*Harvard Law Review* 100 (1986): 313, 314.

I, too, will present the problem as I see it from the perspective of the trial judge and not trespass on the role of historians, philosophers, academicians and futurologists. The question I raise is: may a judge depart from the objective standards of the law when those mandates conflict with the judge's own sense of fairness and decency? Although scholarly legal journals and books are filled with learned disquisitions on the duty of judges to adhere to fixed principles—whether those be found in the language of the Constitution, the original intent of the framers or the language of prior decisions, few, if any, commentators discuss the duty to deviate from rules that offend or violate fundamental principles.

Innumerable philosophers from Socrates to the present time have presented justifications for the citizen condemned by an unjust law submitting to the penalties the legal system provides. Some of these rationalizations ring hollow in the ears of the Vietnam War generation. Others find the notion of a social contract, the maintenance of law and order and obedience to the rule of law sufficient justification for abiding by unjust laws and unjust penalties.[9] There are countless philosophers and lawyers who justify civil disobedience by the citizen to unjust laws and unfair penalties. I have searched in vain for discussions of the duty of a judge faced with the unhappy options of enforcing an unjust law or penalty or violating positive law.

Much of contemporary literature dealing with judicial decision-making, like many of our American contemporary statutes, is designed to remove all discretion from the judge, to compel the magistrate to enforce the law regardless of morality, fairness or human consequences. There is a need for thoughtful discussion of both the process and the goal of a search for ethical values that goes beyond the fashionable posturings of natural law, realism, neutral principles, analysis and deconstructionism. In the 1980s, jurisprudence appears to have become more verbose, rarified, antagonistic and remote from the day-to-day problems of litigants, lawyers and judges. The rift between town and gown has widened to a chasm. "Judge bashing" is a common sport, not only of red-necked political hacks, but also of law professors who seek to instruct judges on how to decide cases.[10]

Rather than recapitulate the well-worn arguments of the various jurisprudential sects, I should like to focus this discussion on two actual cases, one criminal and one civil, and explore the tension between positive law and

---

[9]See, e.g., the view of former Supreme Court Justice Abe Fortas: "[Once a person has been] arrested, charged and convicted, he should be punished by fine or imprisonment, or both, in accordance with the provisions of law, unless the law is invalid in general or as applied. . . . He may, indeed, be right in the eyes of history or morality or philosophy. These are not controlling." A. Fortas, *Concerning Dissent and Civil Disobedience* (New York, 1968), 13.

[10]See the writings of Professors Ronald H. Dworkin, Owen R. Fiss, Stanley Fish, Michael Unger, Mark Tushnet, H.L.A. Hart and John Hart Ely to name only a few of the more prolific academics who have presented elaborate theories of judicial interpretation.

one judge's sense of justice. Probably every legal reader of these pages was schooled in some variant of the case method of pedagogy introduced at the Harvard Law School by Professor Christopher Columbus Langdell. All of us spent our law school years reading learned decisions of appellate courts and attempting to glean from those opinions principles of law. The appellate decision is the end of the litigation process. I suggest that we start much nearer the beginning of the process—at the trial judge's findings of fact and conclusions of law, upon which the appellate court will base its decisions. All the legal positions, policy questions and interpretations of fact are implicit in the findings of the trial judge.

These cases do not involve abortion, affirmative action, religious liberty or the death penalty. They are, rather, typical cases heard in all trial courts of general jurisdiction. Probably there are thousands of such cases heard every day. But the questions of fairness, justice, decency and equality of treatment inherent in these two cases are no less perplexing than those in the notorious Supreme Court cases that have absorbed so much jurisprudential energy.

There is a popular current belief that litigation can be bifurcated into hard and easy cases,[11] and that the vast number of legal cases are easy—a simple application of law to facts and the deduction of a result that is inevitable and right. I suggest that this is a gross misperception. Cases are easy only to those with tunnel vision who fail to see other options and ignore the effects of the "easy" decisions. Frequently, lawyers on the staffs of legal centers for children, the aged, women, the mentally ill and other disadvantaged groups write asking me to refer landmark cases to them. I usually reply that every case is a landmark case if the lawyer has the perception to recognize the implicit issues involved and the ingenuity to cast them into the mold of a justiciable or constitutional question.

In neither of the cases I present were counsel or I, as trial judge, looking for a landmark case. But I could not avoid the question. In the criminal case, Derrick and William, two 19-year-olds, were strolling down a quiet street in a depressed blue collar neighborhood. Linda was sitting on her front doorstep waiting for a friend, her pocketbook on her lap. The youths approached her. One said, "Gimme your purse." The other drew a gun, which was later examined and found to be inoperable. Linda handed them her purse. They opened it, discovered it contained only a nickel in cash and returned it. They strolled away. Linda promptly called the police who within five minutes arrested both youths. It was a bright, clear day. Linda had given a detailed description of both boys. She identified them without hesitation.

They were charged with robbery and conspiracy. They were released on nominal bail. Six months later they came to trial before me. Defense counsel demanded a jury trial because the prosecutor was asking for a mandatory sentence of a minimum of five years imprisonment for each youth and an

---

[11]See, e.g., F. Schauer, "Easy Cases," *Southern California Law Review* 58 (1985): 399.

additional two years because the crime was committed with a firearm. Defense counsel valiantly pursued every possible defense because the penalties were so severe. A jury found both guilty of conspiracy and robbery. There was no error in the trial.

Neither defendant had a prior adult record although both had several minor delinquency adjudications when they were juveniles. Both boys were school dropouts, undereducated, chronically unemployed and occasional drug users. They were typical sons of blue collar families that had lost their solid support of union jobs, close-knit families and social support systems. Derrick's father had deserted the family. Derrick, the eldest, was then 12 years old. His mother had to cope with rearing six small children. William's father, who had also lost his job, was still at home—idle, bitter and brutal. Defense counsel argued that the verdict should be set aside and a new trial granted. This would have been the easy way out. However, the jury had found them guilty. The evidence was clear and sufficient. Courts when instructing juries tell them they must make their findings on the evidence, that in criminal cases the evidence must be beyond a reasonable doubt, but that the jurors are not to conjure up a fanciful doubt in order to avoid an unpleasant duty.

I held the Mandatory Sentencing Act unconstitutional on many grounds. The statute gave discretion for invoking the mandatory sentence to the prosecutor and thus infringed upon judicial discretion. The criteria for mandatory sentences were arbitrary, unreasonable and unrelated to a legitimate public purpose. The Act failed to consider the individual defendant's needs, character and the protection of the public.

I sentenced each of the boys to three years probation conditioned upon attending school and obtaining a high school equivalency diploma, remaining drug free, obtaining a job and paying a $100 fine. The sentences were appealed by the prosecutor. Two years later after both the Pennsylvania Supreme Court[12] and the United States Supreme Court[13] had upheld the constitutionality of the Mandatory Sentencing Act, the cases were remanded to me with instructions to impose the mandatory sentences of a minimum of five years imprisonment.

At that time, both boys were employed. Derrick had obtained his high school diploma and had a steady job in an auto repair shop. He was married; his wife was pregnant. William worked part-time at McDonald's. He had not obtained a high school diploma, although he had faithfully attended high school for a year. Derrick's I.Q. was 107. William's was 84. Derrick is short and slight. He looks like the blond angelic choir boy he was at age 12. William is bigger and tougher. Probably William could survive in prison. Derrick would be raw meat for the tough prisoners who demand homosexual

---

[12]*Com. v. Wright*, 494 A.2d 354 (Pa., 1985).
[13]*McMillan v. Pennsylvania*, 106 S. Ct. 2411 (1986).

relations from small, weak fellow prisoners. I have known far too many young men who have been gang-raped in prison where they were committed for "rehabilitation."

What should a judge of conscience do?[14]

A run of the mill civil case presented a difficult but less harrowing choice between following positive law and obeying the dictates of conscience. Mrs. S. had terminal cancer. The doctors gave her four months to live. The case was rushed to trial. Three years earlier, she had felt a small lump in her breast and immediately went to her gynecologist. He referred her to a board-certified oncologist who ordered a mammogram. The results were inconclusive. Nonetheless, the oncologist did not order a biopsy which would have immediately confirmed a malignancy. Instead, he sent Mrs. S. home telling her that the lump was a benign cyst and that she should not return for a year. Six months later, when the lump was noticeably larger, Mrs. S. consulted another physician who promptly ordered a biopsy and numerous other tests. Unfortunately, the cancer had already metastasized. She underwent a radical mastectomy and radiation treatment. A few months later her ovaries were removed. The cancer then spread to her liver. No further treatment could save her.

During the three years of her illness, the relationship between Mr. and Mrs. S. had deteriorated. Mrs. S. had become deeply depressed and querulous. She had lost her hair and gained almost 100 pounds. She was no longer the slim, pretty, cheerful wife Mr. S. had married. In due course, he found solace in the company of a young divorcee who was a co-worker. Mr. and Mrs. S. had two young children. A malpractice action was brought in the names of Mr. and Mrs. S. and the children. The law was clear that (1) the oncologist was guilty of gross malpractice; (2) Mrs. S. had a valid claim for her losses; (3) Mr. S. had a valid claim for his loss of consortium; and (4) the children had no claim for the loss of the care, companionship and guidance of their mother since she was still alive. That precise issue had been decided by the Pennsylvania Supreme Court only a few months before. Nonetheless, counsel urged me to submit the issue of the children's claim for compensation to the jury. The law was clear that if Mrs. S. were already dead the children would have a right of action for wrongful death. It was apparent to both counsel and me that Mr. S. would promptly remarry and that the compensation for the death of Mrs. S. would be utilized by her successor rather than her motherless children.[15]

---

[14]To refuse to impose a prison sentence on Derrick on the grounds that he would be physically endangered and to sentence William to prison would constitute grossly unequal treatment. Blindly to follow the sentencing mandate and sentence both to prison would be unconscionable although legal and perhaps constitutional.

[15]The extension of loss of consortium to wives is a relatively recent judicial "interpretation" of old English common law doctrine to conform to contemporary concepts. Would the extension of

These are only two of scores and scores of cases in which a trial judge finds that strict adherence to positive law will bring about an unconscionable result.

One turns to the more popular and articulate critics of the courts and judicial policy-making for guidance. Without attempting to find answers to these two specific situations in which there is a tension—indeed, an intolerable tension—between the demands of judicial conscience and adherence to positive law, it is necessary to take note, however briefly, of several popular theories of the judicial function that I find unacceptable.

One such theory is the notion that a trial in a court of law is simply a contest between two litigants. If this were all that is involved, private dispute resolution through mediation, conciliation or alternative private courts such as Judicate and "Rent-a-Judge" would suffice. In the rush to privatism, individuals could hire their own tribunals. In my view, a court has a far more significant function. It does, as Blackstone observed, declare law. It represents the public interest in declaring and enforcing those principles of behavior and individual societal rights that represent the norm of conduct as expressed by the public through the Constitutions of the United States and the several states, statutes, ordinances, rules, regulations and the great body of common law jurisprudence. This is, perhaps, only stating the obvious. A great many contemporary authorities on jurisprudence, however, have expressed a contrary view.

Richard Posner (writing as a professor before he was appointed to the bench) characterized a legal trial as a "competition between plaintiffs and defendants for the favor of the tribunal."[16] This brutal view of the litigation process harks back to John Wigmore's "sporting theory" of a trial as a duel between Hessians (the lawyers) with the judge acting as referee. Professor Drusilla Cornell writes of the legal process: "Law has internal as well as external goods. The goal is to beat the opponent within the rules of the game, as well as to get rich."[17] Professor Roberto Unger declares that judges are merely engaged in "brokering small deals."[18] This cynical and amoral view of the law is perhaps simply a 1980s version of "legal realism" in which it was argued that law and ethics were totally disparate, that judicial decisions

---

the right to children be impermissable judicial legislation or simply appropriate updating of the law?

[16]Note that Posner suggests private law enforcement as being less costly than a public system. R. Posner, *Economic Analysis of Law* (Boston, 1972).

[17]D. Cornell, "Toward a Modern/Postmodern Reconstruction of Ethics," *University of Pennsylvania Law Review* 133 (1985): 291, 318, n. 149.

[18]R. Unger, "The Critical Legal Studies Movement," *Harvard Law Review* 96 (1983): 563, 581. A judge cannot refrain from speculating as to the relation between this cynical view of the legal process as expressed by academics and the shocking instances of gross unethical behavior by some of the brightest and the best young lawyers as well as the widespread disinterest in the 1980s in providing legal services for the disadvantaged.

depend upon the disposition of the judge and that law is no more than prediction of what the court will decide.[19]

No useful purpose would be served by recapitulating the well-worn arguments of proponents of legal realism and of natural law. Suffice it to say, neither position offers much guidance to the perplexed judge who believes that he or she is bound by the mandates of positive law and also the commands of conscience.

Another widely held view that I reject is that ethical values are suspect and that self-interest is the true touchstone or litmus test of individual decision-making. The widely lauded *A Theory of Justice* by John Rawls, although more elegantly phrased, is tacitly based on the assumption that every individual is looking out for number one. Hence, in order to obtain a consensus as to the "good," Rawls creates the fiction of the veil of ignorance so that the individuals making choices do not know their own identities. He assumes that, if one does not know his or her race, age, sex, economic condition or other characteristics, such a person, acting in self-interest, will make choices that will not be prejudicial to any group of which he or she might be a member. A moment's reflection discloses that most people do not act solely out of self-interest. For example, many in high income brackets favor a graduated income tax because they believe it is fair. Many people who do not have children attending public school favor high taxes to support public schools because they believe that all children should be educated. Similarly, some factory owners and corporate shareholders support environmental protection laws even though such laws diminish their profits. In this respect, the legislature, as often happens, is far in advance of the judiciary. The entire body of environmental law, for example, is based on the tacit belief that self-interest is an insufficient postulate for humane government and that the rights of the individual are also furthered by a consideration of communal interest. Self-interest provides neither a truthful nor a desirable predicate for law.

A third position is that in a democratic society groups and individuals have a right to establish their own legal systems.[20]

Fourth, is the belief that the legislature is supreme, that Congress and state legislatures have the right to outlaw whatever they choose without hindrance by the courts.[21]

---

[19]See O. Holmes, "The Path of the Law," in *Collected Legal Papers* (New York, 1920), 173.

[20]See R. Cover, "Foreword: Nomos and Narrative," *Harvard Law Review* 97 (1983): 4. The use of Greek terminology cannot mask the divisive and destructive nature of a theory that each group has the right to establish its own laws. With all its diversity, the American population does have a shared belief in a rule of law. A judge who sees the entire spectrum of the population in jury panels and hears their responses to *voir dire* questioning cannot fail to be impressed with the public's belief in a just legal system and the willingness of most people to sacrifice both time and money to participate in the justice system by serving on juries.

[21]See, e.g., J. Ely, *Democracy and Distrust* (Cambridge, MA, 1980). Dworkin, Perry and Cover concede that there is a necessary role for judicial interpretation but would limit it. It is tempting

Fifth, is the view, often expressed by Attorney-General Edwin Meese, that courts have no interpretive function. While few jurisprudential theorists take so extreme a position, many seek to limit judicial discretion.[22] I suggest that this argument is based on two fallacies, namely, that judicial discretion is undesirable and that the legal system can be structured so tightly as to eliminate discretion. These are fundamental premises of the widespread and popular movement for sentencing guidelines. With little, if any, supporting empirical evidence, former United States District Judge Marvin E. Frankel proposes sentencing guidelines in a little book with the catchy title, *Criminal Sentences: Law Without Order*.[23] His thesis is that judges have too much discretion in sentencing and that this has resulted in widely disparate sentences for the same offenses. Robbery, as usually defined, is the taking of property from another by threat or force, however slight. As we have seen, Derrick and William were properly convicted of robbery even though they took nothing of value and then returned the pocketbook and even though no violence was involved. Convictions for robbery also arise when hundreds of thousands or millions of dollars are taken by brute force that involves violence and serious injury to the victim. I have tried many robbery cases in which the victims were blinded or rendered quadriplegic. Prior to the adoption of sentencing guidelines, judges were able to impose sentences that reflected the obvious differences between a robbery with physical violence and a robbery committed without violence or harm.

Interpretation is an essential part of the judicial function. Few, if any, statutes are so tightly and explicitly drafted that a judge can simply set statutory words in juxtaposition to a factual situation and, ineluctably, without analysis and interpretation, reach a conclusion. Take a simple example, the kind rarely, if ever, considered by those who expound elaborate theories of the judicial function. The Pennsylvania Motor Vehicle Financial Responsibility Act, enacted after careful consideration, provides in pertinent part, "[the owner of the vehicle] ... remains liable for non-economic detriment [pain and suffering] if ... the reasonable value of reasonable and necessary medical and dental services ... is in excess of seven hundred fifty dollars...."[24] It immediately became apparent that courts would have to decide whether the threshold expenditure for medical care must be (1) made before suit was brought; (2) incurred before suit was brought; or (3) reasonably expected to be incurred before suit was brought. Regardless of the judge's beliefs as to being "neutral" and avoiding "judicial

---

to dismiss much of these lengthy, turgid and opaque studies as, in the words of Lord Demming, "boring and vacuous."

[22]See, e.g., K. Davis, *Discretionary Justice: A Preliminary Inquiry* (Baton Rouge, LA, 1969), and Bork, "Neutral Principles." But see C. Pinkele and W. Loutham, *Discretion, Justice and Democracy: A Public Policy Perspective* (Ames, IA, 1985).

[23](New York, 1972).

[24]Pa. Purdons Stat. Ann. § 1009.301.

tyranny,"[25] the judges to whom this issue was presented had to make a decision.

Many of those who would restrict judicial discretion assert that the judiciary is anti-majoritarian and unaccountable. It should be noted that the persons who established the guidelines in most states were consultants hired by the legislatures. These consultants were not democratically elected nor directly answerable to the public. Parole boards that actually determine the length of time served by a prisoner are, in the main, comprised of anonymous bureaucrats, neither selected by nor answerable to the public.

It may be argued that federal judges who are appointed for life are unaccountable.[26] The number of judges who have been impeached is extremely small. The number who have been quietly forced to resign is considerably larger. The notion that federal judges are anti-majoritarian reflects a simplistic view of the appointment process. Although few presidents have been so blatantly ideological as Ronald Reagan in appointing judges, the federal judiciary as a whole reflects the political philosophy of the party in power. As Mr. Dooley sagely observed, the Supreme Court follows the election returns. Certainly in reversing within two years its decision striking down the death penalty the Supreme Court followed the public clamor for capital punishment. The Court admitted that it was influenced by the rash of state legislation quickly enacted to circumvent its earlier ruling. Mr. Justice Stewart, writing for the Court, explained:

> Despite the continuing debate, dating back to the 19th Century, over the morality and utility of capital punishment, it is now evident that a large proportion of American society continues to regard it as an appropriate and necessary criminal sanction.[27]

Whether the courts should reflect popular sentiment or rule on the law uninfluenced by public clamor is an issue beyond the purview of this discussion. A careful reading of opinions on many controversial issues, however, reveals that federal courts are not immune to the public will.

[25]See M. Tushnet, "Following the Rules Laid Down: A Critique of Interpretation and Neutral Principles," *Harvard Law Review* 96 (1983): 781, 784. See also O. Fiss, "Objectivity and Interpretation," *Stanford Law Review* 34 (1982): 739, 744. Fiss's argument that *"any* [his emphasis] judicial interpretation—[is unable to] achieve the measure of objectivity required by the idea of law—" is both preposterous and unattainable.

[26]See, e.g., M. Perry, *The Constitution, the Courts and Human Rights: An Inquiry Into the Legitimacy of Constitutional Policymaking by the Judiciary* (New Haven, CT, 1982) and Ely, *Democracy and Distrust*. Note that in the 1940s a bill was introduced in Congress to establish a commission "to report whether government has departed from the concept of the founding fathers." It is discussed by Felix Frankfurter in "Some Reflections on the Reading of Statutes," *Columbia Law Review* 47 (1947): 527. See also L. Bollinger, *The Tolerant Society* (Oxford/New York, 1986).

[27]*Gregg v. Georgia*, 428 U.S. 153, 179 (1976) overruling *Furman v. Georgia*, 408 U.S. 238 (1972).

Whether or not federal judges are anti-majoritarian, it must be noted that at least 80 percent of all litigation is brought in the state courts where the trial judges are elected. Those judges whose conduct offends the public sensibilities are simply not re-elected. State judges are as majoritarian as the members of the legislature and equally accountable. I suggest that the argument that the judiciary is composed of activist judges flouting the majoritarian policies of the public is absolutely fallacious. The notion that the judiciary is an elite group of Platonic guardians does not bear scrutiny. While prior to the Carter administration the vast majority of federal judges were white, male Protestants whose previous experience had been in large, wealthy law firms, that stereotype is no longer true. State courts also are now more open to women, non-whites and lawyers of much lower income brackets who have had experience in criminal and family law. Whether the intellectual level of the bench is higher or lower as a result of this growing democratization raises a significant question. But it can no longer be said that the judiciary is anti-majoritarian.

The widely discussed incredibly wise, mythical Judge Hercules created by Ronald Dworkin has, I believe, muddled analysis of the judicial function.[28] In answer to this complex and academic view of judicial decision-making, I postulate a judge, Minerva, who is not incredibly wise. However, she knows the law. She also knows a very wide range of human beings. Because she is an elected judge, Minerva understands the political process, its values and its limitations. She also understands the limitations of judicial office. For example, when the chief of police committed a blatantly illegal act, she did not hold him in contempt of court, although that was technically within her jurisdiction. Instead, she prevailed upon his counsel to approve a consent decree. She believed it was more desirable to get the police chief to agree to obey the law and to compensate those he had wronged than to test fragile judicial power by threatening to jail the police chief.

Minerva sits in a busy court of general jurisdiction in a large metropolitan area where she decides, settles or takes guilty pleas in an average of ten cases per week. Each of them presents factual and legal issues. Many have implicit constitutional dimensions. Minerva, of necessity, must be pragmatic. She accepts as givens the doctrine of supremacy of law, that the ratification of a constitution and the enactment of legislation and the promulgation of rules and regulations can create rights and that it is not her function to determine the wisdom of this positive law. Accordingly, she does not have to construct theories of legitimacy for adhering to the law. If she were to attempt such intellectual exercises, she would be unable to decide even one case per month. Minerva does, however, consider that it is her

[28]See R. Dworkin, *Taking Rights Seriously* (Cambridge, MA, 1977). But see the brilliantly witty review of Dworkin's "Laws' Empire" by A. Hutchinson, "Indiana Dworkin and Laws' Empire," *Yale Law Journal* 96 (1987): 637.

function and obligation to weigh competing and conflicting rights, and—on the basis of history, contemporary social conditions, public policy and ethical considerations—to determine which claim is entitled to priority.

Judge Minerva is presented with the case of Baby X in which the natural mother (popularly denominated surrogate mother) and the natural father (the sperm donor) and his wife claim not only custody of the child but exclusive rights to possession of the baby including legal adoption. Here Minerva is faced with a novel factual situation for which there is no positive statutory law and no precedent. Although the facts are unusual, it is by no means exceptional for Judge Minerva to have to decide a case of first impression. It is futile to suggest a "hermeneutic" alternative to interpretation since it is obvious that the framers of the Constitution could not have envisioned this problem. Minerva does not consider whether she has the right to interpret or, as some would characterize it, judicially to legislate. She must reach a decision. Otherwise, the baby would be placed in the limbo of a state institution until the legislature decides to act.[29] Minerva must, therefore, extrapolate from legal principles established at a time when surrogate parenting was not only physically impossible but unthinkable.

The biological father and his wife rely on contract. The principle of contract (two parties bargaining at arms length for a deal, giving consideration for the bargain agreed to) had been accepted in English law long before John Locke. There is also an equally long standing and respected principle that courts will not enforce a contract that is contrary to public policy. Thus, restrictive covenants prohibiting the sale of realty to non-whites, non-Christians and others, although legal when entered into, will not be enforced. Minerva is aware of the many cases in which installment sales contracts were held to be unenforceable despite the written agreement and the consideration paid because one party was not fully informed of the terms, even though they were contained in the printed agreement. She is also mindful of contracts of adhesion that are unenforceable because the weaker party had no free choice in entering into the agreement. Minerva accepts this principle and the long line of precedent without engaging in philosophical theorizing to justify the rule.

She then turns to see whether the surrogate parenting contract is contrary to public policy. Minerva does not fashion public policy but looks to analogous situations to find a declaration of that policy. Sale of human beings, whether *in esse* or *in utero*, was banned by the Thirteenth Amendment. In Minerva's jurisdiction, as in most states, there is a carefully drafted statute regulating the rights of natural mothers and adopting parents. Under this act, the natural mother has 60 days after the birth of the baby within which to change her mind, despite the fact that she had entered into a

---

[29]All too often children are left in institutions and a series of foster homes because courts defer making the hard human choices involved in these legal battles.

contract agreeing to give the baby up for adoption and that consideration was paid by the prospective adopting couple. Minerva concludes that since the natural mother had promptly asserted her right to her baby, the contract is not enforceable.

Minerva now has to decide in accordance with a substantial body of case law which of the two biological parents is entitled to primary custody of the baby. The law is clear that neither the mother nor the father may be deprived of parental rights without clear and convincing evidence of abandonment or unfitness. In the case of Baby X, both mother and father strenuously claim the child. Neither is manifestly an unfit parent. Minerva does not seek to create law but to declare and apply the appropriate law. When divorced or unmarried parents are both married to other spouses, physical custody will be awarded to the parent and spouse according to the doctrine of the "best interests of the child." This vague but sensible standard is not applied mechanically. Financial ability is only one factor to be considered. The tender years doctrine that in awarding custody gave presumptive custody of an infant to the mother has been abolished in Minerva's jurisdiction. Also, the doctrine that in awarding custody the homebound female is to be preferred to the working mother no longer controls. It is also clearly established law that the noncustodial parent must have generous visitation rights. In addition, both parents are obligated to contribute to the support of the child within their respective financial capacities no matter which parent has actual physical custody. Moreover, custody is never finally determined. It can always be re-examined in the light of changed conditions. When the child reaches the age of ten or more, the child's wishes will be given considerable weight. Regardless of Minerva's views as to the correctness of these doctrines, she considers herself bound to follow them.

Despite Dworkin's belief in the "gravitational force of precedent"[30] and the "distributional force of a collective goal," or the theory of the "seamless web" of the law, Minerva knows that she is bound by precedent and that the law is not a seamless web. There are many jagged edges and rents in the fabric that has been continuously unravelled and rewoven over a millennia of decision-making. She knows that these rough spots cannot be planed to aesthetic satisfaction because human behavior is unpredictable, wayward and often violent.

Minerva also knows that economic efficiency, the most effective use of resources for the common good, is ignored by the law every day. Factories close, putting hundreds of people out of work and dislocating not only those families but the entire community. Absent a statute requiring notice of a factory closing, Minerva knows that she cannot take the law into her own hands and compel a plant to continue operations, much as she would like to

---

[30]Dworkin, *Taking Rights Seriously*, 105.

do so. Economic efficiency can play no part in Minerva's decision in the Baby X case.

Minerva finds that Mark Tushnet's statement that "judges no less than legislators [are] political actors motivated primarily by their own interests and values,"[31] is simply a false perception of the judicial function and the behavior of most actual judges.[32] Minerva's colleagues are an average group of judges. Like any other group of persons brought together to perform a common task, they vary. Some are wise, others foolish. Some are conscientious, others lazy. Some are arrogant, others modest. Some are considered liberal, others reactionary. But, with rare exceptions, they know that they are obligated to follow the law despite their personal inclinations, and they do so.

Returning to Mr. Justice Brennan's perspective, the view of judicial decision-making as seen from the bench, I conclude that there is very little judicial tyranny.[33] Except in courts with discretionary jurisdiction, there is no reaching out for cases in which to make law. Even in those courts, perhaps the emphasis should be not on correction of errors in specific cases but upon making law in cases raising novel issues or issues that should be reconsidered.[34] Rather than seeking to limit judicial discretion, I believe that we need a legal philosophy that will permit judges to take a broader view of the human, social and political conflicts they are required to decide. Without in any way detracting from the Lockean view of individual autonomy and liberty, courts need a jurisprudence predicated upon a recognition of ethical values and communitarian goals that are entitled to protection rather than a philosophy predicated upon self interest.

Judges, instead of being characterized as "tyrannical," should be encouraged to consider and recognize claims of individual rights and decency of treatment. The entire structure of appellate courts exists for the correction of manifest error and abuse of judicial discretion. To preclude judges from considering ethical values is to adopt the philosophy of Adolf Eichmann who justified genocide on the ground that he was simply obeying orders. Judges should not, I believe, be constrained by precedent to render indecent or

---

[31]Tushnet, "Following the Rules Laid Down," 784.

[32]A check of the computerized sentencing records of the judges of the Court of Common Pleas, Philadelphia, PA before the enactment of a Mandatory Sentencing Act revealed only statistically insignificant differences among all the judges. Both bleeding hearts and hanging judges sentenced heavily in homicide and forcible rape cases and lightly in retail theft and welfare cases with appropriate sentences between.

[33]The overwhelming majority of judges do follow the law in their decisions. Unfortunately, there are some judges who do behave tyranically in their treatment of counsel, litigants and witnesses. Limiting judicial discretion would not obviate the problem.

[34]A recent perceptive study of the caseload of the United States Supreme Court, S. Estreicher and J. Sexton, *Redefining the Supreme Court* (New Haven, CT, 1986), suggests that the Court hears too many routine cases solely for the purpose of correcting error and should confine itself to those cases in which clarification or advancement of the law is required.

inhumane decisions. Nor should they be required under some theory of hermeneutic interpretation or neutrality blindly to enforce laws or precedents that result in degrading or indecent or unequal treatment of human beings.[35] Sensible judges, if not unduly constrained by mechanical adherence to positive law and precedent, can resolve the tension between law and conscience.

[35]I have refused to sit on cases in which the death penalty has been demanded. The result has been the preservation of my own moral integrity at the price of submitting defendants to a court composed of "death qualified" judges. This may be called the Lady Macbeth syndrome. When Duncan's death was discovered, Lady Macbeth cried out, "Not in my house." Similarly, I say, not in my courtroom. But killing continues. Nonetheless, I do not accept Cover's statement that "judges are people of violence—[they] do not create law but kill it." Cover, "Foreword," 53. The answer, I believe, is to allow sufficient breathing space for judicial interpretation in order to avoid violence and manifest unfairness. As Dean Robert Bennett points out "No norm, no matter how self-consciously articulated by the norm-holder, can except in the most artificial way solve unanticipated problems without the injection of new value judgments." R. Bennett, "The Mission of Moral Reasuring in Constitutional Law," *Southern California Law Review* 58 (1985): 651. This is not to suggest that law can be reduced to the simplicities of Lord Devlin's view as expressed in Shaw's case that judges can base their decisions on what "right-thinking" persons believe. *Shaw v. Director of Public Prosecutions*, 2 All E.R. 446 (1961).

BIBLICAL KINGDOM AND AMERICAN LAW*
Milner S. Ball

This essay is an experiment, a preliminary one at that. My major vocation in recent years has been to venture non-religious theological accounts of American law. So far I have avoided the challenge of describing the status—an ontology—of law and lawyering. I am not sanguine about meeting the demands of such an undertaking. However, one approach to the task might lie through elaboration of the biblical reality of the Kingdom of God. In these pages, I shall attempt a tentative first probing of conditions for raising the question about what the Kingdom of God means for us today, or, more particularly, what the Kingdom of God means for contemporary American law.

This essay is a tribute to Harold J. Berman. I am free to celebrate Professor Berman in this way—by arranging and rearranging fragments in hope of finding clues—for his scholarly stature can scarcely be diminished by any failure in my experiment, and the attempt itself will honor his own willingness to take risks, an example inspiring those of us who explore the critical interaction of religion and law.

I. WHAT IS THE KINGDOM OF GOD?

To ask what the Kingdom of God is for us today is to seek alignment with the question raised by Dietrich Bonhoeffer about "who Christ really is, for us today."[1] Bonhoeffer's question was revolutionary, partly because he presumed it was a genuine, open question that had to be asked, and partly because he presumed that no answer would be either simple or self-evident and might come only in the way he chose to live.[2]

The radically open nature of Bonhoeffer's inquiry can be retained when

---

*This essay is drawn from materials presented as the 1986 Otts Lectures at Davidson College. I am especially indebted to Professor Alexander J. McKelway, as well as to his colleagues and students, for the invitation to deliver these lectures and for the collegial, fruitful response. They gave me substantial help along the way to re-thinking these things all over again. Of course they should not be blamed for failures of mine to advance any further than I have. I do anticipate other essays to issue from that wonderful interchange at Davidson.

[1]D. Bonhoeffer, *Letters and Papers from Prison*, ed. E. Bethge (New York, 1967), 152.

[2]Bonhoeffer believed we were "moving towards a completely religionless time," and that the "religious *a priori*" of Christianity had been removed. He was, therefore, beginning to ask how to speak in a secular way about God. Ibid., 152–53.

revised and raised as a question about the Kingdom of God. There are reasons for the revision.

Positively, the image of Kingdom is central to the Bible. For example, Matthew says the message of both John the Baptist and Jesus was: "Repent, for the kingdom of heaven is close at hand" (Matt. 3:2; 4:17). In Mark, the first words of Jesus's ministry are: "The time has come and the kingdom of God is close at hand" (Mk. 1:15). There are beatitudes and parables and sermons about the Kingdom. The Book of Acts opens with a question about the Kingdom (Acts 1:6) and closes with Paul in Rome "proclaiming the kingdom of God" (Acts 28:31). Elaboration of "the Kingdom of God" is congruent with the texts of the biblical sagas.

Of course, any image can be wrenched from its life-giving context and made an abstraction, an empty conceptual vessel to receive alien ideologies, prejudices and interests. Such misuse of texts is practiced all the time, and I have no special immunity from the temptation to engage in it. The image, or promise, of the Kingdom draws some protection against interpretive abuse from the fact that, in the biblical sagas, the Kingdom is linked to the person of Christ. It is not a neutral, abstract or indeterminate concept.

The term Kingdom, Karl Barth wrote, "does not denote [an] institution or state or sphere but the act and exercise of kingly rule by the being and activity of a royal person."[3] The Kingdom of God is a way of talking about the sovereignty of God or the body and reign of Christ. To revise Bonhoeffer's question is to focus on the overtly political reality—God's active political presence—central in the Bible.

Another, and negative, reason for revising Bonhoeffer's question as one about the Kingdom is that to ask who Jesus Christ is for us today takes unnecessary risks of misinterpretation in the context of today's world. Phrased Bonhoeffer's way, it is too readily heard as a question about subjective religious feeling. The proper inquiry, as I understand it, is political and requires clear disconnection from investigation into individual religious experience.[4]

Here—and the preliminary character of the experiment bears emphasizing again—the concern is with principalities and powers in light of the Kingdom of God. (The particular principality/power at issue is law.)

---

[3]K. Barth, *Church Dogmatics*, trans. G. Thompson; eds. G. Bromiley and T. Torrance, 4 vols. (Edinburgh, 1960), 3: 433.

[4]This emphasis constitutes no departure from Bonhoeffer, nor does the focus on the Kingdom. Bonhoeffer wrote of "a kingdom stronger than war and danger, a kingdom of power and authority, signifying eternal terror and judgment to some, and eternal joy and righteousness to others, not a kingdom of the heart, but one as wide as the earth, not transitory but eternal, a kingdom that makes a way for itself and summons men to itself to prepare its way, a kingdom for which it is worthwhile to risk our lives." Bonhoeffer, *Letters*, 163. Bonhoeffer also had an alternate way of putting the question: "how to claim for Jesus Christ a world that has come of age." Ibid., 189. For Bonhoeffer's further reflections on these and related matters—the meaning of the biblical faith in an autonomous world—see ibid., 188–89, 192–93, 195–97, 198–200, 208.

Discussion of the Kingdom of God in the law school is generally greeted with suspicion edging toward derision, for the professional academic parentage of theology is thought suspect. But, even in the divinity school, such discussion confronts formidable difficulties of text, tense and interpretation.

Some sense of the problem and its dimensions is evident in the well known text from the Book of Revelation: "the kingdom of this world has become the kingdom of the Lord and of his Christ, and he shall reign for ever and ever" (Rev. 11:15). The sentence is uttered as a line in a dramatic projection. It emerges in the course of a description of apocalyptic events. The events are understood as having already occurred, but from an envisioned, projected standpoint. The Kingdom has arrived and is yet to arrive. The author of Revelation sought a language and method reflective of present transcendence.[5]

Various formulae have been devised to address the relationship—and its effects—between the reality of the Kingdom and the reality of this world: Augustine's City of God and city of man; Luther's two kingdoms; Bonhoeffer's ultimate and penultimate; John Calvin's proposal that "our very existence is nothing but a subsistence in God alone" (the kingdom of this world subsists in the Kingdom of God).[6]

The challenge is to invent language responsive to the transcendent sacramental presence of the body discerned in the breaking of the bread. In other words, how do we say today the kingdom of the world has become the Kingdom of God? How do we do so without mistaking the former for the latter—without confusing what is for what shall be? How do we take seriously the particular advent of the Kingdom of God without being understood as suffering the corruption of American civil religion? How can we be taken seriously?

At times, the Gospel of Mark has seemed to me a guiding example. Mark's solution is exemplified by two passages. One is the conclusion: "for they were afraid" (Mk. 16:8). The words walk us up to the empty tomb and leave us there. The text embodies secrecy, a verbal negative space. At the end of the story the resurrection is either a reality for the reader or not, either has purpose or not.

The other passage is Mark 4:12, and Frank Kermode is correct in fixing our attention upon it. According to the story, the disciples had not understood the parables Jesus was telling. Confronted with their failure of comprehension, Jesus explained that parables were necessary "so that [those outside] may see and see again, but not perceive; may hear and hear again, but not understand; otherwise they might be converted and be forgiven."

[5]Note should also be taken of Bonhoeffer's description of God as "beyond in the midst of our life" (ibid., 155) and of Luke 17:17: "The coming of the kingdom does not admit of observation and there will be no one to say 'Look here! Look there!' For, you must know, the Kingdom of God is in the midst of you."

[6]See F. Kermode, *The Genesis of Secrecy* (Cambridge, MA, 1979), 29–34.

This is a harsh, enigmatic, hard-edged explanation. Jesus said he spoke in parables so that the hearer could not understand. Matthew softens the point. He renders Mark's *hina* as *hoti*. According to Matthew, Jesus said he spoke in parables because those outside did not understand (Matt. 13:13). He employed parables out of deference to his audience, to accommodate their incapacity for understanding and to include them by revealing his message. According to Mark, he employed parables in order to conceal and exclude. Mark's sentence as a whole reads: "The secret of the kingdom of God is given to you, but to those who are outside everything comes in parables, so that they may see and see again, but not perceive; may hear and hear again, but not understand; otherwise they might be converted and be forgiven."

Language that has the Kingdom of God as its subject must make room for mystery, secrecy and exclusion as well as for inclusive revelation. Writing instructed by the example of Mark might explore a variety of forms, including juxtaposition, covert communication[7] and supplication.[8] Taking Mark seriously might issue in no writing; indeed, silence may generally be the appropriate first option.[9] The choice will depend upon the circumstance, the constant being the secret in the middle (the intersection of the Kingdom of God with the kingdom of the world, the "beyond in the midst of life"). Critique is also an option, and I choose it because I believe the language of critique to be responsive not only to the example of Mark but also to present need, as the following may help to demonstrate.

II. A Theological Critique of American Law

A critical approach to law must contend with the intimate, mutually supportive relationship of American law and American civil religion. A theological critique of American law necessarily entails a critique of American religion.

A. The First Amendment Alliance

Although the relation of law and religion includes much more than the free exercise and establishment clauses of the First Amendment to the United States Constitution, those clauses are a dominant, convenient locus for analysis of the relation. The First Amendment protects religion. More revealingly, it also protects the government. It attempts to guard the state

---

[7]On covert communication in literature and law, see R. Weisberg, *The Failure of the Word* (New Haven/London, 1984), esp. 131–176.

[8]See, P. Lehmann, *The Transfiguration of Politics* (New York, 1975), 285–287, 348.

[9]See G. Gutierrez, "Theology and Spirituality in a Latin American Context," *Harvard Divinity Bulletin* (June–August, 1984): 4–5.

against the negative effects of religion while gaining for the state the legitimation regarded as a positive effect of religion.

Government does require protection against the destructive effects of religion. Thomas Jefferson once remarked that "millions of innocent men, women, and children, since the introduction of Christianity, have been burnt, tortured, fined, imprisoned. . . ."[10] The republic cannot survive religious turmoil, religious wars and religious persecutions. We have, therefore, what Justice John Paul Stevens mildly referred to as a "political interest in forestalling intolerance."[11]

Neither Jefferson nor James Madison believed that the cause of religious conflict (that is, factiousness) could be removed but that its effects could be contained through sectarian diversity. In Jefferson's handy formula: "The several sects perform the office of a *censor morum* over each other."[12] Since safety lay in multiplicity, all sects were placed on an equal footing for the protection of the body politic.

If the state sought to protect itself against religion, it also—and not so paradoxically—sought to protect itself with religion. It wanted the moral sanction and legitimation which the state has come to expect of religion. There was to be separation of church and state but not of religion and state.[13] Diversity would serve both ends.

From the diversity of contending sects, Jefferson expected true religion to emerge. He favored religion in general, the religion above sects which reason would commend as the pure essence of religion. And this pure, reasonable religion would sanction the state and its law.

The free exercise and nonestablishment of religion would be good for religion and good for the state. This was the American version of the compromise between Constantine and the Church in the early fourth century. By the terms of that ancient alliance, the church received the institutionalization and privilege that accompany imperial favor while the state gained moral status for its force and a moral right to uphold order. The Kingdom of God became an endorsement of the kingdoms of the world.

In American literary tradition, an emblem of this American accommodation is found in the person of the chaplain on board the Bellipotent in Herman Melville's story, *Billy Budd*. Melville describes the chaplain as a "minister of the Prince of Peace serving in the host of the God of War."[14]

[10]T. Jefferson, "Notes on the State of Virginia, Query XVII: Religion," *The Portable Thomas Jefferson*, ed. M. Peterson (New York, 1975), 23, 212.

[11]*Wallace v. Jaffree*, 105 S. Ct. 2479 (1985).

[12]Jefferson, "Notes," 212.

[13]For an illuminating historical study on the uncertainties of the intention of disestablishment, see R. Weisbrod, "On Evidences and Intentions: The More Proof, The More Doubt," *Connecticut Law Review* 18 (1986): 803

[14]H. Melville, "Billy Budd, Sailor," *Billy Budd, Sailor and Other Stories*, ed. H. Beaver (Baltimore, 1970), 398.

He is there, writes Melville, "[b]ecause he indirectly subserves the purpose attested by the cannon; because too he lends the sanction of the religion of the meek to that which practically is the abrogation of everything but brute Force."[15] He is the personification of the endorsement of law by religion.

Religion has not only endorsed the state but has also driven it, as is evident in the way Constantine's troops were inspired to make war in the sign of the Cross. As Richard Slotkin has recently reminded us, animating American policy from the beginning to the present has been the religion by which we seek regeneration through conquest of supposed savages—first the Indians, then laborers, then the urban poor then communists, southeast Asians and Central Americans.[16]

Church and state may be separated but there is an alliance between religion and state. Certainly there is an accommodation between law and religion.[17]

B. The Failure of the Alliance

The First Amendment sought to benefit the state by saving it from the effects of religious intolerance while preserving for it the sanction provided by religion. In consequence the state—especially its law—is saturated with religion. The alliance is ultimately and increasingly a failure.

First, reason has proved no solvent for religious passion. The range of religious beliefs and factions has leapt beyond the bounds of reason. Reason has not contained violent manifestations of these beliefs in the murdering of others for the sake of religion or the bombing of abortion clinics. Sectarian multiplicity under a regime of absolute tolerance is not controlled by reason.

Second, reason has produced no distillation of the pure essence of religion. There is no religion above sects, no composition of religion so abstract, so generalized and vague as to be rendered inoffensive to all our diversity of religions. Therefore, in order to enjoy the sanction of religion, the state has been forced to make religious choices. The state could not remain neutral, nor has it. Its choices have proved incoherent.[18]

While the United States Supreme Court has picked a Presbyterian chaplain,[19] a city creche[20] and Moses with the Ten Commandments as

---

[15]Ibid., 399.

[16]R. Slotkin, *The Fatal Environment* (New York, 1985).

[17]See, e.g., R. Bellah and P. Hammond, *Varities of Civil Religion* (San Francisco, CA, 1980), 161; *Zorach v. Clauson*, 343 U.S. 306, 313 (1952).

[18]See, e.g., the excellent, accessible account in M. Tushnet, "The Constitution of Religion," *Connecticut Law Review* 18 (1986): 701.

[19]*Marsh v. Chambers*, 103 S. Ct. 1330 (1983).

[20]*Lynch v. Donnelly*, 104 S. Ct. 1355 (1984).

interior decoration for the Court building,[21] it has rejected a moment of silence in public schools,[22] certain forms of publicly-supported secular education in parochial schools[23] and a sabbath day right for laborers.[24] The opinions defy principled reconciliation.[25]

Third, the animus behind the logic of First Amendment interpretation has been individualism. Religious diversity is construed as individual free choice, so that the free exercise clause has been read as guaranteeing a kind of cafeteria where individual consumers can line up and choose their fare. Religion is treated as having no claim different from any other constitutionally-protected private choice. As a recent Court opinion has it: "the individual's freedom of conscience [is] the central liberty that unifies the various clauses in the First Amendment. . . ."[26] And this freedom of conscience "embraces the right to select any religious faith or none at all. This conclusion derives support not only from the interest in respecting the individual's freedom of conscience, but also from the conviction that religious beliefs worthy of respect are the product of free and voluntary choice by the faithful."[27]

The general American religion is a religion of the individual. A religion of the individual, however, produces no legitimation for a body politic. When the fundamental commitment is to individualism, a community has no inherent authority. The community has legitimacy only to the degree that it advances individual interests. What remains is a pressure group state in which individualism undoes politics.

[21]See *Wallace v. Jaffree*, 105 S. Ct. 2479 (1985).

[22]Ibid.

[23]*Grand Rapids School District v. Ball*, 105 S. Ct. 3216 (1985).

[24]*Estate of Thornton v. Caldor, Inc.*, 105 S. Ct. 2914 (1985).

[25]Of course, any academic lawyer can attempt an explanation, and I can do so here. The cases can be reconciled on the theory of meaninglessness. The Court permits religious exercises so long as they are meaningless. School children are very impressionable. Even a moment of silence could be made to have religious meaning for them. Therefore, a colorable moment of silence will not be allowed in public grade schools. But prayers will be allowed in the legislature and Moses will be allowed on the interior walls of the Supreme Court because legislators and judges are incorrigible. Religious exercises will have little or no impact upon them and are, therefore, permissible. This theory can be expanded to explain more cases by adding to it a cash flow exception: meaningful exercises of religion will be allowed if they aid the economy. A state right to a day off on the sabbath of one's religion of choice will not be allowed because it is disruptive of the marketplace and expensive for employers. But a government sponsored creche, although it is meaningful and thus poses offense to non-Christians, will be allowed because it induces Christmas shoppers spend more money. In addition to the cynicism of such an attempted explanation of the cases, it suffers from other faults. For example, if the Court is only going to protect religion when it is meaningless—or trivialized as a boost to the economy—then it is impossible to understand why the Constitution singles out religion for specific protection.

[26]*Wallace v. Jaffree*, 2487.

[27]Ibid., 2488.

C. A Theological Alternative

The root cause of the failure of the alliance between religion and the state is not so much the limits of reason or the Supreme Court's confusion as it is the nature of religion. David Hume, Ludwig Andreas Feuerbach, Karl Marx and Sigmund Freud have all taught us that religion arises from fear, promotes intolerance, justifies economic exploitation and precipitates or reinforces debilitating individual and social neuroses.

No criticism of religion has been more thorough than that offered—from the inside—by the theologian Karl Barth. Barth recognized that religion is not only man-made and an illusion but also that it is idolatry, the ultimate expression of human pride. Religion, he said, is man's attempt to justify himself before a capricious God of his own imagining, a God who is the "tedious magnitude known as transcendence, not as a genuine other, nor a true other . . . but an illusory reflection of human freedom, as its projection into the vacuum of utter abstraction."[28] Religion is unbelief and yields neither freedom nor community nor any real legitimacy for law.

Raising the question about what the Kingdom of God is for American law would help to unwind the failing alliance of law and religion. To elaborate the reality of the Kingdom of God would be to elaborate a reality that stands in opposition to religion and religion's attempted legitimation of law. This is so because, I suspect, contemporary portrayal of the Kingdom as a non-religious, biblical reality would disclose two relevant characteristics: the Kingdom of God is a communal reality, and it is predisposed to the cause of the victims of our society.[29]

The Kingdom of God is communal because it is a kingdom, a form of politics—what Jews refer to as "the people" and Christians as "the body of Christ." It is predisposed to victims because, as I have heard it said, "God loves to make his kingdom come among the poor."

I expect the Kingdom of God would be seen to stand in stark contrast to individualistic American civil religion, with its predisposition to the successful and its attempted legitimation of the powers that be. I also expect its advent would be understood as opposing to the victimization of our legal system, a transcendent community predisposed to the cause of the poor. Theological critique of American law would follow from this opposition.

Theological critique of law might be a fit jurisprudential response to the advent of the Kingdom of God. Because law seeks to draw around itself the legitimating cloak of religion, critical analysis of law requires from the outset critical analysis of religion. From there theological critique would proceed to

[28]Barth, *Church Dogmatics*, 3: 479.
[29]See, e.g., "Economic Justice For All: Catholic Social Teaching and the U.S. Economy," *The New York Times* (November 14, 1986), 12.

address whatever in law opposes the authentic community promised in the Kingdom of God.

If criticism is what the Kingdom of God might lead us to *say* in the kingdom of law, then what might we be led correspondingly to *do*? Given the advent of the Kingdom of God, how are we to act as lawyers, as judges, as citizens with responsibility for law?

At least for the time being, it appears to me that episodic action is the companion to critique.

"The faithful," said John Calvin, "have no stopping place in this world."[30] They are always on the move. Calvin once reflected upon the perplexity of Joab, David's general. As Calvin read the story in II Samuel, Joab had hesitated in battle, for he did not know whether God wanted him to win or lose (see II Sam. 10: 6–14). Calvin commended the example of Joab."It is up to God to govern," he said.

> [W]e be not assured whether we shall live today or tomorrow, whether we ought to win a victory, . . . whether we shall prosper in all our affairs; but . . . let us doubt and be in perplexity concerning what God will want to do for one day or one month. If we have a certitude, as we shall have conceived of it in our hearts, this will be nothing but presumption.[31]

That the Kingdom has come and is to come is certain. Uncertain are its particular shapes and requirements from one context to another. Ethical certainties and political programs—since they are conceived in our hearts—are presumptions. Action responsive to the advent of the Kingdom is episodic.

Episodes need not be random and unguided. An episode in Greek tragedy was the action that fell between two choruses. Its root translates: "following upon the entrance," or "coming in beside." The episodes of faith are the coming in beside the Kingdom of God, the following upon its advent, the conforming of this world to that one. They are the acts of the faithful between the *has come* and the *is coming*.

By putting the matter this way, I do not mean to impute special value to disengagement or quiescence. One function of theological critique is precisely to stimulate action, to empower us to take part in the radical change whereby the kingdom of this world is drawn toward the Kingdom of God. From the perspective of the Kingdom of God, governmental and economic cycles, warfare, forces and institutions, including American law, are seen to be contingent. Criticism from this perspective exposes as artifact what was thought to be natural or necessary or inexorable. Criticism thereby encourages us to overcome belittlement.

---

[30]J. Calvin, "Sermons on Second Samuel, Sermon XXXIV" (on Ch. 11), quoted by M. Ball, "The Significance for Political Theory and Action of Calvin's Sermons on Second Samuel," *Calvin Studies* (Davidson, NC, 1982), 40, 49.

[31]Ibid., 48.

When I identify faithful action as episodic, I certainly do not intend to participate in another form of disabling belittlement. Ethical political practice is a necessary response to the advent of the Kingdom of God, which empowers and impels us to action, just episodically and not programatically so.

Three preliminary observations may be offered about the characteristics or guides for this kind of action following upon what has already been said.

First, responsive, episodic action characteristically begins in—and may never move beyond—silent, attentive identity with the victims of present kingdoms. The Kingdom of God is to be discerned taking place in our midst. The clues to it will always be mediated to us through our neighbor and our neighbor's needs. Disciplined receptivity is the first characteristic.

The second is community or collectivity. The Kingdom of God is a kingdom, that is, a communal reality. In praying "Thy kingdom come," believers are not petitioning for individual self-fulfillment but for the rule of a royal messiah. They anticipate a body politic that displaces the nations of this world.

The third characteristic is predisposition to the cause of the poor. If "God loves to make his kingdom come among the poor," then activity responsive to the advent of the Kingdom of God is aligned with the victims of the kingdoms of the world.

The Kingdom of God might be seen to have many concrete consequences for transfigurative activity in law, and a full exposition of the subject would require exploration of examples.

I can imagine drawing one example from the law of relationships between the United States and Indian tribes, which appears to me—as it did to John Marshall—to raise complex, fundamental questions about the justice of the constitutional legal system. Some Indian attorneys liken their situation to that of blacks in the 1920s. Since equal protection jurisprudence, however, like the law of rights generally, is premised upon individual rights, and Indians seek protection of the separate, collective reality of the tribe, a comprehensive jurisprudential theory and litigation strategy will be less available to Indians than they were to blacks 60 years ago.[32]

I can also imagine developing an example from tort law. The dominant public characteristic of civil law is money. Plaintiffs typically sue for damages. The recoveries can be enormous. Pennzoil and Texaco continue to litigate a $10.53 billion judgment. India is suing Union-Carbide for $3.1 billion in the aftermath of the Bhopal catastrophe. Civil litigation is often driven by money. Injury, pain and even love have been made into commodities, each with a price. The money produced by the civil litigation industry and predatory personal injury lawyers has stimulated envy instead of

---

[32]See, e.g., M. Ball, "Constitution, Courts, Indian Tribes," *American Bar Foundation Journal* (1987) (forthcoming).

compassion for victims. Money damages sever responsibility between victims and their families and between victims and the corporate entities that inflict injury. Neither preventive safety nor care for the injured is fostered by the law. It could be argued that having to pay large monetary awards makes industrial actors more responsive, more solicitous of workplace and product safety. But by and large this appears not to have been the case.

If the Kingdom of God has come and is to come and if it is characteristically a community predisposed to the cause of victims, then it would appear necessary to undertake a reversal of priorities in tort law. Safety should be the primary concern. Surely, says Richard Abel, "we think first about the safety of those we love and not about whether they will be compensated if they are injured."[33] Furthermore, when injury does occur, the response ought to be "personal care rather than [consignment of] the victim to the scrap heap of welfare and custodial institutions."[34] Instead of adjudicating the legal-technical issues of damages, fault and cause, civil litigation could then be devoted to the administration of care, and communal, mutual responsibility, or so it might be argued in a full examination of the example.

And I can imagine drawing other examples from criminal law, where there is system overload and collapse but no improvement in resolving the complex problems presented by criminals, their crimes and their victims. No real attempt is being made to undertake even simple first steps, such as exploring the possibilities of restitution rather than imprisonment as a response to crimes against property or requiring the imprisoned to earn high school degrees.

Further examples might focus on lawyer-client relationships or legal education or trial and appellate judging.

My point is that, if we live in a world become the Kingdom of God, the conditions of our lives have been fundamentally altered. Law has a different context. A vocational life that attempts to discern and become a part of the form being taken by the Kingdom of God is a life composed of episodes following upon the advent of a transcendent community predisposed to the cause of the victims.

III. CONCLUSION

The constitutive image of the lawyer is of the advocate, but this is also an image of the royal messiah. There can no longer be a workaday professional world for lawyers where significant ethical-political issues exist only at the remote boundaries. Responsibility and anticipation permeate the

---

[33]R. Abel, "Torts," *The Politics of Law: A Progressive Critique*, ed. D. Kairys (New York, 1982), 185, 196.
[34]Ibid., 199.

whole. The Kingdom of God is in our midst. Every case and every client bears significant potential in its advent—or so a full experiment might hope to demonstrate.

After the treaties of peace ending World War II were signed, a few Japanese soldiers remained out of contact on remote South Pacific islands where they had been dispatched as isolated, forward lookouts to detect enemy movements. They hid in the jungle. News of the end of the war never reached them. Later, when word could be sent, evidently because of their circumstances or their devotion to the emperor, they did not believe what they heard. They fought on. Sightings of such soldiers were reported for as long as two decades after 1945. They lived out their lives unaccepting of the reality that peace had been declared.

An adequate account of what the Kingdom of God is for American jurisprudence would spell out the terms of the armistice for law and lawyering.

THE TENSION BETWEEN LAW IN AMERICA AND THE RELIGIOUS TRADITION*

Thomas L. Shaffer

We need a communal instrument of moral reasoning in the light of faith precisely to defend the decision-maker against the stream of conformity to his own world's self-evidence. Practical moral reasoning, if Christian, must always be expected to be at some point subversive.[1]

John Howard Yoder

The only useful way I know of even to begin to consider tensions between the religious tradition and the law is to describe the religious tradition from within, as it has understood itself. The religious tradition in our culture has not understood itself as a philosophy or a preference or a point of view. It has understood itself as a sequence of facts that those in the tradition learn to remember. Faithfulness to the tradition depends on truthful memory rather than intellectual justification. The religious tradition is not a sub-culture, not a "world within the world," not a constituency. Its principal mandate is to preserve in memory—in teaching, ritual, calendar and narrative—a sequence of events, a "master story."[2]

Law is alien to the religious tradition. Law may become an idol for the religious tradition. A primary tension thus revolves around that which is authoritative for the religious tradition.

The response of the particular people to law is twofold. First, it is a response of caution because this particular, remembering people is wary of circumstances that might impair its memory. Second, it is a response of prophetic witness because the particular, remembering people knows something about the destiny of human persons.[3]

* This essay was originally presented at a conference on "Law and the Ordering of Our Life Together," sponsored by the Rockford Institute Center for Religion and Society. I am grateful for the assistance and advice of Harlan R. Beckley, Emily Albrink Fowler, Mark H. Grunewald, Stanley Hauerwas, Andrew W. McThenia, David K. Millon, Brian C. Murchison, Andrew P. Shaffer, Mary M. Shaffer, Gregory M. Stanton, John Howard Yoder and those who participated in the conference discussions.

[1]J. Yoder, *The Priestly Kingdom* (Notre Dame, 1984), 40.

[2]M. Goldberg, *Jews and Christians: Getting Our Stories Straight* (Nashville, TN, 1985).

[3]I understand or define our "religious tradition" to mean the Hebraic tradition, the tradition of Jews and Christians. The quotations, and the larger position taken in this introduction, are developed in J. Hartt, *A Christian Critique of American Culture* (New York, 1967), and in

I. The Law in Canaan

Tension between law and a religious tradition is presented in the call to a particular people to avoid accommodation to the surrounding culture and to treat with suspicion the law of that culture. This tension is reflected in the story of the children of Israel assembled on the borders of Canaan. It is the story of the response of the particular people to their call and to the law of Canaan.

A. The Tradition of the Particular People

Israel on the borders of Canaan is a powerless people, decimated by plague and battle, by discord and by a generation of wandering and living hand-to-mouth in the desert. One of its two principal leaders, Aaron, is dead. The other, Moses, is dying. But Moses says to them, "You are a people consecrated to the Lord your God; of all the peoples on earth the Lord your God chose you to be the treasured people."[4] He further enjoins them to *consume* the more numerous people occupying Canaan, to take over the land and to hold it as a treasure and a promise from God himself.

The people of Israel are not to *adapt*: "You shall not intermarry with them. . . . You shall tear down their altars, smash their pillars, cut down their sacred posts, and consign their images to the fire. . . . You shall not worship their gods. . . . You shall consign the images of their gods to the fire; you shall not covet the silver and gold on them and keep it for yourselves for that is abhorrent to the Lord your God."[5] Israel is to be—as it was, and as it is—a particular people in Canaan and among the nations.

The gentiles who later became the Christian church laid claim to this particularity. Their story and their picture is the Cross, which is a symbol both of what the nations do to Jews and of what people do to one another in the name of the law.

Jesus before the power of Rome and Moses at the borders of Canaan are signs of insistence on particularity rather than on power. Moses tells Israel at the borders of Canaan to remember, and remembering, to obey. Moses tells them that the purpose of their testing in the desert was neither

---

Goldberg, *Jews and Christians.* Hartt writes: "[T]he church does not behave faithfully when it tries to make the Resurrection somehow intellectually digestible, if not exactly palatable, for the refined sensitivities of contemporary man (who has buried enough victims of his modernity to have little stomach for meeting them all face to face sometime). Rather, the faithful church interprets what man is and ought to become in the light of Resurrection. If someday we all must be confronted by every last one of our victims, many of whom we could not name if we wanted to, it is only because God who brought Jesus Christ from the dead loves them and loves all with the infinite love which will prevail even over our mortal guilt." Hartt, *A Christian Critique,* 135.

[4]Deuteronomy 7:6 (Jewish Publication Society translation).

[5]Deuteronomy 7:5, 16, 25 (Jewish Publication Society translation).

athletic nor moral; it was to prepare them to live in dependence on God.[6] Moses tells them that the occupants of Canaan will be dislodged only little by little. (As it turns out, the Canaanites are not destroyed so much as they are assimilated—which is what happens to the Romans, too. The Torah does not say the Canaanites were to be destroyed; it says they were to be consumed.)

So this particular people has mostly to *be* what it is, a particular people "at odds with dominant assumptions ... chosen, summoned, commanded ... promised ... concrete and specific ... who know so well who they are that they value and celebrate their oddity in the face of every seductive and powerful imperial imperative."[7]

The particular people are, then, wary of the law. They have been told to be wary of it, because the law may be a god in Canaan: "You shall not worship their gods! You shall not even be curious about their gods" (Deuteronomy 12:30). The radical questions for the particular people are (1) whether the law, in American liberal democracy, is in Canaan; and (2) if there, is the law an idol?[8]

---

[6]Thus, I read, there have been centuries of rabbinical sermons on the difference between the *goy kadosh* (holy nation) of Exodus 19:6 and the *am kadosh* of Deuteronomy 28:9. Israel in the desert, in its struggle with God, had begun as a holy *nation*, but it had emerged at the borders of Canaan as a holy *people*.

[7]W. Brueggemann, "Passion and Perspective: Two Dimensions of Education in the Bible," *Theology Today* 42 (1985): 172, 173.

[8]There are two definitional difficulties here: What does "particular people" mean? And how is "law in Canaan" different, as law, from the law that Israel brings with it from Sinai?

"Particular people" is meant to describe Israel's experience from the time of God's promise to Abraham, through 400 years of slavery in Egypt, through the Exodus, Sinai and the generation in the desert. Brueggmann's words, quoted in the text, express the idea: "While Torah acknowledges that 'others' are there and struggles with how Israel is to relate to and be understood in the midst of the others . . . , it is nurture in particularity that is the main focus, a nurture that produces adults who know so well who they are and what is commanded that they value and celebrate their oddity. . . ." Ibid., 173. This particularity is claimed for gentile Christians by the early church in, e.g., Romans 9–11. See F. Mussner, *Tractate on the Jews* (Philadelphia, 1984), 45–51. There is, within Christian ecclesiology, an historical debate about how "particular" the people of God in the church are to be. In my observation, all sides of that debate hold to a significant particularity. On current aspects of this debate that have to do with the Christian ethics of Stanley Hauerwas, see a series of three papers, by W. Miscamble, C.S.C., M. Quirk and S. Hauerwas in *Theology Today* 44 (1986): 69–94.

The law that Israel brings with it from Sinai was law in approximately the modern sense of coercively enforced mandate until the destruction of the Second Temple and the beginning of the Talmudic period. It was not law for the most part, in this modern sense, after that time. I want to distinguish within Judaism and within the history of the church between the normative convictions of the particular people that are enforced with coercion and convictions that are not enforced with coercion but are the content of what Yoder calls "the hermeneutics of peoplehood." That is the argument in the section of this paper that addresses the question of how the church deals with the church. It is, in any case, and within the context of the image and story of Israel at the borders of Canaan, sufficient to say that the law Israel brings from Sinai is not likely to become an idol, since it is God's own Way of Life (Torah). The law (in the modern sense) that

Idols in this imagery are things the Canaanites make with their hands—including, perhaps, wooden figures that can be carried around, as Queequeg carried his little god into his room at the inn on Nantucket, where he prayed to it and Ishmael watched in horror.[9] Ishmael was on the borders of Canaan in that room at the inn; he tried at first not to be curious about this little wooden god. The shifting images—from Canaan to Nantucket and back again—suggest a point: the idols are abhorent only so long as they *are* idols. What makes them idols is determined by how the Canaanites feel about them.

After Israel had established itself in Canaan, the Israelites discovered Canaanite artifacts and wanted to keep them as antiques and momentos (as our parents kept Nazi military decorations). Some of these Canaanite artifacts had been idols (perhaps they were like Queequeg's little wooden god). The rabbis had to decide whether such artifacts could be kept, in view of the stern injunction Moses gave Israel at the borders of Canaan. They ruled that the artifact could be kept by the Israelite who had it, even if it had been an idol, if it could be shown that the Canaanite who had once worshipped it had himself turned from worshipping it, had repudiated it. Mutilation of the idol, for example, would be favorable evidence of such repudiation.[10]

If that distinction can be appropriated on this question of tension between law and the religious tradition, the outcome will be this: the particular people is wary of the law in Canaan (in America); it may be an idol. But it may not be, and in that case the particular people need not be so wary. The way to determine whether the law is an idol is to see whether the people for whom it is the law have come to worship it. If not, the law has no particular danger for the particular people, and, indeed, may have value (as the rabbis, and, indeed, the text of the Torah, recognize moral value in the traditions of the *goyim*).[11]

The particular people's wariness of the law is not entirely mythic. It is evident, for example, in the pastoral letter on the American economy by the Roman Catholic Bishops of the United States.[12] American polity and the

---

is in Canaan may be, but is not necessarily, idolatrous. The particular people who enter Canaan have to determine whether the law there is idolatrous, and then behave accordingly.

[9]H. Melville, *Moby Dick* (New York, 1851), ch. 10.

[10]I hazard an example of modern mutilation of the idols of the law that would be evidence that the person whose law it was (or is) either does not make of the law an idol or, having once done that, has turned from idolatry as the long-dead Canaanite had turned from his wooden artifact. The movement in American jurisprudence called "Legal Realism," and its modern descendant, "Critical Legal Studies," both put marks on the law that would be evidence to my metaphorical rabbi, evidence that it is safe to own the artifact.

[11]Sometimes, when reading the conservative end of the argument against the Critical Legal Studies Movement, I see signs of idolatry—or, at least, I cannot find evidence of mutilation. See further, T. Shaffer, "Levinson builds the Kingdom: Comment on Professing Law," *St. Louis University Law Journal* 31 (1986): 73.

[12]United States Catholic Conference, "Economic Justice for All: Catholic Social Teaching and the U.S. Economy," *Origins* 16 (Nov. 27, 1986): 409.

American economy are, to the Bishops, a means of communication, not an idol. There is ample evidence of mutilation so that they need not be concerned about polity or economy being an idol for those they address. But both polity and economy are (and here the Bishops are relentlessly ambivalent) alien. The Bishops speak of believers "going out into" the economy. They speak of the "virtues of citizenship" as compatible with faith; yet they insist on the traditional distinction in Catholic thought between society and the state. They hold out a vision for humankind that is neither American nor republican but messianic.[13] "The church," they say, "is not bound to any particular economic, political or social system; it has lived with many . . . evaluating each according to moral and ethical principles."[14] This theology is based on the Hebraic understanding that human dignity is a higher value than either prosperity or individual rights; that community is a higher value than individual autonomy; that the moral minimum for the person in a just society is not only economic and political freedom but also adequate material and personal participation in common life. The Bishops neither endorse nor offer a system. They instead identify the system we have as pragmatic and judge it in terms of whether it allows for the particular people to search here for justice. They mean by justice what the Hebrew prophets meant.

B. Government and the Church

As one looks at Israel and Canaan, at the Roman gibbet and the Jewish followers of Jesus who stand looking at the gibbet, the tension between law and the religious tradition is evident in the question of who is responsible for the church. First, there is the particular people tending to itself, the question of what, in Christian terms, the church is to do about the church.[15] It is on this point that I propose to appropriate Yoder's "hermeneutics of peoplehood."[16] Second, there is the question of the government doing something about the church, a sub-topic of standard legal study that is coming to be called "the law of religion."

What the church is to do about the church becomes an issue because of the nature of the claim made by the particular people. What is Israel's claim

---

[13]"The Christian vision is based on the conviction that God has destined the human race and all creation for 'a kingdom of truth and life, of holiness and grace, of justice, love and peace'" (quoting the preface of the Mass for the Feast of Christ the King). Ibid., 425.

[14]Ibid.

[15]There is also the parallel question of the business of Canaan tending to Canaan, of Caesar tending to Caesar, of what the government is to do about the government. Government and the economy it regulates are the apparatus, the *institution*, within American liberal democracy. The tending (or mocking or subverting) of that institution is the business of lawyers. We lawyers are, as Alexis de Toqueville noticed a century and a half ago, the only American aristocracy. A. de Toqueville, *Democracy in America* (New York, 1835), 122–127. Fussing about the government is, always and everywhere, the business of the American legal aristocracy.

[16]Yoder, *The Priestly Kingdom*, 15–45.

at the borders of Canaan? What is the nature of the claim the Christian church made when it appropriated for the gentiles the particularity of Israel? What is most important is that the claim of particularity is not a claim to power or to a right to power. It has nothing to do with *rights*; it is a matter of faithfulness to memory.[17] Israel *hears* (in the classic prayer of the Torah) what the Lord has done and what He has insisted upon; it hears in order to remember slavery in Egypt as well as Exodus and Sinai. Its particularity is that it hears and remembers. The Christian Church likewise hears the words and witnesses the deeds of Christ and remembers and recounts them. Christian theology is, therefore, as Bonhoeffer expressed, the memory of the church.[18] The particularity of the people depends on their memory and faithfulness. Such memory is not a moral boast, not a claim to have *fulfilled* the expectations of God, for we know they have not been fulfilled. Jews pray, on the Day of Atonement, "[We] are not so arrogant and stiffnecked as to say . . . [that] we . . . have not sinned. . . ." The particularity of the people of God is normative, but it is not the boast that the particular people is obedient, nor the claim that it has been obedient.

This point about boasting is important because the claim of particularity has to take history into account. Israel and the church recognize that they have failed; their particular history and their particular histories are histories of failure, of disobedience and of abandonment. Moses said to Israel at the borders of Canaan, "[F]rom the day that you left the land of Egypt until you reached this place, you have continued defiant toward the Lord."[19] The particular people is stiff-necked, as Jewish and Christian Scripture says; but, still, they learn to remember that they are a particular people. When the children of Israel worshipped the golden calf, the Lord said He would destroy them and give to Moses a new people. But Moses argued for the only people he had: what would a *new* people be like? His argument was even that this people was the only people *God* had: what would a new people be like for God? What would the nations say about what the Lord did to the old people? Moses's argument, which was successful, was that not even the Lord could disown this particular people.[20]

---

[17]Why, then, is it even a "claim" To take this memory up as a claim is to acknowledge in some way that the religious tradition feels it necessary to justify itself before "the nations." I think that is true today. It may not have been true for either Moses or the primitive church. But it is true, at least in well-settled habit, of the religious tradition in America. The reason I use the language of *claim* here is not to accede to a demand for Kantian (or epistemological) justification. It is only to attempt to expand on what I mean by particularity. My purpose is, therefore, part of the issue of the church tending to the church, of Israel being Israel. What I want mostly to suggest is that this is not the government's business, that, when the church has made this particularity the government's business, it has not been faithful.

[18]C. Fant, *Bonhoeffer: Worldly Preaching* (Nashville, TN, 1975), 27.

[19]Deuteronomy 9:22–24.

[20]Exodus 32; Deuteronomy 9–10. W. Plaut and B. Bamberger, *The Torah: A Modern Commentary* (New York, 1981), 1384–1404.

What the church should do about the church is important to the tension between the religious tradition and law for two reasons. First, the people of God have failed to remember who they are and have surrendered their particularity to the government. Israel did this when it demanded a king. The early church surrendered its particularity when it baptized Constantine, and the medieval church did so with its pagan theories of church and state. The congregational church in the Reformation surrendered its particularity when it turned its procedures over to local government and, in the name of order, abandoned the procedures it had discovered in the New Testament. Particular people and the particular people itself failed its memory in many ways. Second, particularity includes attention to the processes by which people within the church deal with one another. This, again, is not a matter of moral or communal superiority. It is not a matter of civil liberties, nor of a philosophical view of the human person. It is a matter of remembering how the Lord told the particular people to conduct its own business—and that is with curiosity about and concern for one another, with openness. The reason for this openness is that the God of Israel comes to people in the community by way of other people. In Israel, and in the teaching of Jesus and of St. Paul, teaching authority depends upon the observance of an "open congregational process."[21] The particular people is not dependent on an establishment—on any sort of institution guaranteed by coerced order—but on listening to one another, on the "communal quality of belief."[22] When the procedure is observed, as it is, for example, in post-Talmudic Judaism, validity is sought not in a liberal-democratic "marketplace of ideas" but in the presence of God.

The *midrash* illustrates what an "open congregational process" is among the Jews. On an issue involving levitical purity, Rabbi Eliezer argued forcefully but did not convince the others in his house of study. He called on a carob tree to prove him right, and the carob tree moved, miraculously. He called on a stream of water, and it began to flow backwards. Eliezer's colleagues said that a carob tree and a stream of water cannot serve as proof. Eliezer called on the walls of the house of study, and the walls began to lean downward. Rabbi Joshua said to the walls, "What business is it of yours?" and the walls stopped moving. (However, out of respect for Rabbi Eliezer, the walls did not move back to where they had been.) Rabbi Eliezer then called on God Himself, and a voice came from Heaven saying that Rabbi Eliezer was right. Rabbi Joshua got to his feet and said, quoting the Torah (Deuteronomy 30:12), "It is not in the heavens!"[23] Later, Rabbi Jeremiah

---

[21]Yoder, *The Priestly Kingdom*, ch. 1. Compare the allusions to authority in the Catholic Bishops' letter, "Economic Justice for All."

[22]Yoder, *The Priestly Kingdom*, 24.

[23]In context: "For this Law that I enjoin on you today is not beyond your strength or beyond your reach. It is not in heaven, so that you need to wonder, 'Who will cross the seas for us and bring it back to us, so that we may hear it and keep it?' No, the Word is very near to you, it is in your mouth

said this meant that the Torah had been given on Mount Sinai, once and for all, and, after that, it was for God's people to decide what the words of Torah meant. Rabbi Nathan was told by the prophet Elijah that God heard the argument Rabbi Joshua made that day, and God said, "My children have prevailed against Me!"

That *midrash* established the relevant jurisdiction, but it did not explicate procedure. For this, there is another *midrash*, one that involved an argument between the School of Shammai and the School of Hillel, which occurred a short time before the birth of Jesus. In this case, the voice from Heaven said that both schools were proclaiming the words of God, but that the law should be decided according to the School of Hillel. The scholars wondered how that could be: if both schools taught the words of God, why should one prevail over the other? The Talmud says it was because the Sages of Hillel were tolerant, friendly and modest. "They studied not only their own traditions, but also those of the School of Shammai. Indeed, they transmitted the teachings of the School of Shammai before they transmitted their own teachings."[24]

The tension between law and the religious tradition also arises in asking what the government is to do about the church. What the government usually wants to do about the church is to appropriate its energy, to turn religion into civil religion, to render the church either subservient or irrelevant. For government—notably liberal democratic government—will not countenance a moral authority that interposes itself between the republic and its citizens.

The government's claim to be the sole institution of authority in society is directed against the church, as it is directed against other social groups. It is evident, for example, in the situation of groups of workers in Britain and America. Such groups begin, 200 years ago, in community, and, no doubt, they begin with the memory of their particularity as religious people. The communities in which they begin are civil and economic (that is, all of the workers in a place). They are also "professional" (that is, related to a particular kind of work—a "practice," perhaps, in the way Aristotelians use that word). They seek, as "industrial democracy" forms itself within liberal democracy, to exercise collective influence. Almost as soon as they begin to do that, they are condemned by the government on the ground that they are coercive. They are understood—correctly, I think—as making a radical challenge to the anthropology of liberal democracy, the anthropology that says each of us is radically alone and is best served through governmental guarantees of individual autonomy. The community of workers is under-

---

and in your heart for your observance." Deuteronomy 30:11–14 (Jerusalem Bible). Both of these *midrashim* are translated in J. Petuchowski, *Our Masters Taught* (New York, 1982), 41, 43.
    [24]Ibid.

stood—correctly, I think—as subversive of republican government and heretical within the orthodoxy of Enlightenment politics.

These challenges from associations of workers were met with the legal rhetoric of coercion: no collective moral authority may stand between the republic and its citizens. The legal rubric for this included charges that associations of workers were common law criminal conspiracies and that they interfered with common law freedom of contract. But the meaning of the legal charges was that these associations were an illegitimate locus of power within liberal democracy.

The resolution of this struggle in modern industrial democracies was that these associations of workers were appropriated by the government. They now function through the "distinctively 'republican' device" of state-supervised elections.[25] The organic character they once had, through the commonality of being in a community, through the commonality of sharing a skill or even through common political purposes has been sacrificed to the state's interest in the orderly production of commodities and in industrial peace. Under the label of its interest in civil liberties, the state now supervises even the relation between a labor association and each of its members, one curious feature of which is a legal distinction between the interests of the members of the association and the association's "ideological activities."[26] Wages are the business of state-supervised labor unions; ideology is not.

The swap that labor made is one that appears to have resolved an often violent tension between workers and the government, but one can read modern labor history as a history of government intrusion into the lives of organic communities.[27] "Government impinged on working-class life in the family, the neighborhood and the factory, and in schools, parks and saloons."[28] It impinged pervasively in the work of working-class life.[29] Government did all of this by securing itself from the "ideological activities" that had formed the associations in the first place—"subversive moral reasoning," in Yoder's phrase.

The religious tradition has a similar tendency to trade its particularity for security and influence. The Roman Catholic Bishops of this country, for example, address a similar issue when they speak to business managers in terms of trusteeship and of vocation. The beneficiaries of these trusts the Bishops mention are not all or even principally the investment bankers who

[25]C. Becker, review of Tomlins, *The State and the Unions* (Cambridge, MA, 1985), *Harvard Law Review* 100 (1987): 672.

[26]*Abood v. Detroit Board of Education*, 431 U.S. 209, 236 (1977).

[27]Becker, "Review of Tomlins."

[28]Ibid., 686.

[29]The Roman Catholic Bishops seem to me to have missed this fact. They persist in regarding modern American labor organizations not as institutions, and, in fact, institutions largely under the control of the government, so much as organic associations of workers.

manipulate capital on Wall Street. The vocation is not, when seen truthfully, a call to profit for investors. But if one looks even casually at labor law, or securities law, or the developing law that regulates manipulations of investor power, one finds it hard to detect any principled difference between a worker and a robot.

There is a useful analogy between associations of workers surrendering themselves to the government and the perennial tendency of religious associations to trade their particularity for security and influence. In each case the radical claim is a claim about memory, and in each case—as the Bishops put it—moral substance has to do with the dignity of persons in communities more than with rights in a system of public order.

II. UNDERSTANDING THE TENSION FOR A PARTICULAR PEOPLE

The possibility that law in Canaan may be an idol poses for the particular people the challenge of being faithful to the call of their religious tradition. Such faithfulness contains two responses: caution and witness.

A. Caution

Moses did not tell the spies who had checked out Canaan for him to ask the Canaanites what they thought about Israel's mandate from God. He did not negotiate on the matter of the idols even though, had he really been interested in being responsible for a peaceful and religious public order, he would have. Some accommodation on the matter of idols would evidently have saved the successors of Moses from war, civil strife and apostasy. It would have served the evident interests of both law and religion. But Moses did not negotiate. His mandate was to consume the people and destroy their idols.

There was a sort of security investigation of potential converts in the primitive (Roman) church, in which a person seeking baptism was asked if he had anything to do with the government—whether, for example, he was a soldier or a judge. If he was, he was told he would have to give up being a soldier or a judge. If he wanted to keep his imperial office, he was denied baptism. It would have made sense—as it did later, after Constantine—to have baptized a general or two and lots of judges. It would have led to a more religious and more peaceful public order, but the leaders of the church saw the issue as Moses saw the idols of Canaan—the business of the church is to remember and to celebrate its oddity.[30] The Jews, then and now, will show

---

[30]They did and those who survived were successful, for a while, at being odd. R. Wilken, *The Christians as the Romans Saw Them* (New Haven, CT, 1984). This view of the church is sometimes identified as "sectarian." That designation may be fruitful for ecclesiological discussion. See the essays on the work of Stanley Hauerwas in *Theology Today* 44 (1987): 69–94. For present purposes that designation raises a narrower and simpler question: whether my "particular people" position is an assertion that can be argued within and without the religious

us Christians how that is done.

The particular people will not bow down to the government's idols. This is a significant limitation for participation in American liberal democracy, a limitation that has often been violated by believers.[31] Thomas Jefferson referred to America as God's new Israel. The particular people should, I think, regard that appropriation as idolatrous, and they should consequently be suspicious of Jefferson's political theology. Abraham Lincoln shook his head over such rhetoric and said we Americans were God's almost chosen people. Jefferson's phrase, and phrases like it ("a city on a hill," "the righteous empire") are invitations to idolatry that have been accepted by some Jews and Christians and refused by others.[32]

David Hoffman, the founder of American legal ethics and an eloquent Jeffersonian as well as a Christian, spoke of American law as a temple and of lawyers as priests who served in the temple. "Ministers at a holy altar," he called us.[33] Some of the later excesses of the social-gospel movement, particularly the claim that American democracy *was* the church, were even worse.[34] Those were failures within the particular people that the church claims to be. At such times, and as a consequence of such times, the faithful have had sometimes to say, with Thoreau, that the best people are in jail. It is not a quaint issue, not an historical issue. It has been the moral (and even political) substance of the long, careful pastoral letters that have issued from church leadership (in most of the "mainline" Christian denominations) in the last five years—letters, particularly, about the worship of nuclear weapons and worship of the capitalist economy. Worship—bowing down to idols—is the issue discussed in those pastoral documents.

Issues such as abortion, capital punishment, nuclear weapons and the obsession (a sort of negative idolatry) of the current federal government with

---

tradition. To the extent that the political or social order is idolatrous, my position is limited as an intellectual argument. (But see Genesis 9:1–17.) To the extent that the idols have been mutilated, though, so that witness—moral witness, from the religious tradition—is possible, the "particular people" position is as arguable as any other in the "marketplace of ideas." I elaborate this point in "Moral Theology in Legal Ethics," *Capital University Law Review* 12 (1983): 179. The Roman Catholic Bishops' letter on the economy is an illustration of that fuller sort of moral argument.

[31]Political theology is, of course, a discursive subject within the family of believers. Pastor Neuhaus and my friend and mentor Stanley Hauerwas argue about it: R. Neuhaus, *The Naked Public Square* (Grand Rapids, MI, 1984); S. Hauerwas, *Against the Nations* (Notre Dame, 1985). Their argument is within, and, as far as I can tell, is controlled by, the internal processes I describe above, from the Midrash and from Yoder's *The Priestly Kingdom*. I attempted to assay the jurisprudence of this intrafamilial discussion in my paper, "Jurisprudence in the Light of Hebraic Faith," *Notre Dame Journal of Law, Ethics, and Public Policy* 1 (1984): 77.

[32]M. Marty, *Righteous Empire: The Protestant Experience in America* (New York, 1970).

[33]D. Hoffman, "Resolutions on Professional Deportment," *A Course of Legal Study*, 2d ed. (Baltimore, 1836).

[34]I have been helped on this point by J. Dawson, "The Religion of Democracy in Early Twentieth-Century America," *Journal of Church and State* 27 (1985): 46.

East-West international polity, at the expense of North-South polity (and, therefore, at the expense of human dignity) are all examples of caution in the religious tradition's approach to law. Stanley Hauerwas speaks thus of the people and institutions in America which claim "that Christians . . . must be willing to choose sides and kill in order to preserve the social orders in which they find themselves."[35] "As Christians," he says, "when we accept that alternative it surely means that we are no longer the church that witnesses to God's sovereignty over all nations, but instead we have become part of the world."[36] We have become part of Canaan, kneeling to Canaan's idols. Hauerwas's position is the one I identify as caution in the particular people. When the religious tradition, or some significant part of it, takes a position that refuses, as Hauerwas puts it, "to step aside with the world," the tenor of the religious position taken is caution, wariness, distrust lest what the world offers is an idol.

B. Witness

The second response of a particular people to the law in Canaan is what the religious tradition calls prophetic—appropriating for itself the style and purpose of the Hebrew prophets and particularly the greatest of Israel's teachers and prophets, *Mosheh Rabbenu*, Moses. This response appropriates the religious tradition's most ancient understanding of why it *is* a particular people. Israel and the church are a particular people in order to bring the one God to all of mankind. This people is among the nations for purposes of witness and atonement. The chosen people is a hard-hearted and stiff-necked people, and, in that, it reflects the sinfulness and stubborness of humankind. Israel is sinful and stubborn on the borders of Canaan; the church has been sinful and stubborn in, say, its recurrent spasms of hatred of the Jews and its craven failure during the Holocaust.[37]

But the particular people is also the agent of atonement. It returns—it is able to return—and in turning to witness (*teshuvah*), to covenant and *mitzvot*, it atones for all humankind. It is prophet and priest. It atones for itself, and, vicariously, for the world. The notion of vicarious atonement has been prominent and troublesome in the church, but it is a notion the church appropriated from the Torah. Moses did it first. Moses went up and down the slopes of Sinai, after the Lord said he would destroy all of Israel and give Moses a *new* people. Moses fasted for 120 days, prostrated himself in the dust, argued and changed the mind of the Lord. Israel was not destroyed. Moses was successful. He atoned; he brought Israel and the Lord back to at-one-ment.

[35]S. Hauerwas, *Against the Nations*, 129.

[36]Ibid., 129.

[37]Finally, I suppose, this stiff-necked stubborness and moral failure is a *comfort* to the world. As one of President Carter's friends said, explaining Southern Baptist theology, "People are a bunch of bastards, but God loves them anyway."

A generation later, when Moses told the people who were about to enter Canaan about what he had done at Sinai, he spoke to them as if they had all been there, as if *they* had worshipped the golden calf—although they were the children and grandchildren of those who had worshipped the calf. Moses was an old man about to die. The people who heard him there were different persons, but they were the same particular people. They listened to the agent of their atonement and understood—some of them—some of their Jewish children, and some of their Christian children—that his being prophet and priest for them was an illustration of their being prophet and priest for all of mankind, suffering servants, as Isaiah put it, servants of the Lord.

An example of a prophetic witness is the situation of the communities in America that aggregate wealth, build empires and employ people for the production of goods and services—the business corporations. I have puzzled for some time over the situation of the people who preside over these communities, the situation of the managers and directors of corporate businesses, and this particularly in reference to the manipulations of investor power that are involved in struggles for corporate control. Such people are a focus for the tensions between the religious tradition and American law, and this particularly in reference to the way the religious tradition reaches out from itself not only with caution but also with prophetic witness.

Most of the energy of a modern American law teacher is given to training young people who plan to serve such enterprises as lawyers. Very little of this energy is directed to them as people working in communities where prophetic witness might be possible, let alone to the substance of the prophetic witness. In modern law schools, prophetic witness is not easy to explicate,[38] for such schools have systematically—theologically!—discounted, discouraged and disapproved of the invocation of the religious tradition as important, or even interesting.

The business manager is a person who might be influenced—even through her lawyers—by the particular people's faithfulness, in its remembering that this people does not bow down to the idols of Canaan and, especially, in its remembering that it is a light to the nations, the salt of the earth. If we can agree that such an influence is alive in this business manager, then we can see her as remembering a story that might show us what the tensions between law and the religious tradition are like. I propose to think of her as a bearer of the influence of which Jesus (and other rabbis) spoke, and, therefore, I do not think of her as merely an example or an illustration, because that would be to use this person as if she were a calculator for interest balancing, for costs and benefits. I want to think of her, instead, as a person who stumbles and strives, who fails and has triumphs,

---

[38]I speak of *schools*. Law firms are not nearly so blind, as I try to show in a chapter called "The Profession" in my forthcoming book, *Faith and the Professions* (Provo, UT, 1987).

including failures and triumphs she does not even see for what they are. She is, in other words, as Auden said, on a moral planet, tamed by terror.

The religious tradition speaks to this business manager in one or both of two ways. She is, first of all, addressed as one of the particular people. She may not think of herself in that way. *We* may not think of her in that way, but a person in our culture is unavoidably influenced by the religious tradition.[39] Many of those who act with moral courage do so because of this influence, whether or not they think of themselves as acting from religious motives. I do not recall from the 1950s that the young Jews who were murdered and buried in a dam in Mississippi were talked about as having done what they did because they were Jews. But I think they did. It is no accident, but is evidence of the presence of God, that American Jews are not the most prominent nor the wealthiest group in America, but are, consistently, the most generous in support of charity, with their money, their time and their courage.

We did not talk, in the 1960s, about the immolations of Dag Hammarskjld and Martin Luther King, Jr. as immolations of Christians. But that is what they were—as, perhaps, we now know better than we did then. The altruism of believers can be taken to be the ordinary exercise of civic good will, and often the contributors prefer to have their altruism taken that way. (Dr. King was, I think, an exception.) But, pursued more deeply, they are the actions of members of the particular people. They are the ordinary, daily way that members of a particular people figure out how to live in Canaan and still to live within the memory of the particular people. We only know that for sure when we probe the stories of the contributors, as we did in Hammarskjöld's "Markings," but it is always a possibility—and it may be more common—in lives lived far from the madding crowd.

This is not to argue that every decent action we see is, when probed deeply, a *mitzvah*. It is, rather, to argue that many of them are and to suggest that ordinary goodness may be a sign of the tension between the religious tradition and the law. Sometimes with devotion and with a prayer, no doubt, but more often because almost all of us are affected by the particularity of the Jews and the church—affected even for the better.

This businessperson has a vulnerability to the religious tradition because of where she comes from, and where she comes from speaks to her about how she should go about being the manager of a corporate business enterprise. The recent letter from the Roman Catholic Bishops may cause her, for example, to remember that her position is a *vocation*. She is *called* to do what she is doing, and what she is doing is administering wealth that has been assembled by and from the labor of others. Called by whom? We Catholics used to use the word "vocation" to mean those called to the

---

[39]I make a more extended argument on this point toward the end of T. Shaffer, "The Legal Ethics of Radical Individualism," *Texas Law Review* 65 (1987): 401, 426–428.

sisterhood or the priesthood. It means a personal, oral message from God. I think it usually comes in a dream. The Bishops, and most modern American Roman Catholics, now use the word differently. They are talking about being called out of the church, sent out from the particular people, to do something that is religiously important.

The Bishops did not shrink from spelling out (remembering) the implications of being called out of the church to manage a business. The maximization of profit is not the primary goal of the business, they said.[40] Profit is not preferred to the dignity and well-being of the persons and communities involved in the business. This is with reference to technological innovation, or moving to the Sun Belt, or with reference to the corporate community's response to an external bid for corporate control. To remember that business management is a vocation and a trust is to notice the tension between law and the religious tradition. "In U.S. *law*," the Bishops said, "the primary responsibility of managers is to exercise prudent business judgment in the interest of a profitable return to investors. But *morally* this legal responsibility may be exercised only within the bounds of justice to employees, customers, suppliers and the local community. Corporate mergers and hostile takeovers may bring greater benefits to shareholders, but they often lead to decreased concern for the well-being of local communities and make towns and cities more vulnerable to decisions made from afar."[41]

This is not a liberal-democratic argument. It is not primarily an argument made to "human experience and reason." It is not primarily *any* kind of argument, so much as it is a memory relevant to corporate law (of all things), within the particular people for which Bishops claim to be teachers. Teachers within this people are agents of memory.

The Bishops point out that the corporate business enterprise *is* a community. The influence the religious tradition exercises on this management person is a communal influence. It is the influence of neighborhood and family as well as religious congregation.[42] Because of those things in her life she knows what a community is, and she knows how to want to be in a community with those in her business enterprise. Her ordinary bent—which the Bishops claim for religious memory—is to regard her business as an organic community and to act for the welfare of that community. She can be corrupted, of course, so that she comes to act mostly for the preservation of her own power; but when she is not corrupted she acts from the motivation that the religious tradition calls "the common good." You can only talk about the common good from some substantive memory of what "common" means, and what the Bishops are after here is such a memory in America. This is not memory from the Enlightenment, from Mr. Jefferson's vision of a nation of

[40]Catholic Conference, "Economic Justice for All," 422.

[41]Ibid., 441–442.

[42]That was the thrust of R. Bellah, et al., *Habits of the Heart* (Berkeley, CA, 1985), but I think the authors there understated the differences between the religious tradition and civil religion.

people who would be good because they would be prosperous. This is memory from the religious tradition.

The religious tradition has an exact quarrel here with American law, and the Bishops assert it clearly: the law directs the corporate manager to an immoral course of action. She is called to be a trustee for those whose labor has produced the wealth she manages. Some of these are employees, some customers. Some live in the communities where the business operates, and some have invested their money in the business. A trustee is faithful to all of her beneficiaries. To prefer one and neglect the others is to betray her trust.

The Bishops also turn this point into a social argument, using the same words from the religious tradition—the words "vocation" and "trust." It is, as an argument, made from reason and experience, and perhaps it is even an argument that could be made from within the legal tradition.[43] (Although American law just now is less likely to talk about faithfulness than about balancing interests in a system of social costs and benefits.) The way the Bishops speak of trust is, for example, reminiscent of the way the chancellors spoke of the duty of a trustee in the law of trusts: the trustee has to be faithful to the competing demands of all of his beneficiaries. The beneficiary who is to receive principal after a life or a period of time will, for example, demand trust investments that preserve and increase principal; the beneficiary who receives current income demands investments that bring high income. The trustee's legal duty is to be faithful to both beneficiaries.

I think this argument, when made from the law (or from reason and experience), lacks a depth that the religious tradition is able to remember. There is a depth that realizes a trustee's duty is tragic; the religious tradition is able to bear the possibility that the call to be a trustee (in, say, a corporate business) is a call to tragedy. I don't mean here so much grand Grecian tragedies (although those may come) as I mean the ordinary, daily, bitter tragedies of laying people off from their jobs, of asking workers to take less pay, of deciding against a dividend that investors need. Faithfulness to trust involves ordinary tragedies like those, and Israel and the people of the Cross know they do. Their memory includes tragedy much more prominently than it includes triumph. What the particular people remember about tragedy is that, finally, fate is benign. Fate is the Father Who loves His children. Stanley Hauerwas says—speaking out of the memory that is the religious tradition, not out of the Greek dramatic and philosophical tradition—that

[43]There are many possibilities in our law, as Professor Berman's seminal scholarship continues persuasively to demonstrate. See H. Berman, *Law and Revolution: The Formation of the Western Legal Tradition* (Cambridge, MA, 1983); "Religious Foundations of Law in the West," *Journal of Law and Religion* 1 (1983): 3. I have seen possibilities, in Berman's view of law as fundamentally theological, for an ecumenical, modern, religious jurisprudence. See Shaffer, "Jurisprudence in the Light of Hebraic Faith," 77. My present position on law as (possibly) idolatry is not inconsistent with that earlier venture. An idol is always appealing in a religious way. It would not otherwise be an idol.

tragedy is the triumph of meaning over power.[44] The religious tradition is one of vocation and trust within a community that seeks the dignity of persons. One could say that reason, experience and law can call a trustee to faithfulness, but they cannot show him what to think about evident failure. This is perhaps to say that we do not need the religious tradition for morals, but we may need it to teach us what to do about morals.

The religious tradition is, therefore, paradoxical in its yearning for community. It yearns and yet it remembers that communities are tragic. It has to take into account the stern impassioned stress of a character such as Oliver Cromwell and, at the same time, looking at him, take account of the fact that, as he said, he knew how to deny petitions.

The Bishops' witness, using the words "vocation" and "trust," then, seems to say to the business manager that she cannot possibly be loyal to each of her beneficiaries, but she must be faithful to all of them. She can be faithful to many but can be loyal only to one. Faithfulness is the virtue (the habit) with which a good person negotiates the demands of each of those who wants her to be loyal. Attention to one beneficiary, to the exclusion of the others, is faithless; it is corrupt.

One example of this corruption is the current tendency among federal judges and regulators to evade the stresses of faithfulness with a formula or a principle. For example, the principle being suggested by one influential school of thought about corporate-takeover law is that the manager should resolve the stresses of faithfulness by regarding her enterprise as a set of investments which it is her duty to make profitable. The business press is filled with the arguments of those who insist that corporate managers see themselves in this way. There is also some evidence of broad resistance from corporate managers to that corrupted concept of management loyalty. Ultimately, the difficulty in adopting the point of view that sees the corporation primarily as an investment enterprise is that it corrupts even the profit motive itself. That is perhaps what Richard Neuhaus means when he talks of "the greedy, grasping, wasting ways of a capitalism that destroy memory, tradition and community."[45] It is in consequence and perhaps (as idolatrous) inherently a liquidation of community. Tim Metz, New York news editor for the *Wall Street Journal*, made that argument in his discussion of the recent biography of T. Boone Pickens:

[T]he book's diagnosis of the disease infecting a good part of industrial America rings true, but Mr. Pickens's prescription for the ailment doesn't.

His solution, dramatically underscored in his past takeover moves, is to end waste of assets by wresting them away from incompetent or

[44]S. Hauerwas, *Truthfulness and Tragedy* (Notre Dame, 1977), 73.
[45]*Wall Street Journal* (February 3, 1987), 30, C-5.

unresponsive managements and turning them back to the shareholders—through royalty trusts, share repurchases or takeovers.

In the end . . . that's liquidation. And liquidation is both short sighted and doubly unjust. It's shortsighted because it summarily eliminates the potential long-term shareholder, and by dismembering corporations, it reduces corporate philanthropy [I would include corporate citizenship], which is one of the social benefits of large corporations. It's unjust because it may reward rather than punish the bad manager . . . and because it often snatches jobs away from those rank-and-file employees who already are among the principal victims of mismanagement.[46]

A more subtle and more pernicious form of corruption of managers is the notion that managing a business is a *profession*. This is a familiar sort of corruption to those who study medicine and the law as ways of life. It occurs, for example, when a physician sees himself as having been removed from his organic community (communities) and transported into an institution. It is not the activity, the practice, that produces professionalism, nor the commonality that one feels when applying a difficult skill among colleagues. It is the institution that corrupts the practice, as the bar associations of the 1880s turned the American lawyer from an ethic of responsibility for the common good to an ethic of service to interests or as the aggregations of power in medicine turned those professionals from an ethic of patient well-being to an ethic of patient autonomy.[47]

Either sort of corruption turns my hypothetical manager from the community in which she finds herself toward the demand for loyalty from one constituency. This is what raises the common problem, commonly being talked about, of "how to discipline an autonomous, unresponsive management."[48] The spectre offered here, universally implied in any case, is that of a "management class" that labors mainly for the maintenance of its own power. The usual answer in liberal democracies is to turn the manage-

---

[46]*Wall Street Journal* (March 16, 1987), 20, C-4; *Business Week* reported the successful revival of A. & P., by its chairman, James Wood, through a system of giving employees power to decide what stores should do and a bonus equal roughly to the profit margin that investors usually expect in a business such as Mr. Wood's. The business world—and, indeed, Mr. Wood himself—tends to explain such successes in terms of sharing profits. It was interesting to me that an affected labor leader was quoted in this case as attributing success to the fact that employees were asked seriously what could be done to save this failing business. "You'd be amazed," the labor leader said, "at the willingness of people to participate when they can say anything without fear of reprisal," but also, as Mr. Wood's behavior demonstrated, with the assurance that they will be listened to. *Business Week* (December 22, 1986), 44.

[47]M. Schudson, "Public, Private and Professional Lives: The Correspondence of David Dudley Field and Samuel Bowles," *American Journal of Legal History* 12 (1977): 191. Both the legal and medical stories are discussed in my *Faith and the Professions*, ch. 5.

[48]L. Johnson, "Corporate Takeovers and Corporations: Who Are They For?" *Washington and Lee Law Review* 43 (1986): 781.

ment of business over to the government, in about the same way associations of workers turned their commonality into a part in the engine of industrial democracy. One way to find that result repulsive is to imagine what the consequences of government control will be (to compare the exchange of organic community among workers for the illusory security and faint promise of influence that has come from government bent on maintenance of production and industrial peace). Another and more theoretical way to find that result repulsive is to remember what an organic community is, and to want to preserve such a community, or to find it, or to *return* to it, and then to notice that the one thing law in liberal democracy cannot provide in theory, and has not provided in fact, is community.

The test for a communal approach to the law's treatment of corporate management in the takeover wars would be to seek for the law means of heightening the moral responsibility of managers, by giving them incentives to maintain business community—incentives that, according to my argument, they already have and want to have. These would be alternatives from the religious tradition in the sense in which I have tried to describe it, alternatives to the forces of professionalism (the management class—including the management class of lawyers and judges) and of social Darwinism (which amounts to the same thing, since social Darwinism works only with coercive guarantees it obtains from the government).

The law has sometimes evidenced a jurisprudence of such incentives. Some of the quainter of these include intra-familial immunity from civil liability, protection of parental responsibility for education, care and the support of children, and the rescue doctrine in tort. I mention the quaint legal incentives only to show that the law is not hopeless. Even lawyers know how to encourage and protect communities—even we remember how. There are better examples in business and within the takeover context itself. I am thinking of the recent development of the "silver parachute" and similar worker-protection devices in the practice of preventive corporate-takeover law.[49] These operate to assure that workers in an enterprise which is absorbed in investor wars will keep their human involvement in the business or at least will be paid well (as managers and investors are) for having to give it up. These help to protect the enterprise as community by making it less attractive to raiders, and they help to strengthen the commu-

---

[49]The "silver" or "tin" parachute is an extension of the more common provision of "golden" parachutes for corporate managers. The golden parachute is a contractual provision for severance pay in the event of discharge after merger, and some of them have paid individuals up to $100 million just for leaving. The "silver" or "tin" parachute is a provision for severance pay for workers who are laid off after a successful takeover. The provision is in smaller amounts and for shorter periods of time but is critically expensive for a takeover "raider" because of the large number of workers benefited by such a provision. T. Murray, "Here Comes the Tin Parachute," *Dun's Business Month* (January, 1987): 62.

nity by demonstrating that even employees, even in late twentieth century industrial America, are what Adolph Berle called "stakeholders."[50]

This preventive-law practice does not exclude shareholders. The manager I envision here—the one who knows about communities because she remembers her particular people—seeks, after all, to be faithful. Shareholders have a claim on the faithful manager, but their claim is strongest when it is consonant with claims being made by workers, local communities and consumers. This ordinary, everyday, human fact also shows that it is corrupting or self-deceptive or both to discourage the coincidence of interests or to refuse to recognize the coincidence of interests when it appears in an ordinary way. Both the corruption and the self-deception are frequently the product of defining law and political order in such a way that the highest good of the person is autonomy. The habit of defining autonomy as the highest good (or at least the highest good that the political and legal order can contemplate) is the tendency, if not the goal, in democratic-liberal political thought, as it is the tendency and the goal of the "adversary ethic" in the American legal profession.[51] Abraham Chayes once spoke of the people who fall within a business community as "all those having a relation of sufficient intimacy with the corporation or [are] subject to its power in a sufficiently specified way."[52] Commonality lies deeper than that; evidence of deeper commonality is the fact that the claims of constituencies within the community often coincide. Those who find evidence of God's purpose in such aggregations of people might say, as Karl Barth did, that God finds us where He put us.

This is to see management within a corporation as organic rather than either a commodity or a profession. It also suggests a way to talk about "corporate purpose" with a breadth that comprehends the customs and mores and moral judgments that every business person understands when she or he talks about moral behavior in business life. (My son Andy watched with me a recent television news discussion of the current crop of insider trading cases on Wall Street. At one point, Andy asked, with reference to federal law on the subject, "How could you expect that a person whose ethic is profit would obey a rule like that?" How indeed.)

My hypothetical manager, caught in the winds of a takeover, is invited by the evident tendency of American corporate law to decide in favor of short-term wealth maximization for speculator-shareholders. She is seen— by the law—to be a person who cannot bear to think about the burden of character and ambiguity in human enterprise, who must seek in place of such a burden some secure guide to behavior. The result of the law's escape in this situation, and perhaps the only possible means of escape, is to turn

---

[50]A. Berle, "Corporate Powers as Powers in Trust," *Harvard Law Review* 44 (1931): 1049.

[51]See Shaffer, "The Legal Ethics of Radical Individualism."

[52]A. Chayes, "The Modern Corporation and the Rule of Law," *The Corporation in Modern Society*, ed. E. Mason, (Cambridge, MA, 1960), 25.

corporate management over to the state. Arguing against this escape is what I think of as the ordinary tendency of a corporate manager to act as if she is in a community. There is, then, no decisive tension between investors and management, but there may be a wariness toward investors who are not in the community and not interested in being in it.[53]

The tendency among some academic commentators is to see the situation as providing a choice—either government control or "the market." But that is not a choice; the market *is* the government. The choice there—the one a prophet might notice—is between the law's rejection of the possibility of community in a business enterprise and its recognition of the yearning for community that comes to the manager as a result of the communities she comes from. The problem with the law's coercive support of "the market" (meaning the market in corporate shares, which, when dominated, gives power to determine who managers are) is that it rejects community and demands instead a coerced management loyalty to one of many constituencies in the enterprise. This is to move the dominance of business enterprise from a management that is criticized for self regard to dependence on the state as a guarantor of fairness.[54] Moses warned the children of Israel, as they paused on the borders of Canaan, to be wary of solutions like that, and to remember who they were.

[53]For a moment, the common law allowed corporate managers to make a distinction between speculator-investors and investors who are in the community. See, e.g., *Unocal Corporation v. Mesa Petroleum Co.*, 493 A. 2d 946 (Del., 1985). The federal government, however, quickly pre-empted that state common law judgment, and the law now denies the distinction.

[54]I have profited from using Johnson, "Corporate Takeovers and Corporations; C. Axworthy, "Corporation Law as if Some People Mattered," *University of Toronto Law Journal* 36 (1986): 392; R. Rodes, *Law and Liberation* (Notre Dame, 1986); and from personal conversation with and advice from Professor Johnson.

WRITINGS IN LAW AND RELIGION BY HAROLD J. BERMAN

Harold J. Berman is an acknowledged authority not only in the field of law and religion but also in the fields of Soviet law, comparative law, international trade law, jurisprudence and legal history. This bibliography is restricted to his published and unpublished works that deal, in whole or in part, with the subject of law and religion. A comprehensive bibliography of his writings on Soviet law, international trade law and comparative law is provided in W. Butler, P. Maggs and J. Quigley, eds., *Law After Revolution: Essays on Socialist Law in Honor of H. J. Berman* (Dobbs Ferry, NY, 1988).

A virtually complete collection of Harold Berman's published writings from 1948–1980—comprised of some 200 items—is available on microfiche in both the Langdell Library, Harvard Law School and the Law Library, Emory Law School. A virtually complete collection of course materials prepared by Harold Berman for his courses offered at Harvard Law School and Harvard College from 1948–1985 is also available in Langdell Library.

1938.

"Public Opinion" (unpublished thesis, Dartmouth College).

1939.

"Medieval English Equity" (unpublished thesis, London School of Economics).

1940.

"The Reception of Roman Law and the Reception Literature" (unpublished thesis, Yale University, Department of History).

1948.

"The Spirit of Soviet Law," *Washington Law Review* 23 (1948): 152.

"The Challenge of Soviet Law," *Harvard Law Review* 62 (1948): 220, 449.

1950.

Justice in Russia: An Interpretation of Soviet Law (Cambridge, MA, 1950) (also published in Japanese in Tokyo, 1956).

1955.

"The Editor's Preface," *The Christian Scholar* 38 (1955): 251 (talk at Harvard University Chapel).

1956.

On the Teaching of Law in the Liberal Arts Curriculum (Brooklyn, NY, 1956).

1958.

The Nature and Functions of Law: An Introduction for Students of the Arts and Sciences (Brooklyn, 1958).

"Limited Rule of Law," *Christian Science Monitor* (April 29, 1958): 9.

"The Devil and Soviet Russia," *The American Scholar* 27 (1958): 147.

1959.

"Love for Justice: The Influence of Christianity Upon the Development of Law," *Oklahoma Law Review* 12 (1959): 86.

1960.

"Teaching Law Courses in the Liberal Arts College: A Challenge to the Law Schools," *Journal of Legal Education* 13 (1960): 47.

1961.

"The Historical Background of American Law," *Talks on American Law*, ed. H. Berman (New York, 1961), 3 (translated and published in Portuguese in Rio de Janeiro, 1963; in Arabic in Cairo, 1964; in French in Paris, 1965; in Spanish in Chile and Mexico, 1965; in Vietnamese in Saigon, 1968; in Japanese in Tokyo, 1963 and 1969).

"Philosophical Aspects of America Law," ibid., 293.

1962.

"The Russian Orthodox Church," *Harvard Alumni Bulletin* (November 24, 1962); reprinted in *Christianity and Crisis* 23 (1963): 19.

1963.

Justice in the U.S.S.R.: An Interpretation of Soviet Law (Cambridge, MA, 1963) (a revision and expansion of *Justice in Russia: An Interpretation of Soviet Law*) (also published in Italian in Milan, 1965, and in Spanish in Barcelona, 1967).

1964.

"Law and Love," *Episcopal Theological School Bulletin* 56 (1964).

1966.

The Nature and Functions of Law, 2d ed. (Brooklyn, NY, 1966) (co-author).

1968.

"Legal Reasoning," *International Encyclopedia of the Social Sciences* (New York, 1968); reprinted in *Royalton Review* 10 (1975): 41.

1972.

The Nature and Functions of Law, 3d ed. (Mineola, NY, 1972) (co-author).

1974.

The Interaction of Law and Religion (Nashville/New York, 1974).

The Weightier Matters of the Law (South Royalton, VT, 1974); reprinted in *Royalton Review* 9 (1975): 32 (address at the opening of Vermont Law School).

1975.

"A Conference on Law, Theology and Ethics," *CSCW Report* 33 (1975) (coauthor).

"The Religious Foundations of Western Law," *Catholic University Law Review* 24 (1975): 490.

"The Crisis of the Western Legal Tradition," *Creighton Law Review* 9 (1975): 252.

"The Secularization of American Legal Education in the Nineteenth and Twentieth Centuries," *Journal of Legal Education* 27 (1975): 382.

1976.

"Religion and Law," *Cross Talk* 5 (1976):   .

"The Western Legal Tradition," *Harvard Law School Bulletin* 28 (1976): 21.

1977.

"The Origins of Western Legal Science," *Harvard Law Review* 90 (1977): 894.

"The Use of Law to Guide People to Virtue: A Comparison of Soviet and U.S. Perspectives," *Law, Justice, and the Individual in Society: Psychological and Legal Issues,* eds. J. Tapp and F. Levine (New York, 1975), 75.

"The Prophetic, Pastoral and Priestly Vocation of the Lawyer," *The NICM Journal* 2 (1977); reprinted in *CORAL Newsletter* (July 1, 1977).

"Theological Sources of the Western Legal Tradition," *Revista Juridica de le Universidad de Puerto Rico* 46 (1977): 371.

"On Smashing the Idols of the Law," (unpublished talk delivered at the Association of American Law Schools Meeting, Atlanta, Georgia, December 28, 1977).

1978.

"The Background of the Western Legal Tradition in the Folklaw of the Peoples of Europe," *University of Chicago Law Review* 45 (1978): 533.

1979.

"The Interaction of Law and Religion," *Capital University Law Review* 8 (1979): 345.

"The Weightier Matters of the Law," *Solzhenitsyn at Harvard*, ed. R. Berman (Washington, DC, 1980), 99; reprinted in *Criterion* 19 (1980): 15; *Christian Legal Society Quarterly* 1 (1980): 22.

"Law, Religion and the Present Danger," *Worldview* 22 (1979): 46.

1980.

The Nature and Functions of Law, 4th ed. (Mineola, NY, 1980) (co-author).

"The Interaction of Law and Religion," *Mercer Law Review* 30 (1980): 405.

"The Moral Crisis of the Western Legal Tradition and the Weightier Matters of the Law," *Criterion* 19 (1980): 15.

"Introduction," Chaim Perelman, *Justice, Law and Argument* (Dordrecht, Netherlands, 1980), ix.

1982.

"Atheism and Christianity in the Soviet Union," *Freedom and Faith: The Impact of Law on Religious Liberty*, ed. L. Buzzard (New York, 1982), 127.

1983.

Law and Revolution: The Formation of the Western Legal Tradition (Cambridge, MA, 1983).

"Law and Religion," *Christian Legal Society Quarterly* 4 (1983): 12.

"Urban Law—I," *History of European Ideas* 4 (1983): 275.

"Urban Law—II," *ibid.*, 4: 421.

"Religious Foundations of Law in the West: An Historical Perspective," *The Journal of Law and Religion* 1 (1983): 3.

"Law and Theology," *The Westminster Dictionary of Christian Theology* (Philadelphia, 1983), 322.

1984.

"Law and Belief in Three Revolutions," *Valparaiso Law Review* 18 (1984): 569.

"Some Reflections on the Differences Between Soviet and American Concepts of Relations Between Church and State," *Christian Legal Society Quarterly* 5 (1984): 12.

"Introductory Remarks: Why the History of Western Law Is Not Written," *University of Illinois Law Review* (1984): 511.

"The Relation of Luther's Music to his Theology," (unpublished talk delivered at Emmanuel Church, Boston, MA, March 11, 1984).

"A Sunday Morning Sermon," (unpublished talk delivered at the American Bar Association Meeting, Chicago, IL, August 5, 1984, on the occasion of receiving the Scribes Book Award for 1984 for the book *Law and Revolution: The Formation of the Western Legal Tradition*).

1985.

"The Crisis of Legal Education in America," *Boston College Law Review* 26 (1985): 347.

"Law and Love," (unpublished lecture delivered at a dinner of the Committee of 100 of the Candler School of Theology in Honor of F. M. Bird, November 13, 1985).

"The Influence of Belief Systems on the Historical Development of Law" (unpublished lecture delivered at the Duquesne University School of Law, November 14, 1985).

"Evolution and Revolution in the Western Legal Tradition" (unpublished lecture delivered at a meeting of the Medieval Studies Seminar, Columbia University, November 15, 1985).

"The Interaction of Liberal and Professional Education" (unpublished lectured delivered at the annual dinner of the Gamma of Georgia Chapter of Phi Beta Kappa, Emory University, November 25, 1985).

1986.

"Religion and Law: The First Amendment in Historical Perspective," *Emory Law Journal* 35 (1986): 777; reprinted (with minor revisions) in *Juris: For Jurisprudence and Legal History* 1 (1986): 1.

"Law in the University," *Legal Studies Forum* 10 (1986): 53.

"Pagan Versus Christian Scholarship," *Veritas Reconsidered* (Cambridge, MA, 1987), 12.

"The Struggle for Religious Freedom in the Soviet Union," (unpublished lectured delivered at Boston University, March 13, 1986).

1987.

"Law and Religion: An Overview," *Encyclopedia of Religion*, ed. M. Eliade (New York, 1987), 8: 472.

"Law and Religion in the West," ibid., 8: 463.

"Church and State," ibid., 3: 489 (coauthor).

"The Religious Sources of General Contract Law: An Historical Perspective," *Journal of Law and Religion* 4 (1987): 103.

"Conscience and Law: The Lutheran Reformation and the Western Legal Tradition," *Journal of Law and Religion* 5 (1987): 1306.

"Human Nature and Human Rights" (unpublished lecture delivered at the Conference on Human Nature, University of Pennsylvania, March 11, 1987).

"Law and Revolution" (unpublished lecture delivered at the Mellon Law Seminar on Legal Philosophy and Social Theory, Princeton University, May 7, 1987).

BIOGRAPHICAL SKETCHES OF CONTRIBUTORS

The following biographical sketches include only those works published by the contributor that deal, in whole or in part, with the subject of law and religion.

James Luther Adams Ph.D. University of Chicago (1945); Professor of Theology and Religious Ethics, University of Chicago Divinity School, 1972–74; Distinguished Professor of Social Ethics, Andover Newton Theological School, 1969–72; Professor of Christian Ethics, Harvard Divinity School, 1956–68; Professor of Theology and Religious Ethics, University of Chicago Divinity School, 1943–56; *Selected Publications*: *The Prophethood of all Believers* (Boston, 1986); *Voluntary Associations* (Chicago, 1986); *The Thought of Paul Tillich* (San Francisco, CA, 1986) (coauthor); *Readings on Professionalism* (Carlisle, PA, 1980); *On Being Human Religiously* (Boston, 1976); *Paul Tillich's Philosophy of Culture, Science, and Religion* (New York, 1965; 2d ed., Washington, 1982); "Rudolph Sohm's Theology of Law and the Spirit," *Religion and Culture: Essays in Honor of Paul Tillich*, ed. W. Leibrecht (New York, 1959), 219; "The Social Import of the Professions," *Bulletin of the American Association of Theological Schools* 23 (1958): 152; *Religion and Freedom* (New York, 1958); "Public-Supported Higher Education: A Unitarian View," *Religion in the State University*, ed. H. Allen (Minneapolis, 1950), 68; "Love and Law and the 'Good old Cause'," *The Divinity School News* 17 (August, 1950): 1; "The Law of Nature: Some General Considerations," *Journal of Religion* 25 (1945): 88; "The Law of Nature in Graeco-Roman Thought," *Journal of Religion* 25 (1945): 97; "Orthodox Church and Soviet State," *The Protestant* 6 (1945): 13.

Frank S. Alexander J.D. Harvard (1978); M.T.S. Harvard (1978); Associate Professor of Law, Emory Law School; *Selected Publications*: "Beyond Positivism: A Theological Perspective," *Georgia Law Review* 20 (1986): 1089; "Three Fallacies of Contemporary Jurisprudence," *Loyola L.A. Law Review* 9 (1985): 1; "Demythologizing Law," *Journal of Law and Religion* 3 (1985): 167; "Privileged Communications for Pastoral Counselling," *Journal of Pastoral Care* 39 (1985): 300; "Validity and Function of Law: The Reformation Doctrine of Usus Legis," *Mercer Law Review* 31 (1980): 509.

Milner S. Ball J.D. Georgia (1971); S.T.B. Harvard (1961); Caldwell Professor of Constitutional Law, University of Georgia; *Selected Publications: Lying Down Together: Law, Metaphor, and Theology* (Madison, WI, 1985); "Law Natural: Its Family of Metaphors and its Theology," *Journal of Law and Religion* 3 (1985): 141; "Obligation: Not to the Law but to the Neighbor," *Georgia Law Review* 18 (1984): 911; "Cross and Sword, Victim and Law: A Tentative Response to Leonard Levy's Treason Against God," *Stanford Law Review* 35 (1983): 1007; *The Promise of American Law: A Theological, Humanistic View of Legal Process* (Athens, GA, 1981); "The Politics of God and the Maturation of the Law," *Georgia Law Review* 4 (1970): 555.

William E. Butler M.A. Johns Hopkins (1963); J.D. Harvard (1966); Ph.D. Johns Hopkins (1970); LL.D. London (1979); Professor of Comparative Law, University of London; Director of Center for the Study of Socialist Legal Systems, University College, London; *Selected Publications: Year Book on Socialist Legal Systems* (Dobbs Ferry, NY, 1986-); *Comparative Law and Legal System* (New York, 1985); *Legal System of the Chinese Soviet Republic 1931–1934* (Dobbs Ferry, NY, 1983); *International Law in Comparative Perspective* (Germantown, MD, 1980); *The Soviet Legal System* (Dobbs Ferry, NY, 1977; 2d ed., New York, 1984); *Russian Law* (Leiden, 1977); *The Soviet Union and the Law of the Sea* (Baltimore, 1971).

Charles Donahue, Jr. LL.B. Yale (1965); Professor of Law, Harvard Law School; *Selected Publications*: "Noodt, Titius, and the Natural Law School: The Occupation of Wild Animals and the Intersection of Property and Tort," *Satura Roberto Feenstra*, eds. J. Ankum, J. Spruit, F. Wubbe (Freiburg, 1985), 609; "Church Court Records on the Continent and in England," *Englische und kontinentale Rechtsgeschichte: ein Forschungsprojekt*, eds. H. Coing and K. Nörr, *Comparative Studies in Continental and Anglo-American Legal History* (Berlin, 1985), 1: 63; "Prophecy and Politics: Reflections on a Recent Campaign," *Winter Bulletin* (Portsmouth, RI, 1985): 4; "The Dating of Alexander the Third's Marriage Decretals: Dauvillier Revisited after Fifty Years," *Zeitschrift der Savigny-Stiftung für Rechtsgeschichte (Kan. Ab.)* 99 (1982): 70; "The Canon Law on the Formation of Marriage and Social Practice in the Later Middle Ages," *Journal of Family History* 8 (1983): 144; "Lydwood's Gloss *propriarum uxorum*: Marital Property and the *ius commune* in Fifteenth Century England," *Europäisches Rechtsdenken in Geschichte und Gegenwart: Festschrift für Helmut Coing* (München, 1982), 1: 19; *Select Cases from the Ecclesiastical Court of the Province of Canterbury, c. 1200–1301*, Selden Society 95 (London, 1981) (coauthor); "Proof by Witnesses in the Church Courts of Medieval England: An Imperfect Reception of the Learned Law," *On the Laws and Customs of England: Essays in Honor of Samuel E. Thorne*, eds.

M. Arnold, T. Green, S. Scully, S. White (Chapel Hill, NC, 1981), 127; "The Interaction of Law and Religion in the Middle Ages," *Mercer Law Review* 31 (1980): 466; "What Causes Fundamental Legal Ideas? Marital Property in England and France in the Thirteenth Century," *Michigan Law Review* 78 (1979): 59; Review Article, "Comparative Family Law: Law and Social Change," *Michigan Law Review* 77 (1979): 350; "The Case of the Man Who Fell Into the Tiber: The Roman Law of Marriage at the Time of the Glossators," *American Journal of Legal History* 22 (1978): 1; "Comparative Reflections on the 'New Matrimonial Jurisprudence' of the Roman Catholic Church," *Michigan Law Review* 75 (1977): 994; "Scandal and the Church's New Matrimonial Jurisprudence," *Law and Justice* 52/53 (Hilary/Easter, 1977): 34; "The Policy of Alexander III's Consent Theory of Marriage," *Proceedings of the Fourth International Congress of Medieval Canon Law*, ed. S. Kuttner (1976): 251; "Roman Canon Law in the Medieval English Church: Stubbs v. Maitland Re-Examined after Seventy-Five Years in the Light of Some Records from the Church Courts," *Michigan Law Review* 72 (1974): 647; "Some Thoughts on Michigan's Copy of the Argentoratene Gratian," *Law Quadrangle Notes* 17 (Fall, 1972): 8; "A Case from Archbishop Stratford's Audience Act Book and Some Comments on the Book and its Value," *Bulletin of Medieval Canon Law* (n.s.) 2 (1972): 45 (coauthor).

W. Cole Durham, Jr. J.D. Harvard (1975); Professor of Law, J. Reuben Clark Law School, Brigham Young University; *Selected Publications*: "The Aboriginal and Comparative Law," *American Journal of Comparative Law* (Supp.) 34 (1986): 1; "Accommodation of Conscientious Objection to Abortion Among Nurses: A Case Study of the Nursing Profession," *Brigham Young University Law Review* (1982): 253 (coauthor); "Constitutional Protections for Independent Higher Education: Limited Powers and Institutional Rights," *National Congress on Church-Related Colleges and Universities, Church and College: A Vital Partnership* (Provo, UT, 1980), 3: 69 (coauthor); "Counseling, Consulting and Consent: Abortion and the Doctor-Patient Relationship," *Brigham Young University Law Review* (1978): 783; Note, "Law of War: Humanitarian Law in Armed Conflicts," *Harvard International Law Journal* 14 (1973): 573.

Lois J. Forer J.D. Northwestern (1938); Judge, Court of Common Pleas, Philadelphia, PA; *Selected Publications*: *A Chilling Effect: The Growing Threat of Libel and Invasion of Privacy Actions to the First Amendment* (New York, 1987); *Money and Justice: Who Owns the Courts?* (New York, 1984); *Criminals and Victims: A Trial Judge Reflects on Crime and Punishment* (New York, 1980); "Some Problems in the Administration of Justice in a Secularized Society," *Mercer Law Review* 31 (1980): 448; "Moral Development and Its Failures," *Bulletin of the Menninger Clinic* 44 (5) (1980); "Judicial Responsibility and Moral Values," *Hastings Law Journal* 29

(1978): 1641; "Sentencing and the Death of the Law," *Pennsylvania Bar Association Quarterly* 48 (1977): 241; *The Death of Law* (New York, 1975); *No One Will Listen: How Our Legal System Brutalizes the Youthful Poor* (New York, 1970); "Foundation and Government," *Columbia Law Review* 66 (1966): 988.

John V. Orth J.D. Harvard (1974); M.A. Harvard (1975); Ph.D. Harvard (1979); Professor of Law, University of North Carolina at Chapel Hill; *Selected Publications: The Judicial Power of the United States: Eleventh Amendment in American History* (New York/Oxford, 1987); "English Combination Acts of the Eighteenth Century," *Law and History Review* 5 (1987): 175; "The Virginia State Debt and the Judicial Power of the United States, 1870–1920," *Ambivalent Legacy: A Legal History of the South*, eds. D. Bodenhamer and J. Ely, (Columbia, MS, 1984), 106; "The Law of Strikes, 1847–1871," *Law and Social Change in British History*, eds. J. Guy and H. Beale (London, 1984); "'Forever Separate and Distinct': Separation of Powers in North Carolina," *North Carolina Law Review* 62 (1983): 1.

Thomas L. Shaffer J.D., University of Notre Dame (1961); Robert E. R. Huntley Professor of Law, Washington and Lee University; Dean, University of Notre Dame Law School (1971–75); *Selected Publications*: "Levinson Builds the Kingdom: A Comment on 'Professing Law'," *Saint Louis University Law Review* 31 (1986): 73; "The Profession as Moral Teacher," *St. Mary's University Law Review* 18 (1986): 195; "The Legal Ethics of Radical Individualism," 65 *Texas Law Review* (1987): 963; *Teachers Manual for Text, Readings, and Discussion Topics in American Legal Ethics* (New York, 1985); *Text, Readings, and Discussion Topics in American Legal Ethics* (New York 1985); "Getting Serious About Legal Ethics," *The Bar Examiner* (August, 1985): 3; "For Reconciliation," *Yale Law Journal* 94 (1985): 1660 (coauthor); "Jurisprudence in Light of the Hebraic Faith," *Notre Dame Journal of Law, Ethics, and Public Policy* 1 (1984): 78; "The Legal Ethics of Gentlemen," *Vanderbilt University Law Alumni Magazine* (Summer, 1984): 8; "The Return of the Gentlemen to Professional Ethics," *Queen's University Law Review* 10 (1984): 1; "Moral Theology in Legal Ethics," *Capital University Law Review* 12 (1983): 179; "The Legal Ethics of Servanthood," *Social Responsibility: Journalism, Law, Medicine* 8 (1982): 34; "The Agony of the Church Over Nuclear Weapons," published (in part) as "Onward Christian Soldiers," *Washington Post* (May 2, 1982): C-7, and (in part) as "The Price of Peace," *Notre Dame Magazine* (May, 1982): 65; "The Legal Ethics of the Two Kingdoms," *Valparaiso University Law Review* 17 (1983): 1; "Christian Lawyer Stories and American Legal Ethics," *Mercer Law Review* 33 (1982): 877; "Henry Knox and The Moral Theology of Law Firms," *Washington and Lee Law Review* 38 (1981): 347; "David Hoffman's Law School Lectures, 1822–1833," *Journal of Legal Education* 32 (1982):

127; "The Moral Theology of Atticus Finch," *University of Pittsburgh Law Review* 42 (1981): 181; "David Hoffman on the Bible as a Law Book," *Christian Legal Society Quarterly* (Fall, 1981): 5; *On Being a Christian and a Lawyer: Law for the Innocent* (Provo, UT, 1981); "The Administration of Justice," *Mercer Law Review* 31 (1980): 459; "Law Faculties as Prophets," *Journal of the Legal Profession* 5 (1980): 45; "The Ethics of Estate Planning, Probate Notes," *American College of Probate Counsel* 6 (Spring, 1979): 19; "The Practice of Law as Moral Discourse," *Notre Dame Lawyer* 55 (1979): 231; "Advocacy as Moral Discourse," *North Carolina Law Review* 57 (1979): 101; "Moral Moments in Law School," *Social Responsibility: Journalism, Law, Medicine* 4 (1978): 32; "A Child to Receive the Kindgom," *Marriage Among Christians*, ed. J. Burtchaell (Notre Dame, 1977), 167; "Lawyers, Counselors, Counselors at Law," *American Bar Association Journal* 61 (1975): 854; "Christian Theories of Professional Responsibility," *Southern California Law Review* 48 (1975): 721; "On Making Lawyers More Human," *The Student Lawyer* (September, 1972): 16; "Toward a Jurisprudence for the Law Office," *American Journal of Jurisprudence* 17 (1972): 125 (coauthor); "The New Humanism," *University of Albuquerque Ambassador* (August, 1971); "Abortion, The Law, and Human Life," *Valparaiso University Law Review* 2 (1967): 94.

Douglas E. Sturm D.B. University of Chicago (1953); Ph.D. University of Chicago (1959); Professor of Religion and Political Science, Bucknell University; *Selected Publications*: *Community and Alienation: Essays on Process Thought and Public Life* (Notre Dame, 1987); "Natural Law," *Encyclopedia of Religion*, ed. M. Eliade (New York, 1987), 10: 318; "Religious Sensibility and the Reconstruction of Public Life: Prospectus for a New America," *Religion and American Public Life*, ed. R. Lovin (New York, 1986), 53; "Towards a New Social Covenant: From Commodity to Commonwealth," *Christianity and Capitalism: Perspectives on Religion*, eds. B. Grelle and D. Krueger (Chicago, 1986), 91; "Contextuality and Covenant: The Pertinence of Social Theory and Theology to Bioethics," *Theology and Bioethics: Exploring Foundations and Frontiers*, ed. E. Shelp (Dordrecht, Netherlands, 1985); "Cosmogony and Ethics in the Marxian Tradition: Premise and Destiny of Nature and History," *Cosmogony and Ethical Order: New Studies in Comparative Ethics*, eds. F. Reynolds and R. Lovin (Chicago, 1985), 353; "Jacques Ellul," *A Handbook of Christian Theologians*, eds. M. Marty and D. Peerman (Nashville, 1984), 561; "Corporate Culture and the Common Good: The Need for Thick Description and Critical Interpretation," *Thought: A Review of Culture and Idea* 60 (1985): 141; "The Legal and Political Significance of Martin Luther King's *Letter From a Birmingham Jail*," *Journal of Law and Religion* 2 (1984): 309; "Constitutionalism and Conscientiousness: The Dignity of Objection to Military Service," *Journal of Law and Religion* 1 (1983): 265; "Praxis and

Promise: On the Ethics of Political Theology," *Ethics* 92 (1982): 733; "Two Decades of Moral Theology: Charles E. Curran as Agent of Aggiornamento," *Religious Studies Review* 8 (1982): 16; "American Legal Realism and the Covenantal Myth: Worldviews in the Practice of Law," *Mercer Law Review* 31 (1980): 487; "Modernity and the Meaning of Law: The Importance of the Religious Factor," *Humanities in Society* 2 (1979): 117; "On Meanings of Public Good: An Exploration," *The Journal of Religion* 51 (1978): 13; "The 'Path of the Law' and the Vis Salutis: A Naturalistic Perspective," *Catholic University Law Review* 26 (1976): 35; "Corporations, Constitutions, and Covenants: On Forms of Human Relation and the Problem of Legitimacy," *Journal for the American Academy of Religion* 41 (1973): 331; "On Lawful Revolution or the Spirit of 1776 Revisited," *Bucknell Review* 20 (1972): 117; "Rule of Law and Politics in a Revolutionary Age," *Soundings* 51 (1968): 368; "Three Contexts of Law," *The Journal of Religion* 47 (1967): 127; "Naturalism, Historicism, and Christian Ethics: Toward a Christian Doctrine of Natural Law," *The Journal of Religion* 44 (1964): 40.

Brian Tierney M.A. Cambridge (1951); Ph.D. Cambridge (1951); Hon. Doctor of Theology, Uppsala University, Sweden; Hon. Doctor of Humane Letters, Catholic University of America; Bryce and Edith Bowmar Professor in Humanistic Studies, Cornell University; *Selected Publications*: "Natural Law and Canon Law in Ockham's Dialogus," *Aspects of Late Medieval Government and Society*, ed. J. Rowe (Toronto, 1986), 3; "John Peter Olivi and Papal Inerrancy," *Theological Studies* 46 (1985): 315 ; "Tuck on Rights: Some Medieval Problems," *History of Political Thought* 4 (1983): 429; "The Idea of Representation in the Medieval Councils," *Concilium* (1983): 24; *Religion, Law, and the Growth of Constitutional Thought, 1150–1650* (Cambridge, 1982; Japanese trans., 1986); "Sovereignty and Infallability," *Journal of Ecumenical Studies* 19 (1982): 787; "Public Expediency and Natural Law: A Fourteenth Century Discussion on the Origins of Government and Property," *Authority and Power Studies Presented to Walter Ullmann*, eds. B. Tierney and P. Linehan (Cambridge, 1980); "Ockham's Ambiguous Infallability," *Journal of Ecumenical Studies* 14 (1978): 102; "The Problem of 'Reception' in the Decretists and in Johannes de Torquemada," *Law, Church, and Society*, eds. K. Pennington and R. Somerville (Philadelphia, 1977); "A Scriptural Text in the Decretales and in St. Thomas," *Studia Gratiana* 20 (1976): 361; "Historical Models of Papacy," *Concilium* (1975): 15; "Infallibility and the Medieval Canonists," *Catholic Historical Review* 61 (1975): 265; "Hostiensis and Collegiality," *Monumenta Iuris Canonici*, Series C (1975): 401; "Infallibility in Morals," *Theological Studies* 35 (1974): 507; "On the History of Papal Infallibility," *Theologische Revue* 70 (1974): 186; *Origins of Papal Infallibility, 1150–1350* (Leiden, 1972); *The Middle Ages: Sources and Readings*, 2 vols. (New York, 1970; 2d ed., 1973; 3d ed., 1978; 4th ed., 1982); *A History of the Middle Ages*

(New York, 1970; 2d ed., 1973; 3d ed., 1978; 4th ed., 1982) (coauthor); "The Problem of *Haec Sancta*," *Essays in Honor of Bertie Wilkinson*, eds. T. Sandquist and M. Powicke (Toronto, 1968), 354; *Great Issues in Western Civilization*, 2 vols. (New York, 1967; 2d ed., 1972; 3d ed., 1976) (coauthor); "The Significance of the Council of Constance," *Proceedings of Canon Law Society Conference* (1967): 150; "*Sola Scriptura* and the Canonists," *Studia Gratiana* 11 (1967): 345; "Medieval Canon Law and Western Constitutionalism," *Catholic Historical Review* 62 (1966): 1; "The Continuity of Papal Political Thought in the Thirteenth Century," *Medieval Studies* 17 (1965): 227; "Die konziliare Theorie am Hofe Kaiser Friedrichs II," *Stupor Mundi* (1965): 455; *The Crisis of Church and State, 1050–1300* (Englewood Cliffs, NJ, 1964); "Bracton on Government," *Speculum* 38 (1963): 295; "'The Prince is Not Bound by the Laws': Accursius and the Origins of the Modern State," *Comparative Studies in Society and History* 5 (1963): 378; "*Natura id est Deus*: A Case of Juristic Pantheism?" *Journal of the History of Ideas* 24 (1963): 307; "The Decretists and the Deserving Poor," *Comparative Studies in Society and History* 1 (1959): 360; *Medieval Poor Law* (Berkeley/Los Angeles, 1959); "Pope and Council: Some New Decretist Texts," *Medieval Studies* 19 (1957): 197; "Grosseteste and the Theory of Papal Sovereignty," *Journal of Ecclesiastical History* 6 (1955): 1; *Foundations of the Conciliar Theory* (Cambridge, 1955; reprinted 1970); "Ockham, The Conciliar Theory and the Canonists," *Journal of the History of Ideas* 15 (1954): 40; "The Canonists and the Medieval State," *Review of Politics* 15 (1953): 378; "A Conciliar Theory of the Thirteenth Century," *Catholic Historical Review* 36 (1951): 415.

George Huntston Williams B.D. University of Chicago and Meadville Theological School (1939); Th.D. Union Theological Seminary (1946); Hon. D.D. St. Lawrence University; Hon. Litt. D. Meadville/Lombard; Hon. L.H.D. Loyola University of New Orleans; Hon. D.Cn.L. King's College University, Halifax; Hon. L.H.D. Saint Anselm College (1984); Hon. D.D. University of Edinburgh (1987); Hollis Professor of Divinity Emeritus, Harvard Divinity School; *Selected Publications*: *Divinings: Pointers from the Harvard Heritage 1636–1986* (New York, 1987); *Contours of Church, State, and Society in John Paul II* (Waco, TX, 1983); *The Polish Bretheren, 1601–1685* (Missoula, MT, 1980); *The Writings of Thomas Hooker* (Cambridge, MA, 1975) (coauthor); *The Radical Reformation* (Philadelphia, 1962; enlarged ed., 1980); *Wilderness and Paradise in Christian Throught* (New York, 1962); *Anselm: Communion and Atonement* (St. Louis, MO, 1959); *Spiritual and Anabaptist Writers* (Philadelphia, 1957) (coeditor); *Christology and Church-State Relations in the Fourth Century* (New York, 1951); *The Norman Anonymous of ca. 1100* (Cambridge, MA, 1951); *The Church and the Democratic State and the Crisis in Religious Education* (New York, 1948).

John Witte, Jr. J.D. Harvard (1985); Director, Law and Religion Program, Emory University; *Selected Publications*: "Blest be the Ties that Bind: Covenant and Community in Puritan Thought," *Emory Law Journal* 36 (1987): 579; "The Reformation of Marriage Law in Martin Luther's Germany: Its Significance Then and Now," *Journal of Law and Religion* 4 (2) (1987): 1; "Church and State," *The Encyclopedia of Religion*, ed. M. Eliade (New York, 1987), 3: 489 (coauthor); Editor, H. Dooyeweerd, *A Christian Theory of Social Institutions*, trans. M. Verbrugge (La Jolla, CA/Toronto, 1986); "The First Amendment and Public Schools," *Reformed Journal* 33 (1983): 14.